To my brother, Jimbo

Remembering fondly Cambridge, and looking forward to another occasion to share in martinis + other mimetic desire!

Jon

Praise for
FETHULLAH GÜLEN: A LIFE OF HIZMET

"As the most fascinating and influential Islamic leader alive today, Fethullah Gülen has stirred controversy. Jon Pahl is keenly aware of the accusations that have dogged Gülen, and in this remarkable biography he deals with them as scrupulously and convincingly as a self-confessed admirer of the man and his movement can. More than that, Pahl offers a provocative meditation on the part that religion can play in leading us to serve our fellows rather than setting us apart from one another. Most of all, he tells an inspiring story of a modern saint."
—**Michael Zuckerman, PhD**
Professor of History, University of Pennsylvania

"Jon Pahl has delivered an important gift to the English-speaking world. Often described in the U.S. media as 'the exiled cleric,' Fethullah Gülen's life and Islamic teachings are relatively unknown. Pahl provides a comprehensive history of this one man and his movement of 'service.'"
—**David D. Grafton, PhD**
Professor of Islamic Studies and Christian-Muslim Relations at Hartford Seminary

"Jon Pahl's new book makes a substantial, significant and distinctive contribution to the literature around Fethullah Gülen and the Hizmet movement inspired by his teaching and person. As a biography written by someone with the skills of an historian of religion it differentiates itself clearly from a hagiography. At the same time, it seeks to deploy an appropriately spiritual understanding of a leading Muslim scholar whose life is revered by hundreds of thousands of Muslims and others, and whose teachings have inspired them. In the wake of the July 2016 and following events in Turkey, Fethullah Gülen has become the focus of a campaign of defamation that seeks to justify the misappropriation of assets, summary dismissal from employment, and arbitrary imprisonment of many tens of thousands of people in Turkey, and to the practically enforced exile of many others. In contrast to this, while engaging with a number of the key charges made against Fethullah Gülen, Pahl's summative evaluation of his subject's life in terms of its essentially Qur'anic roots, Sufistic interiority, and consultative engagement with individuals and groups that has resulted in many hundreds of big and small positive initiatives in education, dialogue and the relief of poverty, makes what is a very a timely contribution to public debate. In underlining that, for Fethullah Gülen, both his life and all these things take place within a divine and eternal horizon, Pahl's book also fulfills what its author expresses as his hope for it – namely that it is indeed both 'critically-sound and spiritually-inspiring.'"

—**Paul Weller, PhD**
Emeritus Professor, University of Derby, UK

"Jon Pahl's biography of *Fethullah Gülen, A Life of Hizmet* sheds light on the Hizmet Movement with an extraordinary openness, touching on curious and crucial issues, and responding them in a freely flowing and constructive manner. A must-read that clarifies our understanding on the Hizmet Movement of Islam through the biography of Gülen towards universal values, peace, interfaith, empathy for the world's problems, and altruism in service to community at a most needed time."

—**Züleyha Çolak, PhD**
Lecturer and Coordinator of Turkish Language Program in the Middle Eastern, South Asian, and African Studies Department, Columbia University

"Pahl's book does a masterful job of rich description of the people, places and historical events that shaped the life and spirit of one of the outstanding religious scholars of the modern age and the movement he inspired. Unique and noteworthy in Pahl's biography is the brilliant way in which he places the events in Mr. Gülen's life in the historical context of the swirling and complicated politics of modern day Turkey.

—**Helen Rose Ebaugh, PhD**
Professor Emeritus, University of Houston

"This readable and well-researched book is an appreciative biography by an outsider to the movement that Fethullah Gülen has spawned, and helps us understand the form of Islamic modernism that he represents and why some political leaders find it challenging. If you want to understand Gülen and his movement, this is the place to begin."
—Mark Juergensmeyer, PhD
University of California, Santa Barbara
Author of *Global Rebellion: Religious Challenges to the Secular State*

"Jon Pahl's *Fethullah Gülen: A Life of Hizmet* is the first scholarly study of the Turkish Islamic reformer's emergence into a beloved and controversial global leader of values-based education, transformative business practices, and principled religious pluralism.

"The genius of Pahl's book is his lucid *translation* of Gülen's vision into a contemporary idiom that modern readers can relate to and understand. Akin to Alex Haley's *The Autobiography of Malcolm X,* Pahl effectively analyzes the tension in Gülen's life between creative *fidelity* to a revealed tradition and generous *openness* to present-day education, science, technology, business, and society.

"Eminently readable, bracingly fast-paced, originally researched, and replete with Gülen's own inspirational speeches and writings – this new book is a must read for anyone interested in the relevance of *civic Islam* in the clash between religion and politics in the world today."
—Mark I. Wallace, PhD
Department of Religion, Environmental Studies Program, Swarthmore College, PA

"With clear, interesting, and often moving prose, Jon Pahl narrates the story of Fethullah Gülen, a fascinating person with qualities of Mahatma Gandhi and other great spiritual leaders. As one who has seen outstanding people in the Hizmet movement in a number of countries, this book helps me understand how a great role model can lead to human empowerment and social betterment. Gülen has given women courage and opportunity to be educated and live up to their full potential. Like Martin Luther King, Jr., Gülen has empowered people with education that has led them to civic engagement. This has been helping to transform societies. While dictatorial repression has caused challenges for the Hizmet movement at this time, truth, justice, and compassion will prevail. I am grateful for this important biography which has material that can enrich historical, interfaith, gender, sociological, and religious studies."

—Martha Ann Kirk, Th.D.
Professor, University of the Incarnate Word

FETHULLAH GÜLEN
A LIFE OF HIZMET

WHY A MUSLIM SCHOLAR IN PENNSYLVANIA
MATTERS TO THE WORLD

Jon Pahl

Blue Dome Press
New Jersey

Published by Blue Dome Press
335 Clifton Ave.
Clifton, NJ, 07011, USA
www.bluedomepress.com

978-1-68206-020-9

Library of Congress Cataloging-in-Publication Data

Names: Pahl, Jon, 1958- author.
Title: Fethullah Gülen, a life of hizmet : why a Muslim scholar in
   Pennsylvania matters to the world / Jon Pahl.
Description: Clifton, NJ : Blue Dome Press, [2019] | Includes bibliographical
   references and index.
Identifiers: LCCN 2019004491 (print) | LCCN 2019004558 (ebook) | ISBN
   9781682065259 (ebook) | ISBN 9781682060209 (hardcover)
Subjects: LCSH: Gülen, Fethullah. | Muslim scholars--Turkey--Biography. |
   Islam and culture--Turkey. | Islam--Turkey--20th century.
Classification: LCC BP80.G8 (ebook) | LCC BP80.G8 P34 2019 (print) | DDC
   297.092 [B] --dc23
LC record available at https://lccn.loc.gov/2019004491

Cover photo courtesy of Selahattin Sevi
Cover design by Rodjie P. Ulanday
Jon Pahl's photo on back cover flap by Harle Photography
Maps of Europe, Turkey, and Pennsylvania on page x by Getty Images

Printed in Canada

To Justin, with love

Contents

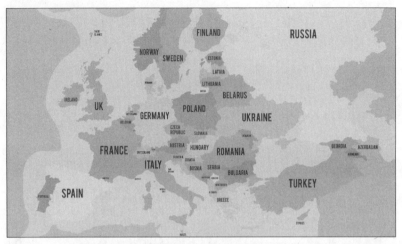

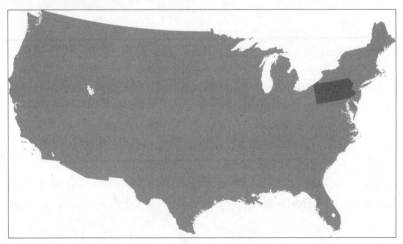

Pronunciation Guide and Glossary

As a general pronunciation guide, the Turkish alphabet has some distinctive sounds:
ş = sh
ğ = silent
h = breathy h--ha
ö and ü = ou and ew, as in German pronunciation
c = short j or soft g sound
ç = long che, as in cheese

Throughout, I have generally used Turkish alphabet, with some phonetic exceptions to ease reading, notably Hodjaefendi (for Hocaefendi), and a few others:

ağabey (also *abi*, pl. *abiler*): "elder brother;" an important informal role within Hizmet

abla (pl. *ablalar*): "elder sister;" an important informal role within Hizmet.

cemaat: gem-aht, "community," widely used to describe the Hizmet movement of people inspired by Fethullah Gülen; also camia, a term favored by Hodjaefendi to describe a more porous, open group, like a "movement" rather than "community."

dershane: ders-han-ay: tutoring center, aka "cram schools" to prepare students for Turkish exams. It also refers to apartments where students affiliated with Hizmet stay during college years and have their reading circles. These apartments used to be called "houses of light" (*ışık evler*).

ghurba: "separation," but more broadly loneliness, being foreign, and renouncing pleasures of world.

Gülen = Gew-len

Hodjaefendi = Ho-ja-ef-en-dee, "honored teacher," used of Fethullah Gülen.

hicret: hij-ret (from *hijrah* in Arabic) "pilgrimage"; leaving one's land for a Godly cause; a key Hizmet ideal.

himmet: voluntary financial support or donation to philanthropic activities, efforts, and projects.

Hizmet: "service," but more broadly work done on behalf of humanity through trusting relationships, for God's pleasure; also the movement of people inspired by Gülen to service.

hoşgörü: "tolerance," but more broadly "principled pluralism;" accepting differences with empathy but working together through dialogue to find common ground.

hüzün: hew-zewn, "melancholy," deep sadness and sorrow; heartache

ihlas: ikh-las, "selflessness," purity, sincerity or integrity.

istişare: (from *istishara* in Arabic) = "mutual consultation;" a central organizing principle and practice in Hizmet.

mütevelli: mew-te-vel-lee, "trustees," donors, business leaders who do *himmet* for Hizmet, and who contribute to decision-making.

rıza-ı ilahi: sometimes just rıza; "resignation," but also "contentment with God's decrees;" doing something for the "pleasure of God," without expecting return.

sohbet: sokh-bet, "conversation," small-group reading discussions; a central organizing principle and practice in Hizmet.

Sufi/Sufism/*tasawwuf*: Islamic spirituality; one who is informed by and practices Islamic spirituality.

uns: "community," or even "intimacy" between a human and God, in Sufism.

PREFACE

I n October, 2006, I received an invitation that would change my life
for the better. The invitation was to an *iftar*, which is the meal to
break the day-long fast of Muslims during Ramadan. The *iftar* was
billed as an "interfaith" event, to be held at the Sheraton Center City
Hotel in Philadelphia, and it came to me from a group called "Dialog
Forum." I did not know who or what "Dialog Forum" was, but I taught
interreligious engagement as a Professor at the Lutheran Seminary in
Philadelphia, I liked a free dinner, and the Sheraton sounded nice.

So, I rsvp'd, and then showed up at the hotel, where I was directed by some signs to a modest downstairs ballroom. Outside of the ballroom I was greeted by a couple of young women sitting at a table laden
with books and other literature. Both the women wore the *hijab*—the
hair-covering that is typical for devout Muslim women. But one of them,
Yasemin—as she identified herself—was exceptionally friendly, and she
quickly checked my name off a list, gave me my name tag, and directed
me into the ballroom. There I mingled with about two-hundred other
people dressed in suits and nice dresses—some of whom I recognized as
colleagues from other universities or colleges in the Philadelphia region.
There was no alcohol, of course. We did have the chance to try some sour
cherry juice—in Turkish, *vişne*—which I had never tasted before. It was
to become one of my favorite beverages.

The dinner was pleasant. Dr. Thomas Michel, who was introduced
as the Jesuit Secretariat for the Vatican's interreligious dialogue unit, was
the keynote speaker. Michel read to us—yes, *read to us*—from a book
entitled *Toward a Global Civilization of Love and Tolerance*, by a man
named Fethullah Gülen (approximate pronunciation, as I heard it that
night: Fet-hoo-la Gew-len) Once I got over the pedantic delivery, though,
I began to listen to what the words were saying. And after the dinner, I
bought a copy of the book from the table out front. And later that night
I started reading it. The next morning, I wrote a brief column thanking

the organizers of the dinner. That column contrasted my experience of hospitality among Muslims with the Christian Islamophobia and U.S. war-making that had marred our culture since 2001 (we were still mired in Iraq). The next day *The Philadelphia Inquirer* published it.[1]

That night was the beginning of the scholarly trajectory, as it gets called, that has led to this biography. During my Ph.D. program at the University of Chicago Divinity School, I had studied "Western Religious Traditions," including Islam. But most of my research has been in the field of American religious history. My publications have generally explored how people of faith in the U.S. have engaged with civil society, for better and for worse. Most recently, I've written primarily about the worse—notably in a book entitled *Empire of Sacrifice: The Religious Origins of American Violence*.[2] And as a professor—first at a small Lutheran liberal arts University, then at the Seminary, and off-and-on as visiting faculty at a large, urban, state-related University (Temple) or in the Ivy League (Princeton), I have sought to integrate my work as a historian with a growing activist commitment to a more just and peaceful world. In that work, I have lived out and tried to reconcile a tension that I see as inherent to the modern world. I have also learned, through my research for this biography, that this tension and effort to reconcile it has also played itself out in dramatic and sometimes tragic ways in the life of Fethullah Gülen.

That tension can be put simply, although it has many facets: a faithful person cannot be rational; a rational person cannot be faithful. In contrast, the paradox that I have lived with and studied, and that the life of Fethullah Gülen illuminates, is that a faithful person *can* be rational, and a rational person *can* be faithful. He would put it even more strongly. It is irrational to be faithless. And it is faithless to be irrational. Gülen would also contend, and I agree, that faithful rationality must express itself in concrete action for justice and peace in the world. We must build bridges, he has argued throughout his life, between the faithful and the scientific, translating the deep trust that religion promotes into practical projects to help alleviate the ample and unnecessary suffering in the world.

I began writing this biography well before Mr. Gülen was a regular figure in the U.S. media. I have often lamented that I was unable to finish the book with greater dispatch. Yet, controversy has been a consistent feature of Gülen's life, as has the persecution of him and those close to him that in recent years has reached a fever pitch. Gülen has also consistently—albeit by very different sources—been misunderstood and been misrepresented. His public reputation has been marred by accusations that upon a little investigation can be revealed to have base (if not corrupt) political motives. Alternatively, people, especially in Turkey, have misunderstood Gülen out of the widespread secular ignorance about how religion, and specifically Islam, operates. This biography aims to correct the record.

I have read everything Mr. Gülen has written that has been translated into English, and all of the secondary sources about Gülen in English—a rather large body of literature—now. And I have studied enough Turkish to make my way through most newspaper stories and other public documents by or about him, with the aid of a good dictionary. I also have had help to translate from Turkish into English some of Gülen's sermons, and to translate some interviews with people close to him. My primary research assistant in that process was a young man who was a spokesperson for Dialog Forum (now Peace Islands Institute) in Philadelphia. His name is Feyzi Eygören. Feyzi has known Mr. Gülen his entire life. Like so many people inspired by Mr. Gülen, while working with me on this book Feyzi was also in graduate school. He recently received his JD from Villanova Law School. But in the summer of 2015, Feyzi and I traveled together for a month in Turkey. We translated some video interviews of people close to Gülen, and then we followed in Gülen's footsteps from Erzurum, to Edirne, to Izmir, and finally to Istanbul. At each stop, we interviewed some of Gülen's oldest and closest colleagues. All told, we gathered about three dozen interviews, and I have done another three dozen since then in the U.S. This book could not have been written without Feyzi's generous (and tireless) efforts.

But the specific genesis of this project, apart from that *iftar* invite, was actually a conference in 2010 at the University of Chicago dedicated to exploring "Islam and Peacebuilding." I had been invited as a speaker, and one evening on the way back to our hotel in a shuttle bus, I had a conversation with M. Sait Yavuz. Sait had been studying for his PhD in history at the University of Maryland, but he had recently moved to Houston to serve as managing director for the Gülen Institute—a think tank. Sait mentioned to me that that the Institute was planning to commission a critical biography of Gülen. I had seen to completion a couple of prior commissioned projects, and I had enjoyed the collaborative nature of that research. I suggested to Sait that we talk more. And within a few months, this project was underway.

So, I have received financial, research, and editorial support in this biography from people close to Mr. Gülen. They have paid for my travel to and from Turkey on three occasions, and to and from several of the schools and other institutions around the globe developed by people inspired by Mr. Gülen—notably in Ghana, Kenya, Uganda, Albania, Australia, and Indonesia. And in 2016-17, I received a modest research fellowship from the Alliance for Shared Values—another Gülen-associated think-tank—to complete the book you are now reading. I am grateful for that support.

I also do not believe that support has changed how I approach or understand Mr. Gülen. In all my interreligious work—now decades deep in experience—I have been guided by a maxim from the sixteenth-century Protestant reformer Martin Luther. That maxim concerns the Eighth Commandment, which reads (in the King James Version that I memorized as a child): "Thou shalt not bear false witness." Luther's interpretation of that Commandment, in his *Small Catechism* (which I also memorized), reads: "We should fear and love God that we may not deceitfully belie, betray, slander, or defame our neighbor, but defend him, speak well of him, and put the best construction on everything." There has been, unfortunately, plenty of slander and defamation of Muslims in recent years. And there has been plenty of slander regarding Fethullah Gülen.

So, I have written a biography that seeks, from the perspective of an outsider to Islam, to "put the best construction on" Gülen's life and the Hizmet movement. That does not mean that what follows is a hagiography. That kind of biography would serve no one well. It would just replace one kind of lies with another. To "put the best construction on everything" in the life of Fethullah Gülen, as I construe it, means to remember self-critically that my perspective is partial. I am an outsider—both to Islam and to the global Hizmet (service) movement associated with Gülen. This perspective is a decided advantage. I can sift the evidence that emerges in association with Gülen's life with all the rigor that I bring to any historical inquiry. I have not hesitated to ask any question of the evidence or in interviews, and I have sought out voices and perspectives that are critical of Gülen. That said, I have also sought to practice a hospitality of mind that mirrors the kind of hospitality I have experienced in being invited and welcomed into a community. And I do seek to correct the historical record when the evidence seems to necessitate doing so. Allowing slanders and falsehoods to stand is not to "put the best construction" on an individual's reputation.

All in all, I have tried to be fair. That has meant integrating my faith convictions as a Lutheran Christian with my skills as a historian of religions to narrate Gülen's story in its contexts. I have engaged, when the evidence takes me there, with areas where Gülen has rightly been critiqued—notably for lack of transparency, for gender-imbalance, and for some nostalgic Turkish nationalism. To "put the best construction on everything" has not meant overlooking anything. I have discovered along the way that the task of understanding how a single life unfolded within a complex and rich culture is a daunting intellectual (and sometimes a personal) challenge. But it has also been a pleasure. With the help of many, many people I have put together the story of how the oldest son of a devout family in Turkey learned to be a religious peacebuilder in the modern world. He did so by helping women and men, as I see it, to reconcile what appear to be profound contradictions, and to live lives of greater integrity than before they became familiar with his life and work. It is, I hope, a story you find both critically-sound and spiritually-inspiring. It is the story of a life of what people in Turkey, and now around the globe, call Hizmet: a life of service.

***

But I began this Preface by saying that my attendance at the *iftar* dinner in 2006 changed my life for the better. It did so because through my research I have met so many fine individual women and men—scholars, citizens, activists, students, teachers, and more, around the globe. I cannot, alas, name them all. To do so would, given current Turkish political persecution of anyone remotely connected to Mr. Gülen, put lives and livelihoods at risk. At times, I have had to change the names of people I interviewed to protect them, although it is also the case that most of the individuals in this biography have been well-known as associates of Gülen. But I am truly grateful for each moment we shared, and for their generosity and honesty. My experience of hospitality as offered by so many around the globe has given me an example of warmth and integrity to which I can only aspire.

I have also been fortunate to receive critical feedback on the book from a wide-range of readers and conversation partners. Alp Aslandoğan, Akın Öztoprak, Ahmet Kurucan, and Hakan Yeşilova were intrepid readers of every word and their fact-checking helped me to avoid many potential pitfalls. They also encouraged me to explore particular avenues of inquiry, and questioned directions that did not make sense to them. We did not always agree, and at times debated vigorously, but in the course of our work together, we became not only colleagues, but friends—*arkadaşlar*. I am truly grateful to each of them for their generous insights, wisdom, and friendship, and especially to Hakan for his editorial expertise. David Grafton, who was my colleague at The Lutheran Theological Seminary at Philadelphia, and who now teaches Christian-Muslim relations at Hartford Seminary, also was a careful and extremely helpful reader of the entire work; hearty thanks to him. Other scholars also read all or part of the work, and/or engaged in conversations with me that were critically constructive. Yasemin Aydın, Züleyha Çolak, Shirley Robbins, TL Hill, Dani Rodrik, and Mustafa Akyol were all conversation partners about interpretive questions that arose, and about narrative arcs and organization. Yasemin was particularly generous with her time and encouraging in her remarks. Mark Wallace was not only a frequent host to me, along with his wife Audrey Beach, at their lovely home in Swarthmore, but Mark was also a valued reader of the manuscript and conversation partner about the project, and beloved friend throughout. Dr. Richard Mandel, Dan and Melissa Muroff, and Andy and Christina Andrews were true friends who howled at the moon with me (sometimes literally) when necessary; deep thanks to them. My Dean at United Lutheran Seminary, Jayakiran Sebastian, has also recognized the importance of this book, and given me steady assistance; thanks to him and to my other colleagues at the seminary. As the project neared completion, Hayrunnisa Kalaç proved particularly helpful at converting my Anglicized spellings back into appropriate Turkish forms, and she and her father also generously shared with me many of the photos that you see in the book. Finally, the good people of Union Congregational United Church of Christ in Green Bay, where I began serving as a pastor in April, 2018, have given me a wonderful community of support, and have been very patient in seeing my scholarly work as an extension of what I do in the congregation. And to my loving wife, Lisa, who actually struggled through Turkish lessons with me one hot summer in Istanbul: ain't no sunshine when you're gone! I dedicate this book to our son, Justin—fellow lover of words and good writing.

All in all, it's been a joy and honor to work on this project in the company of such colleagues and friends. I hope that the biography meets their expectations for it, and I hope it meets the expectations of many others around the world who have encouraged me and given me feedback in conversations and dialogues. The failings of the work are of course mine alone.

INTRODUCTION

How does one tell the story of a man who has been lionized by some as nearly a saint and vilified by others as a terrorist? On a visit to Izmir in 2015, the risks I faced for writing a biography of Fethullah Gülen became apparent to me. As I rode to my room in the hotel elevator after checking in, I happened to be joined by several police officers carrying dossiers. Looking down—avoiding eye contact in typical elevator fashion—I noticed on these dossiers the name of the man I was studying. As I learned in the news over the next two days, the dossiers were probably orders to hunt down and arrest associates of Fethullah Gülen in a sweep that was happening across the city. I prayed that the police did not know who I was or what I was doing. At dinner that night, in the lovely rooftop restaurant of the hotel that had a gorgeous view of Izmir and the Aegean Sea, my meal was ruined a bit by the presence of police sitting at tables in front of and behind me. Upon the advice of my colleagues and friends, I moved hotel rooms every night. Probably I had nothing to fear. I had only written a few modest essays in scholarly publications about Gülen, and I was, of course, an American citizen. But as events over the next few years would show, even an American citizen like Pastor Andrew Brunson could be caught up in the wave of hysteria that led anyone even tangentially connected to Gülen to be a target for arrest and imprisonment.

Political intrigue aside—there will be plenty of time for that in the pages that come—this book has three interrelated aims. The first is to narrate accurately a single life story. This is, I have discovered, more difficult than it appears. I knew before, but have discovered anew, that every human life is irreducibly complex. No person's choices are simple.

No one, to quote an old maxim, is an island. So, while the life of Fethullah Gülen has been singular, it also has been constituted like any life by countless relationships. In what follows, I highlight very selectively some of those relationships. I start with his family, move through some of his long-term associates and friends, and trace down to the present the global network of individuals who have met his ideas, if not his actual person. Readers of biography tend to expect a plot focused on individual heroism or tragedy—and there are those moments in what follows. But the more interesting story, to me, and certainly the one that is more accessible and significant, historically, is the public influence of this singular individual. You might say, then, that this is a public biography. Such an approach makes sense for principled as well as practical reasons. Gülen himself has continually deflected attention from his individual life. He has taught that the primary *jihad* of a Muslim is the struggle to subdue the ego—to remove the obstacle of the "I" that prevents the generation of a "we." And at the heart of his teaching, and perhaps of his life, has been a desire to act in such a way as to seek God's, not his own, pleasure. As a biographer of this distinctive individual, then, I have found it both necessary and important to respect that teaching and desire. Consequently, until I had a complete first draft of this book completed, I chose not to meet the man. This choice struck many of my scholarly counterparts as odd. I suppose it made my research more difficult than it might have been. But I think it was the right choice. When I did meet with him—in two interviews that together made for about three hours of conversation, I could ask both focused and informed questions. Those meetings did not substantially alter the lines of interpretation I had already developed. They did clear up some detail, and they added some nuance. They also confirmed my general sense of his personality gained from the public record. Still, readers interested in a biography that "gets inside" the subjectivity of a figure are bound to be disappointed by my effort here. Yet this is the story of one life; a story that I hope is both accurate to the evidence, and with explanatory power in its contexts.

The second aim of the book, then, is to describe for an educated reader the history of an Islamic (and interfaith) movement that took root in this singular life but now has significance well beyond it. Another way to put this aim is to say that I have crafted through biography and a very focused history an introduction to Islam for non-Muslim readers. I write unapologetically as a non-Muslim. But I also write with decades behind me spent in dialogue with Muslims, and I have studied and taught Islam in countless classrooms with a wide variety of students. It has also of course been impossible not to be aware, as I write, that some readers may harbor fear or stereotypes about Muslims, consciously or unconsciously. Such fear and stereotypes have circulated widely and freely in the English-speaking world, of late, stoked first by the appalling behavior of terrorists who claimed to act in the name of God, but also exacerbated and amplified by the governments, militaries, and attendant corporations which have benefited from the continued circulation of these falsehoods and fears. I hope that the questions I have brought to Gülen's life-story might be questions that others bring to Islam more broadly. I know I will not persuade either terrorists or war-profiteers. But my effort in this book has been to write for the vast majority of people of good will who might honestly wonder whether Islam is truly a religion of peace. As the subtitle of the book has it, then, this is the story of a life of *hizmet*—a life of service. But that subtitle contains an ambiguity. On the one hand, it refers to Gülen's own *hizmet*: to the work he has done as a preacher and teacher, and to the relationships he has forged with people near and far. On the other hand, it refers to the movement called Hizmet—and to the service of those inspired by Gülen. So, this is both the biography of an individual and the history of an unmistakably Islamic movement that I believe represents the nonviolent heart of the tradition.

My third aim, then, is to narrate the history of how an individual life and a movement contributed to building peace. Oddly, this may be the most difficult aim to achieve. Just as there is profound misunderstanding of Gülen and of Islam in popular English-speaking discourse, so too is there strong bias against seeing religions as catalysts for peace—unless the religion (however defined) happens to be one's own. I am of the school that everyone has something like a religion. I am also of the conviction that those religions that are least recognized as such are also the most dangerous. "Religions: kill people dead," goes the t-shirt. Yet deaths directly attributable to any of the historic religious traditions of humanity—indigenous, Hindu, Buddhist, Jewish, Christian, or Muslim, to name just a few, pale in comparison to the deaths that the "religions" of greed, nationalism, lust, envy, or glory, to name just a few, have produced. And those "religions" cut across the historic traditions, and in fact undermine and contradict them at countless points. Just as religion is not necessarily irrational, as Gülen has consistently contended, neither is it inherently violent. So, my aim in what follows is to show how, from the historical record, the religious life of Fethullah Gülen and the religious movement inspired by him has contributed to a more just, peaceful world. Whether the evidence supports that view is finally for readers to judge. But I am making my wager plain.

The central question that animates the book is: how did a pious Muslim boy born in 1938 in a tiny and remote Turkish village come to inspire a global movement of millions of individuals dedicated to literacy, social enterprise, and interreligious dialogue? A related question follows immediately: how did Fethullah Gülen, that pious Muslim boy who became a global religious leader, also motivate animosity that has led him to be jailed repeatedly, to be monitored by police and intelligence agencies, and (most recently) to be slandered as a "terrorist?" These questions are historical and biographical, but I focus my approach through a problem that cuts across disciplines, namely the capacities of religious leaders to provoke violence, and their capacity to promote peace. It's widely recognized that religions can produce violence. The Crusades and the terrorist attacks on 9/11 happened. It's less well-known that the leading peacebuilders of the past century worked largely, if never exclusively, from religious motives. Among them were, from many potential candidates: Mohandas Gandhi, Jane Addams, Rosa Parks, Badshah Khan, Desmond Tutu, Thich Nhat Hanh, Leymah Gbowee. Too often, religions get stereotyped only for their violent tendencies. Those tendencies are real, and tragic when mobilized. But no less real are the capacities of religious traditions to promote goodness, beauty, truth—and other life-giving practices. They have done so for billions of people for millennia. And they have done so for increasing numbers of people over the course of the twentieth and early twenty-first centuries (the U.S. and Western Europe are largely outliers to this trend). Interestingly, while religious peacebuilders like those on the list above earn accolades in retrospect, during their life-times they often experienced opposition, slander, resistance, imprisonment, and persecution, if not martyrdom.

So, in the pages that follow we'll explore events as they happened over the course of Fethullah Gülen's life, but we'll also try to understand how his life gained the significance it has come to have (positively and otherwise) for so many. As a work of history, questions of cause and effect are central. What were the causes that brought Fethullah Gülen to prominence? How did this boy, now an old man, develop the influence that has made him like a saint, to some, and hated, by others? Of course, my answers to these questions are hypotheses. Like any scientific hypotheses, mine must be guided by the evidence. I will thus follow the trails left by primary source documents, statements of contemporaries, and interpretations of fact by many other scholars to draw my conclusions. My method has been that of any intellectual explorer. I've observed, read, analyzed, listened, and learned—and then narrated. I have also sought to be as self-critical as critical. I have listened to allies of Gülen, and to those who disagree with him. The answers I have reached led me to see Gülen's life as marked by five key elements, patterns, or relationships: 1) integrity of participation in the *nonviolent practices* of Islam; 2) *principled pluralism*—manifest in a commitment to dialogue; 3) what I call *engaged empathy*—deep feeling for the suffering of the world, and willingness to engage on behalf of alleviating that suffering; 4) a commitment to spiritual and scientific *literacy*; and 5) an organizational model of *social enterprise*. Studying Gülen's life and discovering these five aspects of his work has been an exciting intellectual endeavor that has occupied now more than eight years of my life. I hope it is exciting to read as you explore along with me.

Gülen's life has certainly had more than its share of excitement. Despite oft-stated efforts to stay out of the limelight—fame, for him, following Said Nursi, is a "poisonous honey"—Gülen has frequently found himself on large world stages. There were good reasons for *Time* Magazine to name him one of the world's one-hundred most influential figures in 2013. But the attention has also on occasion turned unpleasant, notably when he was imprisoned or when those close to him have been persecuted. Given that his unpleasant encounters with influence have often had political causes, one might also expect a political explanation for his historical significance. Could he have had a grand ambition for political power? Or a strategic plan guided by careful market research, at least? But as I read the evidence, Fethullah Gülen's life has not been, primarily, political. His influence has stemmed, rather, from the fact that he has been a particularly consistent and authentic Muslim and at the same time he has been a modern thinker who motivated Muslims to embrace and to contribute to the contemporary world. Such a simple explanation is not sufficient to explain Fethullah Gülen's life and significance. Those inspired by him have had many reasons for being so inspired. Those who have hated him, in contrast, have almost always done so for political reasons. To interpret Gülen primarily through a political lens, then, is to mistake or to misrepresent the main point of his life—which has been to be a faithful Muslim who applies the faith for a modern, global age. Throughout my research, I have heard repeatedly from those close to Gülen that they were drawn to him by his sincerity or integrity as a Muslim. And I have heard equally consistently by those critical of Gülen that he had a "hidden agenda," or that he organized a "parallel state." I have found no concrete and unbiased evidence to support the latter kind of conspiracy theorizing. My conclusion? If authenticity and integrity has mattered in the modern world, then Fethullah Gülen's life would seem to be a singular case-study of it in a Turkish Muslim vein. The truly frightening prospect, to me, as those federal police in Izmir just "doing their job" and "hunting down terrorists" might suggest, is that authenticity and integrity may not matter anymore, in some contexts.

One problem that has impeded fair understanding of Gülen is that many Western readers understand as little about Turkey as they do about Islam. Another is that few people perceive or appreciate the peacebuilding potential of religious traditions. That may be the case even when they draw upon the resources of one of these traditions to find peace for themselves. Consequently, this Introduction must spend a bit of time, before outlining the content of each chapter, in exploring the three contexts in which Gülen gained his significance: Islam and its practices; twentieth century Turkey; and the rise of religious peacebuilding. So, Gülen was born in 1938 to a devout family in the small village of Korucuk, in Northeastern Turkey, near the larger town of Erzurum. From his childhood, he was a Muslim devoted to the oneness of God and to the witness of the prophet—the creedal affirmation that is the first of the five pillars of Islam. Such an emphasis on unity is not without historical significance. Since the age of 4, Fethullah has spent hours every day in prayer—the second of the five pillars of Islam. The significance of this practice should not be overlooked. Prayer is not magic, but it is a source of cultural power. Prayer has influence on the practice of other believers, and in Gülen's case as a decided sign of his authenticity as a

Muslim. Gülen has also made *Hajj*—the pilgrimage to Mecca that is a third pillar of Islam, three times. This, too, may have social and historical significance. As globalization has shrunk the world, sacred places have taken on extraordinary and sometimes explosive significance—think of Jerusalem. The fourth pillar of Islam is the month-long fast of Ramadan—and Gülen has scrupulously observed this fast. He has also preached and written on how fasting produces peace, among other benefits. Finally—by way of demonstrating his Islamic *bona fides*, Gülen has practiced and inspired extraordinary forms of *zakat*—the financial frugality and charity that is a fifth of the core practices of pious Muslims around the world. Again, Gülen's faithful observance of these *theological* and *ritual* foundations of Islam may be more important historically to explain his significance than many scholars have recognized. I call these theological and ritual foundations in the life of Fethullah Gülen *nonviolent practices*—because that is, in the end, what they are. Such beliefs and practices cultivate sociable habits such as patience, hospitality, delayed gratification, cooperation, charity, and other virtues, and they are inherently nonviolent. No one has ever killed another while bowing toward Mecca. In the language that I will use throughout this book, then, Gülen has sought to show through his life and teachings how *nonviolent practices* such as prayer, pilgrimage, and charity can help Muslims to grow a more just and peaceful world.[1]

Of course, commitment to these five nonviolent practices is widespread among Muslims. Gaining an introductory understanding of Gülen's life and significance, then, also requires understanding something about the modern Turkish context in which he lived for most of his life. From the time Gülen was born up until today, then, the Republic of Turkey has experienced both dramatic changes and durable continuities. It is tricky to describe these changes and continuities, for the changes have come rapidly and sometimes violently, and the continuities have sometimes been oppressive. In 1923 Mustafa Kemal Atatürk—a military hero who in the first decades of the twentieth century had defended (often brutally) the integrity of the Ottoman Empire from European colonial assault and from internal corruption, began to institute a series of changes that transformed the religiously-based Ottoman Sultanate and Caliphate into a secular Republic known as Turkey. Between 1924 and his death in 1938, Atatürk imposed (and that fact is important) a broad program of reform known as "*laicism*." "*Laicism*" is a French term of Latin origin meaning "of the people." As the term suggests, however, its historical origin hearkens not to the people of Anatolia—the name of the peninsula that largely constitutes Turkey today, but to the people of the French Revolution. Like that Revolution, Atatürk's in Turkey sought—and largely succeeded, to diminish the role of religion in public life. Put positively, Atatürk's vision was to salvage some vestige of the Ottoman Empire by establishing a modern, secular Republic. He did so to a large degree. And he did so in a remarkably short span of time. The official Republic of Turkey that the adult Fethullah Gülen lived in would have been all but unrecognizable to his grandfather and grandmother—in language, government, and culture. Women gained the vote in 1929. Turkey became a NATO member in 1952. It joined the European Economic Community (a precursor of the EU) as an Associate Member in 1964. And from 1970 to the present Turkey has experienced rapid economic development as the State-Owned Enterprises that Atatürk established in the 1920s and 30s were privatized under liberalizing political and economic policies.

But if change marked official Turkey through Atatürk's forced reforms, continuities endured in the everyday lives of many Turks, especially in the villages of the rural east and north. Among those continuities were the practices of Islam. If Atatürk cultivated devotion to himself as a modern strong man in the mold of nearby Josef Stalin of Russia, he also found it necessary to allow certain practices of Islam to continue across Anatolia, even while trying to stamp them out. Another continuity between Ottoman and Republican Turkey—perhaps more durable even than the practices of Islam—was the existence of networks of patronage. These networks circulated resources among a minority elite.[2] Elisabeth Özdalga, a scholar of modern Turkish history, put it well: "The state has not been able to integrate individual citizens ... [and] the state has more often than not deterred civil initiatives through various repressive measures."[3] For instance, patriarchy—the domination of public life by men—had officially ended in the new Republic. Women had access to legal freedoms beyond those in many Western European countries. But in practice men continued to run things, now in boundaries defined by the State, as well as by culture. An elite endured. The military had replaced the pashas, imams, preachers, and leaders of *Sufi* brotherhoods—males all, as primary cultural authorities. Politicians inhabited a decidedly secondary tier of power. Succinctly, for most of Fethullah Gülen's life the military was the guardian of Atatürk's legacy of *laicist* strong-man tactics.

Consequently, the military intervened in coups three (some would say five, and others would see six) times during Gülen's life. The undisputed coups were on 27 May 1960, 12 March 1971, and 12 September 1980 (the specific dates are known by every educated Turk, and are infamous, or revered, depending on your take on Turkish politics). The 4th intervention, dubbed by some a "post-modern" coup, occurred on 28 February 1997. On that date, the National Security Council—the political branch of the military, released a memorandum that led to a series of political resignations, and that (re)imposed restrictions on religious practice. The fifth came in the form of an "e-memorandum" in 2007 when the General Staff released a statement on its website with comments on the presidential elections and their staunch position as a "party" in arguments about "secularism." After this statement, the presidential election failed, and a general election was called. And a sixth "failed coup," "staged coup," or "silent coup" (again depending on your perspective), took place on July 15, 2016. That event, which was a military fiasco that led to over two-hundred deaths, resulted in accusations that Gülen and those inspired by him had conspired to conduct it. How, you might ask, could a Muslim preacher and scholar who had consistently preached peace (as we shall see), and who had repeatedly been the *victim* of prior coups at the hands of the military (as we shall also see), and who was (finally) living at the time in isolation in the Pocono Mountains of Pennsylvania, come to be accused of being a conspirator *along with the military* to carry out a coup in Turkey? Excellent question! I will explore in Chapter 5 my reasons for thinking that these accusations of conspiring to overthrow the government against Gülen are patently untrue. And I will also explore the quite real disruptions and trauma for Gülen and for many people inspired by him that followed from these accusations. And I will make clear, finally, that it was unmistakable that the "failed coup" primarily benefited President (formerly Prime Minister) Recep Tayyip Erdoğan. Whatever the causes behind the events of July 15, 2016, then, and it will likely take historians decades to sort them out, there can be little question that Erdoğan drew upon a long legacy of authoritarian politics in Turkey to stay in power. He did so by curbing free-doms of association, the press, and property that had previously marked Turkey's democratic progress. That this strong-man was now dressed up with a veneer of democratic and Islamic practice did not change the ev-idence.

There are ample ironies in this brief narration of the recent history of Turkey. The military coups of the mid-twentieth century had resolved quite real instability and social chaos, if not quite anarchy, in the Repub-lic of Turkey. Generally, they did so by appealing to a "threat to national security." This phrase had been shrewdly tucked into affirmations of free speech and association affirmed in a 1961 Constitution. And until 2015 the military had generally seen Islam as the primary "threat" to national security (Communism filled in as another scapegoat during the Cold War). By 2015, however, the government under Prime Minister and then President Erdoğan now claimed the mantle of Islam. Erdoğan came to power as Mayor of Istanbul as an avowed political Islamist. Then, once in power on the national scene, he largely de-fanged the military through a series of prosecutions too complex to get into at this point. The upshot was that Fethullah Gülen, and people inspired by him, who had once considered Erdoğan somewhat of an ally in their efforts to bridge Islam and modern democracy, now became scapegoats and targets for an in-tense campaign of hate-speech and political persecution.

Tragically, though, this targeting of a group of Muslims as ene-mies of the state also represented a certain continuity within Turkish history. Since Atatürk, the government ostensibly controlled religion: all religious schools, and all imams and preachers, had to be licensed by the State. At times, Gülen's career had benefitted from patrons in high political places. Far more often, however, Gülen had suffered from po-litical persecution. But whatever Gülen's political standing, his support among ordinary people grew continuously and consistently. The popu-lar practices of Turkish Muslims had a way of surviving the oppression of the secular regime. And increasingly, as Gülen and those inspired by him expanded into global networks, they forged communities of prac-tice that some scholars have dubbed "civil Islam." This "civil Islam," or an Islam whose social significance came from below and that was compat-ible with democracy, should be contrasted with the "political Islam," or an Islam imposed from above, that fueled, for example, the 1979 Islamic

Revolution in Turkey's neighbor, Iran, and that was the original model for Erdoğan. After encountering resistance along his political Islamist path—even briefly winding up in jail in 1979—Erdoğan rose to power by clothing himself as a democrat and advocate for civil Islam. By 2017, however, having integrated many in the Muslim heartlands of the country into his political base, he then moved ruthlessly to silence dissent and to secure authoritarian control of every facet of Turkish life. He did so by offering Gülen as a foil or scapegoat to placate the secular military to his left, and to placate the political Islamists and nationalists to his right. Such scapegoating was nothing new for Gülen. He had experienced troubles repeatedly in his life, as we shall see. But for the many individuals drawn to Gülen's vision of a modern, educated, market-based, and internationalist civil Islam, and who had supported Erdoğan's apparent integration of Islam with democracy in Turkey, this new persecution by one who claimed to practice the same faith seemed particularly virulent, surprising, and painful.

In any event, it was in this volatile context that Fethullah Gülen was born and emerged as a public leader. It was during his years in Izmir (1966-1971) that people began to identify collectively with the one they called *Hodjaefendi*—honored teacher—and a movement began to emerge. Most of the people in this movement have been Turkish, and within Turkey those people have been called many things—among them some not very flattering. But one term that Gülen has used for them, and that seems to me accurate to the historical record, characterizes them as people of *hizmet*. *Hizmet* is a Turkish term with Arabic roots that means "service." Beyond whatever political entanglements within Turkey that have ensnared them, then, these people inspired by Gülen have sought to live lives of service. They have, as of 2018, put *hizmet* into practice and brought the teachings of Fethullah Gülen to Africa, Asia, Australia, Europe, and North and South America. At the heart of that experiment in Hizmet, wherever it has happened, has been the effort to maintain integrity as Muslims and to advocate for and advance secular knowledge, democratic ideals, and economic development. Put slightly differently, as he developed as a preacher and teacher, Fethullah Gülen increasingly affirmed that one could be both a faithful Muslim and a loyal citizen of a diverse, secular, democracy; indeed, at times people inspired by him made it seem as if the one quite necessarily implied the other. Such a

paradoxical conjunction of what to many observers seem to be oppo-
sites—Islam/secularity, religion/science, faith/democracy—had marked
Gülen's teaching from the beginning of his career. Negotiating those tensions continues to be central to people of Hizmet around the world. For
the purposes of short-hand, I call the attempts by Gülen and people of
Hizmet to be both faithful Muslims and good citizens—which also has
included participation in and advocacy for interreligious dialogue, *principled pluralism*. We shall explore this theme of principled pluralism as
an aspect of Gülen's life and the Hizmet movement more fully in Chapter
Four. Gülen's effort to foster a generation of Muslims committed to their
faith and yet willing to dialogue with anyone has been a fascinating dra-
ma that is still very much ongoing around the globe.

The people who came to participate in Hizmet did not all arrive
on the same path. Some learned indirectly, through the example of local
leaders who may (or may not) have been directly influenced by Gülen.
Others learned more directly through Gülen's teachings and counsel as
articulated in sermons, public lectures, small-group talks, books and
articles, and individual consultation. Gülen has steadfastly disavowed
"leadership" of any kind. He has resisted the idea that a movement
should carry his name (as it has in many academic circles). At the same
time, Gülen has clearly identified with the people who have chosen to
devote themselves to God and to building civil society through his inspiration. He has been a teacher, in a distinctive adaptation of the practices
of a *Sufi sheikh*, throughout his life. Undoubtedly, despite his disavowals,
a key puzzle I have had to explore in seeking to understand Gülen's life
and influence is this relationship between movement "leader" and followers. How much is Hizmet dependent upon one individual—and how
much is it institutionalized? One piece to figuring out this puzzle may be
found in a somewhat startling feature of Gülen's life: while preaching or
praying he frequently cried. The people who gathered with him in prayer
sometimes cried, as well—often to the point of sobbing and other forms
of emotional release. This was unusual if not unprecedented in Turkish
public worship—especially among men, although some similar things
had happened in select *Sufi* lodges. The sociologist Max Weber identified
this kind of leadership as "charismatic."[4] And while there is undoubtedly
an element of charisma in Gülen's personality, the attraction people felt
to him is often difficult for citizens of Europe and the U.S. to compre-

hend. Gülen can thus be a target for resentment, misunderstanding, and caricature, as *The New Yorker* journalist Dexter Filkins aptly demonstrated in a religiously-tone-deaf 2016 essay.[5] The bond that has been forged between Hodjaefendi and those inspired by him goes beyond individual charisma, I suggest, to what I call engaged empathy. Engaged empathy is deep feeling for the suffering of the world that motivates people to organize themselves to alleviate that suffering. Something like this is encouraged in the teachings of many religious traditions. It is also a key aspect of religious peacebuilding. And the engaged empathy that Gülen has taught and inspired has been extended among people of Hizmet into manifold practices, businesses, and institutions. If Gülen's significance thus stemmed from the ways he advanced among Turks the non-violent practices of Islam, and from how he encouraged principled pluralism, his influence also grew through his emphasis upon engaged empathy.

In the context of secularizing Turkey, Gülen served as what political scientists have identified as a "Thermidorean" figure.[6] He allowed for and articulated the cooling of Revolutionary fervor by creating an opening for the public expression of Islam in secular Turkey; an opening politically exploited and mobilized by President Erdoğan. Through Gülen, rural and newly-urban Turkish Muslims were able to resolve deep tensions and address quite real suffering that the Republic exposed or neglected. For second-generation Republican Turks who were middle class or poorer, the economic promises of secularism lacked the substance of Muslim tradition. So what Gülen offered people, and what Erdoğan exploited, was a bridge between Islam and modernity. This bridge contrasted with the way Atatürk had *forced* modernity upon Turkey at the expense of Islam. One historian suggested that in recent decades Turkey has seen a "paradoxical Islamization of secular society and the internal secularization of Islamic thought."[7] That Gülen played a key role in this mutual process is unmistakable.

As a Thermidorean figure, then, Gülen has lived in a fragile, marginal zone. He was liable to suffer under shifting political winds. And as is well-known, he has lived in self-imposed exile in the United States since 1999. He might, if things had gone differently, have been welcomed back into Turkey for the waning years of his life as an exemplar of how Turkish Islam could show to a very troubled region how to integrate modernity and Islam. Such a possibility—that as of 2018 seemed remote—explains why then President Obama made his first official State visit to the Republic of Turkey in 2009. But that happy scenario is not how events unfurled. Instead, both Gülen and those who have identified with him in Hizmet—who had been disparaged at various times as *Fethullahcılar* ("Fethullah-followers") or "Gülenists," have most recently been dubbed members of the FETO—the Fethullah Terrorist Organization. This absurdity has more than a touch of Orwellian doublespeak to it. Gülen has consistently, and publicly, denounced terrorism.[8] Yet to be slandered puts Gülen in very good company in the history of religions. Those most dedicated to peace have often drawn the most profound hatred from those in political power. And yet, ironically, through their patient and principled persistence, those slandered and persecuted have often found ways to prevail against their ostensibly more powerful persecutors. Gandhi was not exactly loved by the British Raj, and yet his nonviolent *satyagraha* (truth-force) movement eventually overthrew the empire and brought democracy to India. Similarly, each time Gülen was persecuted over the decades—and it happened repeatedly, he and the movement associated with him emerged stronger than prior to the persecution. Enemy-status drew attention to Gülen. This attention allowed people to decide for themselves about what they discovered about him. The assaults unleashed by the Erdoğan regime since 2012 were unprecedented in their scope and destructive intent. Peoples' lives were irreparably harmed. Consistently, however, whenever the State had sought to suppress Gülen and Hizmet, events rebounded to the advantage of Hizmet and of Gülen's legacy.

It is of course impossible to predict the future—and a historian's crystal ball is no clearer than anyone else's. But even and perhaps especially after the Erdoğan crackdown a shared suffering of political oppression produced for Gülen and people of Hizmet a growing network of allies and co-workers; in Turkish *arkadaşlar*. This word, "friends," was common for Gülen and within Hizmet. Sometimes these friendships were intentional and strategic—as when Gülen encouraged his students and associates to build schools in various places across Turkey in the 1970s and 1980s, and when he encouraged them to do the same around the globe after 1990. These students then brought their students by the bus or plane-load to Izmir or to Istanbul to hear Hodjaefendi and to meet other friends. Sometimes friendships happened informally—as when businessmen learned about Gülen or Hizmet, and then contributed their skills to the building of schools, dormitories, hospitals, media corporations, and much more (and turned a profit while also doing good). All in all, through Hodjaefendi and Hizmet Turks carved out a network that allowed them to link spirituality with secularity. This network provided an alternative to the secularist faith-in-the nation (whoever its strong-man was) that was (and remains) the operative piety of the Turkish Republic. That President Erdoğan clothed his own ruthless political machinations and economic greed in Islamic garb did not resolve the enduring problem that practicing Muslims faced: how to be both faithful and modern, without sacrificing the integrity of either.

. Because of this network of friendships that swirled loosely around Gülen, the Hizmet movement was often known in Turkish as simply *cemaat*: "the community." This relatively neutral designation of informal associations strikes me as apt. Gülen developed relationships organically; hierarchies that developed around him—and they did, were constantly shifting. His influence grew steadily from the late '60s, but over the decades the movement also expanded to a point where the "leader" became, while still a source of inspiration, in many ways a follower—learning about initiatives around the world after they had been instituted. Hizmet developed a life of its own as Muslims put into practice the teaching of engaged empathy.

Outsiders might find analogies helpful to understand the historical development of this community. One scholar has suggested the English Puritans, with some good reasons (as we shall see).[9] But the Puritans were quite clearly a political movement. There was no mistaking Oliver Crowell's ambitions. Gülen, in contrast, has consistently disavowed politics. A better analogy to understand Gülen and Hizmet, then, may be with nineteenth-century Protestant revivalists, such as Charles Grandison Finney. In ways akin to how Christian revivalists like Finney (who founded Oberlin College) helped democratize nineteenth-century America and Europe, Gülen put into words the sufferings of ordinary people and encouraged them to participate faithfully in an emerging liberal economic and political order.[10] An even more enduring analogy, however, initially suggested by Phyllis E. Bernard, may be to another English-American religious movement, namely the Quakers, officially the Society of Friends.[11] This seventeenth-century Protestant reform movement had a clear (even zealous) religious foundation, drew the ire of authorities in both England and the American colonies, and eventually merged a peaceful spirituality with a pragmatic and business-minded rationality. And just as Quakers and Christian revivalists (emotional in their own idioms) paved the way for missionary-movements that spread Christianity, markets, and democracy around the globe, so too has Gülen motivated Muslim activists to carry his ideals—which he would of course call God's work, around the world. To call this engaged empathy is to call it too little, but I hope it advances understanding of Gülen's significance beyond mere Weberian "charisma."

Another, and perhaps the key, aspect of Gülen's contextual significance is his consistent advocacy for rigorous secular education for both boys and girls. Again in common with both Quakers and nineteenth-century Christian revivalists, Gülen has inspired people of Hizmet to work to advance universal literacy as understood in spiritual and scientific terms. Gülen's life-story exemplifies the conjunction. His own formal education ended in second grade. Atatürk's secular revolution did not privilege schools in places like Korucuk. Gülen's family, and especially his father, clearly preferred literacy in Islam to the kind of co-educational, secular education the Republic mandated. Through a series of teachers that included both his mother and his father, Gülen developed a deep familiarity with classical Islamic and Turkish sources that is impressive to anyone familiar with the literature. But Gülen also began discovering limits to this strictly Islamic formation. Two important influences pushed Gülen to link Islam with scientific inquiry. The first was a book of Qur'anic exegesis: the *Risale-i Nur* of Kurdish Muslim reformer Said Nursi. Nursi prescribed scientific inquiry for every Muslim. He was convinced that science confirmed, rather than conflicted with, revelation. Gülen first studied this work seriously in 1956, and it continues to be central to his intellectual life. The second influence that pushed Gülen's intellectual development was, ironically, an Army commander. This officer met Gülen during his mandatory military service from 1961 to 1963, and he encouraged the young preacher to study Western philosophy, literature, and science. What Gülen discovered from these two influences (among many others), and has consistently taught since, is that theology was not opposed to science, and that God's truth was mutually apparent in nature and the Qur'an. To harmonize religion and science like this may seem paradoxical for Western readers, where a "warfare" between science and religion has been declared by some intellectuals, and has been perpetuated by others. But perhaps the chief significance of Fethullah Gülen's life has been to promote among pious and devout Muslims the embrace of scientific and technical mastery. The evidence here is in the accomplishments of the thousands of students—men and women, he has motivated to go on to careers in the sciences and social sciences. We shall meet some of them in the pages to follow. We shall also see a few examples from the vast network of tutoring centers, elementary and secondary schools, math and science academies, colleges and universities that spread from a single institution in Izmir in 1968 to roughly 1,200 schools in 180 different countries by 2016. Almost universally, these schools were not *madrasa*s or schools for Islamic studies. Instead, they followed the secular curricula of the countries where they were built. Any Islam present in them was Islam by example. For Fethullah Gülen and the people inspired by him, then, embracing depth in Islamic scholarship and practice with mastery of scientific rationality was the kind of literacy that was at the heart of Hizmet.

All of this sounds very nice—and was historically significant by any register. But it could also be a recipe for personal aggrandizement, in the fashion of cult leaders who surround themselves with fawning devotees who hand over their lives and resources to enrich the leader. Gülen, in contrast, has lived a life of voluntary simplicity. He never married, he owns nothing, and he has always lived in modest residences. I have heard various descriptions of Gülen's simple living asserted repeatedly in interviews. At first these puzzled me; what difference does it make that he lived in a hut for a few years in Izmir, or slept in the corner of a mosque in Edirne? But gradually, as I heard the stories repeated, by bankers and contractors and farmers and teachers, it became clear that Gülen's asceticism, coupled with explicit teaching, encouraged others to take that spirit and to make it their own through various enterprises that both did well and did good. Max Weber (again) called that (inaccurately) the Protestant Ethic.[12] In fact, Catholics have been at least as good as Protestants at capitalism, as have Jews, Hindus, Muslims, and (increasingly) Buddhists. But the point remains: religious asceticism can fuel rather than impede participation in market economies, business, and finance. Perhaps religious asceticism—or at least a moral horizon—can also regulate, constrain, and moderate the destructive consequences of unfettered greed. There can be no doubt that Gülen's lifestyle has been consistently modest. His family home, no longer standing in Korucuk, was a one-story, five-room brick square that at times during his childhood slept a dozen or more—his parents, grandparents, seven siblings (after they were all born), aunts and uncles, nieces and nephews, and a steady stream of visitors—mostly imams and scholars. And he did in fact live in a window-box (in Edirne), a plywood shanty (in Izmir), and (since 1999) in a single room in a retreat center in Wind Gap, Pennsylvania (on the edge of the Poconos). He eats little, and he sleeps little. He has been arrested and taken into custody, and for at least six years was on the run from the military junta in Turkey. And yet he has encouraged those to whom he preached, if not his own family, to generate wealth to alleviate suffering.

People inspired by Gülen have taken his preaching about wealth-generation and put it into practice, to the tune of billions of dollars, even with recent attempts to sequester their assets by the Turkish government. Those closest to Gülen have lived simple if not austere lifestyles. They have done so both for reasons of principle and to discourage accusations of graft. Gülen's earliest followers in Izmir were small-business owners, at best. But Hizmet over the decades has also come to express itself in banking, publishing, media, and other trades and enterprises that were consistent with the aims of service as articulated in Gülen's teaching. A school in Uganda, for example, like the one built as Turkish Light Academy in 2007 (now just Light Academy), could not be completed without architects, engineers, construction contractors, tradesmen, laborers, information technology designers—and that's just the building. To operate the school required teachers, administrators, and the multitude of support services—from curriculum to cafeteria to sporting equipment to uniforms—that go along with educational enterprises. Repeatedly, organizations begun by people of Hizmet "seeded" other enterprises in the regions where they were planted. Such economic activity benefited local residents through salaries and contracts, and it benefited local governments through taxes. At the same time, wealth generation also led to more Hizmet projects, in a kind of virtuous cycle—to borrow a phrase from the economist Robert Reich.[13] Individuals chose to make donations, or foundations expanded into new arenas, and profits were then plowed back into new projects. To be clear: not all the businesses associated with Hizmet have been non-profits. Most have been non-profit educational or dialogue foundations, or non-governmental organizations such as Kimse Yok Mu or Embrace Relief—two of the names for global poverty-alleviation agencies associated with Hizmet. But all the Hizmet-related businesses operated along the lines of what Nobel laureate Muhammad Yunus identified as "social businesses."[14] That is, Hizmet has promoted business practices that both seek a strong bottom-line and hope to contribute to the well-being of society by solving social problems. From Said Nursi, Gülen learned that three primary problems plagued the modern world: ignorance, disunity, and poverty. Gülen then taught that this unholy trinity could be remedied through positive action to promote education, to engage dialogue, and to generate wealth. And as Yunus has perhaps articulated more clearly than anyone, such an organizational model of social business or social enterprise has the potential, well beyond its existence within Hizmet, to transform capitalism in the direction of greater justice. Conveniently, or at least poetically, within Hizmet this financial pattern has been dubbed *himmet*. *Himmet* is a Turkish word, originally from Arabic (*himma*), which refers in the *Sufi* context to inner spiritual resolve and dedication to attain the Divine. It also connotes the spiritual support by a saintly person to those who ask for it. *Himmet* in the Hizmet context has come to mean the voluntary altruistic financial support, fundraising, or donations to philanthropic activities, efforts, and projects. Stemming from Fethullah Gülen's own embrace of voluntary simplicity, then, *himmet* through *hizmet* has engaged people around the globe in practices of wealth-generation on behalf of the common good. What was first a Turkish Muslim movement has now become a global (and increasingly interreligious) version of social enterprise.

***

So, here is the broadest, satellite-view of our map: I will narrate Fethullah Gülen's life-story in five chapters, each chapter highlighting an element or set of relationships from his life and teaching that highlights his historical significance, and that suggests he and the movement he has inspired belong among the ranks of other historic peacebuilders: 1) *a commitment to spiritual and scientific literacy*; 2) *integrity of participation in the nonviolent practices of Islam*; 3) *engaged empathy*; 4) *principled pluralism*; and 5) *a business model of social enterprise*. But do these five aspects of Gülen's life, or five kinds of relationships, in fact mark him as a peacebuilder, as I claim?

Fortunately, an emerging science of peace and conflict studies is beginning to make it quite clear what breeds peace, and what leads to violence and war.[15] Violence—which we can define simply as harm to or destruction of life—is often misunderstood. All violence harms or kills. Street violence harms or kills immediately. Wars and terrorist acts do the same collectively and often indiscriminately. But there are kinds of harm to life that result from social policies and cultural patterns. These systemic kinds of violence kill slowly, with psychological and spiritual suffering to go along with the physical. Policies that perpetuate inequality and poverty and erode dignity are violent. Cultural and language patterns that stereotype, dehumanize, and create "us vs. them" dualisms can do real harm. And religious practices that promote self-righteousness and fear are violent. Fethullah Gülen's life and teachings, and the global Hizmet movement, have aimed to expose and to reduce especially these latter kinds of systemic or cultural violence. Historically, again, those in power have frequently targeted peacebuilders precisely because they challenged the structures and systems that keep people in fear and turned against each other. Peacebuilders are inherently (if not confrontationally) radical. As the word denotes, they seek to address the roots of injustices, conflicts, and wars.

In this light, Gülen's life and teaching accords closely with patterns that scholars of peace and justice studies see at the root of peaceful societies.[16] Gülen and people of Hizmet have not contributed to peacebuilding primarily by protesting, which is often how the public imagines peacebuilding. Rather, Gülen and people of Hizmet have contributed to peacebuilding by way of patient and proactive work, through the five kinds of relationships or practices sketched above. These patient practices—teaching, praying, conversing, and so forth, do not, alas, always make for dramatic reading or journalistic headlines. Yet peace, in this view, happens precisely when these practices can be engaged. Peace is not, in other words, some utopian prospect. Peace is the quite real ways that people have discovered to live together and to cooperate. Peace exists, succinctly, when people have the potential to flourish. The story I tell in the pages that follow describes both how Fethullah Gülen came to flourish as an individual, and how people have found ways to flourish through his teachings by building agencies and organizations that promoted peace.

At root, then, beyond participation in the nonviolent practices of Islam, beyond principled pluralism, beyond engaged empathy, beyond literacy, and beyond social enterprise, the story I tell about the life of Fethullah Gülen as a life of *hizmet* highlights the role of trust in forging more just and peaceful societies. In Turkish, again, the word *hizmet* means, literally, "service." But "service" in English can suggest passivity or deference to power. In the life of Fethullah Gülen, *hizmet* points to the way spiritual power translates into practical action: into peacebuilding through discernible and consistent practices. Hizmet, then, in an actual translation of what it has meant in the life of Gülen and those inspired by him, means the active work of human beings who learned to trust each other. This trust was forged through obstacles. It took courage. I call this kind of peace, manifest as trust, deep peace. Deep peace is not merely the absence of war. That I call basic peace; it is the least every government should provide. Nor is deep peace merely the kind of economic justice and social equity that marks good societies. That I call policy peace; and it is certainly to be desired and worked toward by any hopeful person and citizen. Rather, deep peace in the life of Fethullah Gülen shows how religions can provide people a peace that surpasses understanding, as the Apostle Paul put it.[17] This deep peace and the relationships it fosters can also motivate and support human beings to extraordinary acts of commitment on behalf of living out and realizing a tradition and its vision of the good life, no matter what. The most succinct way to describe the story I tell in the pages to follow, then, is as the story of deep peace in the life of Fethullah Gülen.

That story, again, has five chapters. The organization is both chronological and topical. Chapter One, "Learning—Erzurum and Edirne, 1938-1966," focuses on the earliest years of Fethullah Gülen's life, and what I think will be his strongest legacy—his embrace of and advocacy for literacy. The chapter begins by raising a question that was asked implicitly throughout his early career: "can anything good come out of Erzurum?" Fethullah Gülen grew up, in other words, in a backwater. And yet, the first section of the chapter documents how, in the words of Fethullah's sister Nurhayat: "we were a happy family." Up until he was fourteen, Fethullah lived with his extended family that included his grandparents, Şamil and Munise, his father Ramiz and mother Refia, and (eventually) seven siblings. The family stressed learning. His mother Refia was Fethullah's first Qur'an teacher, and Ramiz was himself an imam. The young Fethullah experienced his first *hatim*—or complete recitation of the Qur'an, at age 4. He became a *hafiz*—one who had memorized the Qur'an, by age 14. At age 15, Gülen left home to attend Qur'an school, first at Erzurum Kurşunlu Mosque, and then at various mosques around Erzurum province. Throughout his early years, he also studied with noted *Sufi* teachers of the Hanafi School—the most mainstream school of jurisprudence for Sunni Muslims. Among the most important of his teachers were Muhammed Lütfi, the imam of Alvarlı, a village nearby his hometown of Korucuk, and Osman Bektaş. His fellow students, like Hatem Bilgili, recalled Fethullah as an avid, and gifted, student. During his time in Qur'an school Gülen also became acquainted with the works of Said Nursi, and he began to read deeply in Rumi—the thirteenth century *Sufi* poet. Both Nursi and Rumi's influences can be found throughout Gülen's life and work. The chapter then traces Gülen's earliest appointments as an imam—in Edirne and Kırklareli—towns in Thrace Province in northwest Turkey. There Gülen quickly developed a reputation as a powerful preacher, and people began flocking to hear his emotional and rationally-engaging sermons. However, for some in the police and security forces, his growing reputation was challenging to the status quo. The regime saw any popular religious figure as a threat. It was between appointments in Edirne and Kırklareli that Gülen completed his mandatory military service. He served first in Ankara, and then in İskenderun (on Turkey's Mediterranean coast). At the latter, at the urging of one commander, he began to read in Western classics and humanistic literature. The military, however, was the bastion of secularism in Turkey, and although Gülen found one commander supportive, he also experienced at least one officer who reported him as a threat to the secular state. It was during his military service that the first of the many military coups to mark his life disrupted Turkish politics and threw his livelihood into question. His health suffered under the pressure, and he had to take a three month leave of absence, although he eventually completed his military service without further incident. By the time of his appointment to Izmir in 1966, Gülen's reputation for both scholarship and preaching was growing, yet, while under a close scrutiny by the secularist status quo which always had a check on any religious figure. Chapter One concludes with attention to how Gülen's advocacy for learning has led to a global network of schools. It includes the stories of two women who became leaders in Hizmet through these educational initiatives. One served as principal of a school in Albania, and then as a teacher at schools in Vietnam and Kenya; the other served as an editor and Islamic teacher in Istanbul.

Chapter Two: "We Were Young, 1966-1971," focuses on how during his years in Izmir Fethullah Gülen developed a growing reputation as a teacher who could bring people together, in the context of a Turkish culture riven by ideological conflict. The late sixties were a time of political awakening for many young people around the globe, and Turkey was no exception. Protests, marches, and riots marked every Turkish city, including Izmir. Some of them veered into violence. In contrast to this ideologically-laden conflict among youth, Gülen taught nonviolence, both indirectly through the five nonviolent pillars of Islam, but also directly through example and counsel. "The *Shahadah* in a *Sohbet*: Spiritual Food," describes how Gülen adapted a practice of Said Nursi—small group textual study, called a *sohbet*, to teach central Islamic principles like the *Shahadah* or creed. This section of the chapter then extends to how individuals around the world—including Muslim women in the U.S.—came to understand such study as a kind of "spiritual food." The next section of the chapter, "I had never prayed like this in my life!" focuses on how Gülen's practice of prayer drew people to him. His practice of prayer—not only five times a day, but as a lifestyle that permeates his entire time—marked Gülen as an individual with profound spiritual power. People saw him as spiritually literate. The third section of the chapter describes Gülen's first pilgrimage to Mecca, in 1968. What Fethullah Gülen drew from this experience was that Muslims could take the spirit of the pilgrimage, and its palpable sense of Muslim unity, and extend it in service to humanity wherever they might be. The fourth pillar of Islam, and the fourth section of the chapter, focuses on Fethullah Gülen's practice of Ramadan—the annual month-long fast by Muslims. For Gülen, for whom the Ramadan fast was something he looked forward to every year, the practice of fasting was a way to awaken spiritually by taming the ego and its incessant desires. The feasting with which the fast ended every night, in contrast, in a meal called an iftar, was a way to share bounty with one's neighbors, and thereby to make new friends. The chapter concludes with a section, "*Zakat* and Its Opposite: Organizing *Mütevelli* and Getting Arrested." It sketches Gülen's early teaching about money, and how he engaged the fifth nonviolent pillar of Islam, called *zakat* (charity) to guide Muslims in their use of financial resources. Among Gülen's followers during these early years were small business-men, who formed themselves into foundations, governed by trustees, called *mütevelli*. These *mütevelli* became the financial backbone of an emerging Hizmet movement, just as they also became targets, along with Gülen, for those opposed to any role for Islam in Turkish civil society. Nevertheless, during these years *mütevelli* provided, and raised, funds for students, summer camps, and for other initiatives which would later become dormitories, tutoring centers, and (eventually) schools—all of which were provided to young people by subsidy or scholarship. These were years of exciting growth for both Gülen as an individual, and for those drawn to him. They were years when (as one participant put it), "we were young." These were also years that ended with Gülen in prison and charged as an enemy of the state, following a military coup.

Chapter Three: "Empathy and Tears—The Aegean, 1971-80," high-lights the growth of Hizmet throughout the Aegean region in the 1970s. The chapter concentrates especially on Gülen's preaching, during which he and entire mosques filled with people would break into tears. This cry-ing reflected many things. But it signaled how Gülen awakened in people a deep identification with suffering—empathy. For some, no doubt, this suffering was internal; Turkey still gave faithful Muslims plenty of rea-sons to groan. But as Gülen gained in popularity during these decades, rather than focusing inwardly and building a self-interested power-base, he increasingly moved empathy outward—in service toward others. He taught young people, especially, who flocked to hear him preach, to live for a cause, when ideological groups and militaries driven by Cold War dualisms were often asking youth to die for their causes. Gülen and his followers advanced engaged empathy by embracing creative use of me-dia and modern technologies, and by institutionalizing and expanding the networks of hizmet begun in the prior decade. Gülen's sermons were recorded and distributed, and as a state-appointed preacher he delivered sermons to large crowds during this decade throughout the Aegean region. But the message he communicated consistently deflected attention (and resources) away from himself and toward the causes of literacy, the practice of Islam, and the alleviation of suffering. The Hizmet movement developed, in short, among people who recognized suffering when they saw it, and who were willing to forego short-term pleasure for long-term personal and social benefit. And engaged empathy spread as oppression grew. Once again, the decade ended with another military coup, and with Gülen briefly detained by police.

Chapter Four: "Melancholy and Dialoue—Istanbul, 1980-1999" focuses on how Gülen became a nationally-recognized figure from an Istanbul base. He did so as an advocate for dialogue, or as an exponent of what we have called principled pluralism. Gülen's childhood was provincial—and he still speaks the language of "heart" that characterizes many rural and local citizens of many cultures. But especially through a series of public initiatives, forums, and dialogues that were begun under a relatively more tolerant and even friendly political regime in Turkey, Gülen also articulated a cosmopolitan global ethic that motivated people inspired by him to go out into the world and to work in diverse cultural contexts. This outward movement began in formerly Soviet Republics with large Turkic-speaking and largely Muslim communities—often countries with linguistic, cultural, and ancestral ties. But since the 1990s the global outreach of Hizmet has grown into a truly global movement—with representation on every continent. Gülen of course grounded this global ethic theologically—as the Turkish word *hoşgörü* can summarize nicely. *Hoşgörü* often gets translated as "tolerance," but that doesn't accurately convey the significance of the term, implying as "tolerance" does a degree of condescension. Properly, *hoşgörü* means to "see all others as God sees them," namely as fellow creatures who reflect God's own beauty, and goodness, and mercy. A faithful Muslim, Gülen taught, could dialogue with anyone. There is no question of Gülen's credentials as a principled Muslim. But he also articulated—and those inspired by him increasingly learned from their encounters with diversity, to grant to others what Rabbi Jonathan Sacks has called "the dignity of difference."[18] Such an ethic has challenged both exclusivist Islamism and relativist secularism, to use categories popularized by Harvard's Diana Eck.[19] And that challenge explains to a large degree why Gülen has become a target of both Islamists and secularists. But, in any event, *hoşgörü* within

Hizmet put into practice the kind of deepening devotion within one's own tradition that resulted, at its best, from honest and open encounter with another. The chapter ends, once again, with Gülen under pressure from militarist-minded elitist and nationalist authorities, and on trial as a "threat to the state."

Chapter Five: "Hizmet Global—America, 1999-" addresses Gülen's life since moving to America in 1999 and how it has been marked by the capacity to inspire volunteers to organize for social enterprises. Gülen's teaching about poverty and wealth evolved to connect the ancient and common Islamic practice of *zakat* or charity with the most future-oriented dynamics of capitalist organization. It is this latter legacy that is perhaps the most surprising from Gülen's biography. A Muslim boy coming from a backwards rural village inspired a global network of people building bridges of dialogue and peace by wealth-generation to solve social problems: profits consistent with the prophets, or *himmet* (dedication; spiritual, financial support) for Hizmet. At the center of this model of organization was the practice of *istişare* or "mutual consultation." Akin to the way Quakers conducted business, by seeking consensus, Gülen has invited Muslims to practice *istişare* in whatever projects they undertook. What this model lacked in efficiency it made up for in trust: *istişare* generated networks of agencies, institutions, and businesses around the globe where people learned to trust one another. Even while Gülen's direct influence waned on the Hizmet movement as it grew, people of Hizmet practiced *istişare* as new opportunities for social enterprises were recognized and developed in Asia, Australia, the Balkans, Northern Europe, and the Americas. Implicit within Gülen's biography and within Hizmet, in short, was something beyond mere "market Islam," as one recent study suggested.[20] More radically, *himmet* for Hizmet suggested a way across traditions to mobilize and to direct the energies and capital of business on behalf of enhancing the capacities of human flourishing, rather than only to enrich the greed of a few.[21] The chapter, and the book, concludes with attention to how this model of organization thus challenged the increasingly documented greedy machinations of the Turkish regime, leading to the slandering of Gülen as a "terrorist," and the scapegoating of people of Hizmet.

All in all, the life of Fethullah Gülen has been the life of a faithful Muslim preacher and teacher committed to service to humanity: a life of *hizmet*. That he has been slandered and persecuted is a tragedy in the historical record—akin to the tragedies that have befallen many peacebuilders in history. While I have thus clearly taken sides in the contemporary debate over Gülen's significance, I also have sought to tell the story of this one man's life as honestly as I can. I believe he must be understood as both less, and more, than a political figure. His primary significance is spiritual and cultural. He arose in a context where Turkish Muslims recognized his integrity and were drawn to him—while at the same time those in power also recognized in him a threat to their privileged networks of patronage. I hope this book promotes greater understanding of Gülen's work. It is my expectation that he will eventually be recognized as belonging among other better known twentieth century religious peacebuilders, even though it is not likely that he will live to see the peace that his teachings encouraged and anticipated, or live to see his reputation secured. But that is to get ahead of the story. It begins in 1938 in a small village in northeastern Turkey, when a son was born to a man named Ramiz and a woman named Refia.

CHAPTER ONE

LEARNING - ERZURUM AND EDIRNE, 1938–1966

Education is the most effective and common tongue for relations with others. We are trying our best to do this; we have no other intention.[1]

M. Fethullah Gülen

C an anything good come out of Erzurum? This question lingered throughout Fethullah Gülen's early life. Erzurum is a province in Northeastern Turkey, near Armenia and Georgia. The province incorporates the city of Erzurum—an ancient settlement which had more than 300,000 residents in 2017, and which features Atatürk University—one of the largest in Turkey. But most of Erzurum Province is sparsely populated by very poor rural villages tucked onto the plains between the Caucasus mountain ranges.

The entire area is high altitude, with the thin, fresh air and brighter colors of any plateau. Erzurum's elevation is at roughly 6,500 feet above sea level, and the mountain ranges to the North and South of Erzurum feature peaks of over 10,000 feet, including *Büyük Ejder* (literally "the big dragon") in the Palandöken range. In the brief summer, the region is a pale green. Because the soil is highly alkaline, few trees grow aside from an occasional scrub pine. Driving west from Erzurum, toward the village of Korucuk where Fethullah Gülen was born in 1938, one's eyes welcome the rare stream bed and its deciduous trees, where caravans on the Silk Road, which winds through the region, would stop for the night.

Korucuk lies in the Pasinler Valley. It was, and is, a farming village. An occasional poplar tree provides some shade in the summer, and a wind-break from drifting snow in the winter, but otherwise the village is open to the breezes and sunshine when the weather is gentle, to gusts and torrents when it storms. In summer, stacks of hay bales line the side of the road. The summer breezes of Korucuk, and all of Erzurum province for that matter, are laden with the sweet smell of hay. But in Korucuk those sweet breezes also often give way to fragrances a tad more on the sour side. In fact, dung is collected in sprawling piles or stacks of bricks alongside the sheds and houses of the village. The dung piles sometimes spill into the single paved street of the village. The dung bricks will be used to light cooking fires year-round, and to warm homes during the long winters.

The minaret of the local mosque is visible from anywhere in Korucuk, and the sound of the *adhan*—the call to prayer, can be heard from any corner of the village. There are maybe 50 houses in Korucuk, housing 250 people—about the same number that Fethullah Gülen recalls from his boyhood.[2] Most of these houses are in various stages of decay, or, to put it positively, are being "worked on." Tin rooftops are common, as are some tarps. Some have mud and stone foundations that date back decades, if not centuries. Most haven't been painted in years, if ever. Few are more than one, low story. On the lovely summer day that I visited Korucuk in 2015 I was greeted with warm hospitality by a distant relative of Gülen's. As we sat on blankets behind his home, he treated me to a refreshing glass of his homemade yogurt-drink (*ayran*). Still, I could not escape the conclusion that by and large Korucuk—and Erzurum Province overall, is a harsh, stark place populated by hard-working people. Few of the residents older than thirty who I met possessed all their teeth (although their smiles were more than ready). I realized why people might wonder: can anything good come out of here?

Yet in one reporting, at least, Gülen remembered his former village home fondly. His chores as a child included letting out to pasture the 2 or 3 (at most) cows, and herding a few sheep, that the family kept for subsistence. And of-course when he traveled to relatives nearby he also helped with whatever work was necessary in the fields.[3] Thus, with the perspective of almost fifty years, he wrote in 1994:

> The deep silence, contemplative calm, and magical nature that surround our imagination when thinking about our old villages no longer exists.
>
> The slice of silence that we sense and become exhilarated by today

in a cove or a grove was always the natural and permanent atmosphere of our old villages. There was such a warm bond and sweet
balance between former villages and cities that villagers did not envy
the city and city dwellers, and city dwellers did not look down upon
villagers. In fact, city dwellers sometimes actually came to live in the
villages. The village, considered a small city at that time, was a place of
divine beauty where city dwellers went for amusement and relaxation,
and to be close to nature. A pleasant silence and calm always dom-
inated the old villages. The morning sunlight, the mewing of sheep
and lambs, and the cries of insects and birds would strike our hearts
in sweet waves of pleasure and add their voices to nature's deep, inner
music. In the evening, existence would shroud itself in the covers of
dusk, a mysterious condition that would cast a spell on people and
produce dreams. The nights always resonated with a song of silence
and calm.

In this world—the next-door neighbor to the next world—the call
to prayer and the prayer litanies, the language of the beyond, would
call us to a different concert and take us [into] a deeper and more
spiritual atmosphere. As long as we sense thoughts and ideas belonging to that sacred period, we cannot break with our past and remain
detached from our future.[4]

Less romantically, according to a different report, upon one return
to his village of origin (probably in 1988), Gülen remarked that "In the
past, the villages grew roses. Now they grow dung."[5] And even more
starkly, in another interview Gülen once said: "I grew up in a place that
resembled 'ruined towns, ruined homes' ... 'homeless deserts, headless
communities, days without work, evenings with no thought for tomorrow, domination, oppression."[6] Could anything good come out of Erzurum?

"We were a happy family"

On the western edge of Korucuk, just as one approaches the village, is an
overgrown cemetery. Thistles, wildflowers and a few straggly roses grow
amidst the barely trodden paths. Those paths wind between worn head-
stones that mark the passing of generations. A small rectangular stone
outline, about a foot high, traces the exact spot where a body lay. Tomb-

stones—usually a larger one at the head, and a smaller one at the feet, are inscribed sometimes with Arabic, sometimes with old Ottoman script, and occasionally with the new (since the 1920s) Latin alphabet. Occasionally, a tall stone almost to the height of a person marks the tomb of an imam, scholar, or *Sufi sheikh*. These markers also have two rectangles for feet, and a head in the shape of a turban—about as close as any Muslim representation comes to incorporating the human form. Such stones are rare in the Korucuk cemetery. But one of them is in a small, 12 foot by 12-foot square enclosure—outlined by three rows of modest cement blocks with a wrought-iron fence atop, that is the Gülen family plot.

The presence of this spiritual leader's tomb in the Gülen family burial place points to an important fact: Fethullah inherited a legacy of spirituality. He recalled in an interview that: "The first person from our family to settle in Korucuk was my great-grandfather Molla Ahmet, son of Hurşid Ağa, son of Halil Efendi. Molla Ahmet was an extraordinary person distinguished by his knowledge and piety. During the last 30 years of his life, he never stretched out his legs to lie on a bed and sleep. It was said that when he became sleepy, he would sit down, rest his forehead on his right hand, and nap a little."[7] This emphasis on his great-grandfather's personal piety—even to the point of ascetic extreme—mirrors the actual difficult circumstances that in all-likelihood led to the family's migration to the Pasinler Valley.

The original location of the Gülen family was Ahlat—a town on the Western shore of Lake Van, very close to Turkey's eastern borders with Armenia, Azerbaijan, and Iran, and to the south and east of Korucuk. In 1877-78, the Caucasus region—in which Erzurum generally resides, was the eastern front of a war between Christian forces loyal to the Russian Empire and Muslims from among the Ottoman Turks. The war was brutal. Russians advanced to the City of Erzurum and besieged it in November, 1877. The siege failed, in part, at least according to legend, due to the heroic efforts of Nene Hatun—a young woman who took up a rifle and a hatchet against the Russians to avenge the death of her brother. Having failed to take Erzurum, the Russians then moved East to Kars, closer to Russia. The Gülen family migration followed the path left behind by this Russian strategy: they went where the Russians weren't. Some of the Armenian Christians of Erzurum Province (nearly 40% by some reckoning), who had lived in relative peace under the Muslim Ot-

tomans for centuries, sided with the Russians during the 1877-78 conflict. They then fled the Erzurum region along with the Russian Army, as
Muslims flowed into the region from occupied territories. These events
led to one of the worst human tragedies during WWI, which for Armenians was a genocide. Today, many Turks recognize this turbulent time
as a horrible stain in history, mourning for their losses as well as for the
great suffering of Armenians. While some countries, like France, call it
genocide, some other countries, like the US, do not. All agree that violence and bloodshed accompanied the "liberation" of Turkey by Atatürk
and his armies in the early twentieth century. And nobody disputes that
Eastern Turkey was a particularly brutalized region.

So, the Gülen family knew war and its costs. It is not, however, a
warrior's monument that is in the Gülen cemetery plot in Korucuk. It is
a pious scholar's—Molla Ahmet, Fethullah Gülen's great-grandfather—
who first settled in Korucuk. That the Gülen family would embrace religion and spirituality can, and should, be understood as a counterpart
and alternative to the war-making that tore apart the region of his origin
and forced his family's migration.[8] An early story about Gülen's grandfather, Şamil, the son of Molla Ahmet, can give one glimpse into the
family's mentality. Just before World War I, a large earthquake shook
the Erzurum region. Korucuk suffered. People fled their homes, many
of which were rendered unstable. They slept in large open areas such as
the local threshing floor, in fear of aftershocks. However, as winter approached, this of course became impossible. Erzurum experiences heavy
snowfall—as much as 3 meters (nearly ten feet) annually, and the ground
is covered with snow for on average 150 days each year.

Şamil Gülen was among those sleeping on the threshing floor. One
evening as he was on his way there, he encountered the local imam—a
man named Mehmet. Imam Mehmet told Şamil: "Go home and sleep.
If even one rock falls, bring it and throw it at my head." Gülen was of
course surprised (but probably grateful) for this advice. He asked the
imam how he could be so certain. The imam then shared a dream he had
experienced:

> Last night the Prophet came to our village. The Four Righteous Ca-
> liphs were behind him. Ali ibn Abi Talib had many stakes in his hands.
> I immediately ran to them. Turning to me, the Prophet asked, "Is this

village yours, Molla Mehmet?" I said, "Yes, O Messenger of God, it is mine." Then the Prophet turned towards Ali and said, "O Ali! Pound a stake in this village so it will not shake again."

The imam then repeated his imperative to Şamil Gülen: "Go home and sleep." Buoyed with confidence in the words of his imam, and even more by a visit to his village by the Prophet and his Companions, Fethullah Gülen's grandfather went back to his home, and slept.[9]

Now—for some, such stories may sound as much legend as fact. The city of Erzurum *was* nearly destroyed by an earthquake in 1859, and another in 1983 did considerable damage to the region. An earthquake in the Lake District of Van on October 23, 2011 killed nearly 500. But this story can help us begin to understand how for Fethullah Gülen, in line with the Islamic devotion of his family, learning was not narrowly understood. Learning for Gülen could include attention to what Freud (in) famously dubbed "the unconscious." Gülen himself explained: "Dreams usually comprise images that are somehow related to past or future circumstances, seen either clearly or symbolically, through windows opening onto the world of truth ... Every dream, like a light or a signpost from the worlds beyond, may remove a darkness and indicate a direction."[10] Understandably, any Muslim theologian will interpret dreams differently than Freudians who, in Gülen's vivid imagery, see human beings as "a swamp of animal impulses." And Gülen is careful to warn that dreams are not necessary to "see the worlds beyond," lest the unscrupulous exploit them, or the naïve depend upon them. But generally-speaking, "thousands of inspirations flow to the heart during dreams."[11] An attentive and disciplined interpreter, drawing primarily on knowledge of the Qur'an and Sunnah (the tradition of the Prophet's teachings), could secondarily come to trust in what one might learn from dreams, among other sources. His grandfather Şamil was an example. Learning happened in classrooms, yes; but not only there. If his grandfather could trust in an imam's dream, then dreams might also bear meaning for young Fethullah.

In fact, as a child Gülen learned that silence and listening—simply paying attention—is crucial to learning. Fethullah's older sister Nurhayat recalled that when other children went outside to play, young Gülen stayed behind with the adults to listen in on their discussions and debates.[12] Fethullah himself remembered that his grandmother, Munise was a particularly good listener. "I grasped my grandmother even before my father and mother," Gülen writes. "Her quietness and depth, like calm seas, affected me greatly. ... She was a unique woman who spoke very little and tried to reflect Islam fully with her state of being."[13] By describing his grandmother as "quiet," Gülen meant to describe the depth of her spirituality; that she did not worry about worldly matters. To some, this might appear to reflect gender bias. And Gülen's attitudes about gender have evolved to be more progressive over time. He has consistently advocated for full education for both boys and girls, but he was raised in a rather rigidly patriarchal culture. Unlike the Apostle Paul, however, who notoriously wrote that the women of Corinth should "be silent" in church (1 Corinthians 14:34), Gülen applied the example of his soft-spoken grandmother universally. "Talking too much," Gülen once wrote, "is a personality defect stemming from mental and spiritual imbalance."[14] Now, coming from a preacher and teacher who spent a good portion of his adult life talking, these words carry more than a touch of irony. But behind this counsel to guard one's speech is a broader principle that has been repeatedly stressed by Gülen: to be self-critical. Islamic scholar Zeki Sarıtoprak identifies self-criticism for Gülen with the *Sufi* principle of *muhasaba-i nafs*: "questioning yourself before being questioned."[15] Gülen himself clarifies the notion: "A sensible person is not one who claims infallibility and therefore is indifferent to others' ideas. Rather, a truly sensible person is one who corrects his or her errors and makes use of others' ideas in acknowledgement of the fact that human beings are prone to error." Succinctly, and with a good dose of common sense, Gülen uses a Turkish folk saying which also has Islamic resonance to clinch the point: "Those who speak a lot make many mistakes."[16] As we shall see in Chapter Five, this willingness to listen quietly and attentively—learned first from his grandmother, Munise—was a crucial component that led people to trust Fethullah Gülen, and that led to what is now a global movement.

First encounter with death

From his grandfather Şamil and grandmother Munise, then, the young Fethullah learned that Islamic learning was deep and broad, including even experiences like dreams, and he learned to guard his tongue and to listen attentively. The death of the two of them within an hour of each other, on January 10, 1954, affected the fifteen-year old Gülen profoundly. He had known the two since his birth. At the time, he was studying Arabic in Hasankale (now Pasinler)—a town about ten miles from Korucuk. He walked back and forth every day. On the day of his grandparents' death, however, Gülen recalls being in Erzurum (fifteen miles from Korucuk) to take some exams. He describes learning of his grandparents' death as follows:

> The world collapsed over me. I was traumatized. After my classes end-ed, I hit the road [on foot]. Of course, I couldn't make it to their fu-neral [a Muslim is ideally buried within 24 hours of death]. I cried for days. I prayed day and night, saying 'My God! Please kill me, too, so I can return to my grandparents.' I was totally unable to accept their deaths. The reason I was so traumatized was because the members of our family had very strong ties to each other.[17]

For many children, the death of their grandparents is their first experience of death. Gülen knew them both intimately.

Young Gülen had every reason to hope that his pious grandparents would be in paradise. That hope was behind his own prayer to die. Still, articulating such a wish to die can sound very strange to secular ears. It becomes less strange when one tries to imagine the point of view of a devout Muslim youth in rural Anatolia in 1954 who had no doubts about heaven. Death is of course a challenge to learn from for anyone. From the perspective of maturity, Gülen drew at least six teaching points from the fact of death. They are worth exploring briefly here. They might help us to understand the intensity of his youthful grief, as he reflected upon it across the decades. The topic is, of course, perennial. Some of the points Gülen makes are conventional, some perhaps surprising. But together they illumine both his grounding in Islam, and his integration of secular learning—when facing the unmistakable destiny of every hu-man being.

First, Gülen writes, "death is not a final exhaustion of nature, [but] ... a transformation, a change of place, state, and dimension; a comple-tion of service, a release from [life's] burden, to attain peace and ease." This neatly combines biology with theology. It acknowledges both death's finality and its character as transformation of matter. Yet, second, since "death is a separation from life and the living, it affects our minds and those sentiments that make us human. It is impossible to deny such an influence, to silence the heart in the face of death. Death arouses considerable tumult in our hearts and minds." One can easily hear the anguish of the teenage Gülen in this description. Third, however, believers "view death as an advancement, perfection, an acquisition of a higher essence and nature. Since death carries the fruit of eternal existence and bliss, it is also a great blessing and a Divine gift." Again—this belief was part of Fethullah's awareness from his childhood. To some, this is mere denial. But for others, it is the heart of faith—to affirm that an apparently indifferent cosmos is in fact governed by a merciful and generous Purpose for every individual.

Fourth, "death is the time when one being resigns and hands over its affairs to its successors." Here, again, Gülen interprets biology psychologically, or perhaps anthropologically; death clears the field for new people, new ideas, new actions. Fifth, "death may also be understood as silent advice, in the sense that nothing is self-existent." Here, Gülen gives the fact of mortality social significance, as evident in every funeral gathering: we need each other. All matter is connected to the energy that animates it. By analogy, all creation is connected to the Creator. Finally,

> Consider the subject from another angle. If there were no death, would we not live in a hell of unrelieved terror as we faced an endless existence without a break or relief? How could we measure the worth or value of anyone or anything, conserve or concentrate our energy, make or carry out an intention, if time was limitless? If such a situation existed, those who now mourn the fact of transience and death would mourn their absence. Moreover, we would not experience creation's inexhaustible variety, with all the prompts and images it gives to the human mind of beauty, freshness, and loss with renewability. How, in the absence of such a panorama of novelty within stability, could the human mind be inspired to contemplate that which lies beyond and sustains the visible world? How could we seek and worship the One who creates and provides for the whole?[18]

Of course, few fifteen-year olds would be likely to formulate such ideas. But they suggest how, over a lifetime of being informed by both faith and modern science, Gülen came to reflect on the loss of his grand-

parents—and, naturally, many losses since then. And as astute observers of Western culture (such as Ernest Becker) have long suggested, the
denial of death is not only a problem for religious people.[19] There are
plenty of ways that atheists and materialists have found to deny their
fragile destiny.[20] When young Fethullah articulated a *desire* to be with
his grandparents who had died, then, he articulated a realistic and understandable, albeit intense, version of the pining that anyone feels after
losing a loved one.

Parents

Gülen's father's name was Ramiz. A picture of him taken in the late
1960s or early 1970s shows him as a balding, somewhat gaunt man with
heavy-lidded eyes, thick eyebrows, and a bushy white beard. He had
large ears, and a long thin nose (as opposed to Fethullah's wider nose).
His mouth shows just the hint of a smile as he looks at the camera. Like
his son, Ramiz served as an imam—first in Korucuk, then briefly in the
nearby villages, and finally in Erzurum, where, after his death on September 20, 1974, a mosque was named in his honor. About his father,
Gülen recalled:

> He lived a careful life. He was very careful in observing his prayers.
> His eyes were teary too. He never wasted his time. When he came
> home from the fields, he used to open up a book and read until dinner
> was ready, with his moccasins on his feet.... My father was a person
> who filled up his time with auspicious and abundant things and a per-
> son who attached importance to thinking. He was opposed to living
> an empty life. He was an eager man. He had learned how to read and
> write through his own efforts.... Those times were times when Turkish
> culture had been forgotten and left in the wilderness in some places
> [that is—Atatürk's reforms had imposed a cultural revolution that fa-
> vored the West]. My dad learned Arabic and Persian in two years and
> improved his knowledge [these languages were officially outlawed].
> He was very interested in knowledge and his situation had a deep im-
> pact on me. Knowing what he went through in that age for the sake of
> knowledge has made me more mature.[21]

Recall again the context. Atatürk had died in 1938, but his secularization program continued its frequently ruthless course. Certain kinds of learning—even languages other than Turkish, were outlawed. Public displays of Islam, aside from those mandated by the State, were banned. But as Gülen's description of his father Ramiz' life makes plain, on the popular level—and certainly in villages like Korucuk—Islam continued to thrive. It did so largely in study groups and meetings—which had to gather cautiously not to come under the radar of the authoritarian state—where Arabic and Persian were among the tools of the tradition.

Beginning in 1950, then, under a new political regime, Muslims like Ramiz Gülen also began to reassert themselves in public life. Some of the *Sufi* orders—shut down in 1925—reemerged, and their lodges or meeting houses opened for prayer, sometimes in the guise of tourist attractions or museums. Among the *Sufi* brotherhoods that experienced a resurgence in the 1950s were the Kadiri, Nakşibendi, and Mevlevi (dervish) orders.[22] All three had centers throughout Turkey, and all three would be important in Fethullah Gülen's intellectual development. Even more importantly for Gülen, a new community emerged around the teaching of Said Nursi (1877-1960). Informed by *Sufi* thought—he was educated by masters of Nakşibendi and Kadiri orders—Nursi was initially active in support of the Republic, but became disillusioned and critical of the direction of the new regime. For this, he spent time in jail, where he wrote prolifically, advocating for Muslims to embrace modern science, and for science to be shaped by the ethics of Islam. Although his writings were banned, they proliferated in small group study circles. Over time, in recognition of his scholarly superiority Nursi would come to be called "Bediüzzaman": "the most unique person of the time." Sometimes he would simply be called Üstad: "the teacher." A great many Turks came to follow Nursi, and many scholars see a direct link between the "Nur" movement, as it was called, and the career of Fethullah Gülen.[23] All in all, then, if the 1950s created an opening for a reformer like Nursi, it was still a time when the practice of Islam could get you thrown into a Turkish jail. As Fethullah remembered the life of his father, "what he went through," to acquire knowledge, he saw oppression.

That oppression could be severe, and at times was simply petty. Police or gendarmes—county officials—could arrest anyone suspected of violating the Kemalist orthodoxy. They looked for men who wore traditional head coverings (a turban or fez), rather than the Western fedoras and top-hats that Atatürk favored. Salih Gülen, one of Fethullah's younger brothers, recalled an occasion when the police stopped his father while he was trying to teach. They forced Ramiz to remove his turban, accusing him: "are you still following that old-time religion?"[24] Another widely circulated story can explain a consistent confusion in Fethullah Gülen's biography.[25] It can also illustrate the lengths a faithful Muslim like Ramiz had to go to practice the most basic matters of faith— such as the right to choose the name of his child. Shortly after Fethullah was born in 1938, Ramiz went to republican officials to register the birth of his son, as required by law. The name he had chosen was Muhammed Fethullah. The official objected that the name was too Islamic. Rather than fight with the official, Ramiz left. Three years later, when another son was born, Ramiz had been elected as a village official. He had also befriended a local military sergeant. Political scientist Mustafa Gökhan Şahin explains that this time Ramiz "took his military sergeant friend to the registry office with him. The Military sergeant ordered the officer to name the children the way Ramiz wanted. However, after the sergeant left, the registry officer named Fethullah without Muhammed and the other child [Ramiz' second son] Seyfullah (sword of God) instead of Sıbgatullah ("Paint" of God) as the father originally wanted. That's why Gülen's official birthday is April 27, 1941, roughly 3 years later than the actual one."[26]

From all accounts, the Gülen household was a peaceful one. That is not to say that there were no negotiations among the family members. Alp Aslandoğan, Executive Director of a Hizmet-affiliated NGO, recalled how in one of his talks Gülen remembered from his childhood only one instance of disagreement between his mother and father— when his mother went to the market without informing Ramiz. Generally, in mid-twentieth-century Turkish village life, women set the tone for domestic matters, but patriarchy prevailed in public. Aslandoğan also remembered a story Fethullah told about how women in the Gülen household strove for, if not enforced, family harmony. On one occasion, when Ramiz was beginning to appear upset with his wife, Gülen's grandmother Munise reportedly said to her son Ramiz: "If you say a single bad word, scold, or mistrust my daughter, I'm not going to make my milk lawful to you." This warning, according to Aslandoğan, invoked a hadith—or saying of the Prophet and his Companions. It reads:

A man came to the Prophet and said, "O Messenger of God! Who among the people is the most worthy of my good companionship?" The Prophet (PBUH) said: "Your mother." The man said, "Then who?" The Prophet said: "Then your mother." The man further asked, "Then who?" The Prophet said: "Then your mother."[27]

The point was clear enough—mothers (and women generally) deserved respect. Aslandoğan drew the conclusion about the Gülen family dynamic: "This incident arose because of merely the *hint* of a harsh word. Hodjaefendi's family members were respectful to each other. They gave each other dignity."[28] Or as Gülen's older sister Nurhayat put it simply: "we were a happy family."[29]

The Gülen family may have been happy, and were well-regarded in the region, but they were hardly rich. There was usually enough food, but rarely too much. Still, their home was frequently host to both extended family and visiting scholars. Ramiz apparently had a strong reputation throughout Erzurum Province, as both a scholar and a man of moral scruples. There are many stories recounting Ramiz' moral scrupulosity. One of them, for instance, recalls that Ramiz would tie shut the mouths of his livestock as he herded them, so that they would not eat the grains or grasses of his neighbors as they walked through the fields around Korucuk and Alvar.[30] As a scholar, Gülen recalled about his father in an interview that:

Although raised in a small village amidst material poverty, scarcity, and drought ... [my father had the reputation of one who] seemed to have received a "royal upbringing." ... [He had] an agile mind that revealed itself in subtleties ... My father constantly adorned his comments with witty remarks he had heard or made up, [but] ... I was impressed that he would never step over the line of what was proper. In both his love and his anger, he protected that boundary. He was bound to the Prophet's Companions to the extreme, and instilled in me and my siblings his love of them.[31]

Ramiz' job was to serve in the post where he was appointed by the State—leading prayer, preaching, and (within the limits of the law) teaching. He served in Korucuk until 1949—when Fethullah was 11. After that he was appointed imam in Alvar—a nearby village. That appointment ended rather abruptly sometime in the early 1950s. After brief service in Çiçekli—yet another village in the Pasinler Valley, Ramiz was appointed in 1956 to be an imam in Erzurum. He lived there for the rest of his life—with occasional visits to see his son, which will be described at the appropriate junctures.

Gülen's mother, Refia, has been the subject of a recent biography.[32] That book was written in part to counter misrepresentations about her origins, including a charge that she was Jewish (which would explain, to those prone to conspiracy theories, why her son would be friendly to Israel and seek to build bridges between Muslims and Jews). In fact, Refia was born in 1913 in Sığırlı village of Erzurum Province. She was the youngest daughter of her mother, Hatice, and father, Seyid Ahmet—a family with a long legacy in the region. The marriage between Refia and Ramiz was arranged by their families—far and away the common pattern in the Erzurum region then, and, in many cases, down to today. It was consummated in 1935, after a three-year engagement. The couple had eleven children—eight of whom lived to adulthood. There were six boys. Fethullah was the oldest, and his younger brothers were Seyfullah/Sıbgatullah (b. 1942, d. 2014), Mesih (b. 1944), Hasbi (b. 1946, d. 2012), Salih (b. 1949), and Kutbettin (b. 1955). There were two sisters—Nurhayat (b. 1936) and Fazilet (b. 1951).

A picture of Refia Gülen from sometime in the 1980s shows her with downcast eyes as she knits. Fethullah inherited his mother's broad nose and sweeping forehead. In the picture Refia wears a white scarf that cascades down over her shoulders. She also wears two rings—one on each hand. A well-worn prayer book or small Qur'an sits on a shelf behind her. Her face is creased, eyebrows heavy, and she appears to be avidly concentrating. Like her son, Refia put piety above politics. She was the first to teach her son to pray, and in fact she was also her son's first Qur'an teacher. She did not, however, limit her teaching to within the family. Gülen explains: "She taught the Qur'an to all the village women and to me at a time when even reading it was difficult."[33] Refia Gülen engaged, to be clear, in civil disobedience. Using Arabic was forbidden. She could have been arrested and thrown in jail. Gathering a group of women to study together added to the risk. Yet, faith mattered more than unjust politics.

As is well known, learning the Qur'an involved reciting it. In an interview, Refia recalled that Fethullah started learning to recite with her at age 4, and he finished reciting Qur'an in about a month. The occasion was celebrated as his "first *hatim*." The Gülen family sponsored a feast for the village, and Gülen recalled that some guests told him that this was his "wedding day." He remembered, not surprisingly, being embarrassed by this. He also remembered that he cried. This is surely an early memory for a child to recall. But in an interview I did with him in 2018, Gülen remembered the day vividly. Such an imprint suggests that Gülen experienced from an early age a tension between devotion and public recognition. That tension that would play itself out in many ways throughout his life. The episode suggests more importantly that literacy (broadly understood) was important to the principal people in young Gülen's life—his parents. The few books in the household, Gülen recalled, were "either worn or torn from being read so often."[34]

Naturally, Refia Gülen also performed other tasks of being a mother. Her daughter, Nurhayat, who was two years older than Fethullah, described a typical day in the Gülen household during the 1940s:

> My mother would wake me and Hodjaefendi up at 3:30 or 4 in the morning to pray. She would start teaching us Qur'an, although we didn't have much time in the morning because she also had to cook, clean, do laundry. She worked very hard. We'd never say no if she asked us to do something. At times there would be twenty-five people in the house—our entire family—uncles, aunts, children, and 4 or 5 visiting *hodja*s as guests. Hodjaefendi would always talk and discuss with our guests. He wouldn't play. From the *hodja*s he'd learn about the prophets—how Islam expanded. Then he'd come and tell these stories to my grandmother, who would cry profusely. We'd say, "[Fethullah]—why are you making her cry so much?" He went to the mosque with the grownups. At night, then my mother would teach us some more about Qur'an, and my father would teach more detailed lessons.[35]

Refia kept busy, in short, and the Gülen household was one organized around prayer and learning.

Not everything was work. The family was affectionate. In a reflection published in 2005, some of Gülen's experience with his own mom perhaps comes through:

If there is someone who hugs, cuddles, kisses, and caresses us, who
relieve[s] our feelings of sadness and dejection, who shares our wor-
ries, who prefers us to eat in her place, us to be dressed well instead
of her, who feels her hunger or fullness when we are hungry or full,
who bears unimaginable hardships ... for our happiness and joy, who
shows us the way for our body to develop, our will to strengthen, for
our intelligence to become sharp and perspicacious, for our horizons
to be oriented to the Hereafter—a person who does all these without
expecting, openly or secretly, anything in return—that person is none
other than our mother.[36]

These vivid descriptions of physical affection, maternal empathy,
and intellectual, physical, and spiritual encouragement—characterize
well what we know of Gülen's earliest relationship with his mom. The
two remained close throughout her life. After Ramiz died in 1974, Refia moved to Izmir, where Fethullah was then preaching. Her son visited her frequently there, and he would go to Erzurum to see her during
summers. Refia took pride in her son, who was becoming increasingly
famous. She lived to the age of 80, and she died on June 28, 1993. She
is buried close to where her son preached, at a site he last visited before
departing Turkey in 1999, in Karşıyaka Cemetery, high on a hill above
Izmir.

Fethullah lived with his nuclear family only until age 14 or 15—
when he moved to study full-time in various *madrasa*s (theological
schools) and with various *Sufi* mentors—about which more shortly.
While at home, chores, meals, hospitality, and conversation marked
young Gülen's life. But one constant in his experience was the music of
chanting the Qur'an—in prayers and recitation. By the time he left home,
or shortly thereafter, he became a *hafız*, or one who had memorized the
entire Qur'an. Such memorization happened in part through chanting.
The Qur'an, in short, is sung—in lilting, melismatic repetition of the
poetry and prose of the text. Many have speculated about music as a
"universal language." The power of the Qur'an in Islam—and it has extraordinary power—is in part the way it draws upon this universal power of music (especially given that other kinds of music are not often featured in Islamic worship). More specifically, then, Fethullah Gülen grew
up with a musical, as well as a poetic, literacy through his study of the

Qur'an. This is a literacy of a different type from sheer mathematical or instrumental reasoning. As an adult, Gülen wrote of the Qur'an that:

> Every word is aimed at the *latifatu'r-Rabbaniyah*, or "the spiritual intellects or faculties," that can directly perceive the spiritual realities that the mind cannot grasp. These faculties include the *qalb* (the spiritual faculty of the "heart"), *sır* (the faculty of the "secret"—the spiritual faculty that is more subtle than the "heart"), *khafi* (the private—the faculty that is more subtle than the "secret") and *akhfa* (the more private—the most subtle faculty). These subtleties are the actual target of the words expressed. If words cause any kind of contradiction or variation of meaning between these subtleties, this indicates a deficiency in the words. While reserving their differing degrees of deficiency, there is such a deficiency in almost all human declarations. The Qur'an, however, is superior and exempt from such deficiencies.[37]

It is no doubt difficult for many raised with scientific rationality to understand such an assertion. One simple (and deficient) way to explain it is that the truth of the Qur'an is like the truth of music—and it was that kind of truth that Gülen first learned in his family.

It was not only the chanting of Qur'an that filled the air with music in the Gülen household. Nurhayat remembered that her mother did not sing much, "because she didn't want us to be spoiled." That says something about the value placed on musical beauty in the household. But Nurhayat did recall singing together with Fethullah and his brother Sıbgatullah a "song of the foods." This little jingle—which Nurhayat sang for me when I visited with her in 2015, and Fethullah recited verbatim when I interviewed him in 2018, taught children the names of various edible items, from bread to tomatoes, in a celebration of abundance. As I heard Nurhayat sing the melody in her aged voice, and as she remembered her singing it with her brothers as a girl, we both began to cry. Fethullah, too, grew misty when we remembered the song, and his sister and late brother, together.

Although the song celebrated abundance, in fact the dinner plates in the Gülen household could be spare. "Nobody could be picky," Nurhayat said. As for the singing, Nurhayat offered that her voice and Fethullah's harmonized well together. She also recalled that Fethullah once told his younger brother Sıbgatullah, when he tried to join Fethullah and Nurhayat's melodies: "your voice doesn't blend too well with ours."[38] Perhaps this was brotherly teasing. Perhaps Sıbgatullah really couldn't sing. Perhaps Fethullah had high standards. But the point is simply this: through multiple media, across multiple generations, young Fethullah learned to learn in a happy family. His more formal schooling, somewhat in contrast, left him short of some of the skills he would later come to value. It was only when he left Erzurum that he came to realize how deep was his inheritance, and how there were limits to the provincial and parochial worldview he had been taught. Could anything good come out of Erzurum?

Learning in all things

Fethullah Gülen's formal, secular schooling lasted no further than the 4th grade. Nevertheless, there are some stories from these years that help us understand how Gülen's character began to take shape. Belma [Sönmez] Özbatur was his elementary school teacher. She began teaching in the public school in Korucuk in 1948, when she was twenty. She remembered Fethullah as among her first classes. When she arrived in Korucuk, in November, it was snowing so heavily that she could barely see the houses in the village from the road. And then when it came time for school to begin, she couldn't find the students. They were all sequestered in an Islamic school. The Republic had recently imposed standards for secular schooling. Villagers were hardly compliant in their acceptance of these rulings. Belma recalled that the village was "very poor." None of the students had uniforms or even complete sets of clothing to wear to class. All of them had long, unkempt hair. One of her initial acts after receiving her first paycheck, she recalled, was to pay the local barber to give the boys hair-cuts.[39]

Belma had vivid memories of her most famous student, as she recalled him in an interview recorded in 2006:

> Fethullah Gülen was a different student. He was hard-working, a gentleman—a child who looked at things from afar. He was earnest. For us, being a military officer connoted a spirit of nation and fraternity. Fethullah had these feelings strongly, that's why I wished that [someday] he'd be an officer. This village had seen the Russian war. They packed the grandmothers, grandfathers in a room and torched them

live. I was told about these events. So, people of Korucuk had this enthusiasm, fondness, and respect for the [Turkish] soldiers.

He'd look and smile from afar; he'd laugh out loud rarely when
he was happy. He wasn't rowdy like the other students. He'd sit near
a window at the back. . . He'd come join us in sports and gymnastics,
too. . . He wouldn't jump into things; he'd watch them—but once he
made a decision he'd go and do it.

He was big; white [pale]—he'd look in my eyes. Without finishing
4th grade he had to leave [when his father was invited to be imam in
Alvar] ... But his father and whole family were self-educated people
who read in religious studies.

One day he came to visit me. He would call me "my teacher." I told
him: "Fethullah—why don't you come [back]? Continue—please finish your school." I knew his family had to go, but I wanted to continue
to teach him.[40]

The teacher was proud of her student, and she clearly recognized
ability in him early on, even anticipating that he'd become an officer—
which was, for a secular Turk, the highest praise. He was a well-man-
nered boy. But once Belma remembered that when he got mixed up with
one schoolyard tussle, she "slightly pulled his ear," and then she said,
surprised: "You, too, Fethullah? I don't ever want to see this again!"[41]
And, generally, she didn't.

When Gülen was 11—or in 1949, the family moved 8 miles from
Korucuk to another village, Alvar, where Ramiz was appointed as an
imam. Gülen recalled from this time: "When my father was an imam at
Alvar village, I learned how to read the Qur'an with the correct pronunciation and rhythm from Hacı Sıdkı Efendi of Hasankale, our district. I
did not have a place to stay in Hasankale, so I had to walk back and forth
on the 7 to 8 km [4 mile] road."[42] Many adults remember such hardships
from their childhood—walking miles to school, uphill both ways, in the
snow, even in summer. No doubt Fethullah struggled during some of his
walks, too. But over the brief three years that the family was in Alvar,
Gülen clearly grew in stature. It was during this period that he preached
his first sermon. Murat Alptekin's account is as follows:

On one Ramadan evening his father Ramiz Efendi was supposed to
give a sermon after dinner. [Fethullah] was one of those who arrived

at the mosque early. The congregation had just gathered together. Kazım Efendi, who was respected for his spiritual qualities by the prominent men of Alvar, looked at Gülen. Their eyes met. Kazım Efendi
stood up, and taking Ramiz Efendi's turban and cloak, he put them on
the boy amidst the astounded looks of the congregation. Gülen was
also astonished. He was very young to give a sermon before this big
crowd ... However, when the sermon began, the congregation, who
could not make sense of Kazım Efendi putting a 14-year-old boy on
the pulpit, began to listen to his words in amazement. The subjects
were one thing, but the person explaining them was something else.
The sermon of a 14-year-old boy had captured the hearts of the congregation, and some had swooned due to the voice rising from the
pulpit.[43]

Now, there is more than a touch of the hagiographical here. Some
details may be exaggerated—reading into this event in a provincial village the kinds of responses that people had to Hodjaefendi's sermons
later in his life.

But his sister Nurhayat also recalled that Fethullah's first sermon
came at Alvar, probably in 1952 (Gülen was 14). It would have been late
Spring or early Summer (Ramadan that year was between May 25 and
June 24). As Nurhayat remembered: "His first sermon was at Alvar ... It
was the *tarawih* prayer in one of the nights of Ramadan. Hodjaefendi
gave a sermon after the prayer. Normally the women did not go to the
mosque. Our father would not allow us to go... But I went secretly. That's
when I first heard him." When I asked Nurhayat whether she remembered what she heard Fethullah say that night she responded:

> We really didn't know Hodjaefendi was going to preach. I had a sign.
> It was a dream. Normally, when you roll dough onto a platter, after
> a while you turn it upside down. Well, in this dream I rolled dough
> onto a platter and when I turned it upside down there was sun under-
> neath it! I woke up—and went to my father. Sıbgatullah was next to
> me. I told my dream to my father. He said, "There will be a big âlim
> [scholar] that will come out of this house. He will educate people for
> good for this world and for the afterworld." Sıbgatullah said "that will
> be me." Then even though I saw this dream, I just remember hearing
> Hodjaefendi's voice and seeing him through the window—the women

were upstairs [in the mosque].[44]

Now, again, for some, the lines here between fiction, fantasy, theology, and history might blur quite quickly. But it was at Alvar that Fethullah Gülen's career as a preacher began.

According to at least one account, however, it was not exactly peace that followed Fethullah's early sermonizing. The circumstances that led the family to depart Alvar are not completely certain. In his official web biography, Gülen simply reports: "My father had to leave Alvar. After a period of time in Artuzu, he settled in Erzurum."[45] This brief account hints at trouble. Ramiz *had to leave* Alvar. The causes are unclear, and the sources conflict. Did young Fethullah's speaking at the pulpit disturb some locals? Was it something he said? Did some in Alvar become jealous of the Gülen family? Or was Fethullah too moralizing at a young age? All have some resonance in the historical record, scant as it is. But the details are less important than the general point: an experience of controversy may have colored young Gülen's first foray into preaching. It would not be his last.

Alvar

In Alvar, Hodjaefendi studied Islamic spirituality, *Sufism*, with a local teacher, Imam Muhammed Lütfi. Lütfi has been the subject of several biographies, and his influence on Gülen was profound. Lütfi was a "pure wellspring," Gülen put it.[46] He came from a distinguished family, in the lineage of the Prophet. He was recognized as a *Sufi sheikh*, as was his father, Hüseyin Kındığı Efendi, and brother, Vehbi Efendi. When Lütfi's brother died, the Imam of Alvar (as Lütfi was known) wrote a brief couplet that as an adult Gülen recalled—having lost several of his own brothers by then: "I drifted apart from beautiful ones, now I woe with this longing."[47] That is a succinct and accurate lament for the loss of a sister or brother. The next chapter will describe more fully the kind of prayer that Lütfi led, namely "circles of remembrance" or *zikir*. Gülen also recognized that "both the *Nakşibendi* and *Kadiri* orders of *Sufism* inspired" Lütfi—landing him squarely in traditions with centuries of continuity. Love for the Prophet was one of Lütfi's distinctive teachings imparted to Gülen, as in this poem also penned by the Imam of Alvar:

O the Sacred Witness, O the Sun embellishing the universe
Your clothes are melodious, your eyebrows are lovely
A strand of your hair is dearer than the entire world
Your hair disseminates a pure fragrance to both worlds.[48]

Such extravagance marked some expressions of *Sufism*, so much so that popular attachment to the places and relics of the Prophet (among other practices) made it suspect to secularists, and to those inclined to more sober worship. Gülen explains: "Eulogies in praise of the Prophet would often be recited in [Lütfi's] presence; he and all the people there would burst into ecstasy. Sometimes he lamented in such a way and his voice rose to such a high pitch while reciting the following stanza that the place where he was would resonate with the awe of God and everybody in the circle would shake:"[49]

This heart is so fond of you, O beloved: why?
Your beauty is shining like the bright day: why?
Your eyebrow is like the 'two-bow-length's nearness to God"
Your face brings to our minds the chapter of Ar-Rahman
(The All-Merciful): why?[50]

Such couplets, that Gülen recalled from memory, clearly evoked the associative logic and extravagance of mysticism. For now, the point is simply this: learning for young Gülen happened in a *Sufi* way. He was introduced to *Sufism* through circles of learning (prayer) as well as through formal study. Again—we'll pay more attention to these practices, and to Lütfi, in Chapter Two.

Still—there are two stories about Lütfi's influence on the young Gülen that definitely belong here. The first Gülen related as follows:

I was about fourteen or fifteen years old. I had a good friend whom I truly liked. One day he said, "There are some centers of learning ... in Istanbul where one can be educated for six months to obtain a certificate and be qualified to preach and deliver sermons."[51] My friend convinced me with these words. I packed my belongings without asking the teacher who was responsible for me and the great imam, and then left for the train station with that friend of mine.[52]

Fortunately for Fethullah—and for the remainder of this biography, another friend had warned Fethullah's father about his son's impetuous plan to move to Istanbul. Ramiz arranged for a cousin to stop Fethullah at the train station. A meeting with Imam Lütfi soon followed. "I had never seen him so angry before," Gülen remembered. "He said, 'I swear to God, if you had left, you would perish!' Those words he uttered are still ringing in my ears." Gülen was puzzled at the time about the intensity of the imam's reaction. Did he really think Fethullah would perish? Istanbul was a big place, and a youth could easily get lost. Or was there a deeper meaning—that the imam thought Fethullah had a destiny that he had to work through during his time in Alvar and Erzurum, and that leaving too soon would interrupt? Eventually, Gülen came to realize that it was fortunate that he remained with Lütfi, who "protected me under his spiritual shelter."[53]

The other story is lighter, but also with long-term significance. It hints that his master's ways were filled with wisdom on how to avoid conflicts. According to one of Lütfi's biographers, a man showed up drunk one Friday for prayer. He caused a scene. Lütfi, however, did not condemn his besotted brother, but also did not let him go unaccountable. The Imam of Alvar turned people's attention away from scandal and toward introspection: "This man is intoxicated with one sin," he admitted to his congregation. But then he went on: "If all the sins the rest of us committed were intoxicating beverages, then we'd see if *anybody* was sober in this mosque!"[54] Those who were without sin, the imam might have paraphrased Jesus, can throw the first moralizing stone. Lütfi died in 1956— while Gülen was still a young man. But we shall see him again—given the influence his *Sufism* continued to exert in Gülen's life and work.

Beginning in 1953, Gülen began studying in Erzurum. It was the first time he lived apart from his parents. In an interview, he recalled vividly the moment of his arrival in Erzurum, and some of the circumstances of his youthful existence:

> Sadi bey (grandson of the Imam of Alvar, Muhammed Lütfi—himself a young man of barely 20) was teaching at the Erzurum Kurşunlu Mosque school. This school is a small one with a wooden ceiling. Five or six people stayed in a nearly two-rug-sized place. My dad had left me there for the first time. I was holding a small chest in my arms, and that was all the stuff I had.

We had a gas stove. We used to prepare and eat our dinner where we slept. Those who had the opportunity would go to the Kırık Çeşme Baths and bathe when necessary. They would give tickets to some poor students there, who would use those tickets. Some rich people paid for them. When there weren't any tickets, there would be a lot of hardship.[55]

It's not difficult to imagine the hardship of five or six adolescent boys sharing a single small room under these conditions.

Gülen's father sent him some "modest pocket money" from his earnings as an *imam*, but it was rarely enough. "We were really poor," Gülen simply put it, "and we sometimes could not find basic foods to eat, like bread and cheese, for a few days." Gülen remembered one particularly difficult stretch, when

We were starving, [and] we went to the *Sufi* lodge, three or four students together. ... There was a shed beside the *Sufi* lodge used for storing food. Through the spaces of the wooden wall, we saw watermelons inside. The Imam was praying inside. After a while, the door opened and he said, "Come in boys, let me slice a watermelon for you."

This was the Imam of Alvar, now also living in Erzurum. He was "an immense figure of deep spirituality, [and] understanding of others," said Gülen. His "heart could sense beyond the physical reality." When the Imam died in 1956, Gülen went with the funeral procession from Erzurum to Alvar, in the middle of winter, to bury his beloved *sheikh*. "Although I failed to fully benefit from him, I am so thankful to my Lord for the blessing of having known him."[56]

Despite hunger and other hardships, Gülen developed a reputation for fastidiousness. "I used to pay a lot of attention to my attire," he remembered. "I used to wear clean and somewhat luxurious clothes for those days. I used to starve for days, but nobody ever saw me wearing un-ironed pants or unpolished shoes. When I couldn't find an iron, I used to put my pants under the bed and the weight would make them look as if they had been ironed." Fethullah took some abuse from his peers for this behavior. He recalled one student, whose sartorial habits leaned toward the rumpled look associated with scholars everywhere, who told Gülen "My friend, why don't you be a little more religious!" Gülen was aghast.

Such moralizing alienated. Was Islam about the style of one's clothing? "I still cannot understand," Hodjaefendi put it years later, "the connection between wearing ironed pants and being religious."[57] Islam wasn't about moralistic trivia, ironed or otherwise.

During his years in Erzurum, until 1959, he studied with various teachers—notably Osman Bektaş—and in various mosque schools (*madrasas*). Among them were the schools next to the Kemhan and Taş Mescit Mosques. He did not stay only at the schools—as in his first residence at Kurşunlu Mosque school—but also boarded in rooms with friends and extended family. At one point, he lived in the Muratpaşa Mosque and Ahmediye Madrasa in Erzurum.

Generally, though, the curriculum at all mosque schools, which were largely underground and unsanctioned, although widely known about, focused on classical Arabic grammatical and theological disciplines. Young men (universally—women could study in separate schools) spent hours every day in dictionary studies (*lugat*), rhetoric (*belagat*), logic (*mantık*), philosophical theology (*kelam*), Qur'anic commentary (*tefsir*), jurisprudence (*fikh*), and legal theory and methodology (*usul*). Fethullah excelled. He mastered and/or memorized classical grammar books such as *Emsile*, *Bina*, *Maksud*, and *Izhar* within a few months.[58] One of Gülen's classmates from these Erzurum years, Hatem Bilgili, had known Fethullah since he was five years old. He recalled that Gülen had a "photographic memory." "He was not a normal student," Bilgili went on. "It would take us about 5-10 hours to study a lesson; Hodjaefendi would get it in 5-10 minutes." Bilgili picked up a book to show me Gülen's reading style. He opened the book, moved his finger across and down the page, and then the next, flipped the page, and then the next, and so on. As fast as the eye moved across the script, the material was scanned, and the eye moved on. "So, he would speed read?" I asked. "Yes," Bilgili replied. Bilgili also emphasized that he and Fethullah and the other students had to study under scrutiny from the police. "To write and read the Qur'an was illegal," he said, "and we would need to hide the books. Most of my grandfather's books rotted in wells because that's where they were hidden; even in the school we would need to hide the books, in an oven, underground."[59] Again—whether or not Gülen had a photographic memory as a young man is difficult to verify. But that he was an exceptional student is equally difficult to contest. His abilities began to be more widely recognized. He began traveling to other mosques to lecture and to meet with colleagues. Such lecture tours were especially common during Ramadan. In 1957, at the age of nineteen, Fethullah made trips to speak in the cities of Amasya, Tokat, and Sivas. These were all small cities located to the north and west of Erzurum, on the way to the capital of Ankara. Fethullah's world was expanding.

That world was, however, still almost exclusively an Islamic world. Gülen, we might say, was being *trained*. Just as Christian ministers are expected to acquire training in scriptural interpretation, church history, and systematic theology, so did Gülen encounter a range of classical Islamic disciplines and thinkers in his *madrasa* education. A few broad strokes regarding those influences deserve mention here. Other more detailed sketches will appear at appropriate junctures in the following chapters. Broadly speaking, then, Gülen's theological education was into the Hanafi "branch" of the Sunni "denomination," if one may be excused for speaking in those inaccurate but perhaps helpful terms. As is well-known, Muslims fall into two main "denominational" groupings—Sunni (80-90%) and Shia (10-20%). The Sunni also divide themselves, again speaking very broadly, into four branches or schools of thought (the Arabic word for the discipline is *fiqh*, "jurisprudence"): Hanbali, Maliki, Shafi'i, and Hanafi. Unlike Christians, however, Muslim denominations and branches do not take institutional (much less national) form. Some schools, such as the Hanbali—which is the smallest in number, *are* closely identified with a particular regime, in this case with Saudi Arabia. Yet each school also can be further differentiated. The Hanbali, for instance, come in Salafi or Wahhabi varieties (the two are sometimes conflated, and both have gained notoriety for strictness and anti-Western zeal). In any event, to say that Gülen's education formed him in the Hanafi school of jurisprudence is not to say a great deal—but it is to say something important. It is, perhaps most notably, to say that he is not Hanbali—either Salafi, or Wahhabi.

More positively, to say that Gülen was trained as a Hanafi is to say that he was trained in the school of thought shared by the greatest number of Sunni Muslims in the world. Ramiz Gülen was Hanafi. So was the Imam of Alvar. So was Rumi, whose importance for Gülen we have already noted, and as we shall have reason to see again. So was Abu'l Husain al-Quduri (d. 1037), Imam Rabbani (d. 1624), and Khalid-i Baghdadi (1779-1827). Writings by all these distinguished Hanafi scholars informed Gülen's thought.[60] But just as a Protestant Christian theologian might cite Roman Catholic or Eastern Orthodox sources, Gülen also has drawn (by way of example, from among dozens of other possibilities) on Abu al-Hassan Kharaqani (d. 1033) and Al-Ghazali (d. 1111). Both Kharaqani and Ghazali were from the Shafi'i school, with the latter perhaps the most important theologian of medieval Islam.[61] Succinctly, Gülen studied classical scholars from all the schools of thought. He concentrated or specialized in Hanafi jurisprudence.

Further complicating the picture of influences on Gülen's early training is the ferment that was taking place among Muslims in the wake of the fall of the Ottoman Empire. The Ottomans had, unevenly but effectively, consolidated for centuries much of the Muslim world. In the absence of the Ottomans, nation-states or other regimes (for instance monarchies) gained strength, or in some cases were imposed by colonizing forces. But along with these political changes came theological reflection on how Islam ought to proceed in the absence of the unity it enjoyed under the Ottomans. Two broad streams intermingled and diverged in various individuals and contexts. As we suggested in the Introduction, the first broad solution was "political Islam" (aka "Islamism"). Advocates for this approach sought a unity of religion and politics from the "top-down" in government-led (and/or revolutionary) Islam. Advocates of the second approach, "civil Islam," granted legitimacy to a secular state or nation, and then sought to shape Muslim individuals who would renew and reform those societies from the "bottom-up," for instance through education.[62] Gülen studied plenty of political Islamists, and expressed affinity with a few. The Muslim Brotherhood in Egypt, which was founded in 1928, is a good case. It was organized initially as a youth club by schoolteacher Hassan al-Banna, and eventually combined political party activism with social services such as hospitals, foundations, and relief agencies. The latter, minus the political party, was something Gülen would advocate for, in due course.[63] Within the Brotherhood, Sayyid Qutb (1906-1966) became an influential voice. Gülen studied both his commentary on scripture, *In the Shade of the Qur'an* (1951-65) and *Milestones* (1964). The latter emphasized the political role of *shari'ah* (broadly, state-integrated Muslim law) in forging strong Muslim societies. Qutb also spent a decade in jail, accused of plotting to kill

Gamal Abdel Nasser, Egypt's President. He was eventually convicted and hanged. Gülen expressed sympathy for Qutb's exegesis, but differed with his political platform, and denounced his embrace of violence. Qutb also drew heavily from another source with which Gülen was made acquainted in his early education, Ibn Taymiyyah—a thirteenth-century jurist who is often credited with having great influence on Salafism, providing theological legitimation for the unified religious-political regime in Saudi Arabia—in a pattern now widely emulated in the Middle East (and beyond). Similarly, Gülen studied the works of Abul Ala Maududi (1903-1979), who worked in British-ruled India. Maududi helped forge the Jamaat-e-Islami—an international Muslim group with very strong representation across Asia, and that was crucial in Pakistan's development as an Islamic Republic in 1956. Finally, in this quick survey of potential political Islamist influences on Gülen's early education, he was of course aware of the turmoil just beginning in Turkey's neighbor, Iran. That turmoil eventually led to the 1979 revolution that overthrew the secular (and corrupt) Shah, and that generated yet another "Islamic Republic." All these currents informed the young Gülen, and they could have provided sources for his own vision.

In fact, over time Gülen consistently distanced himself from political Islam, and became one of the leading global voices for civil Islam. Looking back with critical eyes honed over decades, Gülen came to recognize some of the limitations of his training in the *madrasas*. Typically, he turned to metaphysics and theology rather than politics to make the case: "I do not fully understand the late *madrasa* system of studying certain things in the name of rhetorical principles and what they are good for," he said. "We were offered lots of things," he went on. "Perhaps, they were useful in terms of providing materials for dialectic reasoning, but not to construct a modern line of thought... I early noticed that the madrasa did not have a modern line of rationale, a mathematical foundation, or at least a root in Baconian logic." The result was that the madrasa

> estranged the natural sciences and research, despite injunctions in the Qur'an and the Sunna... While God says, "We will show them Our manifest signs in the horizons of the universe and within their own selves" (Fussilat 41:53), we hardly saw research, examinations, and en-

gagements with the nature of things. Although the Qur'an was read, the book of nature was left to the side... A clash emerged in the society, and the mind separated from the heart. Consequently, the book of the Universe was put in one place, and the book of the Qur'an was put in another.[64]

To attempt to unite mind and heart in learning, studying both the book of the Universe and the book of the Qur'an, would become a hallmark of Gülen's life, and eventually of the global Hizmet movement.

As for political Islam, Gülen took a different approach, accepting secular government, working within the rule of law, and supporting democracy. He looked back on his development in 2016, when asked about his supposed "political" aims:

I ... served as a preacher for nearly 30 years before coming to the U.S. and my friends continued to publish my talks after I settled here. There are over 70 books based on my articles and talks. It is natural that in Turkish government there are people who share some of my views just as there are those who don't share them.

My teaching has always been to act within [the] law and in an ethical way. If anybody who follows my works acts illegally or unethically, or if they disobey the lawful orders of their superiors, that is a betrayal of my teachings and I fully support their being investigated and facing the consequences.

If there is no discrimination, government institutions reflect the colors and patterns of its society. We know that in Turkish government institutions there are people of various political and religious orientations, such as nationalists, neonationalists, Maoists, Kemalists, Alevis, leftists, sympathizers of *Sufi* orders and others. For decades, none of these groups could be transparent about their identities except the Kemalists because of political profiling and discrimination.

...

It is the constitutional right of every Turkish citizen to serve in their government institutions if they are qualified to do so. To accuse anybody of having a nefarious goal without evidence is slander. If people are afraid to reveal their identity for fear of reprisals, it is the regime's problem, not theirs.

As far as my discourse is concerned, I have never advocated for regime change in Turkey. To the contrary, 22 years ago, in 1994, I told publicly that there will be no return from democracy in Turkey or elsewhere in the world. This was both a prediction and a commitment to democracy.[65]

As we shall have ample occasion to see, Gülen's commitment to democracy was consistent, as was his commitment to uniting secular education with the practice of civil Islam. It was during his years in Erzurum, in any event, that Gülen picked up the studies he had left behind in Korucuk and with his teacher Belma. Eventually, he would pass external exams verifying his competency in the topics covered in the secular secondary school curriculum of Turkey.[66]

Risale-i Nur

If there were many sources that shaped Gülen's effort to unite "mind" and "heart" in learning as an advocate for civil Islam, none was more crucial than a single text—albeit one with 6,000 pages. This was the *Risale-i-Nur Külliyatı*, "The Epistles of Light," penned by Said Nursi.[67] Nursi (1877-1960) was a remarkably complex and intriguing character. An ethnic Kurd, and at heart a *Sufi* theologian and reformer of Islam, he fought against the Russian forces in WWI, and he supported the resistance against the invading British forces. When Atatürk came to power, Nursi initially supported him. As he became aware of the more ruthless secularism of the new regime, however, Nursi grew critical of it. For his criticism, he "spent half of his life in exile or in prison," according to one historian. Like the young Gülen, though, Nursi was not simply an Islamist who opposed secularism. He "was critical of traditional Islamic learning," too. His prodigious *Risale-i-Nur*, which he wrote largely while in exile, was a Qur'anic commentary that "sought to prove that science and rationalism are compatible with religious beliefs." More fully:

> [Nursi] wanted "to protect the people from unbelief," and "[to protect] those in the *madrasa*s from fanaticism." In short, his writings had three interrelated goals: (1) to raise Muslims' religious consciousness (self-transformation is very important); (2) to refute the dominant intellectual discourses of materialism and positivism; and (3) to recover collective memory by revising the shared grammar of society, Islam.

This faith movement empower[ed] communal life by stressing the power of knowledge, freedom, and initiative to build stable Muslim selves and communities.[68]

Very similar goals would be realized in the Hizmet movement inspired by Fethullah Gülen.

Exactly when the young Gülen first learned of Nursi is unclear. The most prominent story has it that while he was a student in Erzurum, probably in 1956, Gülen was invited by another student, Mehmet Kırkıncı, to go hear a lecture by Muzaffer Arslan, one of Nursi's disciples.[69] Gülen liked what he heard, the story goes on, started reading Nursi in earnest, and kept going to lectures when one of Nursi's disciples came to the region. This seems likely enough. But it was not as simple as it sounds. According to the regime, Nursi was an outlaw—both as a Kurd, and as an outspoken Muslim. His books—in outlawed Arabic script—were, then, illegal. Historian M. Hakan Yavuz explains:

> Because the state banned all reading and discussion of his works, copies of his commentaries were scribed by hand and distributed via a confidential network, known as the *nur postacıları*, the postmen of the epistle. This secretive solidarity network became the foundation of the "textual communities" known as *dershanes*, which in turn became one of the embryos of civil society in Turkey. His followers made more copies of his work and distributed them widely throughout Anatolia.[70]

It is not too strong to say that civil Islam in Turkey started in these *dershanes*. They were, again following Yavuz, part of the "transition from an oral culture to a print culture" within Turkish Islam. This transition would be complicated, and accelerated, as media burgeoned in the late twentieth and early twenty-first centuries, but all in all it is difficult to overestimate the influence of Nursi on Gülen and the Hizmet movement.

Edirne

By 1958, then, Fethullah Gülen's formal theological education was completed. The twenty-year old young man applied for and received the traditional Islamic *ijaza* (license to teach).[71] This gave Fethullah mobility as a lecturer. As he recalled it later, "My father certainly wanted me to get out of Erzurum. My mother was always opposed to this. But finally my father got his way. By obtaining my mother's consent, too, it was decided that I should go to Edirne. In Edirne, there was Hüseyin Top *Hodja*. He was our relative [on his mother's side]."[72] Top facilitated for Fethullah to teach (he got his preaching license soon afterwards) in Edirne. For the next seven years, on and off, and with many twists and turns along the way, Gülen began to develop in and around Edirne a reputation for excellence as a teacher and preacher that eventually inspired a global movement.

Edirne in 1958 was a city of about 75,000 people. Located in the far northwestern corner of Turkey, very close to borders with Greece, to the South, and Bulgaria, to the North, Edirne had an ancient history. It was a city oft-disputed. It took its name from a conqueror—the second-century Roman Emperor Hadrian (of which the Turkish "Edirne" is an etymological variant). For nearly a century, from 1363-1453, it was the heavily defended capital of the Ottoman Empire. And in the Balkan Wars of 1912-13, Ottoman soldiers in Edirne were overrun. Thousands were captured and imprisoned under brutally cold and impoverished conditions. Many died. Those who survived, including Şükrü Paşa, who is a great uncle of Gülen, were liberated after nearly a year in captivity by Enver Paşa (d. 1922), one of the "Young Turks." Enver was responsible for allying Turkey with Germany during World War I. He was also responsible (not single-handedly, of course) for the atrocities against Armenians during the same time-period. It was only in 1922, then, that Turks permanently reclaimed Edirne. But the memories of that brutal imprisonment and military defeat lingered. So, it is no surprise that one can find high on a hill in the Sarayiçi district of Edirne the Balkan Wars Memorial. Located there is Turkey's version of a Tomb of the Unknown Soldier. And yet, for all this history of warring as a backdrop, even a quick glance of the Edirne skyline from the vantage of the Balkans War Memorial makes it apparent that Edirne is a city of mosques.

Among the dozens whose minarets rise above Edirne, the most famous without question is Selimiye. This extraordinary building, with central dome higher and wider than that of Istanbul's Hagia Sophia (Ayasofya in Turkish), was completed in 1575, and designed by the famed architect Sinan (d. 1588). It is a monument to Ottoman power. Edirne had ceded rights as capital of the Empire to Istanbul by the time Selimiye was completed, but the mosque was (and is) a stunning *tour de force* in stone and marble, arches and domes. But in 1959 Fethullah Gülen did not begin his teaching and preaching career at Selimiye. Nor did he begin his vocation at the Eski Cami (the Old Mosque) just steps away from Selimiye, which dated to the early fourteenth century. Nor did he begin his career teaching and preaching in a third Ottoman mosque near the center of Edirne, the Burmalı Cami—so called because one of its minarets is wrapped by a number of earth red helices that twist from top to bottom. Gülen would eventually serve there, in the mosque better known by its proper name of Üç Şerefeli—named after another minaret, which is unique with its three balconies. Üç Şerefeli is a distinctive monument in its own right. Art historian Laurelie Rae puts it well: "[its] uniqueness was more powerful than the splendor of Selimiye Mosque. Perhaps I felt Üç Şerefeli was intended for the Ottoman people whereas the Selimiye Mosque was built for the Ottoman Empire."[73] But Üç Şerefeli is not where Gülen's vocation began. Nor, finally, did Gülen begin his teaching at the forest-encircled Darü-l Hadis Mosque—although he would end up there eventually, too. No, the first mosque at which Fethullah Gülen began to teach and preach in Edirne was the tiny, backwater Akmescit Mosque in Yıldırım district. The boy from Erzurum had found an Erzurum-like mosque in Edirne.

When I visited the Akmescit Mosque in 2015, the imam was vacuuming the threadbare carpet. It is a decidedly modest structure; perhaps the most modest mosque I have ever entered in Turkey. There was room, maybe, for fifty men in prayer on the carpet. About half that many women could pray in the balcony. The pulpit was five feet above the ground, three or four steps up. The walls were thin, the carpet worn, the paint in need of touching up. To be sure, when Gülen arrived in 1958 the mosque was new. In fact, it had been commissioned a few years earlier by Refia Gülen's cousin, Hüseyin Top, who was an imam in that neighborhood. And as Gülen himself had reported, after he passed the test at the Mufti's office, Top asked that Hodjaefendi be assigned to this new mosque during the upcoming month of Ramadan (with Refia's permission, and to satisfy Ramiz' ambition for his son to get out of Erzurum). Still, even in 2015 the neighborhood was all-but rural. I saw a tractor in the street, and there were two farmer's carts laden with vegetables and other produce within walking distance of the mosque. Again, it was, in 1958, new. And it was not, at least literally, Erzurum.

Fethullah was not there for long, although not for lack of trying to keep him by members of his first congregation. At the end of his first month "neighborhood residents went to see Hüseyin Top and asked him to convince Gülen to remain as their imam: 'He is a close relative of yours. We like him very much. He is unique with his knowledge, virtues, and oratory skills. We request that he continue as imam at our mosque.'"[74] The fact that Gülen worked without a salary probably did not hurt his appeal. Still, three obstacles were in the way. The first was the State: Gülen was not yet licensed to preach. The second was the State: since WWI, all males over the age of twenty were required to serve at least eighteen months in military service. The third was the State: all clergy held state-appointed positions regardless of local preferences. The first obstacle Gülen overcame within a few months after his arrival in Edirne, when he traveled to Ankara and passed the State-sponsored exam to be licensed as a preacher. He then applied for the position of *müftü* (*mufti* – provincial head of religious affairs) of Edirne, but the second obstacle still loomed, and would prove difficult to overcome, as we shall see. And the third obstacle was overcome, or at least endured, when he took a test for available positions in Edirne and was assigned by the Presidency of Religious Affairs in Ankara (the government bureaucracy responsible for all religious matters) to join the staff in the center-city Üç Şerefeli Mosque, the "mosque with three balconies." It was a definite promotion.

He would serve there for about two-and-a-half years. As a center-city mosque, Üç Şerefeli drew a clientele that included professional and public figures. Gülen developed a reputation as a preacher who connected Islam to daily life. His Friday sermons touched upon law and economics, among other subjects. He preached to both men and women. And he began what is now a common practice in the U.S., but was not common within Islam and Turkey at the time: he announced the topic of his weekly sermon in advance on a sign outside of the mosque. He also developed a reputation for his ascetic lifestyle. He lived within the mosque in a small corner window nook—about 4'x8'. It had no heat, no electricity, and only the most modest furnishings. It was cold in winter—Edirne is quite far north. It was hot in summer. Gülen spent his days in prayer, study, and sermon preparation, on which he spent hours. He also socialized with extended family, close friends, and other Edirne residents—including politicians, businessmen, and police.[75] "I developed my habits there," Gülen simply put it about his years in Edirne. One of his habits was buying books and magazines—both for his own reading and to give as gifts. His modest salary and tendency to generosity meant, Gülen recalled, that during his years in Edirne he "often had financial difficulties." Still, despite the problem of making a living on his modest salary, and "despite my solitary lifestyle" in Edirne, as he remembered it, "I had good relations with prominent people in Edirne." Gülen remembered in particular that "I had a close friendship with Resul Bey, the Chief of Police. I also struck up friendship with patrons of the city's coffee-shops... In fact, ... a colonel from the Black Sea, once told me: 'We're fellow countrymen. You can't be from Erzurum!'"[76] It was meant as a compliment. But he *was* from Erzurum. Indeed, throughout his time in Edirne he was called "the *Hodja* (teacher) from Erzurum." That was not a compliment, although it also carried an element of affection: "Look at this new preacher. And, do you believe it, he's from Erzurum!" So he was. What was unclear, yet, was where he was going. There was one obstacle remaining before he could, he might have imagined, settle into his life as a preacher: he had not yet completed his mandatory military service. Consequently, the young man in his twenties left Edirne in November, 1961, and set out for Mamak military base in Ankara.

There are scant public records that document what Gülen learned during his mandatory military service. Gülen recalls that he reported on November 11, 1961, and we know that he served until 1963, which completed his obligation to the State. But we also know that his service was not without interruptions, struggles, and difficulties. A military coup—the first of many in Gülen's lifetime—had roiled Turkey on May 27, 1960. That coup ended the decade-long rule of the Democrat Party, led by Prime Minister Adnan Menderes. Menderes was then hanged after a trial by the military regime in September, 1961, just two months before Gülen's service began. Ankara was of course the capital of the Republic. By being assigned there, Gülen entered a cauldron of political intrigue. During his decade in power, Menderes had created a slight opening for religious liberties within the Republic. Most notably, he had returned the *adhan* or public call to prayer that was broadcast five times per day from every mosque in Turkey, back to Arabic from Turkish. That language change had been one of Atatürk's most prominent, and least popular, innovations. But the coup had once again put Muslims on the defensive, and among the military leaders most hostile to religion was a colonel by the name of Talat Aydemir. As Gülen remembered him, Aydemir could "have been another Mussolini. He and his supporters were all potential dictators, and they mocked spirituality." That was the climate in Ankara when Gülen began his military service. So, Fethullah knew to be wary when the commander who was his immediate supervisor came to him and asked: "Are you the *Hodja*?" The commander's wife was ill. He wanted to bring her to Gülen to have the young imam read prayers for her. Gülen remembered replying: "I don't know how to 'read' like that. If you believe reading will be effective, you can do it.' Later," Gülen went on, "I came to understand that he had been testing me." That is, would this *Hodja* from Erzurum practice superstition? Was he an Islamist threat to the Republic and its virtue?[77]

Gülen was in Ankara for eight months, or nearly half of his service. After that, lots were drawn and he landed in İskenderun—a naval base on Turkey's southeastern Mediterranean coast. It could have been a plush, albeit hot, appointment. It got hotter for Gülen. He preached on Fridays at İskenderun's central mosque. One of the local newspapers reported on his preaching in a way that aggravated authorities—a pattern that would happen repeatedly in his life. A sermon that people hadn't really heard became the basis for charges by people who didn't really know him. He was briefly taken into disciplinary detention during his military service, because he was, in his own words, "delivering sermons." He further clarified that a commander, who was respectful of religious observance, allowed him to preach, with the commander in attendance. As the commander was preparing to leave their unit, he hugged Gülen in tears and said that Gülen would face repression. His prediction came true. Gülen's detention was brief—only ten days as a "disciplinary measure." The charges were then dropped.[78] But it would be the first, not the last, detention for Fethullah Gülen.

The repression took its toll on the still very young preacher. As he recalled it, after a time in İskenderun, between the heat and the trauma: "I was so malnourished that I had to be hospitalized for exhaustion and jaundice."[79] A brief return to Erzurum to recuperate followed—about which more shortly.

Context is crucial. Throughout the history of the Republic, the Turkish military had been the home for its elites. Generals were the ones who were at the cutting edge of change. Menderes over a decade of increasingly authoritarian rule, had not only sought to create a slight open-ing for Muslims in public life. He also sought to liberalize the Turkish economy and to advance Turkey's relations with the West. Most notably, Turkey joined NATO in 1952. Many benefits flowed from this alliance. As historian Carter Vaughn Findley put it, starkly: "Between 1948 and 1968, U.S. military aid to Turkey totaled nearly $2.5 billion, aside from perhaps another $1.5 billion in Western economic aid. The Turkey of the 1950s could not have experienced growth in both its economy and its military without such investment."[80] This "turn to the West" under Menderes decisively shaped what it meant to be Turkish. To be among the elites who shaped society meant to be familiar with European (and, increasingly, with American) mores. And America, flush off the Allied victories over Germany and Japan in World War II, was nothing if not a military power. In that milieu, the overt practice of Islam was, more or less, an impediment in the eyes of the elite, particularly the generals.

And two perhaps contradictory developments in American cul-ture in the early 1960s inexorably shaped Turkish culture, and the life of Fethullah Gülen. The first was anti-Communism. The second was in-vestment in education. First things first: Gülen probably inherited from his family no great love for Russia. The proximity of the Soviet Union to Erzurum, and the history of Russian incursions there, made Anatolian Turks suspicious of, if not outright hostile to, the Great Bear to the North. One effort to prevent a possible Russian influence was the Turkish An-ti-Communist League (TKMD), which many Turks supported. It was a time when you were either a Communist or an anti-Communist. Gülen, as a devout Muslim, naturally inclined to the second group. Although being anti-anything was hardly Gülen's primary aspiration, he was brief-ly a part of the discussion in those years whether to establish a branch of TKMD in Erzurum. The discussions went nowhere, and Gülen had little to do with anti-Communism throughout the rest of his life.

The TKMD of course had roots in the Cold War of the 1950s, where nations around the world had to pick sides. Some Turkish anti-Commu-nists also reportedly had support from the West for counter-insurgency activities.[81] Conspiracy theorists, naturally, find in Gülen's brief partic-ipation in discussions about opening a branch of an anti-Communist League a smoking gun of his pernicious political persuasion. It is true that there is very little in Gülen's thought, even in his early writings, that might be perceived as friendly to State-driven, Khrushchev-style Communism. But it is also true that there is little if anything that is overtly hostile to Russia, or to Marxism as a political ideology, for that matter. Naturally, as a Muslim, Gülen was no fan of Soviet atheism. So, if he was an anti-Communist—and that should be a very large IF, he was so for reasons of geography, history, and theology—more than politics. That Gülen dabbled in this overtly political League early in his career, and that this dabbling happened to coincide with American interests, was probably a coincidence. There is no evidence of anything more to it. For instance, many of the TKMD participants went on the establish the right-wing Nationalist Action Party (MHP) in 1969. Gülen had nothing to do with that development.

The American investment in education during this period had a more lasting imprint around the world. On the wave of enrollments due to the GI Bill, and due to the booming U.S. economy, American universities blossomed in the 1960s into some of the best in the Western world. And Western learning unmistakably focused, during that decade, on the "great books" of the classical arts and sciences. Gülen became a part of this global cultural trend. He did so through the influence of an unlikely, but not unimaginable, source: a military commander. Gülen had read widely and deeply in Islamic sources. He was not as well-versed in sources beyond Islamic theology and philosophy. So, it was fortunate, as he recalled it, that during his time at İskenderun "there was a very good commander who insisted that I read the Western classics."[82] Gülen followed his commander's order. A list of the Western authors that Gülen came to be comfortable referencing (not always favorably) in his teaching and preaching would include Camus, Dante, Dostoyevsky, Freud, Pascal, and Shakespeare—among many others.

Philosopher Jill Carroll has studied some of the Western influences that appear in Gülen's writing. She found links between Gülen's thought and Plato, Immanuel Kant, and even Jean-Paul Sartre. These influences are not always direct, and they are (to a degree) mutually exclusive. It's hard to imagine Kant and Sartre sharing a congenial dinner table, much less philosophical harmony. Rather, as Carroll explains, she groups

> Gülen with these other humanistic thinkers because his work, like
> theirs, focuses on central issues of human existence that have long

been part of humanistic discourse in both its religious and non-religious forms. In other words, these thinkers are concerned with basic questions about the nature of human reality, the good human life, the state, and morality. Moreover, they reach similar conclusions regarding many of these issues and questions after deliberating about them from within their own traditions and cultural contexts.[83]

Gülen became an Islamic humanist. This was mainly through Muslim influences. But perhaps the commander deserves credit, too, for his advice to Gülen to read classics.

During the leave of absence that his health required in 1963, alluded to earlier, Gülen returned to Erzurum. He was there for three months. He was not, it would seem, an invalid. "While I was in Erzurum," he recalled, "I went back and forth to the Halk Evi (People's House)." The Halk Evi movement was one of Atatürk's attempts to supplant Islam with something different. The houses were found all over Turkey. The one in Erzurum was typical—a combination of hotel, dormitory, performance venue, and coffee-shop.[84] Gülen also recalled that during his convalescence his mother was particularly eager to see him married. Refia told Fethullah, according to one source, that "it would be a good idea for you to tie the knot." The dialogue about that matter was, as Gülen remembered it, brief, albeit with a touch of humor. "Mother," Fethullah replied, "I have already tied the knot with service [hizmet] to Islam. If you tie the knot for me, too, I won't be able to move!"[85] Nevertheless, this was not the last attempt his parents would make to get Fethullah married.

But the most significant development during his convalescence in Erzurum was that he was invited to participate in a seminar on Mevlana Rumi, held at the People's House. He considered it an honor. There were many distinguished guests. "I was too young" to really belong on the program, he recalled. But the young preacher also brought a distinctive point of view. "All the speakers before me had tried to show Mevlana as a pantheist," he remembered. "[So, I tried] to give the image of Mevlana as a true Islamic personage."[86] This is not, we should be clear, to say that Gülen presented Rumi as a "conservative." Rather, it was that the style of thought that led others to see Rumi as a pantheist was in fact what Gülen held to be at the heart of authentic Islam.

References to Rumi, and to classical Turkish and Islamic poetry more broadly, dot Gülen's writing frequently. Theologian Ori Soltes has described, in a way designed to make the connection between Rumi and Gülen apparent to an American Christian (largely) readership:

> As a practicing *Sufi*—an adherent of Muslim mysticism—Gülen is comfortable with paradox and has shaped his thinking in accordance with the paradoxes that are inherent in mysticism. God is within us and God is unimaginably beyond us. God is inaccessible, yet the hidden most recesses of God are accessible. As the mystic seeks God, God seeks the mystic. We must seek God from deep within our own tradition; there are myriad traditions from which paths lead to ... God.[87]

Soltes here uses shorthand terms like "*Sufi*," "mysticism," and "paradox," to signify the deep influence from the poetry of Rumi in the life and thought of Fethullah Gülen.

More concretely, that influence centered on the practice of love. Perhaps Gülen's military service had provided him with an important lesson by showing him how *not* to be a Muslim; by showing him the limits of power as force. Perhaps his encounter with the military had brought home the imperative of love that Rumi so eloquently and passionately articulated. The long passage below is from much later in Gülen's life (1999), but it is a good example of the influence of Rumi on Gülen's thinking:

> The level of our understanding and appreciation of one another depends on how well we recognize the qualities and riches that each person possesses. We can summarize this concept with a thought based on a saying of the Prophet, peace and blessings be upon him: "A Believer is a mirror of another believer." We can enlarge on this saying as "a human is a mirror of another human." If we are able to succeed in doing this, as well as being able to understand and appreciate the riches hidden within every person, we will also understand how to relate these riches to their true Owner, and thus we will accept that anything in this universe that is beautiful, affectionate, or loving belongs to [God]. A soul that can sense this depth says, as did Rumi presenting us tales from the language of the heart: "Come, come and join us, as we are the people of love devoted to God! Come, come through the door of love and join us and sit with us. Come, let us speak to one an-

other through our hearts. Let us speak secretly, without ears and eyes. Let us laugh together without lips or sound, let us laugh like the roses. Like thought, let us see each other without any words or sound. Since we are all the same, let us call each other from our hearts, we won't use lips or tongue. As our hands are clasped together, let us talk about it."
... Islamic thought sees each one of us as a different manifestation of a unique ore, as different aspects of one reality. Indeed, the people who have gathered around common points ... resemble the limbs of a body. The hand does not need to compete with the foot, the tongue does not criticize the lips, the eye does not see the mistakes of the ears, the heart does not struggle with the mind.

As we are all limbs of the same body, we should cease [any] duality that violates our very union.[88]

Gülen would draw repeatedly on Rumi's profound sense of loving unity as manifested in the entire universe in coming years.

Gülen went back to İskenderun to complete his military service in late 1963. The status quo was disturbed, again, by his presence. Such conflicts foreshadowed much of his life. He preached at various mosques, and people flocked to hear him. According to one source:

One day he went to a mosque to give a sermon. He led the Friday prayer. When he left the mosque, he saw something strange. The mosque was surrounded by soldiers on all sides. One of the commanders shouted, "Shoot this guy."
Just at that moment Gülen ran to the squadron commander, saluted and surrendered. Thus, the big incident planned by a commander who could not tolerate him was prevented.
Unsuccessful in inciting an incident as he had planned, the commander's animosity towards Gülen increased even more. He was arrested, and an investigation began. . . [Eventually] Gülen was released and he continued to perform his military duty.[89]

After completing (one is tempted to say "surviving") his military service, Gülen again returned to Erzurum for a brief visit with his family, before returning to his call in Edirne.

Now, however, Gülen was appointed "imam by proxy" at Dar'ül Hadis Mosque; he shared the pulpit with another imam who was ill. In addition to his preaching, Gülen also served as instructor in the Qur'an school associated with the mosque. Gülen benefited during this second period in Edirne from the friendship and support of a patron, Suat Yıldırım, who had been appointed *müftü* or chief imam of Edirne. In fact, Gülen lived in a house with Yıldırım. It did not protect him from surveillance and harassment from the secular authorities. Recall again the context. The government still frowned upon any religious leader who did anything other than their "official," mandated duties. Gülen was proving to be charismatic. He was drawing especially young people to Qur'anic studies at Dar'ül Hadis. In addition to his regular preaching and teaching, Gülen was also organizing informal theological conversations or chats—*sohbetler*, about which more in Chapter 2. In any event, sometime in 1964 "the police raided the mosque and detained many people, including Gülen." The case came to trial. Witnesses testified on Gülen's behalf, and against him. A few accused Gülen of inciting revolution and violence. Gülen spoke in his own defense, asserting that there were many present in the courtroom who had heard him preach on behalf of "peace, harmony, and safety," and who had heard him affirm that "it does not become Muslims to incite disorder." Several of the witnesses against Gülen were caught in contradictions. Eventually, he was exonerated of all charges and released. But as one source drew the sobering conclusion: "The provincial administrators did not leave Gülen alone and Edirne became an unbearable place. Eventually [in early 1965] he was appointed to Kırklareli."[90]

Kırklareli was a different province, but it was still in Thrace, and it was only 56 miles to the east from the city where Gülen had found things unbearable. Not surprisingly, given the short distance, and the growing reputation of the *Hodja* from Erzurum, he was always under constant watch by the state. One notable event from this time-period was when Gülen invited poet Necip Fazıl Kısakürek to the Kırklar Mosque. Gülen may have intended this invitation as a respite from continued hostility by the police. How dangerous could a poet be? In fact, it probably made things worse. Kısakürek, who died in 1983, was by 1965 as well-known for his political leanings as for his poetry. In the 1940s he had founded and edited a journal, *Great East*, which was dedicated, as the title suggests, to the thesis that the East had a source of civilization as deserving of glorification as the West. Kısakürek understood Islam (particularly in its *Sufi*, Nakşibendi, forms) to be the solution to social problems; hence leading some to label him an "Islamist."[91] Kısakürek was, to be sure, no fan of the Kemalist regime; in turn, the Kemalist establishment was not exactly a fan of his. Kısakürek saw both capitalism and communism as "Western" ideologies to be opposed, but he emphasized especially the weaknesses of communism. He anticipated the disintegration of the Soviet Union (forty years before it happened), and he foresaw that the collapse of Communism could be an opportunity for Muslims to re-establish influence and to gain power. And yet, for all his political leanings, Kısakürek was immensely popular across observant Muslim communities as a poet.[92] So, the invitation was, at least, a sign that Gülen was gaining in influence.

The "*Hodja* from Erzurum"'s tenure in Kırklareli was brief, barely a year. It ended with a twenty-day "Anatolian tour." He visited and spoke at various mosques in central Turkey, ending in the capital of Ankara. There he scheduled a meeting with Yaşar Tunagür, who was a Deputy in the Presidency of Religious Affairs, and who was becoming a friend—in an alliance that would prove very helpful to Gülen over the years. He now had an advocate in high places. Tunagür had recently moved to Ankara from Izmir—where he had served as preacher and teacher at Kestanepazarı Mosque. Not coincidentally, after yet another brief period in Erzurum, Gülen would be appointed to this mosque.[93] And it was in Izmir that the nucleus of Hizmet, as a civil society movement, would take off. That movement focused, not surprisingly, on learning. Fethullah Gülen had found in education a path to a wider world than his upbringing in Erzurum had provided him. He would pass that commitment to learning on to all who came into his orbit.

Education around the world

The preamble to the Constitution of UNESCO—the United Nations Educational, Scientific, and Cultural Organization—reads, in part, that "since wars begin in the minds of men, it is in the minds of men that the defenses of peace must be constructed."[94] Here, if anywhere, given that it has been almost universally *men* who have started and waged war, the gender specific language is appropriate. But in the educational efforts inspired by Fethullah Gülen, with roots in his earliest career, there were no such limits on learning, by gender or any other social distinction. From very modest beginnings, both women and men, from across classes and races, joined efforts inspired by the *Hodja* from Erzurum to engage in learning that united "mind" and "heart." Within a few short decades, they then developed educational efforts around the globe. How did this happen? As an extension of Fethullah Gülen's life-story, then, as a way to draw out the crucial significance of his life in the arena of learning, some attention to these efforts will wrap up this first chapter.

Simply put, for Gülen learning built peace. In a succinct essay, social scientists Muhammed Çetin and Alp Aslandoğan outlined several key components of Gülen's educational philosophy worth attending to briefly.[95] The most important is simply that for Gülen learning is valued. Too often, in many educational contexts, learning is transactional or instrumental. Schools become sorting and sifting centers, rather than places where people meet to learn for its intrinsic, relational value.[96] Within Hizmet, and certainly for Gülen in his stated commitments: "the main duty and purpose of human life is to seek understanding." Even more strongly: "A school is a kind of place of worship." And, in a sentence that reflects both idealism and realism: "Educating people is the most sacred, but also the most difficult, task in life."[97] What this has meant, historically, is nicely summarized by political scientist İhsan Yılmaz. Gülen's

> pluralistic, inclusivist, and peacebuilding ideas have enabled the Hizmet Movement to successfully turn its moral, spiritual, intellectual, financial and human resources into effective social capital and utilized this social capital in establishing educational institutions from primary school to university levels in more than 140 countries. The movement's stance toward pluralism, diversity, tolerance, acceptance, civil society, secularism and democracy shows that the movement generates a bridging social capital, extremely helpful for peacebuilding and establishing sustainable peace through education.[98]

Yılmaz' language of "bridging social capital" is distinctive. It finds roots in the work of Harvard sociologist Robert Putnam. According to Putnam, social capital is basically the "value of social networks, partly stemming from the norms of trust and reciprocity that flourish through these networks." Putnam has argued, with ample evidence, that religions specialize in producing social capital in two ways. The first is that they produce "bonding" social capital, which, as the term implies, creates strong relationships between people of similar interests, identities, ethnicities, and so forth. "Bridging" social capital, on the other hand, points to those "social ties that link people together with others across a cleavage that typically divides society (like race, or class, or religion)."[99] Gülen's life-story points to the power of education to generate social capital that both bonds and bridges. As we shall see, a movement that bound individuals together in trust began around Gülen's teaching. But that movement was not exclusivist. People drawn to Gülen also sought to engage students across economic divides, and across religious differences, with no "strings" attached aside from valuing learning. The Hizmet-related schools, in short, constituted an almost textbook case in the production of social capital. It is impossible, of course, historically to isolate this kind of effect in any one biographical cause. Gülen studied under scholars of religion and spiritual masters, but he did not have the benefit of formal education; this might be a factor to help explain the high value he placed on learning. Few people are as aware of the value of a phenomenon as those who have been deprived of it. So, the simple commitment to value education for its intrinsic purpose is a first mark of Gülen's educational philosophy.

A second, still following Aslandoğan and Çetin, is that Gülen's philosophy of education recognized and emphasized how learning contributed to a healthy civil society. The educational endeavors associated with Hizmet and inspired by Fethullah Gülen sought to establish a "community service spirit in the field of education," Aslandoğan and Çetin wrote.[100] There is a paradox between these two aspects of Gülen's educational philosophy that Gülen himself put sharply: "Although knowledge is a value in itself," he wrote, "the purpose of learning is to make knowledge a guide in life and illuminate the road to human betterment."[101] Uniting mind and heart in learning would bring rigor to the acquisition of knowledge. But it would also produce a commitment to utilize knowledge to benefit the human community through service, through hizmet. Thus, in a quote to which we shall return (and which echoes directly a teaching of Said Nursi): "our three greatest enemies [in society] are ignorance, poverty, and disunity ... Ignorance can be defeated through education, poverty through work and the possession of capital, and disunity through unity, dialogue, and tolerance. As the solution of every problem in this life ultimately depends on human beings, education is the most effective vehicle."[102]

As always, to understand these assertions, and how they emerged out of Gülen's biography, it is crucial to recognize his context. Public education in Turkey was shaped throughout Gülen's life largely by "top-down" policies. These policies were dictated by the statist elitist establishment, and they existed especially to benefit those connected to that establishment (notably the children of military officers and bureaucratic elite). This top-down approach did produce results—literacy rates in Turkey rose dramatically over the course of the twentieth-century.[103] But that top-down approach also challenged (to put it mildly) many of the cultural patterns among individuals raised in (or drawn to) Islam. In contrast, Gülen's educational philosophy focused on organizing from the "bottom-up." The schools and other educational efforts associated with Gülen generally began by identifying talented individuals who had been excluded from elite education. Those schools (and tutoring centers) then created pathways for these young people to flourish more fully than in the "top-down" system. For almost the entire duration of his formative years, this was how Gülen himself had learned: informal mentorships that taught what was not taught at school. He learned away from a state's autocratic control, through mutually accountable grassroots relationships. We shall pay more attention to how this kind of educational experience led to a distinctive organizational network within the Hizmet movement more broadly in Chapter Five. For now, the point is simply this: Gülen's educational philosophy saw learning as intrinsically valuable, but also saw education serving a purpose in shaping virtuous, altruistic, and engaged citizens.

A third feature of Gülen's educational philosophy, then, and what animated Hizmet perhaps more than any other feature, was an effort to produce, in the words of Aslandoğan and Çetin, "a synthesis of the heart and the mind, tradition and modernity ... the spiritual and the intellectual."[104] A dichotomy between faith and intellect had been set up in Western societies since at least the eighteenth-century Enlightenment, with its most notable by-product being the so-called "warfare" between science and religion. For Gülen, however, as we have already seen repeatedly, any apparent contradiction between "head" (scientific rationality) and "heart" (religious tradition) was false. He wrote:

There can be no conflict among the Qur'an, the Divine Scripture, (coming from God's Attribute of Speech), the universe (coming from His Attributes of Power and Will), and the sciences that examine them ... In other words, if we can be forgiven for using such a prosaic comparison, the universe is just a large Qur'an that has been physically created by God for our instruction. In return, as it is an expression of the laws of the universe in yet another form, the Qur'an is a universe that has been codified and written down. In its actual meaning, religion does not oppose or limit science or scientific work.[105]

This may be the most difficult feature of Fethullah Gülen's biography for many Western readers to understand. It is also the most important feature to comprehend.

Over the decades, millions of people began applying to their own lives Gülen's commitment to link head and heart, science and religion. This chapter will conclude with a couple of their stories. Nurten Kutlu became familiar with Gülen in the early 1990s. She was not raised in a religious household, but while in college at Marmara University she saw some of the women of Hizmet who wore the *hijab*, and yet who were also educated. "When I saw that," she said, "that combination of [being] educated and religious, having an open mind but also open hearts, [I knew that I didn't] have to be scared to be religious." Such fear was intentionally cultivated in secular Turkey, where it was illegal for a woman to wear the *hijab* in schools, and where public expressions of religion generally were considered in poor taste, at best. While still in college, Kutlu started reading Gülen's works. She dove into the *Risale-i Nur*. She began volunteering in one of the tutoring centers that the movement had set up (more about these in coming chapters). She began working on a master's degree.

Then, she met Gülen in 1993. Kutlu was with a group of teachers and mentors who came to visit Gülen. Their purpose was to share the good news that some of their students scored top at the university entrance test. "He was gentle," she recalled. She also remembered that he said he appreciated their work. He encouraged them to keep studying and volunteering. And he acknowledged to them that sometimes men, including in the Hizmet movement, might serve as obstacles to women's full participation. "They grew up with the Eastern society and rules—with their father's education," she summarized what Gülen said. Kutlu then said, "I am somewhat of a feminist," and, about Gülen she offered, "I think he's a feminist." Kutlu then began working as a teacher in Izmir, where she experienced some of the patriarchy that Gülen had warned her about: women struggled to be heard by administrators. Still, her capacity for leadership was recognized. In 1998, she moved to Albania to be the Headmaster and Dormitory Principal at Mehmet Akif Girls' School. She served in that role until 2001. It wasn't easy—Albania's atheist past made life challenging. "Those three years seemed like 10," she suggested. Yet, she married while in Albania. Her husband was also connected to Hizmet. Together, they moved to Vietnam. There they opened a school together. That was eleven years. And, in 2012, she and her family moved again, this time to Kenya—where she served four years in a relief and educational foundation. Throughout, as she put it, "we want to combine secular education with being faithful. You can do both together. And we did!" As of 2016, Kutlu was living in the United States. But she longed to go back on *hijrah* (moving to places other than one's home town or country). "Without *hijrah* there is no Hizmet," as she put it.[106] Nurten Kutlu's story neatly tracks the rather astonishing effects—in one single life, that followed from Fethullah Gülen's effort to foster a kind of learning that bridged head and heart. And it undoubtedly came out of Erzurum.

The second story of how learning in Hizmet flowed from the life of Fethullah Gülen is that of Emine Eroğlu. She also became familiar with Gülen and Hizmet while in college in the late 1980s. She was a student in the city of Trabzon at Black Sea University. "I was on a spiritual journey," Eroğlu said, "I needed some guidance. That search caused pain in my heart. I came across one of Mr. Gülen's sermons, listened to it, and his articulation, his rhetoric, being able to marry mind and heart, and his convincing arguments that offered hope to [people]—that attracted me." She began more intensive reading. Upon graduation from college she "made an unconventional decision" and chose an unofficial program for her spiritual education for three years—studying Islamic *fiqh* [jurisprudence] and *tafsir* [Qur'anic exegesis]. It was "unconventional" because it was not exactly a promising career path for a young woman in secular Turkey. Still, she spent three years in her studies, and over the same time also deepened her prayer life. Later, she taught for three years at a Hizmet-inspired school in Dagestan (a Russian republic adjacent to Georgia and Azerbaijan). She then moved to Istanbul to Fatih University (a Hizmet-related school), where she eventually earned her Master's in Turkish Literature. That was followed by a stint at Marmara University, one of Turkey's most prestigious, where she started her PhD in the same field, but was not allowed to complete her degree because of the headscarf ban—about which more, later. Throughout, Eroğlu continued reading theology. But eventually she was hired as an editor at a publishing house in Istanbul, where she served until 2016.

But Eroğlu did not merely learn for her own sake. She began applying what she had learned. Notably, she began holding public teaching events, seminars, or reading circles—*sohbets* (about which more in Chapter Two). "I gave *sohbets* in Bursa, Trabzon—larger cities," she said. "When people would come to the city, they would see to it that they had a *sohbet* with me," she recalled with understandable pride. Such public leadership by a woman in religion was not unheard of in Islam—Gülen's mom had been his first religious teacher. But that was private, away from sight and in fear of the regime. These were public gatherings—although also carefully-advertised to avoid raising suspicions among authorities. But in any event, a student had become a teacher, and learning spread. "I'm one of those who was fortunate to meet with many of the people of Hizmet," Eroğlu said. "I've witnessed how Hizmet helps people to bring out their inner beauty. Hizmet helps people to calm themselves ... and to do *tebliğ*—to spread the good word of Islam." This work was done, Eroğlu emphasized, through nonviolence. It started with a struggle with one's self and any obstacles that existed to a loving relationship with God and others. This was the true meaning, she made sure to clarify, of that controverted term *jihad* [struggle]. "I learned this from Hodjaefendi," she explained. She then reiterated a very well-known Turkish Muslim maxim, that Gülen himself often cited: "Without hands against those who strike you, without speech against those who curse you."[107] This was not a simple lesson to learn, in Turkey or anywhere in the world.

The stories of these two women who followed Fethullah Gülen into lives of learning and service are impressive enough on their own. But individuals need institutions to secure sustainable significance. We'll pay much more attention to the institutions and organizing methods associated with Fethullah Gülen in Chapter Five. But, for now, at least one of those sets of institutions—the Hizmet-related schools in Southeastern Turkey and Northern Iraq, merit attention. As is well known, the Kurdish community that lives in Southeastern Turkey, Northern Syria and Iraq has been torn by conflict repeatedly since the founding of the Republic of Turkey. State-sponsored military incursions have been common, and terrorist groups have organized in reaction. Despite this decided lack of peace, and in some ways precisely because of it, people of Hizmet set out there to build schools. Martha Ann Kirk, a Professor of Humanities and Theology at University of the Incarnate Word in San Antonio, Texas, traveled to Southeastern Turkey in 2008 to study the work of these Gülen-inspired institutions.[108] The range of institutions Kirk discovered was impressive: tutoring centers; nursery, primary, and secondary schools; after-school programs; high schools; and dormitories (more on these in Chapter Two). These educational initiatives existed for both girls and boys. They built bridges across ethnic and language barriers—with education in English, Turkish, Kurdish, and Arabic. Schools existed in cities and towns such as Şanlıurfa, Mardin, Mazıdağı, Derik, Boyaklı, Midyat, Batman, Binatlı, Bismil, and Diyarbakır, among others. Many of these places had been centers of activity by the PKK—a Kurdish militant group. Yet the schools taught non-violence.

For instance, Kirk described the work of an educational and charitable agency called Derköy. Derköy served the town of Derik—which had a population of about 18,000 in 2008. More than 40,000 lived in surrounding villages.[109] Derköy was led in 2008 by Ömer Ay and his wife. The Ays grew up in the Black Sea region and became familiar with Gülen's work in the early 1990s. "Destroying is easy," Ömer offered to Kirk, "but building something new is difficult. We are trying to mend broken hearts. We emphasize that instead of blaming each other, we must learn to understand each other." The agency was built from the ground-up. It was not without risk. "We went to businessmen who previously supported the PKK," Ay recalled, "and told them that it is essential that the new generation learns how to live in peace. Now some of those businessmen are funding the construction of a dormitory that will allow students from the villages to come here and get a high school education. Fewer and fewer young people have joined the PKK since we have been giving them other opportunities."[110] Nobody was keeping those statistics, but in 2008 (during what historians have called the "Kurdish opening" in

Turkish policy) that seemed likely. And numbers from countless other conflicted regions supported Ay's contention: education eroded extremism.[111] Yet this kind of bridge-building stoked suspicion. It also provoked resistance from those who benefited from the status-quo of conflict and militarization. Nevertheless, "I have been a follower of Gülen for 15 years," Ay told Kirk. "But Gülen has been teaching this way of life for 40 years. I keep reading his books and trying to practice this non-violence."[112] It was a powerful kind of learning, indeed, that translated reading into non-violent living and then tried to build institutions to pass it on.

And, to be clear, Derköy served girls as well as boys. A man from Derik named Eyüp Tacer was a small-business (furniture store) owner. He had three daughters and a son. "Gülen changed our minds about girls," he said. "They are important for our future. I think that girls are more intelligent than boys if given the opportunity."[113] Such a generalization was of course not likely to persuade someone disinclined even to give girls the opportunity to learn—as was the case throughout Southeastern Turkey even into the twenty-first century. Literacy among girls there was still barely forty per cent.[114] But two of Tacer's daughters, who had been students through Derköy, were studying medicine in 2008. Perhaps their work in healing could be persuasive—when words failed.

***

Such learning that leads to service—to *hizmet*, is the road that Gülen himself walked in his earliest years. From his poor but scholarly family in Korucuk, through his mosque schooling in Erzurum, to his mentoring by *Sufi sheikhs* like the Imam of Alvar, Fethullah Gülen spent his earliest years deeply engaged in Islamic learning. In time, however, Gülen also began to discover some gaps in that learning. He encountered and embraced the thought of Said Nursi, and he was pushed during the years of his military service in Ankara and İskenderun to broaden his education to incorporate modern thought more intentionally. As he began his preaching career in Edirne and Kırklareli, he also began encountering resistance to his efforts to bridge Islam with civil society, to unite heart and mind without violating either. He wrestled throughout these years with his provincial background: could anything good come out of Erzurum? In fact, shortly after arriving in Edirne, Gülen realized that he had to change. He discovered that he could not, as he put it, "preach Erzurum in Edirne."[115] So, he changed. He became more social. He sought out contacts in business and professions, and he even made some friends (not only enemies) in high places. He participated in public seminars on figures like Rumi, and he invited a controversial speaker to his mosque. He even took his first teaching tour to mosques throughout Anatolia. Looking back at those gradual changes, it may seem easy to recognize the road from Erzurum to Derik. Indeed, with the benefit of hindsight, it may seem that it was a simple matter for Fethullah Gülen to walk that path of learning that united heart and mind. It may seem inevitable that Gülen would eventually inspire so many others to their own efforts on behalf of nonviolent peacebuilding through education. But that path was hardly self-evident to the young Fethullah Gülen. Turkey in 1966 was a country torn by ideological conflict and political violence. And before his path was at all clear, the young preacher from Erzurum was called into the heart of that turmoil, to the cosmopolitan city of Izmir.

CHAPTER TWO

"WE WERE YOUNG" - IZMIR, 1966–1971

The city of Izmir—the former Greek city of Smyrna—has long been among the most cosmopolitan trading centers on the Aegean Sea. Wrapped around the Bay of Izmir, the city sparkles. On the skyline, thousands of red-tile-roofed residences juxtapose with steel and glass skyscrapers. The twin Folkart Towers, which look like huge, wavy computer flash drives, are the tallest of these skyscrapers, rising six hundred feet into the clear (usually) blue sky in the Bayraklı district—five miles northeast of the city center of Konak. To the southeast of Konak is the vista from Kadifekale Castle—a medieval fortress. This ruin sits atop Mount Pagos, which is the highest natural point in Izmir. Mount Pagos soars steeply up from the ancient Smyrna *agora*, which is dotted with Greco-Roman ruins. From this spot, one can see the hills leading to Efes (Ephesus) to the South. To the north are the hills leading to Bergama (Pergamum). And directly in front is the bright aqua bay, with cruise ships and tankers passing to and fro. Izmir sparkles.

On street-level, in the city center of Konak, and especially in the ancient bazaar of Kemeraltı, the mood changes. Here, it is easy to imagine the Izmir that Fethullah Gülen was called to in 1966. It is easy in Kemeraltı, in fact, to imagine Izmir as timeless. The cosmopolitan city takes on flesh. Men in skinny wool suits and women in colorful silk hijabs wind their way through narrow walk-ways and alleys. Low-hanging, colorful canvas awnings, or graceful stone arches, protect shopkeepers and shoppers from the blazing sun. *Köfte* and kebab vendors hawk their wares. The smell of roasted lamb, beef, and chicken wafts in the air. Fish vendors display the day's catch from the nearby sea. Tomatoes and olives, apricots and plums, pistachios, and almonds fill old wooden bins.

Boys and girls walk arm in arm down uneven stone paths. Those paths are periodically intersected by grated iron drains, down which flow the detritus of centuries.

Fethullah Gülen first walked the streets of Izmir on March 11, 1966. He was called to serve as administrator of Kestanepazarı dormitory—a residence and Qur'anic study center for middle and high school students preparing to become imams. The dormitory was connected to a seventeenth-century mosque, where Gülen would also preach. The mosque was located a few dozen stone steps above the Kemeraltı bazaar. From the tiled courtyard of the mosque one could see the shops below, in a pattern common in the ancient world, where religion and commerce easily intersected. Although Izmir grew between 1966 and the present—from roughly 600,000 to its current 2.8 million residents—one thing about it stayed consistent. It harbored a reputation for temptation. And so, when told of his assignment to Izmir, Fethullah Gülen—the boy from Erzurum—now a young man of twenty-seven, reportedly replied: "I will be drowned there."[1]

In fact, he flourished. It was in Izmir that many of the initiatives now associated with Hizmet began. Here, as conflict roiled Turkey between Communists and Nationalists, Secularists and Islamists, Rightists and Leftists, with riots in the streets like the student protests that erupted across the United States and Europe during the same time-period, Gülen charted a course for Hizmet with anchor points in the five pillars of Islam. It would seem obvious. Yet, starting in Izmir, Gülen initiated a movement that took the basic practices of Islam and the peace those practices had brought to people for a thousand years, and applied these practices in ways that seemed to many Muslims startlingly modern. Throughout, nonviolence was the non-negotiable norm. In contrast to the ideological conflict into which youth were being drawn across Turkey, the teaching of this powerfully-spoken, but personally modest, young imam was like the caravanserais that welcomed merchants and sailors on the trade routes that ran through Izmir from at least the time of Herodotus in 475 BCE: an oasis.

The *Shahadah* in a *Sohbet*: "spiritual food"

The most consistent feature of Gülen's life has been teaching the *Shahadah*, or confession of faith that is the foundation pillar of Islam. Every

Muslim confesses the oneness of God and that Muhammad was God's prophet: *La ilaha illallah, Muhammadur rasulullah.* "There is none worthy of worship except God." This affirmation peppers Gülen's writings, directly and indirectly. And so daily, often several times a day, in addition to his formal Qur'anic instruction for imam students, Gülen would gather together in Izmir a small group of students to read together and to discuss informally important topics. These gatherings were called a *sohbet*, literally a "conversation." Said Nursi had revived this method of small-group study, which had roots in the early days of Islam. Fethullah Gülen perfected it. The *sohbet* quickly became perhaps the chief method for gathering people to Hizmet. The earliest *sohbet* led by Fethullah Gülen in Izmir would have had five or six students in attendance. By the time Gülen left Izmir, in 1972, they involved hundreds, in dozens of different small groups. The *Shahadah* spread through a *sohbet*.

In the absence of transcripts from these early discussions, some key passages from Gülen's writings—in an imagined conversation—can convey the spirit if not the letter of the first *sohbet*s (sometimes the Turkish plural, *sohbetler*, is also used). Eleven young men, all dressed in pressed pants, shirts, and ties (Gülen's attention to neatness having become the norm), have gathered in the heat of the afternoon. It is just after the midday prayer and before the sun sets over Izmir. A few are eager students at the imam school. More are local small-business owners or tradesmen just ending their workday. They sit in a living room of an apartment rented by college students connected to the dormitory at Kestanepazarı mosque. It is hot in the room—still near 90 degrees Fahrenheit. None smoke. None drink alcohol. Tea flows freely. The young men converse in groups of two or three, until the one they call Hodjaefendi enters the room. Gülen sits at the head of the informal circle. A hush settles, and the reading begins. It is a passage from Nursi's *Risale-i Nur*, *The Gleams: Reflections on Qur'anic Wisdom and Spirituality*. On this afternoon, the specific text to be discussed is "The Twenty-Third Gleam: On the Nature of Refuting Naturalistic Atheism." Gülen asks one of the young men to read the passage, which begins: "The way of disbelieving naturalists is extremely irrational and based on superstitious beliefs."[2] Nursi's logic turns conventional secular wisdom upside-down. Usually, naturalists accused *religious believers* of superstition. Atatürk, for instance, reportedly said that "I have no religion, and at times I wish all religions at the bottom of the sea ... My people are going to learn the principles of democracy, the dictates of truth and the teachings of science. Superstition must go."[3] But then, as if to demonstrate that religion *can* be rational, Gülen and the young men discuss for the remainder of an hour (or so) the honest question that atheism raises: "does God exist?"

Gülen begins with an almost direct paraphrase of Nursi: "The existence of God is too evident to need any argument." In good rhetorical fashion, this overstates the case to "set the floor" of an argument. Gülen then admits that in an age of materialism, for some, it is *not* clear that God exists. There is a ripple of recognition in the room. Hodjaefendi then suggests that not knowing is *not* negating. He pauses to let the point settle in. This differentiates agnosticism from atheism. It inclines to the side of God's existence those who may not be decided, but who entertain doubts. Gülen then continues:

> No one has ever proven God's non-existence, for to do so is impossible, whereas countless arguments prove [divine] existence. This point may be clarified through the following comparison: Imagine a palace with 1,000 entrances, 999 of which are open and one of which appears to be closed. Given this, it would be unreasonable to claim that the palace is inaccessible. Unbelievers ... [pay] attention only to the door that is seemingly closed. The doors to God's existence are open to everybody, providing they sincerely intend to enter through them.[4]

For Gülen, God's existence can be argued based on evidence, but belief in God is ultimately a matter of personal, interior, or subjective faith; a matter of intention. This argument—developed for Christians by Martin Luther in the sixteenth century, and popularized across Europe by romantics and idealists ever since—was also very much part of Atatürk's secularization project. Immediately after decrying superstition, which was the point of his many secularizing projects, Atatürk went on: "Let [people] worship as they will ... so long as it does not interfere with sane reason."[5] Belief in God was fine, this meant, and religion was *primarily* private. It is an argument that the young men find agreeable on many levels. Many of them have had to keep their religion private, or risk consequences at work or at home.

But, we can then imagine the *sohbet* continuing as a student asks: "But does this not make God *merely* subjective?" Gülen then goes on to summarize over a dozen classical arguments for the existence of God. We will explore only a few of them. First, then, he argues that "everything is contingent, for it is equally possible that they will exist or not." Things all relate to each other, and appear to occur spontaneously, but this is not quite ever the case. There must be something that *determines* whether something exists or not. "Necessarily," Gülen concludes, "this is God." Gülen here mirrors the first argument for God's existence that Roman Catholic-theologian Saint Thomas Aquinas developed. Both build on the philosophy of Aristotle and his theory of causes. The room in Izmir is quiet now except for the breathing of the brothers, the sounds of the city below them, and a slight breeze blowing through the open windows of the apartment.

But a student then asks, reasonably: "Events have multiple causes. How can we say that the thing that causes something to exist must necessarily be God?" Gülen replies:

> Whatever has been created has a purpose. Take the example of ecology. Everything, no matter how apparently insignificant, has a significant role and purpose ... Nothing is in vain; rather, every item, activity and event has many purposes ... Since only humanity can understand those purposes, the wisdom and purposiveness in creation necessarily points to God.

Aristotle is again behind the scene. Gülen now contends not only that God is the First Cause or Creator, but also that God is the Final Cause, or purpose, of everything. After all, the purpose of something is part of its reason for being. The *reason* something exists, obviously, is also evidence that it does exist. And there are, of course, countless "reasons" for the existence of God, or purposes to which people have put belief in a deity.

But there are also, of course, countless "gods." People have been known to fight over them. So perhaps a student of Hocaefendi asks: "But what of evil? If God exists, why do bad things happen?" At this point, Gülen turns the argument. The problem again is perception. Human constructs of God might compete, but cooperation is also real. "All things in the universe, regardless of distance, help each other," Gülen suggests. "This mutual helping is ... comprehensive," he continues. "Our bodily cells, members, and systems work together to keep us alive. Soil and air, water and heat, and [even] bacteria cooperate with each other to benefit plants. Such activities, which display [design] and conscious purpose, by unconscious beings, suggest the existence of a miraculous arranger. That one is God." God is the ultimate cooperator. We either see that cooperation, work with it, or not.

The conversation has gone on for nearly an hour. It is unlike the way any imam has ever engaged these young men before. They are eager to hear more. But one stubborn soul blurts out: "Who created God?" It is a blasphemous question. Yet Gülen neither silences it nor expresses frustration with it. He furrows his brow a bit, and he leans back in his couch. Humans perceive causes and effects, Gülen points out. But part of what "God" means, he continues, is that God is "Self-Existent and Self-Subsistent." The *Shahadah,* he recalls to nods of recognition around the room, affirms above all that God is one. All people share a common Creator. The Creator of everything cannot be just another effect. Everything, including the question of who created God, Gülen says with a gentle smile to the young man who asked the impertinent question, comes from God. Hodjaefendi wraps up the argument like this: "All causes begin in [God]. In truth, created things are '0's' that will never add up to anything, unless God bestows real value or existence by placing a positive '1' before the '0.'"

Again, it is the unity of God that is crucial to the *Shahadah,* and to Muslims; and within Islam the question of God's unity follows from the question of God's existence like water flows into the sea. The assertion of unity also has a decided edge. It defines Muslim distinctiveness. For a person raised a Christian or a Jew—and there were both in Izmir in 1966—a logical final question in our imagined *sohbet* would be: "Is 'God' the same as 'Allah?'" To that question Gülen says: "God, with a capital G, is not an exact equivalent of the term *Allah,* although we use it for practical reasons [in translation] ... *Allah* is the essential personal name of God, and comprises all [God's] Beautiful Names." There are 99 of these names, and all of them are comprehended in *Allah.* "When *Allah* is said," Gülen continues,

> the One, the Supreme Being, the Creator, the Owner, the Sustainer, the All-Powerful, the All-Knowing, the All-Encompassing, whose Names and Attributes are manifested in creation, comes to mind. This

term also refers to [God's] absolute Oneness as well as ... having no defect or partner.

The conversation has reached familiar ground; a staple of Muslim faith about which there is no controversy. Gülen nods to the young men of the *sohbet*, and rises as he offers a Qur'anic benediction to the young men: "(In acknowledgement of their imperfection, and their perception of the truth of the matter,) the angels said: "All Glorified are You (in that You are absolutely above having any defect and doing anything meaningless, and Yours are all the attributes of perfection). We have no knowledge save what You have taught us. Surely You are the All-Knowing, the All-Wise" (2:32). The chat is over. As Gülen moves toward the door, and as the young men rise to follow him, individual conversations break out again between smaller groups—all talking at once. They have been made *to think*. At least one who entertained doubts about the existence of God is now less doubtful. That one is also more willing than he was before to work with others who seem convinced that God not only exists, but that God has something for them to do together. Soon, the number of students at the *sohbet*s in Izmir grew. Men were drawn into chats with *Hodjaefendi*, and women were led in chats with other elders. In a Turkey being torn apart by ideological clashes, the *Shahada* in a *sohbet* secured a sense of peace.

Down to today, the *sohbet* system—if we can speak of it in these terms—has been one of the primary ways people became, and stayed, connected to Hizmet around the globe. These small-group reading circles were not just intellectual exercises. They created networks of support for men and women, usually meeting separately, sometimes meeting together. Sociologist Margaret Rausch, for instance, has described her fieldwork among the women's *sohbetler* of Kansas City in the early years of the twenty-first century. According to Rausch,

> the women participants' engagements with the teachings of [Gülen] and their involvement in activities and institutions established by other participants have led to improvements in their personal lives, to their access to the public sphere, and to their aspirations to make a mark ... in the society where they are residing and working.[6]

As described by Rausch, the practices of the *sohbet*s have been more-or-less continuous from the 1960s to the present.

A small group of fifteen women—thirteen of them married, the other two living in one of the Hizmet dormitories (more about them shortly), gathered together weekly, usually in the evenings—after work or classes. Some were still students, some worked outside the home, and five were stay-at-home moms. Most wore head scarves. One participant described the process:

> Sohbetler in the U.S. and Turkey are almost the same. We gather and one abla [older sister] reads an Islamic book. It could be a book by Gülen, an interpretation of the Qur'an or Risale-i Nur. We discuss whatever we read and try to figure out the implications of reading and ways we can apply those to real life. Sohbetler are interactional. They are not like lectures. Everybody who attends tells what she understood. There is a very nice and harmonious atmosphere ... Sometimes we go jogging, eat delicious food after the sohbet and have fun together. When I was in college, during daytime, I was always busy with courses and worldly issues. When I returned home and attended the sohbetler, the abla kept me focused on the other world, on my responsibilities and on the idea of struggling to be a better person. I felt like I was getting my spiritual food from sohbetler.[7]

Understanding, conversation, even fun made the Shahadah in a sohbet like spiritual food.

Rausch drew out of her field work three ways that young women found value in the sohbets, from the 1960s to the present. Such chats encouraged young women to live for high ideals (constantly striving), to make progress through piety, and to seek the resources of "ablalar [older sisters] as role models." Each deserves brief attention, through the voices of the young women themselves. Gülen has consistently stressed higher education for women as well as men. One of the women Rausch interviewed commented:

> When I read Gülen's teachings about education, they rang a bell with me since I really believe in the power of knowledge. Gülen's interpretation of the very first revelation to Prophet Muhammad (peace be upon him) is very unique and gave me a fresh perspective. The first revelation begins: "Read! In the Name of your Lord, Who has created

(all that exists)." Gülen emphasizes that this command from God is very relevant today and that it illustrates the importance of education. I have applied this concept to my life by embracing books even more than I had before [encountering Gülen's thought] and by targeting the goal of attending medical school.[8]

Not all the women inspired by Hodjaefendi, of course, aimed to be MD's. Others found roles in more direct service (*hizmet*), or in dialogue activities. But the idea of living for "higher ideals" was consistent. Another young woman remarked:

> Being involved in these [service] activities with people who share the same values has changed my life for the better because it makes me feel like part of something big and important instead of feeling alone and isolated ... We motivate each other and help each other to sustain our conviction and our dynamics ... [Few of our goals are] a one-person-job, [so] this is where a few sets of hands, legs and brains come in very handy!"[9]

Women participated in the *sohbetler* for friendship, in short: to foster mutual accountability and to inspire each other to succeed.

One of the participants shared with Rausch a startling metaphor to describe what the *sohbetler*, and her participation in Hizmet more broadly, meant to her. The *sohbetler* inspired her to be like "a bucket with a hole" in it, she said. As Rausch followed up to question this image, the woman explained: water in a solid bucket can grow stagnant, even become contaminated. But a bucket with a hole in it must continually be replenished. Like water that flows in a river, a bucket with a hole in it can be life-giving and flowing."[10] Another woman in the group explained further, citing one of Gülen's favorite paradoxes: "Daily life is a constant struggle. We believe that [a] human being has the ability to be even better than angels and at the same time fall lower than devils. God gave us the ability to separate what is good and bad and let us [be] free in our choice ... Making each day different [a bucket with a hole in it] means trying to improve spiritually."[11] This did not mean, emphatically, that spiritual improvement was at the expense of secular progress. In fact, the two belonged together. For these women, progress happened *through* piety, rather than piety being an impediment to progress. It was a point Gülen stressed repeatedly.

Along with friendship and motivation, according to Rausch, the *sohbetler* gave young women the support of those they called *ablalar*— older sisters. Just as Gülen himself, as a young imam, served as an *abi* (older brother) through chats in Izmir, so did some of the more mature young women within Hizmet mentor others. One younger sister explained:

> *Ablalar* try to affect us both by being a role model, a living example, and by persuasion. When you see them around always helping others, you just admire them and want to be like them. Some *ablalar* have considerable knowledge about Islam, Gülen's books and they try to share what they know with us ... Sometimes they kindly warn you if you make a mistake ... I can [say] that the most influential point of *ablalar* is they exercise what they tell us, you actually see them living according to their beliefs.[12]

It is worth pointing out that the emphasis in this narrative is on how ablalar *try* (twice) to be good influences. Still, Rausch draws a sage conclusion. These women "are aware of the common view of liberal secularists in Turkey [and elsewhere] that a woman who consciously chooses to veil has a veiled mind."[13] So by gathering in *sohbetler*, and through encounters with their *ablalar*, the women of Hizmet marshaled collective power. They practiced their agency—to use a sociological buzzword—to dispel the stereotype about a veiled head being the sign of a veiled mind.

Still, they were fighting an uphill battle in 1966, and it remained so. The simple goal, as one young woman put it, was to "serve [*hizmet*] God by serving society, and to do whatever you do for the sake of God, for becoming closer to God." Such a goal struck some as suspicious. After all, the *Shahadah* was uncompromising. There was One God who required a life of service. Could this belief really *empower* women? According to Margaret Rausch, it did. The women she studied who gathered in *sohbets* did so to make faith in one God:

> integrally intertwined with their daily life activities, their ongoing personal development, their education and career goals and their interpersonal interactions and relationships. In their view ... their constant pursuit of God's approval and their unceasing endeavor for self-re-

newal and improvement all serve as a means of support and a source of enrichment. It is their faith and piety that provides the foundation for establishing equitable, healthy and mutual enriching forms of interpersonal interaction at every level in their lives.[14]

By joining with one another in chats that provided them with "spiritual food," women gained encouragement to face the challenges of everyday life. And those challenges could be considerable. Turkey in the 1960s—and through much of the late twentieth century—was not always a congenial place for public piety. Yet along with gathering to affirm the *Shahadah* in a *sohbet*, the young men and women gathered around and inspired by Fethullah Gülen gathered together to pray. Such a practice would seem harmless. It is nonviolent by definition. But prayer stoked controversies in modern Turkey that were almost as heated as those swirling around the head scarf. The example of Hodjaefendi, however, was clear. The spiritual food that was at the base of the pyramid for him, from the time of his childhood until the present, was prayer.

"I had never prayed like this in my life!"

Hizmet grew dramatically once Gülen landed in Izmir in 1966. Among those drawn to him were İsmail Büyükçelebi, Alaattin Kırkan, and Yusuf Pekmezci. Büyükçelebi was a student in the imam-hatip school. Pekmezci was in the textile business. Kırkan was a tailor. Within weeks of his arrival in Izmir, Gülen had discovered that people were recording his sermons and circulating the cassette tapes. He protested, but the practice went on anyway. Soon, people who had heard these tapes—from all over Turkey, began arriving by busloads to hear Hodjaefendi preach. Gülen was developing a following that the authorities could not help but notice. Not everyone in Izmir, in other words, was thrilled by the arrival of the imam from Erzurum. Gülen was different. His ways were austere. He slept in a small hut that was assembled in the corner of the Kestanepazarı mosque courtyard. The square footage was barely enough to accommodate him lying down, and it had neither heat nor running water. Furthermore, Gülen was scrupulously frugal with money. By the accounts of many of his earliest associates, he spent nearly his entire modest salary on food and other creature comforts for his students. He even paid the mosque back for the water that he used.[15] Such austerities did not endear him to all his professional colleagues. Spiritual people are not immune to professional jealousy. The police, and the local governor, took careful notes.

Aside from the *sohbets* and his teaching, while in Izmir the young Gülen led and participated in the central functions of any imam—leading public prayer and preaching. We have already seen in Chapter One, how Hodjaefendi's influential and passionate preaching at a young age startled some people in the village of Alvar, and we shall have occasion to pay closer attention to the role of preaching in Gülen's life in Chapter Three. But for now, our topic is prayer. Muslims have a general term for prayer, *dua*, literally "supplication," that refers to personal invocations. But the pillar of Islam, required of every faithful Muslim, is *Salah*—which is the obligatory, five-times per-day prayers within Islam (Turks use the Persian word *namaz*). Every day while in Izmir—as in fact every day of his life since the age of 4—Gülen structured his day around *Salah*. It should not be necessary to assert, but is, that prayer is a manifestation of nonviolence. Nobody has ever been killed by praying (that is not to say, alas, that people have not been killed *while* praying). But *Salah* was a profound source of personal power for Gülen. In time, it became a profound source of collective power for Muslim men and women in Turkey who followed Gülen's example.

It is important to set this practice of non-violence in context. Atatürk and his followers—although never putting it quite so clearly, sought to stamp out public prayer in Turkey. They did so primarily by changing the language in which it was conducted from Arabic to Turkish. The move was counterintuitive: wouldn't prayer in the vernacular *draw* people to mosques? In fact, it set a generation adrift. The Qur'an is in Arabic, and prayers wherever Muslims gather have been in Arabic. But under Atatürk, even the call to prayer—the *adhan*—that has been universally delivered in Arabic since the time of Muhammad wherever Muslims have lived, was changed to Turkish. That experiment lasted for 18 years—from 1932-1950. Along with a general attitude that disapproved of any public religious practice, this linguistic shuffle had stifled the prayer life of many Turkish Muslims.

Gülen's own prayer life was shaped by this context of official secular oppression, just as he sought, in Izmir, to revive the practice of public prayer. One of his early books, *Selected Prayers of Prophet Muhammad* and *Great Muslim Saints*, gathered together brief, classical prayers for use on various occasions. Along with describing and documenting the appropriate prayers to be said during Salah, about which more shortly, Gülen's book also offered prayers for many everyday life moments. One section of the prayer book, for instance, invited people to remember God during travel—with specific petitions for embarking, arriving, and returning home. It even included a prayer for if one became afraid during travel. That may have come in handy for young Izmir businessmen or women flying on airplanes for the first time in the 1960s and 70s.[16] A key element of public prayer is what is called *wudu*—ritual purification or ablution with water, often in a fountain or other form of running water. Every mosque will have some designated area for *wudu* (abdest in Turkish). This ritual washing happens according to a set of practices that varies depending upon the particular tradition one follows (just as Christians vary in whether to sprinkle or immerse people in baptism). Generally, though, in *wudu* one washes the hands, arms (to the elbow), face (including ears, mouth, and nose), head (at least sprinkling the hair with water), and feet (up to the ankles). One may recite the bismillah while performing *wudu*, or ablution, which is simple and direct. It begins: "In the name of Allah, the Merciful, the Compassionate." It is the beginning of every chapter of the Qur'an, and it a phrase used to begin almost any occasion among Muslims. Gülen's prayer then asked God's favor for matters that might be quite relevant to Izmir or any business leaders: "O Allah! Forgive me for my sins, make my home spacious, and bless my provision." Remembering God in relationship to these everyday matters—a home and food for one's family, was anything but common among Izmir residents in 1966.

Even more pointedly, though, the context of oppression of prayer meant that Gülen recommended that people turn their homes into places of worship. Interpreting the Qur'an 10:87, he counseled those drawn to him to "make your homes places to turn to God." The rationale was practical. "When it is impossible for you to worship God in the open," Gülen reflected, "adopt your houses as places of worship. ... [And] when your places of worship are banned from fulfilling their functions, convert your houses into places of worship to perform your duty."[17] Turkey was of course hardly the only place where people who pray have suffered. And many Turks who may not necessarily have prayed would still ask guests to remove their shoes before entering their home—as you would do in visiting a mosque. But by emphasizing that one could (and should) pray at home, and that one could (and should) consider the home a sacred place, Gülen also helped Turks to negotiate the oft-repressive tenor toward prayer in official Turkish policy. This emphasis on prayer at home was also consistent with strengthening women's practice of prayer, since Muslim women traditionally prayed more often at home than in public, for various reasons.[18]

But if Gülen sought to revive prayer through recommending specific supplications, and by recommending that Turks make their homes into sacred places, he also sought to revive practice of the five daily prayers of *Salah*.[19] These five prayers are used as a measuring-stick of faithfulness in most Islamic communities. Of course, in 1960s Izmir, as today, there were plenty of barriers to realizing a steady prayer life. Work, school (which did not include breaks for prayer), and even soccer competed for peoples' attention. Summers were particularly difficult, especially for youth. Students in the imam school were not immune to distractions, Gülen observed, and they would begin to relax their practice during the hot-season. Consequently, as a way simultaneously to strengthen the practice of prayer, to have some fun, and to give parents a break—he consulted with a group of business leaders in Izmir and together they decided to begin a summer camp. Over the course of the twentieth century the youth summer camp had become an institution within Christian cultures—the YMCA was the most notable example. Camping was not widespread among Muslims.

İsmail Büyükçelebi was in middle school when Gülen arrived in 1966. He recalled that the first summer camp happened in a forest near Buca—not far from Izmir. Students attended for four weeks. One of the benefits, of course, was that, as a captive group, the young people could be encouraged to pray *Salah* regularly and more consciously away from the distractions of city life. Gülen did not want mere rote participation, however, and the summer camp allowed for teaching *about* prayer as well as its practice. Büyükçelebi explained:

> He would continue the kind of lessons [he gave in imam school and *sohbets*] during the summer. He always talked about praying with intention. A person who takes their ablution seriously with care; their

Salah carefully and slowly—these obligations are required, but some-times people hurry through them. But Hodjaefendi has a subjective *Salah* condition: if you see yourself not doing parts of the *Salah* in depth with all of the sincerity you have—you must do it again. If you don't get it right—do it twice, or three times—until you have it from the bottom of your heart, sincerely.[20]

It's not that at these summer camps Gülen was a prayer-monitor, observing the rights and wrongs of the young Muslims. That would have been contrary to the spirit of nonviolence inherent in the practice. Of course, collective pressure made participation more likely—that's com-mon in any small group. But in prayer, Gülen would be at the front of the group, usually—leading, with his back to the young men. Büyükçelebi continued:

> I've prayed behind him many times ... [He taught us] that the Prophet
> lived a life of prayer. [The Prophet] had certain supplications when he
> woke up, went to sleep, left house, into market ... His life was a prayer.
> Hodjaefendi's intention is making sure this becomes alive again—in
> the community.[21]

Lively prayer cannot be forced prayer. Beginning with his students from the imam school, including Büyükçelebi, Gülen moved the prac-tices of the mosque into the woods. In coming decades, summer camps became regular features for both boys and girls of Hizmet. We'll attend to them, and Gülen's participation in them, again in Chapter Three.

Salah—in camp or in the mosque, by men or women, is a physical process that follows in a step-by-step practice. Gülen himself put it this way:

> God told the Prophet how to pray, and we are told to follow his exam-
> ple. There are certain rules to follow. Before beginning, we must purify
> ourselves with the proper ablution [*wudu*]... Then we say *Allahu ak-*
> *bar*, meaning that nothing is greater than God. Standing in a peaceful,
> respectful stillness, with hands joined together on our chest, indicates
> our complete surrender. Concentrating as fully and deeply as possible
> allows us to experience ... the Prophet's ascension in our spirit ... Ris-
> ing-up inwardly, we bow down physically to renew our surrender and
> express our humility. As we do so, we experience a different stage in

our servanthood and so prostrate in fuller reverence and humility.[22]

What is vital to recognize here, again, is the nonviolence and even anti-violence implicit in this practice. A humble person is a peaceful person. Nobody could kill another while bowing down to God. Indeed, at the end of public prayer, after the series of prescribed postures and practices (each cycle of which is called a *rak'ah*, of which there are normally between two and four per prayer), the supplicant turns to right and then left and says, "*As-salamu alaykum wa rahmatullah*," "Peace and mercy of God be with you."

Of course, as with most ritual, repetition is part of the point. The brain changes slowly but surely from its animal habits of fight or flight into something recognizably human through habits of patient practice like repeated prayer. It helps to be in a community of practice—which is the idea behind every assembly—Jewish, Christian, Muslim or otherwise. Gülen put it this way:

> *Salah* ... [is when] patience is put into practice ... It is also the most appropriate and propitious ground for social agreement and harmony and the clearest sign of the formation of a Muslim community ... Everyone who is able to make belief a part of their nature through *Salah* and ... dive into the depths of the life of the heart through it, and see themselves as an inseparable part of a community like a firm, solid structure in its warm and peaceful clime, can easily overcome the hardships along the path of servanthood.[23]

So, prayer, in addition to bringing personal peace, could build a community of peace. That was Gülen's wager in reviving the practice of prayer.

Restrictions in Turkey, however, made fulfilling *salah* especially difficult for women. The laws changed many times. Generally, though, wearing a headscarf (*hijab*) in a public place—like a school or government office—had been frowned upon and forbidden, if not illegal, since the time of Atatürk. For prayer, however, both Muslim men and women must dress modestly. Women are required to cover their heads. This meant that if a woman wanted to pray, and wanted to work, she had some choices to make. Either she went without prayer—a choice some made, or she went without work—a choice for many others. A third way—especially after the informal prohibition became official as law in 1980, was to veil and to unveil several times a day—a nuisance, to say the least. Interestingly, given the negative consequences of any of these choices, for many women in Turkey the right to wear a veil in public became a feminist cause. This was contrary to the stereotype circulated in European and American public media, where veiling was often represented as a sign of oppression. The issue was volatile in Turkey, even recently. In May 1999, for instance, Merve Kavakçı, who had been elected to Parliament, stirred controversy (to put it mildly) by showing up for work in a blue headscarf. She understood her act as representing all faithful Muslim women and their rights to work and to education. She hoped (if not expected) to take her oath of office wearing her headscarf. Instead, she was booed and hissed at, and had to retire without ever serving. Kavakçı lost her Turkish citizenship and moved to the U.S. Over time, though, with the new regime under Prime Minister and then President Erdoğan, Merve Kavakçı became the Ambassador for Turkey in Malaysia, her daughter Mariam Kavakçı became an adviser to President Erdoğan, and Ravza Kavakçı (Merve Kavakçı's sister) became a member of Parliament, wearing a headscarf.[24]

But it was in the 1960s, and especially in cities like Izmir, Istanbul, and the capital of Ankara, that the headscarf debate became particularly heated. The Hizmet movement was not officially a major player; Gülen has consistently claimed that wearing *hijab* was a matter of personal preference not crucial to the essentials of Islamic faith (*usul*) (although many if not most of the women I have met with who have connections to Hizmet have chosen to veil). But the issue came to a head (sorry) in 1968 when Hatice Babacan was expelled from study at the University of Ankara School of Divinity for refusing to remove her *hijab* in the classroom. That incident led to protests across the country. Many men supported a woman's right to dress as they chose, and others took sides with the secularists. Novelist Orhan Pamuk's Nobel-winning novel, *Snow*, documented some of the volatility associated with the headscarf issue in Turkey. Züleyha Çolak, a scholar of modern Turkey who has also been inspired by Gülen's teaching, recalled that the ban divided society and even families. For instance, she grew up with secularist parents. They struggled to understand their daughter as she felt increasingly drawn to Islam and to wearing the hijab. Fortunately, as she put it, her father had "taught me to think for myself, to have an open mind." That spirit eventually led him to understand (if not to agree with) her point of view. So, as a young woman in high school she recalled how she would "walk to school wearing my head scarf, come up to the gate of the school" and then make a very public demonstration of removing it. This took courage. It drew attention to the lack of connection between Islam and public institutions in Turkey. Eventually, the compromises she faced made it impossible for her to stay in Turkey; she too emigrated to the U.S.[25] Such a disconnect between piety and politics was felt by many women over the decades in Turkey, especially since the 1960s. Not all have had the courage of a Hatice Babacan, Züleyha Çolak, or Merve Kavakçı. But many in countless small ways participated in a struggle to be the same person (or at least to wear the same clothes) at prayer and in public life.

One of the attractions of prayer that Gülen emphasized was its beauty and music. For Christians accustomed to Bach chorales or the crashing cymbals of praise bands, the lilt of an imam issuing the *adhan*, or the melismatic chanting of an imam leading prayer, might seem modest. In part, that's the point. No prayer leader would want to draw attention to one's chanting rather than toward God. Yet there is unmistakable beauty, and art, in the practice of leading prayer. Gülen frequently invoked music metaphors in his own teaching, and indirectly, at least, alluded to the music of prayer in passages like the following:

> Even if we should let ourselves be swept along by our daily lives, the calls for prayer, songs that exalt God, the various sounds of prayer, the recitation of the names of God, those who give [God] thanks, calling out [God's] Uniqueness, letting this spill from the windows of the mosques, all draw us to their climate; they paint our souls with their hues, they give a tambour-like voice to our hearts, they make them sigh like a flute.[26]

The music of prayer was another one of the ways that the human senses were engaged nonviolently in this religious practice. Prayer reminded participants of a loving (and even lovely) God of peace.

So, through direct teaching, through the innovation of a summer camp, and through example, Fethullah Gülen set out during his years in Izmir to renew among Muslims the practice of prayer. The Hizmet movement itself of course suggests that the effort proved effective, and the story of Alaattin Kırkan can illustrate how Gülen's practice of prayer influenced an individual life. Kırkan, born in 1948, hailed from Ödemiş—a town known for its macho guys; for its fighters. As a youth, Kırkan looked up to these toughs. When his family moved to Izmir in 1960, he trained to be a tailor. As a young man from a family of modest means, he could not afford his own shop, so in April, 1966 he became an assistant to "the second best tailor in Izmir," as he put it. Many of his clients "had strong knuckles," Kırkan recalled. When "they had fights in the coffeehouses," he remembered, "not only the fists would fly. The chairs would go, too." Kırkan was a Muslim, but he was also attracted to being one of those macho guys.

After a few months as an assistant, Kırkan found a partner with whom he opened his own shop. The partner, however, was both a tough guy and one of those Turks indoctrinated in the Kemalist mentality, who automatically looked down upon religion. One day shortly after the new store opened, Kırkan pulled out a prayer rug to pray. His partner noticed. "What's that?" the secular colleague asked. "What does it look like?" Kırkan replied. His partner then said: "It looks like you're going to pray." And then, Kırkan remembered, his partner went on, "with a belittling voice: 'If you're going to pray, I hear there's a new preacher in Kestanepazarı, and I hear he cries like a girl. Why don't you go pray with him?'" Kırkan adds the (nonviolent) punch line: "So that secularist without knowing it became my teacher."

The next Friday, following his curiosity, and in defiance of his partner, Kırkan went to the big noon prayer led by Gülen at Kestanepazarı. Although Islam mandates prayer five times every day, Friday noon is a prayer that is necessary to be observed as a congregation. Kırkan's story continues:

> Although I wasn't very old, I had seen many *hodja*s before this. But that was the first time I saw a crying *hodja*. It's very hard to explain that moment ... Part of it was his clothing [the tailor notices]. ... His socks were milky white. His pants were milky white. His robe was milky white. His *sarık* (turban) was milky white. Is there anyone else like that? His eyes were teary ... It was clear he had passion ... His concern was the human person ... He was crying for us. He was crying for humanity. And just like the companion Ali, he said, "The Muslims are

my brothers, and the non-Muslims are my human brothers." He cried a lot. He was the man who cried for us ... I ran back the second week.[27]

There would be no fighting in this tailor's life. We'll explore more fully the meaning of Gülen's tears in Chapter Three. But, for now, the point to draw out is simply this: the eighteen-year-old tailor once pulled toward macho fighters became, through prayer, one of the first to embrace Hizmet. He stayed close to Gülen throughout his life.

Yusuf Pekmezci, who between 1963 and 1968 was on the Board of the Kestanepazarı Dormitory, also discovered that growing close to Fethullah Gülen and reviving his practice of prayer meant putting down his fists. Pekmezci was in his twenties and had developed a good business trading in textiles throughout Turkey and Europe. He was drawn to Gülen from the moment Hodjaefendi arrived in Izmir. Yet Pekmezci, who hailed from the conservative city of Konya, was also a nationalist— part of the strengthening right wing in Turkey. He prayed, but his politics bordered on the fascist. He hated Communists. Along with many other young people, he was also willing to take to the streets to fight them. And the Communists were strong in Izmir. As he described it, protests and counter-protests were common, including riots, vandalism, and street fights. Shortly after Gülen arrived in Izmir, Pekmezci was headed to one of these street fights with his gang:

> One day there's a forum in the town center. The Communists were gathering. I went there with 20 people behind me. My men. And then I heard someone call me from the back: "Yusuf Bey!" [bey is a term of respect, similar, perhaps, to "Mister" in English]. It was Fethullah Gülen. He said again: "Yusuf Bey," and then I remembered the voice and knew it was Hodjaefendi. He asked me, "What are you doing here?" I said: "We came to fight." Hodjaefendi said: "With who?" Pekmezci replied: "With the leftists [solcu in Turkish]!" Hodjaefendi simply asked: "Why?' Pekmezci said: "Because they're leftists." Hodjaefendi said: "You shall not fight!" Pekmezci protested: "Hodja, I have 20 people here. We came to fight." Hodjaefendi again asked: "Who are you fighting? Pekmezci said: "The leftists!" Gülen then asked one more time: "Why are you fighting?" And Pekmezci, exasperated, said again: "Because they're leftists!" Then Gülen asked a powerful, if simple question: "What are you?" Pekmezci said: "I'm a rightist." Hodjae-

fendi then said: "Don't you want any leftists?"[28]

In other words, was Islam only for "rightists?" Gülen had more than a political struggle in mind.

Still, Pekmezci was not immediately persuaded. Gülen's questioning gave him pause--but Pekmezci had the certainty of any ideologue. So, he told Gülen: "I don't want any leftists." Gülen then said: "Yusuf bey, you're doing the same thing. Leftist is the same as rightist. You're citizens of the same country. Why are you fighting?" As Pekmezci recalled it, Hodjaefendi then went on, in words that could be found in one form or another in many of his writings:

> We're all brothers; there are rightists and there are leftists. If you don't want a leftist, it's like you don't want half of the body that God has created for you. Don't you want your left ear *and* your right ear? If you don't want your left ear, then maybe you should cut it off. Throw it away. Live with just your right side. In God's creation, there's a right side and a left side. We're all people. We must see the dignity in each other. Brother—think![29]

Pekmezci concluded: "I did; I was silent. He made me think." As he was doing so, Hodjaefendi asked him to "walk away. Let's go," Gülen said. Pekmezci protested one last time: "But I can't. They'll say I walked away." So, he said to Hodjaefendi: "Stay here with me. Let me organize these guys, and then I'll come." And after a few words to his nationalist colleagues, Pekmezci left the rally. He walked back to Kestanepazarı with Gülen. It was the last of his work as a nationalist agitator.[30] The power of prayer set a context for living beyond politics.

Such a high purpose for prayer was consistent with the way Gülen learned about prayer in his studies of *Sufism*. There are scholarly debates about how to define a *Sufi*, or *Sufism*, but sparing a considerable amount of time to pray is certainly a part of it.[31] One of the chief marks of many *Sufi* communities, then, and certainly in the life of Fethullah Gülen, was the practice of voluntary prayers. These prayers went beyond the mandated five-times per day *Salah* to include prayers such as *tahajjud* (midnight prayer), and *awrad,* which is also called *dhikr* (remembrance). *Dhikr* has been a particularly important practice in Gülen's life, and in the Hizmet community more broadly. It involves among other things sitting in the direction of Mecca or as a circle and singing invocations. These invocations might be the *Shahadah*, or glorifications of God, or simply the name of God—Allah. In *dhikr*, a person in prayer might also recite (or recall silently) any (or all) of the other ninety-nine beautiful names of God, such as *as-Salam*, the Peace, or *an-Nur*, the Light. Often, *dhikr* involves the use of strings of prayer beads—like a rosary used by Roman Catholics, or the beads called *mala* used by Hindus. These beads—called *tesbih* in Turkish—can be simple strings of seeds, or ornate works of fine wood or stones. Gülen has dozens of these prayer strings--given to him as gifts, or that he collected in his travels among different communities. Some of these Muslim prayer strings have one-hundred beads. Other smaller collections have thirty-four beads—with one for Allah and thirty-three to be touched three-times for a complete cycle. *Dhikr* in any event involves repeating, like a mantra, a verse or name or the names of God, over and over and over—along with other supplications. The goal is simply to remember the presence of God. And the prayer can become ecstatic.

Dhikr might also involve chanting, and music. Gülen recalled vividly the "circles of remembrance" of his *Sufi* mentor, the Imam of Alvar. His long description of them is worth quoting in full, as a window into the kind of prayer that shaped him:

> The Imam of Alvar was a person with a deep inner world, a man of God overflowing with love and enthusiasm. His state at circles of remembrance was a living example of this richness of heart. Both the Naqshbandi and Qadiri orders inspired him, and it was possible to witness both types of remembrance at the mosque. In the *Sufi* tradition, the head of the circles goes to the contributors to teach them to say the words of remembrance. Since that blessed person [the Imam of Alvar] was very old in those days, he would not go through the circle but sit somewhere, like the prime one among prayer beads and behold those in the circle from there. Anyway, a short while later those in the circle would become enraptured and unable to realize their surroundings. There would be some people who choked with tears and even fainted. Despite his serious health problems, the Imam of Alvar would sit with folded legs (as in the Prayer) on the sheik[h]'s mat for two to three hours. Religious poems, eulogies in praise of the Prophet as well as litanies would be recited from his work, *Khulasatu'l-Haqaiq* (Sum-

mary of Truths), with a rhythm of a simple frame drum (*daire*). There was a hafiz—memorizer of the Qur'an—with a very beautiful voice in the village. He was the one who beat the frame drum. At that moment, the Imam of Alvar would be oriented to God Almighty with his entire being. Sometimes he would be entranced with the sublime atmosphere generated by the hymns, effect a similar mood in those around him, and would kindle in hearts the fire of love for the Divine. When a few people lost themselves in ecstasy, or someone became enthusiastic with tearful eyes, this would pass to the other participants and form an atmosphere of love and enthusiasm in everyone. Such powerful atmospheres, that even though I witnessed these in my childhood, I am still under their effect.[32]

Fethullah Gülen, then, whether one calls him a *Sufi* or not, was shaped by *Sufi* practices such as *dhikr*.

More substantively, he has organized his day around prayer. Theologian Salih Yücel described the pattern of a typical day in Gülen's life, going back to his time in Izmir (if not before). "Gülen's schedule," Yücel wrote:

is based on daily *salat* (obligatory prayer), which is always performed in congregation on time [i.e., at the appointed hour and minute]. He would [awaken] ... an hour before dawn ... [to] pray *tahajjud,* read the Qur'an, supplicate in the way of the Prophet Muhammad, and make *awrad* or *dhikr* (remembrance of God), which includes reciting the Names of God. After every obligatory prayer, he would make supplication for those who requested that he pray for them. Then, he would perform *fajr* (morning prayer) in congregation. After prayer, he would again make *awrad* and *dhikr* for fifteen to twenty minutes.... He would [then] converse with visitors for a few minutes before his teaching session would begin. He would ask his students to read from Said Nursi's *Risale-i Nur* collection and expound on the specific reading. The study period would last approximately an hour. Following that, he would breakfast with those around him. After breakfast, he would return to his room to rest until mid-day.

I asked those around him what does he do during his free time. I was told that Gülen spent his time taking a short nap, performing *ishraq* supererogatory prayer, reading different books, writing essays about portions of his books or poetry, and contemplating the activities of his movement. About two hours before *zuhr* [mid-day] prayer, he teaches *tafsir* (commentary of Qur'an), *hadith*s, *fiqh* (jurisprudence) and *aqidah* (theology and history of Islam) to selected students who graduated from divinity schools. The study circle is similar to the traditionalists' way, during which students would sit on the ground, but using modern technology such as computers and projector.

Around noon, he would leave his room and watch the news for fifteen to twenty minutes. He would converse with those around him for half an hour. He would prepare for *zuhr* (noon prayer) and pray in congregation. After performing *zuhr*, Gülen would make *awrad* and *dhikr* for at least twenty minutes. While having lunch with others, he would answer questions from his audience about [various topics] ... I noticed that he would hesitate to respond to political questions. Sometimes, he would ask those around him about their family or profession and, occasionally, make comments. He would give special attention to the elderly and young children.

After conversation, he would return to his room to read books or prepare his future own publications; at times, he would invite individuals to discuss their requests further with him. He would then pray *asr* (afternoon prayer) in congregation and make *awrad* and *dhikr*. There would be another short question and answer session, lasting about half an hour. He would then walk on the treadmill in his room for forty minutes. While on the treadmill, he would make *dhikr*. After the congregational *maghrib* (dusk prayer), he might or might not eat with others. After the congregational *isha* (night prayer), he would return to his room and continue his writing, supplicating, and *dhikr* until 11:00 p.m. Sometimes, he would speak privately with visitors after *isha* prayer.[33]

Not politics or economics but *prayer* has been the consistent marker for time in Fethullah Gülen's life from Kestanepazarı Mosque in Izmir to the present. Such a commitment to the practice of prayer both aligns him with the vast mainstream of orthodox Islam—the *sunnah*, or tradition of the Prophet—but also with an even broader stream of nonviolent spiritual practice. It's sad to have to emphasize the simple point, and I apologize to readers who "get it," but the emphasis is in fact necessary: peacebuilders pray, and prayer is a nonviolent practice.

Even more: prayer has power. The power of prayer is neither political (necessarily) nor miraculous (necessarily). Personally, prayer builds
confidence. The repetition of prayer comforts a troubled mind with the
solace of the familiar. Culturally, prayer builds trust. Communing with
God and others can make any challenge seem surmountable. And socially, prayer builds movements. For instance, Zahit Yılmaz owned a small
business when he first encountered Gülen in the early 1970s. He was pious, but not particularly active in his faith. That changed when he prayed
with Gülen. He described his memory of the moment:

> It seems to me that when Hodjaefendi comes out to prayer, it's like he's
> walking to the main stage. When he starts the prayer it's like you for-
> get everything. You are concentrating on the prayer, and you feel like
> you're somewhere else. You remember your sins and want to prostrate
> as soon as possible ... When we prostrate, some sob, some cough, some
> it's as if they're laughing—there's a sound coming from everyone ... It's
> as if your sins of years are cleansed with *wudu*, it's like your inner-sins
> are cleansed with your tears. One time I remember we had prostrated,
> and I asked, 'aren't we going to get up?' We had done twenty-three
> supplications to God—ordinarily there are 3. I had never prayed like
> this in my life.[34]

That experience of prayer with Fethullah Gülen in Izmir led to a
lifetime of commitment to Hizmet for this person. He and his son and
his grandsons—all of whom I met on a visit in 2015, were grateful for
their association with Hodjafendi. They supported Hizmet financially.
He even had a fine collection of Fethullah Gülen memorabilia. And yet
their loyalty to the one who had showed them how to live a life of prayer
came at a cost. In 2016, he was one of thousands to be arrested and imprisoned, following the so-called coup. His crime? He was an associate
of a "terrorist."

Hajj and *hijrah*: taking Hizmet where there is no Hizmet

A third "pillar" of Islamic practice, after confession and prayer, is *Hajj*—
or pilgrimage to Mecca. This five-day festival has been held annually in
Saudi Arabia since the seventh century—although devout Muslims trace
elements of the event back to Abraham, Hagar, and Ishmael. Whatever

its origins, the *Hajj* for both men and women involves a series of mandatory practices, some quite arduous. The schedule includes, of course,
prayer five times per day, but also includes travel and overnight camping at several sites near Mecca. It also allows a good bit of free time for
meditation, conversation, networking, and rest. At the center of the *Hajj*,
quite literally, is the Ka'ba—a cube structure in the central courtyard of
the Great Mosque in Mecca. It is toward this structure that Muslims pray
during *salah*. About the Ka'ba the Qur'an says: "God has made the Ka'ba,
the Sacred House, a standard and maintenance for the people" (5:97).
For Muslims, this is no ordinary place; it is the projection of the "eternal
seat" of the Divine on the face of the earth, and therefore eternal. As is
well-known, one of mandatory practices for every pilgrim during *Hajj*
is circumambulation of the Ka'ba. This is called *tawaf*, literally "circling,"
and a pilgrim must perform *tawaf* (counterclockwise) seven times at the
beginning, and seven times at the end, of the *Hajj*. Annually, as of 2016,
more than 1.5 million Muslims made these circles. Such a central focus
in worship on a single sacred space is a truly fascinating practice in the
history of religions. Jerusalem, Rome, and Benares, among other cities,
play similar roles. But because Sunni Islam lacks any *other* central authority structure (such as a Pope or Council), and because the centrality
of Mecca is reinforced multiple times per day for devout Muslims, there
is truly nothing quite like the role of the Ka'ba in other historic religious
traditions. The Ka'ba, Mecca, and the duty to make *Hajj*, then (if one is
financially and physically able to do so), is an embodied representation
of the oneness of God and a vision of human harmony, in a single place.
When Muslims pray toward Mecca, as they do somewhere practically
every moment of the day, they visually and physically represent what
they confess about God and what they hope for all people—the unity of
peace.

Fethullah Gülen—who has traveled to Mecca for pilgrimage on
three occasions, first performed the *Hajj* in 1968 while on the staff of Kestanepazarı dormitory and mosque. Murat Alptekin explains, with more
than a touch of melodrama, how it happened:

> His greatest dream was to see the places where the Messenger of God
> grew up and lived via Hajj. However, financial resources did not allow
> for it. One day while he was teaching students at Kestanepazarı, one of

the students asked, "Sir, are you thinking about going on *Hajj*?"

This question was like salt on his wound. Unable to hold back his tears ... Gülen began to cry. He thought, "Who am I to be able to go on *Hajj*?" He was so sad he could not finish the lesson. Crying, he left the classroom, [and] went to his room. ... Just at that time a student knocked on his door and said, "Sir, there is a telephone call for you."

Gülen took the phone feeling the sadness awakened by the yearning he felt to make the *Hajj*. The person calling was Lütfi Doğan, the President of Religious Affairs. ... He said, "We have decided with our friends to send three people to Hajj this year on behalf of the Presidency of Religious Affairs ... You are one of the three people chosen."

Astounded by this news, Gülen thought he was dreaming.[35]

It was, in fact, a dream soon realized.

As this turn of events also suggests, Gülen was becoming a favorite of at least some individuals in the religious bureaucracy. The Presidency of Religious Affairs could make, or break, careers. It no doubt helped Gülen's situation that by 1968 he was supported by Izmir business leaders—some of whom accompanied Gülen on the *Hajj*. One of them was Yusuf Pekmezci. Pekmezci—from whom we last heard as he was about to go to battle in the streets of Izmir in 1966—had the means to pay his own way to Mecca. He recalled that the small contingent that traveled with Gülen had regular conversations with him, and that Gülen did not hesitate to instruct his fellow pilgrims in the course of their travels: "We stayed at a hotel. There are people everywhere, and I said, 'Look at all these people—they all came here because they believe in God!' Hodjafendi then turned to me and said: 'Do you think that we're higher than anyone else because we're here in the house of God? Look at all these people—thank God for them. But [what's important] is to help people in need.'" *Hajj*, for Gülen, was not only about visiting a physical place. If it did not deepen compassion, it was just touring. Another anecdote from Pekmezci reinforced and clarified the point. "We were sitting next to the Ka'ba," he recalled. "We go home to sleep, but Hodjaefendi takes a coat and stays there all night. We sleep. He prays. The next day I came to find him—I was going to *wudu* for afternoon prayer. He said: 'I'm here.' I saw a disturbance in the crowd, and I wanted to ask Hodjaefendi about it. I said, 'What's that?' He said, 'Here, in this place, you're not going to see anything, hear anything, or say anything.'" In other words, for Hodjaefendi the *Hajj* was not about the physical senses alone. The Hajj was about one's concentration, about one's intention, about one's *focus*; it was as much a spiritual as a physical journey.[36] Or as Pekmezci drew the conclusion: "I saw that from Hodjaefendi in 1968; we were just people visiting a place; he [was] looking at the heart."[37]

Gülen had taught that *Hajj* was more than a physical process in sermons, *sohbet*s, and essays, but the lesson took a while to sink in. "*Hajj*, or Pilgrimage to the House of God in Makkah," he wrote, "is an expression of gratitude to God in return for both the bodily health and the property [God] has bestowed on us. Therefore, the person who intends to perform *Hajj* says: "I intend to perform *Hajj* for the sake of God."[38] Saying one intended to perform *Hajj* "for the sake of God" was not just a pious platitude. It had practical import. It meant that travel to the sacred place was less about any personal benefit that one might derive, and more about service—about *hizmet*. Since God of course needs nothing, performing *Hajj for the sake of God* inevitably meant performing it with the intention to benefit other humans. As one adage that has circulated widely among people inspired by Gülen put it: the meaning of pilgrimage (and journeying more broadly—*hijrah*—about which more shortly) is to "take *hizmet* where there is no *hizmet*." Although Mecca was a destination, it was for Gülen a new beginning. If presence in the sacred place increased God-awareness in some way, then that had to be translated into practical action. If one entered Mecca with an attitude of gratitude, which Gülen surely did, how could he not then leave without intensified motivation to extend that grace to others? "All throughout the duty of *Hajj*," Gülen offered in a sermon that referred to his own pilgrimage:

> one must sit, stand, walk, and do everything with the consciousness of doing them for the sake of God; they should keep up this consciousness while opening their hands before the Ka'ba, putting their faces to the Gate of Repentance (Multazam), greeting or kissing the Black Stone, going to Mina, staying in Arafat, and passing to Muzdalifa. In short, they should carry out all of the required acts for the sake of God and thus try to render their valuable seconds by compacting years' worth into them.[39]

Each of these actions--such as kissing the Black Stone embedded in a wall of the Ka'ba, is a non-mandatory step in the *Hajj*—a discrete moment. But just as space could be compressed in one sacred place, so to speak, Gülen was suggesting that time could be compressed from multiple moments into a singular unity. Gülen left Mecca a changed man.

It's not that he didn't appreciate his first visit to Mecca. As anthropologist Victor Turner famously put it: "Any pilgrim is half-tourist, and a tourist is half-pilgrim." Gülen was no different. Thus, he wrote, in a sentiment worthy of a post-card, that "the moment of seeing the Ka'ba for the first time is a magical one." But more often than such touristic observations, he turned the pilgrimage outwards—not to personal experience, but towards the community:

> People who go to these holy places during the blessed days can pray for themselves and their families alike. However, the Muslims' condition, especially during our times, bears much greater significance than our personal matters do. The condition of Muslim lands is obvious and clear; we have never been so miserable throughout the history of Islam. We cannot stand on our own two feet, and we are trying to stand behind notions brought forth by others, whose real aim we aren't aware of. Most of the time, this type of foundation is pulled away from under our feet and we inevitably topple over. Bediüzzaman [Said Nursi], who suffered in agony about this condition, states that thinking about the Muslim world naturally prevents him from thinking about himself. In this respect, the Muslims who find the opportunity to go to *Hajj* and see the Ka'ba for the first time, should open up their hands and beg the Almighty, "My Lord, grant deliverance to, have mercy on and grant forgiveness to the followers of Your Messenger! My God, enable Muslims (the *ummah*) to straighten up! Show them the ways to a revival!"[40]

What Gülen drew from his first *Hajj*, perhaps, was increased urgency, and sharpened focus. Just as Malcolm X returned from his own pilgrimage in 1964 with a sharpened direction to his own practice of Islam, so did Fethullah Gülen in 1968. He saw the *Hajj* above all as a theological encounter ("for the sake of God") on behalf of spiritual awakening to intensify commitment to the purpose of service.

Fethullah Gülen's *Hajj*, then, was less about what he did in Saudi Arabia than what he brought back for others. By 1968, of course, Muslims who had gathered for the pilgrimage in Mecca left the sacred place and returned to every country on Earth (Indonesia, for instance, has had the largest Muslim population among nations since 1971). And those who returned to their communities could now bear the honorific term: "*Hajji.*" The pilgrimage brought with it obligations. "When I was in Medina," Gülen recalled,

> the words of a person with a deep love for the noble Prophet pierced through my heart. He was saying 'O Messenger of God, I have been here for days, I haven't heard a sound from you. Now I am about to leave for the Ka'ba. What am I supposed to say if they ask me what I brought from here?' He said so many similar things of this kind that it was impossible not to be moved. So we had better look for such experiences to move our hearts and remind ourselves that we might not find another chance for such a journey again.[41]

This was not quite to say that "we may never pass this way, again," but it was close. Gülen's encounter with the permanence of the sacred places of Islam—the Ka'ba has been there for a very long time—made him more aware than before of the impermanence of his individual life. In journeying to Mecca, he was of course transported physically. But a corresponding spiritual transport moved him even more fully than before the journey from self-interest to solidarity on behalf of service to humanity.

In fact, Gülen's transformation through the *Hajj* incarnated (so to speak) the *Sufi* understanding of what is called *sayr u suluk* (journeying and initiation). Gülen was still a young man in 1968—not quite 30. He had been honored by the Presidency of Religious Affairs to make the pilgrimage. What were the expectations for him afterwards? As Gülen explained the *Sufi* doctrine of journeying and initiation, it was a four-step process. Any spiritual journey involved "journeying toward God," "journeying in God," "journeying with or in the company of God," and finally, "journeying from God." Unless "God" was equivalent to the "State," a blasphemous notion he would never have countenanced, Gülen was not likely to be co-opted into narrow political affiliation even by the generosity of a Presidency of Religious Affairs. In fact, the four steps of journeying and initiation within *Sufism* had one goal: to diminish self (the ego) and to expand God-awareness. For instance, to explain the third step, "journeying with or in the company of God," Gülen quoted Nasimi (a fourteenth-century Azerbaijani *Sufi* poet):

> *The space where I am has developed into no-space;*
> *This body of mine has wholly become a soul;*
> *God's look has manifested Itself to me*
> *And I have seen myself intoxicated with His meeting.*
> *A call has come to me from the Ultimate Truth:*
> *"Come, o lover, you are intimate with Us!*
> *This is the station of intimacy;*
> *I have found you a faithful one."*[42]

Such language of being a "lover" of God and "intoxicated" with meeting God has often made some literalists uneasy. Gülen even made the analogy explicit: "This is ... the station where, like a wine glass, one becomes filled with and emptied of [God's] love, loving and urging others to love [God] madly. One who overflows with the gifts of this station regards any speech that is not about [God] as being a mere waste of words."[43] Recall Gülen's counsel to his fellow *Hajji* Yusuf Pekmezci in Mecca: "'Here, in this place, you're not going to see anything, hear anything, or say anything" but God.

And yet, no one can maintain such consciousness perpetually. The fourth step in a Sufi's journey/initiation, then, was "journeying *from* God." We have reached, perhaps, the heart of Hizmet. "Every kind and act of worship," Gülen once wrote, "is gratitude to God in return for the bounties He has bestowed upon us." In this fourth step of journeying and initiation, then, a person "turns toward the realm of multiplicity with new interpretations of the way of unity after having reached unity.... Such returning travelers devote their life to saving others from 'dungeons.'"[44] Saving people from dungeons sounds like exciting but dangerous work. There are many ways to do so; as many dungeons as people dig for ourselves. There are, as Gülen put it, many "tasks incumbent upon the travelers upon their return to people from God." But in all these tasks— teaching, labor, professions like medicine or law, research in the sciences or humanities, even businesses that supported the common good, for example—a *Hajji* could now "see unity in multiplicity and multiplicity in unity." This paradox seems obscure, but it may be the central experience of the *Hajj*. While on pilgrimage, individuals all dress the same—in simple white robes called *ihram* (which refers to the pilgrim's state of "purity" as well as the clothing itself). But this unity contains multiplicity. The pilgrims come from different places. Each has a distinct face. In fact, men and women pray together on *Hajj*, side-by-side, in the same rows, and women cannot wear a *burqa* or *niqab* that hides their faces. Yet for all their multiplicity, all pilgrims focus on the one God, circling around the Ka'ba in a stunning, physical display of unity.

For Fethullah Gülen, it may have been on his first *Hajj* that he recognized the theological significance of the circles he had participated in as a youth. Not surprisingly, in fact, when writing about journeying and initiation, Gülen quoted from his Erzurum teacher, Muhammed Lütfi, the Imam of Alvar, who called out in words that Gülen never forgot:

> *O you who are seeking God's gift!*
> *Come to this circle, join the circle.*
> *O you who are passionately pursuing God's light,*
> *Come to this circle, join the circle.*[45]

The *Hajj* in 1968 expanded, for Fethullah Gülen, the kinds of circles he could join. It consequently expanded the meaning of being a Muslim for him.

Travel—including of course to the major pilgrimage of the *Hajj*—has marked people of Hizmet since Gülen's time in Izmir, as an expression of their practice of Islam. As sociologist David Tittensor clarified:

> Travel has an important place within Islamic faith and tradition with regard to connecting with the divine. One of the five pillars of Islam is that all Muslims must make the *hajj* (pilgrimage) to Mecca during their lifetime if they are physically able and can afford the expense. Alongside this, there is the doctrine of *hijra* (migration), where one is obligated to migrate from a land if they are not able to practice their faith freely, and the non-obligatory but widespread folk practice of *ziyaras* (visits to shrines). Closely associated with travel is the search for *ilm* (knowledge). Both the Qur'an and the hadith direct the believer to undertake *rihla* (travel) in the world that God created in order to better understand the creator. The former contains numerous verses that exhort the reader to "travel on the earth and see" (3:137; 6:11; 12:109; 16:36; 29:20; 30:9; 30:42). ... In like fashion, the hadith litera-

ture, which reports the life and deeds of the Prophet Muhammad, and which was written after his death, builds on this Qur'anic thread, with many related tales extolling the need for both travel and knowledge. Al-Tirmidhi (d. 892) relates the story in which the Prophet explained that "those who go out in search of knowledge will be in the path of God until they return" and there is the now famous hadith in which Muhammad is purported to have uttered the injunction "seek knowledge even as far as China."... Subsequently, the importance of travel became embedded in the consciousness of Muslims and was regarded as a pious activity that brings God's approval and grace.[46]

As we shall see in subsequent chapters, people inspired by Gülen embraced his teaching about journeying and initiation. They took on the challenge of travel to countless corners of the globe on behalf of Islam. It is not too strong to say they became missionaries, so long as the word "missionary" is understood not in the sense of arrogant or imperialist proselytizing but rather in terms of persuasive service to humanity.[47]

For just one example, Derya Yazıcı was born in Germany, but her family had roots in Erzurum. She lived as a youth in Bursa—a city due south of Istanbul across the Marmara Sea. She studied at Marmara University in Istanbul, where she became familiar with Fethullah Gülen. Her certification as a teacher was followed shortly by getting married, after which she and her husband then served over more than two decades in various Hizmet-related institutions—usually tutoring centers or schools, in Cyprus, Mongolia, and across Turkey—Ankara, Konya, and Kayseri. They came to the U.S. in 2015. She explained:

> With the *hijra* [literally "migration"—pilgrimage, i.e. hajj, can be considered a form of migration] ... we go with the understanding in our hearts that we are taking Hizmet where it's not known. That's the message from our Prophet, and from Hodjaefendi. At the same time, everybody looks for something in their life, and whenever I change a place, I learn different cultures and people. I'm learning a lot, too! That is making me whole—I add something new to myself. Leaving a place is difficult—you don't know if you will ever see [those people] again. Memories can be lost. But at the same time, you look forward to the new—to new places, and new people. So, moving brings both sadness and joy combined.[48]

Yazıcı then went on to indicate one of the unexpected outcomes of moving so often, with a touch of humor. "With a lot of moving around I always have 2 recurring dreams," she said: "In one, we are moving from place to place, but we are missing the plane, or can't get packed, or the seat on the plane is broken, etcetera, or 2) My teaching experience surfaces—I'm late for classes, students are waiting for me, and I can't get there! These two dreams (nightmares, I suppose) are the same everywhere!"[49] Many teachers could relate similar bad dreams. But her point was simply this—movement and journeying within Hizmet, among those inspired by Fethullah Gülen, was to "take Hizmet where there is no Hizmet." And we may speculate that Gülen's first *Hajj* might have contributed to this conviction—and then he began sharing with others.

There can be little doubt that the journey that is *Hajj* is among the most profound nonviolent practices of religious peacebuilding on the planet. As alluded to briefly already, perhaps the most famous account of the significance of the pilgrimage is found in the life-story of Malcolm X. Malcolm had been part of Elijah Muhammad's black nationalist version of Islam prior to his pilgrimage in 1964. He recalled, in a letter home, that:

> Never have I witnessed such sincere hospitality and overwhelming spirit of true brotherhood as is practiced by people of all colors and races here in this ancient Holy Land, the home of Abraham, Muhammad and all the other Prophets of the Holy Scriptures. For the past week, I have been utterly speechless and spellbound by the graciousness I see displayed all around me by people of all colors.
>
> I have been blessed to visit the Holy City of Mecca, I have made my seven circuits around the Ka'ba ... I drank water from the well of *Zamzam*. I ran seven times back and forth between the hills of Mt. Al-Safa and Al-Marwah. I have prayed in the ancient city of Mina, and I have prayed on Mt. Arafat.
>
> There were tens of thousands of pilgrims, from all over the world. They were of all colors, from blue-eyed blondes to black-skinned Africans. But we were all participating in the same ritual, displaying a spirit of unity and brotherhood that my experiences in America had led me to believe never could exist between the white and non-white.
>
> America needs to understand Islam, because this is the one religion that erases from its society the race problem.[50]

Upon his return to the United States, Malcolm X put this lesson into practice. His new focus led to what is now the largest orthodox group of African American Muslims. His was, perhaps, an exceptional experience, filtered through an extraordinary genius.

But it may not be far beyond the norm. A 2008 Harvard study, "Estimating the Impact of the Hajj: Religion and Tolerance in Islam's Global Gathering," studied the significance of the *Hajj* among ordinary Pakistani Muslims. It concluded:

> We find that participation in the *Hajj* increases observance of global Islamic practices such as prayer and fasting while decreasing participation in localized practices and beliefs such as the use of amulets and dowry. It increases belief in equality and harmony among ethnic groups and Islamic sects and leads to more favorable attitudes toward women, including greater acceptance of female education and employment. Increased unity within the Islamic world is not accompanied by antipathy toward non-Muslims. Instead, Hajjis show increased belief in peace, and in equality and harmony among adherents of different religions.[51]

For Fethullah Gülen, far from drawing him into any mere political allegiance, his participation in the *Hajj* in 1968 contributed to his awareness, perhaps more strongly than before, how *as a Muslim* he was also a citizen of the world.

But while religions like Islam are global in scope, they take root locally. Thus, during his time in Izmir, Gülen began an initiative that demonstrated what he had brought back from his "journeying from God." A physician close to Gülen, who was with Hodjaefendi from the time he came to Izmir in 1966, recalled that Gülen once said: "To go from one place where there *is* Hizmet to a place where there is *no* Hizmet to *create* Hizmet is to do pilgrimage."[52] That is, pilgrimage was not just tied to a specific place: it was what one *did* with the pilgrimage that mattered. Murat Alptekin clarified this expanded notion of pilgrimage: "Gülen ... tried unconventional ways to explain Islam. [For example], when he saw that many people who did not come to the mosque killed time smoking heavily and playing cards at coffee houses, he began to give talks at these places."[53] A smoky coffeehouse could be a place of service as surely as a hotel in Mecca. So, Gülen started going to coffeehouses around Izmir to give talks—informal *sohbet*s, or casual sermons. He was accompanied to these talks by a few students and some favorably-inclined shop-keepers. Yusuf Pekmezci was among them. Pekmezci remembered that:

> Hodjaefendi looked at the mosques and asked, "where do the young people go?" We said, "Hodjaefendi, the young people go to the coffeehouses and [movie] theaters." Hodjaefendi said, "We can't go to the theaters, but we can go to the coffeehouses. We can try to explain things to our friends. Maybe they don't know. We cannot force people to come to the mosque. We have to go to them. This is not something we have initiated; this is something going back to all the Prophets. Every prophet went to the places where the people were. Since we are the servants of God, and since I'm a government worker, it's not right to just say, 'they have to come to me.' So, let's go to the coffeehouses![54]

Pekmezci was among those who tried to dissuade Gülen. "That's a really bad idea," he recalled saying to him. "People smoke there, play cards. People will ask, 'What's a *hodja* [teacher] doing in a coffeehouse?'" Gülen acknowledged the concerns, but then said:

> You're worried about what people will think. My concern is what God thinks. The prophets went to the people. The people didn't listen. They derided them. They did bad things to them. But no prophet gave up on going to them. ... We need to give our respect to these people because they [too] are created by God. Nobody is greater than another. What we know we must share. If they ask, and we know, we'll explain. And we might have things to learn from them.

"So that's," Pekmezci explained, "how we started going to the coffeehouses."[55]

Eventually, these meetings spread to dozens of coffee houses in Izmir and the Aegean. The first, however, was held in the Mersinli district in Izmir. Pekmezci, having been persuaded somewhat of the value of the experiment, was the advance scout tasked to set it up. He went to the coffee-shop owner to pitch the idea. He first offered the owner 300 Lira to host the event, then 600, then 900. At that point, the owner said, as Pekmezci recalled it: "Why are you telling me numbers as if you're bidding on something? That guy there [pointing to a regular patron] drinks one tea and talks until the morning. Why are you offering this much money? Come, drink your tea, and talk!" So, they had a first site. Pekmezci, upon Gülen's request, asked one condition—that nobody play games (backgammon, for instance) while Gülen spoke. The owner agreed. Pekmezci offered him the cash, again. The owner replied: "What's your hurry? Let's see what you're selling!" So, the meeting was set. Pekmezci recalled that getting Hodjaefendi to the coffeehouse itself was a challenge. He had no car, and the busses didn't run there. So, they went on foot. They left Kestanapazarı following afternoon prayer, stopped at a mosque near the coffeehouse for sunset prayer, and then walked the remainder of the distance to the coffee-shop (a total of 6-7 km, Pekmezci recalled). Pekmezci remembered that they were greeted by the coffeehouse owner with the words: "Ok, go ahead, talk!"[56] And so Gülen talked. Naturally, not all the patrons were pleased by this intrusion into their gaming; some "grumbled." But those who remained were invited to "ask every kind of question that came to mind." The discussion "lasted three and a half hours. No one got bored," one source concluded, with a judgment no historian could verify.[57] Pekmezci, more vividly, recalled that "some of the [patrons] asked in the middle [of Gülen's discourse], 'Does he talk somewhere else?'... They were happy. They didn't play games." Indeed, according to Pekmezci, some of the patrons from this meeting, and from the others that began to happen elsewhere around Izmir, "started coming to the mosque." And at least, Pekmezci concluded, "we never heard of someone taking offense at Hodjaefendi because he was going to coffeehouses."[58] By 1968, then, Fethullah Gülen was a young man on the move. He had brought back from his first *Hajj* a commitment to "take Hizmet where there is no Hizmet." And it grew in as unexpected a place as an Izmir coffeehouse.

Ramadan: fasting and feasting to awaken spiritually and to make new friends

By 1968, a small circle of maybe one-hundred people had gathered as intimate friends around Fethullah Gülen.[59] Many of them were or had been his students. Others were small-business operators, store managers, or laborers. Almost all were inspired by his preaching—about which we will say much more in the following chapter. If that one-hundred formed the core of what would become the Hizmet community, many thousands more had heard of the *Hodja* from Erzurum. They had come to hear him preach in Izmir out of serious religious concern or mere curiosity. A few of those thousands sought out Gülen for advice and counsel. Some of them would become the core *mütevelli* (literally "trustees,") the financial supporters who sponsored Hizmet projects. For roughly five years Gülen continued to reside in his small hut in the Kestanepazarı courtyard. He studied and taught students about the unity of God and other subjects. He prayed and led prayer. And he administered a dormitory—now as a *Hajji*: one who had completed the sacred pilgrimage.

If the pillar of Islam that is *Hajj* emphasizes movement, meeting, and change, the nonviolent practice that is the month-long fast of Ramadan would seem to be a counterpoint. As is well-known, during the month of Ramadan (which shifts annually due to the Muslim lunar calendar), Muslims are pledged to abstain from food and drink (including water) from sunrise to sundown. This is no easy task in any season. It is especially grueling in Turkey's summer, when a hot sun may shine for as many as sixteen hours. As one popular Muslim quip has it: "Ramadan is a full-time job." It is not only about abnegation and asceticism, however. According to journalist Reem Akkad: "We fast because we want to feel for those who are less fortunate; we fast so that we remember how blessed we are." Ramadan, then, like the *Hajj*, is a nonviolent practice with a focus. It can foster empathy (the key topic in the next chapter) and memory. But Akkad goes on: "there's also something deeper. The core reason I fast is that I believe that is what God has asked of me, as a means to increase my faith and draw nearer to my soul. Ramadan takes attention away from the physical and focuses it on the spiritual. ... The pangs of hunger are a reminder that I am much more than my physical self."[60] This may seem counter-intuitive: how can giving up the matter that we need to live lead attention away from it? But such is the report of many, including Fethullah Gülen, who for each of his five years in Izmir was both a practitioner of Ramadan and a teacher who illuminated how this intensely physical practice contributed to deep spiritual peace.

That he was young—in some cases only a few years older than his students, helped his effort to teach the traditional practices of nonviolence to other young people. Yusuf Pekmezci recalled that "Usually when we thought of a *hodja* we expected an old man with a beard." Gülen did not sport a beard; consciously choosing to eschew a mark of Muslim "authenticity" in some circles. He also dressed in simple, modern, Western clothing—again, in contrast to some self-styled Muslim leaders who favored traditional Arab garb. And he was not yet 30, or as Pekmezci puts it, "of course Hodjaefendi came as a young preacher. He was about my age. That drew me. I tried to be devout, but we'd fight until the morning—rightist versus leftist. His lifestyle affected me. His explanations and lifestyle complemented each other."[61] Far more than simply sporting a beard, Gülen gained legitimacy by practicing what he preached about Ramadan—and other subjects.

Ramadan is, traditionally, a family event. Before the sun rises, a meal is shared—a meal rich in protein and with plenty of liquids, since that is the only sustenance to carry an individual for an entire day. Some Muslims, such as students, then go back to sleep for a while. Others head directly to work. At the end of the day, as the sun sets, preparation begins for the *iftar* meal—literally "break-fast." Sometimes this is just a brief meal—traditionally begun with a date, prior to evening prayers at a mosque. A full meal then follows the prayers. During Ramadan, there are also special prayers that are only performed during this season—giving them a distinctive significance, perhaps somewhat like Christmas carols for Christians.[62] It was during one of these prayers in 1953, as we noted in the prior chapter, that Fethullah Gülen preached his first sermon.

So, despite the physical struggles, the shared hunger of Ramadan generates for those who observe it some serious pleasures. One is obviously dedicated family time: families gather together to eat and to pray. Over the course of a month, this practice may provide occasion to disrupt unhealthy family patterns and to renew affection; shared struggle has been known to bind people together. Similarly, there is an undeniably *festive* air surrounding every *iftar* meal. It is considered especially auspicious to share an *iftar* with others, including (notably) strangers. So, Ramadan has a way of spilling into the practice of hospitality. Some Muslim families have been known to host guests *every* evening for a month. There is also a notable conviviality in societies where people are fasting collectively. People gather to gain strength for their practice. They gather to offer encouragement to each other to endure. Mosques are fuller during Ramadan than during the other eleven months of the year. Finally, the three-day celebration that ends Ramadan, the Festival of 'Eid al-Fitr, is the most joyous of Muslim holidays.[63]

In the context of 1960s Izmir, torn by strife between nationalists and Communists, Islamists and secularists, Gülen recalled, with the benefit of hindsight, exactly this conviviality of the Ramadan celebrations of his childhood:

> I remember well that during my childhood when there was as yet no electricity in cities, people walked to mosques with kerosene lamps in the darkness of night. We imagined that Ramadan was walking around in the alleys in the lights of those lamps. Under the influence of poetry, meaning and deep spirituality which Ramadan poured into our souls, we desired that it should never come to an end. Nevertheless, despite our heartfelt desire, it flew away and the festive day followed it with all its pomp.[64]

More abstractly, but in the same vein, Gülen also described how Ramadan actually became *attractive* for participants. Ramadan could be, he suggested, even personified as a pleasant guest:

> Throughout Ramadan a sacred excitement ... can be sensed in the air. Dawn brings new light and promise; day comes with breeze; evenings loom on the horizon, with their divinely arrayed colors, nights enveloped in a mystery of silence; they whisper to us of a private meeting with the Absolute Beloved; they lead us to transcendental ways of life and [offer] compositions of paradisiacal melodies for those who are capable of hearing them. The nights keep on revealing things.... Like circles joining one another, these mysterious utterings sometimes turn out to be such impressive orations that all ... hold their tongues and stand in astonishment while listening to these sermons that consist of neither letters nor word. ... Therefore, we would never wish for Ramadan to leave us, [but] in spite of this, it goes. It leaves like a guest; it has arrived and spent a pleasant time with us, staying for a while. As with everything, it comes one by one, it goes on in the same way... and then the 'Eid comes to us as the royal heir of the full harvest of this magnificent month.[65]

Ramadan, in short, helped build deep peace. Its benefits for Gülen went well beyond the ordinary physical needs that abstinence would have seemed to exacerbate.

In Izmir in the 1960s, such an understanding of Islamic practice that connected the faith to nonviolence was as necessary as it was rare. Secularists had sought to de-politicize Islam, which many Muslims—notably those soon to be tagged "Islamists"—resisted by re-politicizing it. Both were caught in a reductionist trap. Both imagined politics as the ultimate guarantor of security and even salvation. Gülen's practice of Ramadan, and his teaching about it, suggested that Islam, and life itself for that matter, was about something more significant than mere politics. Call it a relationship with the Absolute Beloved. Thus, Gülen contended, perhaps with his experiences of political conflict in Izmir in mind, that

> the month of Ramadan appears on our horizons with its charming beauties with fasting, the Prayers of *Tarawih* [one of those special prayers], the fast-breaking dinners, and the pre-dawn meals. Ramadan brings about a heavenly atmosphere of its own. Even at times when different tensions follow one another, violence and aggression become excessive, contradiction is seen as virtue, and ice-cold winds blow between the masses, Ramadan makes its influence by reconditioning souls, fostering sound hearts, feelings, and thoughts, along with abating every kind of hardness and harshness. Muslims [thus] show serious respect toward this month, when peace and gentleness perceptibly prevail. For this reason, in spite of different adversities, if we give our willpower its due and manage to open our heart to this very special and distinguished segment of time with heartfelt trust in its blessings, and thus become oriented to it with sincere belief, awe and respect, then it will cuddle us and shower us with blessings. Anger, violence, and rages will cease, and an atmosphere of peace and reconciliation will prevail.[66]

Again, in many places in the 1960s and 1970s, such teaching that linked religion and peace presented a sharp contrast to the violence tearing apart societies.

Yet Ramadan for Gülen was not just some idealistic project. It was eminently practical. Its basis was trust—across political divisions. Thus, he suggested to those who listened to him that

> in order to put these ideas [about Ramadan] into practice, believers—a Muslim family residing in an apartment for instance—should

invite their neighbors to a fast-breaking dinner, no matter what their philosophy of life is. ... Similarly, Muslims who teach at schools and universities or work at other establishments can contribute to societal peace by opening their table to everyone, without discriminating between different sections of society. We should make use of this blessed month in such a fruitful way, to the degree of not having any fast-breaking dinners without guests. These dinners should be enriched with abundance and diversity of guests, rather than richness of dishes. As it is known, the Messenger of God stated, "A meal for two suffices for three, and a meal for three suffices for four."[67]

Ramadan fostered hospitality. During that month, one could let go of one's cherished prejudices. For Fethullah Gülen, Ramadan was the best season for *hizmet*.

Yet for all its social benefits—making new friends through the practice of hospitality—and for all its physical rigor, Ramadan was finally for Gülen about increasing spiritual awareness. It required focus and intensity and discipline. Consequently, the ultimate purpose of the month was for Muslims to let go of thoughts or practices that distracted from God-awareness. For instance, one student of Gülen's, writing about his practice in later years—after Gülen had moved to Pennsylvania in 1999, recalled that in 2011 Gülen was

> in *itikaf*, or religious seclusion, for the whole of Ramadan [ordinarily, *itikaf* is the last 10 days of Ramadan]. He would not leave his floor. He had stopped reading newspapers, and even when he was informed about important developments in the world, he always responded with the language of the Quran.... He kept his mind and heart busy only with God and our duties as the servants of God. He gave a lecture on Quranic commentary in the early morning and late afternoon and declined to speak on any matter other than that of the Quran. If anyone mentioned the oppression of the Syrian regime, he replied with prayer; if anyone reminded him of a past event, he replied with the name of Allah; if anybody suggested a future possibility, he said "Allah knows best." Nothing – no question and no news – would distract him from his state of mental fasting.[68]

Obviously, it would be impossible to manage a socially active

movement given such withdrawal. But that kind of intensity for the sake
of spiritual growth was a familiar practice in many religious traditions.
Christian monks and nuns took vows of poverty and silence. Hindu and
Buddhist ascetics withdrew into the forest. Ramadan was a month-long
nonviolent practice central to Fethullah Gülen's life during his years in
Izmir; and every year after.

Zakat and its opposite: organizing mütevelli, and getting arrested

Sadly, such a withdrawal by Fethullah Gülen soon became a matter not
of choice, but of coercion. Conflict in Izmir and throughout Turkey escalated as the 1960s gave way to the new decade. A general strike in Spring
1970 was organized by the Confederation of Revolutionary Workers'
Unions. That strike was met by violence from anti-Communist groups.
College campuses and youth across the country were polarized and politicized. Sometimes the violence was anti-American; often it was rooted
in deep ideological divisions between labor, management, the military,
and the government. That government, under Prime Minister Süleyman
Demirel, had accomplished some small gains in infrastructure development, but also had demonstrated grinding incompetence. For instance,
the national budget for 1970 was submitted three months late. Yet Demirel was a survivor. He frequently flipped policy positions and changed
alliances. Among his best known rhetorical flourishes was the phrase
"Dün dündür, bugün bugündür," which means "Yesterday was yesterday,
today is today."[69] But as violence escalated in 1970, even that flexibility
fell short. Events came to a crest between December 1970 and March
1971. In December, students rioted at Ankara University, and someone
bombed both the Labor Party headquarters and Demirel's car (he wasn't
in it). Then, another group of students started a gun-battle with police at
Hacettepe University in Ankara. Demirel then had two-hundred leftist
students arrested. In response, on March 4 leftist students kidnapped
four American soldiers and held them for ransom. Leftists considered
Demirel a stooge of the U.S. government, whose anti-Communism had
of course stoked the conflict in Vietnam, which was perhaps at its height
in 1971. Back in Turkey, police stormed a dormitory at Ankara University to free the U.S. soldiers, but killed two students in the process. Fi-

nally, on 12 March 1971, the military intervened. It came to be called
the "Coup by Memorandum." High-ranking Generals issued a Memorandum that made several demands of the government. Those demands
left Süleyman Demirel little choice but to resign. By doing so, he saved
himself the fate of the Prime Minister under the previous coup, Adnan
Menderes, who had been hanged. The Generals then cracked down under martial law. They shuttered newspapers and magazines. And in the
coming months they arrested thousands—politicians and union leaders,
academics and public intellectuals, leftists and rightists, Communists
and Muslims. Among those arrested was Fethullah Gülen, along with
some of those closest to him.[70]

But that brief narrative gets ahead of the story, just a bit. What
made Gülen a target of the military regime in 1971 was nothing specific
to his teachings or practice. Indeed, there was nothing in his teachings
(had the Generals read them) or practice (had they bothered to study
them) that threatened the stability of the Turkish Republic. What made
Gülen a target was that there were now people who supported him with
their time, talents, and financial resources. He was a political threat, in
short, even if Gülen himself continuously disavowed political aims. The
individuals who supported Gülen were dubbed *mütevelli* in Turkish, or
"trustees." They were organized informally, organically, but gave an Islamic slant to a typical mode of business organizing—the foundation.
Gülen "Islamicized," if you will, a modern mode of financial support.
In the process, he anticipated the kinds of changes in capitalism that
individuals such as Muhammad Yunus and others have called "social
business" or "social enterprises."[71] We will pay some detailed attention to
this organizing process in Chapter Five. But for now, to understand how
financial resources began to concentrate themselves around projects
connected to Hizmet, we need to understand, briefly, how Gülen helped
modern Turks rediscover the fifth and final pillar of Islamic practice—
zakat, usually translated as "alms," "tithe" or "charity."

Historians of Islam Greg Barton, Paul Weller, and İhsan Yılmaz put
it succinctly, albeit with the wisdom of hindsight, in their Introduction
to an important collection of essays, *The Muslim World and Politics in
Transition: Creative Contributions of the Gülen Movement*:

Gülen encourages businessmen sympathetic to his cause to donate from their money as seed capital to establish schools [and other businesses] in many different countries. This appeal is based on one of the five fundamental pillars of Islam, which is that of *zakat* (tithing). It is expected that Muslims who are able should donate (as *zakat*) at least two-and-a-half per cent of their wealth every year. Muslims traditionally donate their *zakat* to poor families or use it to establish mosques and schools that teach religious texts. Gülen reinterpreted this tradition, advocating that the giving of money to establish secular educational institutions and to support scholarships to students [and other social businesses] is also *zakat* and can therefore be considered as an act of worship.[72]

In fact, to call this interpretation of *zakat* a "reinterpretation" is not entirely accurate.

For much of the history of Islam, there has been little separation between "secular" and "religious" purposes for *zakat*. Within contemporary Saudi Arabia, for instance, general taxes and *zakat* are all collected by the Ministry of Finance. The ruling monarchy then can use resources that come from that Ministry for whatever purposes they decide (although no doubt accountants could manage to identify one revenue stream from another, as needed).[73] More to the point, perhaps, within Turkish history the Ottoman sultan and pashas also easily shifted tax and *zakat* funds from one purpose to another, or created new kinds of funds and trusts for philanthropic purposes in a unity of sacred and secular causes that might befuddle modern readers and auditors. These trusts were often called in Arabic *waqf*, plural *awqaf*, which was in Turkish *vakıf*, "foundations." These foundations existed to provide support for Ottoman subjects in areas of food, housing, education and other "social welfare" arenas not covered by the government or for-profit ventures. And they were administered by groups of individuals who bore (among other titles) the name of *mütevelli*, "trustees." Indeed, the concentration of resources in foundations associated with *Sufi* Lodges was no doubt one of the sources of Atatürk's frustration with them.[74] So what Gülen began doing in Izmir, as he gathered some business leaders around him to support the work of Kestanepazarı School and Dormitory, was to restore or to *renew* the practice of *zakat* through foundations that emerged organically under the changed circumstances of a secular republic. What was significant, practically, was this: those business leaders were now engaged actively and enthusiastically in *zakat*. Even more significant, finally: resources were now being collected and channeled for charitable projects and administration by the *mütevelli*—the trustees who were friendly to Fethullah Gülen, in ways that gave them financial freedom from dependence on support from the State.

Again, Chapter Five will explore more fully the origins and significance of this aspect of Fethullah Gülen's life and work—basically, the theological grounds for his organizing—in the concept of *istişare* or mutual consultation, and some of the social enterprises that he inspired and that spread around the world. For now, we can conclude Chapter Two with some brief attention to the broader significance of these economic ventures in the context of 1970s Izmir and beyond. As should be clear, by now, a central economic tension within Turkey in 1970 was between Communist and anti-Communist factions. These factions had their own issues local to Turkey, but they also reflected broader global geo-political tensions. Historically, of course, Turkey had often been the bridge, and sometimes the battlefield, between European and Russian cultures. By reviving the *vakıf* tradition within Islam, Gülen resolved this tension on behalf of *social* (as opposed to merely "free" or merely "Statist") enterprises. That is, businesses now answered to an *Islamic* criterion neither American nor Russian. This criterion provided them a moral horizon along with the classical profit motive associated with typical capitalism. Thus, scholar Elisabeth Özdalga, in an influential article, identified the distinctive economic ethic of Gülen and those inspired by him, with a nod to Max Weber, as "worldly asceticism" in Islamic guise.[75] By this, Özdalga meant to point out how Gülen's engagement with the Islamic practice of money-management—which at one level is what *zakat* is all about—mirrored the way (as Weber saw it) Christian reformers like Luther and Calvin mobilized Protestants (with Catholics not far behind) to accumulate capital so as both to live well *and* to do good.[76] Gülen, of course, accomplished this mobilization through Islamic, not Christian, idioms, and in the context of modern Turkey, not pre-modern Europe.[77] But pushing the analogy even further, historian M. Hakan Yavuz saw Gülen and the broader Hizmet movement as "the Turkish Puritans." This was meant to be a flattering description. More specifically, Yavuz writes, Gülen's goals are to sharpen Muslim self-consciousness, to deepen the meaning of the shared idioms and practices of society, to empower excluded social groups through education and networks, and to bring just and peaceful solutions to the social and psychological problems of society. Gülen, as a social innovator, focuses on the public sphere more than on the private sphere and seeks to turn Islam and Islamic networks into social capital. The Gülen movement does not constitute a series of reactionary convulsions of the marginalized sector of the Turkish population, but is rather a bourgeoning middle-class movement that seeks to utilize new economic and social spaces.[78]

Indeed, writing optimistically (in 2003), Yavuz concluded that "a stable Turkey presupposes a balance between Islamic values and the Kemalist political system; the Gülen movement offers a way to achieve this balance."[79]

In fact, the events of 12 March 1971 might have foreshadowed that this was not to be Gülen's fate in Turkey. Charity and the peacebuilding potential of *zakat* met its opposite in the violence of a military coup. Gülen was arrested on May 3, 1971. The circumstances were, as one source reported them, unusual:

> One day when Gülen returned home, he saw that there were police inside. They said, "Welcome," to him. In order both to assuage his hunger a little and to learn their real intentions, Gülen asked, "Will I be late if I eat something?" Indicating that he might be held for a long time, the police replied: "Fill your stomach; it's not known when you'll be back here."[80]

By this time, Gülen had moved from his shanty in the Kestanepazarı courtyard and was living in a room in a new dormitory built by trustees in Güzelyalı—another Izmir neighborhood. But the police had tracked him down. Gülen's brother Sıbgatullah, living in Erzurum, recalled the trauma: "Then they detained Hodjaefendi in 1971 during the coup. At the same time my two brothers Mesih and Salih were put into jail as well. They picked them up during a *sohbet*. They let out the other brothers, but Hodjaefendi stayed in detention for six and a half months. One time I took my dad for a visit to the prison [in Izmir]. I took a couple of days off [from work]. My brother was in jail.... What could you do?"[81] Faced with the persecution of an innocent man, his brother, "what could you do," indeed. Sıbgatullah's memory was accurate. Gülen stayed in pre-trial detention until November 9, 1971.

He was charged under Article 163 of the Turkey Criminal Code Law No. 765, for what U.S. lawyer James Harrington calls the "rather broad and vague charge of 'carrying out propaganda' to undermine the secular Turkish State and replace it with a religious one."[82] More specifically, but no less definitively, the indictment claimed that Gülen was guilty of an attempt at "changing the social, political, and economic basis of the regime in Turkey; founding an association and secret community for this purpose and thereby taking advantage of the people's religious feelings for this purpose."[83] He was, of course, a preacher and teacher. It is the rare preacher or teacher who is not, at some level, propagating something. Preachers have also been known to try to get people to associate with each other. And preachers tend to draw on people's feelings to try to change society for the better. As for the charge of eroding secularism—Gülen was nothing if not a faithful Muslim. He followed the nonviolent practices of the five pillars of Islam—as this chapter has (I hope) demonstrated. And if being a faithful Muslim was necessarily opposed to living in a secular society, then *most* Turks were guilty, more or less. Nevertheless, when Gülen was released in November, he continued to serve as a preacher in venues across the Aegean. But his case had not yet been decided, but merely continued to be adjudicated at some future date. The charges would be dropped, eventually, thanks to a general amnesty three years later. The uncertainty over those three years foreshadowed what would be a difficult decade to come for Fethullah Gülen. Ironically, however, it would also be a decade of growth for what became the Hizmet movement. This growth came despite (and in some ways perhaps because of) the persecution of the one they now called Hodjaefendi—honored teacher. That growth happened because Fethullah Gülen articulated for Turkish Muslims the reality of the suffering many of them had experienced. He also offered them (as the Buddha had once offered in his own milieu) a way out of that suffering. So, Chapter Three in the life of Fethullah Gülen must take up the matter of engaged empathy—or, more poetically, take up the topic of Hodjaefendi's tears.

Chapter Three

Empathy and Tears - The Aegean, 1971–1980

Many women and men in the Turkish Republic had good reasons to cry in the decade of the 1970s. Martial law meant citizens lived with the threat of arrest for any association that might appear to threaten the heavily-armed regime. Yet, despite this shroud, life went on. People ate, drank, laughed, walked, talked and prayed. They lived their lives seeking solace and dignity. Nobel laureate Orhan Pamuk's novel, *The Museum of Innocence*, which begins in 1975, accurately captures the tenor of the times in Turkey. It also, indirectly at least, highlights some of the dynamics in Fethullah Gülen's life and influence during this decade. In his novel, Pamuk describes the love of a well-to-do thirty-year old Turkish man, Kemal, for a slightly younger shop-girl, Füsun. Kemal's is a complicated romance. Even though Füsun marries another man, Kemal cannot forget her and starts collecting mementos of Füsun to keep his love alive before they got tragically separated. This collection eventually becomes The Museum of Innocence.[1]

Now, what makes *The Museum of Innocence* an apt, if imperfect, way to understand the life and significance of Fethullah Gülen in the 1970s is that Gülen, like Kemal, devoted himself to the objects and practices of love. This meant, in Gülen's case, that regardless of what was happening politically in Turkey, he continued patiently and passionately to teach *hizmet* (service). He sought to engage people in positive action—*müspet hareket* is the Turkish phrase. In Kemal's case, Pamuk put it like this: "I have no desire," the novelist wrote, "to interrupt my story with descriptions of the street clashes between fervent nationalists and fervent Communists at that time, except to say what we were witnessing was an extension of the cold war." Turkey's travails mirrored those elsewhere. Kemal, Füsun, Fethullah Gülen, and the thousands increasingly drawn to Gülen's teaching during this decade can stand in, then, for the

Turkish every-man and every-woman in the 1970s, torn by Cold War conflict, but living as best they could. Kemal, Füsun, Fethullah Gülen and those inspired by him struggled to realize their loves—for themselves, for each other, and (for Gülen and for people of Hizmet) for God. Fethullah Gülen refused to interrupt his calling to teach and to preach by getting bogged down in mere politics. He instead sought to orient people to those most basic relationships and practices that might alleviate their suffering. This often meant (as a writer tries to alleviate suffering through her words) orienting people to how they might work to alleviate the suffering of another. Pamuk put it like this, in an interview: "There is a kind of *Sufi* ... quality to this love for the world. I identify with Kemal's attention as a lover to his beloved because it is like a novelist's attention to words. In the end, being a novelist, in a way, is loving the world, caressing the world with words."[2] In the case of Gülen, he loved the Beloved, too. And the caresses he offered Turks during the 1970s were not only in a "kind of" *Sufi* way. That love came through especially in his preaching and teaching. People gathered to hear him. When Hodjaefendi did not travel to visit them, they came to him. They came on busses from all over the country to hear him in Izmir. They crowded the streets outside of mosques. They listened in on loud speakers when they couldn't get in the doors. And when he preached, he cried. And people cried with him.

Gülen began the decade under the shroud of the military coup. The Martial Law court sentenced him for house arrest in Sinop, but it was overruled by the court of appeals, and then charges were dropped because of an intervening amnesty law in 1974. Despite this shroud, Gülen kept a busy public schedule.[3] He filled pulpits in the decade throughout the Aegean and Marmara regions—notably in Edremit, Manisa, and Bornova. Audio tapes of his sermons (which had been recorded since 1966 by sympathizers, especially by Cahit Erdoğan) circulated throughout the country. Eventually he went on a national tour. He preached in many of the most prestigious pulpits in Turkey, including in 1977 at Sultanahmet Mosque in Istanbul. When Gülen spoke at this magnificent house of prayer leading politicians attended, including then Prime Minister Süleyman Demirel. In addition to Hodjaefendi's growing individual stature as a preacher, the 1970s also saw initiatives that Gülen had recommended in the late 1960s begin to bear fruit. Most were dedicated to assisting young people. Many Turks in the rising middle classes sought ways to provide an excellent secular education for their children *and* to keep them faithful Muslims. It was a tricky balancing act. But Gülen's teachings provided a ready theological and practical path. So, people around Gülen began setting up dormitories near college campuses, like the one Hodjaefendi had lived in during the late '60s, and they began establishing summer camps like the one he had begun in Buca. These camps and dorms served dual purposes. They provided youth (and their increasingly flush parents) an Islamic alternative to what many faithful Muslims perceived as ideological indoctrination into Communism or nationalism at government-run schools. And they provided venues for Muslim youth to continue their secular education as readers, writers, and *thinkers* attuned to scientific methods. These successful start-ups, for that is what they were, quickly spread across the nation. In short order, as their sustainability became clear, they gave rise to other initiatives—notably university prep courses and scholarship funds for needy students. These two latter initiatives, along with the dormitories (and, in the following decade, schools) became very effective channels for the work of the *mütevelli* or trustees, who organized themselves for the purposes of fundraising and business development in each locale where the Hizmet teaching took root.

As for Gülen himself, for all the flurry of activity it was also a time of loneliness. Immediately after his release from prison in 1972, he returned briefly to Erzurum to visit his family. It was a bittersweet reunion. His father was decidedly aging. He would die in two years. His mother, similarly, missed the comfort of her oldest and most well-known son; she would move to Izmir to be near him after the death of her husband Ramiz in 1974. In 1973, Gülen again made *Hajj*—this time not sponsored by the government, but by a friend for whom he made *hajj* as a surrogate for his aged mother, a common practice in Islam. As is often the case with second visits, the gloss in Mecca was not quite as bright as the first time; there are few recorded reflections from Gülen's return trip there. And in 1977 Gülen visited and lectured in the burgeoning Turkish communities in Germany—an important first step for Hizmet outside of the Anatolian peninsula. But just as Turkey itself was unsettled—the role of Prime Minister changed hands ten times during the decade—Gülen frequently expressed a deep sadness. For all his growing fame, he was, in many ways, a stranger in his own land. The Arabic term for the phenomenon is *ghurba*. Its reconciliation in the life of Fethullah Gülen, and among people of Hizmet, came through what we shall call engaged empathy. For those who came to hear Fethullah Gülen in the 1970s, some of whom were people like Kemal and Füsun, they often found release from *ghurba* through Hodjaefendi's tears.

Ghurba

If Fethullah Gülen lived with *ghurba* in the 1970s, it was not only due to his being like a stranger in his own land – it was his decision to live a solitary life, away from all worldly pleasures, including marriage. It's not that there weren't opportunities. In 1961, while in Edirne, he preached to a women-only congregation two times a week. One anecdote recalled that early in his tenure there, he rented an apartment in a residential district. Often, he stayed at the mosque teaching or studying until late at night. As he walked home, he would often pass neighborhood women (and, no doubt, men) who were relaxing outdoors in the summer heat—the Edirne equivalents of Füsun and Kemal. The possibility of impropriety must at least have crossed Gülen's mind, because he began his residence in the window-box of the Üç Şerefeli mosque shortly thereafter. Another anecdote accurately described how Gülen comported himself with scrupulous modesty when in the company of the women of Edirne. As is common in mosques down to today, for reasons of modesty women were consigned to the balcony or back rows of mosques during prayers, unless they were gathered in a same-sex group. So when Gülen lectured to the women of Edirne twice a week, he also reportedly requested that the women avert their gazes from him, which he also promised to do in return.[4]

Such scruples may have been Hodjaefendi's understandable response to the efforts, if not pressure, of many to arrange for him a suitable partner. Gülen's childhood friend Hatem Bilgili recalled that "there were a lot of people, a lot of families, who tried to set him up." Among them were his parents. Bilgili remembered that:

> I was going to Edirne in 1961. Ramiz [Fethullah's father] gave me a letter outside the Madrasa. He said, "give this letter to Fethullah." And he said, "whoever he wants to marry, I will arrange it. If she is tired I will carry her on my right shoulder and my left—and if I'm tired I will carry her on my back. I will ask nothing from Fethullah." So, [Bilgili

continues] I went to him, and I gave him the letter. Fethullah read it. And he wrote a letter. I read it. "This is too disrespectful," I told him. He looked at the letter. He ripped it up. He wrote a 2nd letter. I pointed out something disrespectful in it. He ripped that letter up, too. After the 3rd letter, he said to me, "if you say something about this letter, I will break your bones." But I remember the last letter. In that one, he sent respects to his relatives, and I remember this one specific passage. It affected me. I never could attain to that standard. I will remember that part until my death. Hodjaefendi wrote: "I have divorced this world and everything related to it. My only goal in this life is to live the Qur'an and to help others live the Qur'an. This is my only purpose."[5]

Such an intensity coincides in this story with a clear sense of humor: Fethullah didn't have to break Hatem's bones. More humor comes through in a match-making account from a few years later, when Fethullah's brother Sıbgatullah recalled that "our mom thought that if we got Fethullah married we'd be able to make him stay in Erzurum. A couple of families came to my parents with a request for their daughter to marry Hodjaefendi. Eventually my dad came to Hodjaefendi in Izmir and told him that they wanted to get him married. Hodjaefendi said, 'if you really want to get somebody married, get Sıbgatullah!'" Fethullah's gambit succeeded. Sıbgatullah goes on: "Finally, my dad agreed. 'Hodjaefendi gave his turn to you,' [he told me]. So, I got married and now we have nine children. *Maşhallah*!"[6] "*Maşhallah*" in Arabic literally means "what God wanted has happened." But the phrase is commonly used among Muslims to acknowledge and give thanks to God for something good, along the lines of "what a blessing!"

But *ghurba* was Fethullah's fate. There had been unmarried scholars and *sheikh*s within Islam in the past. Among them were al-Bistami (d. 874), al-Tabari (d. 923), and Ibn Taymiyyah (d. 1328). Gülen's *ghurba* had precedents.[7] In fact, the term has a deep resonance in Islam. It is characteristic of a *chosen* way of life within some branches of *Sufism*. Choosing not to marry might be a way to prepare oneself for other kinds of estrangements—getting sent to prison, for example, or being betrayed by fellow Muslims. Gülen's father Ramiz no doubt experienced *ghurba*. He probably taught the concept to his son. In one story, Abdullah Birlik, whose father was among Gülen's earliest and closest associates, recalled that while Fethullah was in prison in 1971, Ramiz came to Izmir to visit. He attended Fethullah's trial. Birlik goes on: "One day during court, the time for witnesses for the prosecution appeared, and religious officials were called. Twenty-three people were called. They all lied. Ramiz was really sad. These were respected people who had lied about his son and my dad. Then my mom saw ... that Ramiz was sad, and she asked him: "Why are you sad?" And Ramiz replied: "Today in court there was a bazaar for faith, and everyone sold out."[8] That kind of *ghurba* was all too common in 1970s Turkey.

In fact—it's been part of the culture since the founding of the Republic. When the government took over religion, religious officials (some of them, at least) understandably felt pressured to give the government what they thought the government wanted. Another individual, aside from Gülen, who resisted this "selling out" was Said Nursi (1877-1960). We have encountered him before, and we will see him again. Nursi was a Turkish Kurd. Being Kurdish often has produced estrangement within Turkey. Nursi spent much of his life in jail or in exile. According to historian Yvonne Haddad, Nursi's life was a model for Gülen in how to turn *ghurba* into something positive. Gülen learned from Nursi how it was "possible to conquer the profound sense of loneliness and alienation experienced ... in an alien and hostile environment." Nursi bequeathed to Gülen "a paradigm for survival, for seeking solace and affirmation from God by attempting to dwell in [God's] presence. In the process, the experience of *ghurba*, estrangement, is transformed into *uns*, companionship."[9] In other words, if one's Beloved was God, then the absence of earthly love was merely a transitory phenomenon. Eternal love made temporal *ghurba* endurable.

Yet, loving God in a material world is not exactly a natural skill. Gülen described *ghurba* in a way that recognized the challenge: "Literally meaning the state of being a foreigner, homelessness, loneliness, separation, and being a stranger in one's own land," Gülen wrote, "*ghurba* ... has been defined in the language of Sufism as renouncing the world with the charms to which one feels attachment on the way to the All-True, All-Desired and Sought One, or living a life dedicated to the other world though surrounded by this world and its charms."[10] Gülen, aware that some Muslims saw *Sufism* as lacking grounding in orthodox Islam, demonstrated the presence of *ghurba* both in the Qur'an and the Sunna. The Prophet

Muhammad experienced it, he suggested, as did his companions. Muhammad had felt *ghurba* when he had to live among "those unaware of spirituality and spiritual states." He and his Companions knew estrangement when they had to "suffer among wicked transgressors." They knew loneliness when they had to endure scorn from "the rude and ignorant ... bigots, who [restricted] themselves only to the outward wording" of religion, while disregarding its central teachings of mercy and compassion.[11] There were plenty of analogies to those examples that Gülen's listeners could draw upon from their own experience. Even more pointedly, and poignantly, Gülen quoted a *hadith* from *Sahih Muslim*—one of the most authoritative collections of the sayings of the Prophet and his Companions. It reads: "Islam began helpless and with the helpless and those treated as outlandish and outsiders, and it will return to the same condition of helplessness and being represented and revived by those who will be treated as outlandish and outsiders. Glad tidings to the outsiders who try to improve in a time when all [others] are engaged in destruction and corruption."[12] Again, the contemporary resonances were (and are) plentiful. Authentic Islam was not likely to be found among the proud and powerful, but among the outlandish outsiders. And yet for these spiritual elites, *ghurba* became a source of courage and strength. As Gülen concluded: "Those who feel this separation rise to friendship with God, without ever feeling themselves completely alone."[13]

Gülen's experience of and understanding of *ghurba* can be illuminated by another, perhaps better-known concept within Sufism, namely *Fana Fi'llah*, or "Annihilation in God." *Fana* can be difficult for some Westerners to comprehend, much as the Buddhist and Hindu notions of "no-self" and *nirvana* (literally, "cessation"), can appear challenging to individualistically-oriented cultures. Yet the prospect that one can become so fully a friend of the ultimate Power in the universe that one's private ego or self is annihilated in the flow of love is, perhaps when put that way, not so hard to comprehend. And when preaching in the 1970s, Fethullah Gülen clearly expressed something like *fana*, as did those who heard him. Thus, as Gülen put it,

> that hero of annihilation ... sees that all things other than God are but drops from the endless ocean of the Divine Existence, although [she] cannot distinguish the drop from the ocean, a particle from the sun,

a mirror from what is reflected in it because [she] is deeply immersed in God's Existence.[14]

Those who experienced this kind of religion, then, may

> express their sensation of Divine Existence and Oneness, joy and plea-sure, they [may] express the favor of God's company, and the excite-ment of feeling [God] by sometimes crying or screaming, sometimes by losing themselves and fainting, and sometimes by going into ecsta-sies and dancing. All of these happen during the spiritual journey on the hills of the heart.[15]

So *fana* and ecstatic expression may be part of *ghurba*, too—*ghur-ba* becoming *uns*, companionship. And it is this kind of experience that many people reported who heard Gülen preach during the 1970s.

Gülen as preacher

Ahmet Tekin was one of them. He heard Gülen preach in many places. But he remembered especially his preaching in Bornova, where Gülen was appointed in 1976. Bornova is a college district of Izmir. It is home to several universities. College students constituted a considerable per-centage of Gülen's regular audience for sermons there. Tekin recalled that "ever since the Bornova mosque was built, [we] never saw youth [at prayer] like when Hodjaefendi [preached]." And what happened when Gülen preached was a physical manifestation of *ghurba*. "When Hod-jaefendi would start praying, there would be an orchestra of crying," he remembered. "It was like you could see the angels behind him," he con-tinued with a touch of hyperbole. More specifically:

> Hodjaefendi would cry every time he'd mention Allah, or the Prophet. The mosque was so full that people couldn't prostrate. We'd bump into each others' feet. Just when Hodjaefendi would say "Allahu Akbar," the sobbing would start. When he'd go from *ayet* [verse] to *ayet*, the sobbing would not stop. When Hodjaefendi started crying everyone else would start. We'd cry because he cried. I don't understand that emotion…. It's hard for [anyone] to understand.[16]

Hard to understand, or not, tears became a characteristic of Gülen's public persona.

To be fair, the tears didn't start only in the 1970s. Necdet İçel was an imam born in 1955 in a Turkish village named Korucuk, albeit not the village of the same name in which Gülen had been born in 1938. When he was ten, in 1966, İçel heard Fethullah Gülen preach his very first sermon in Izmir. He recalled:

> I went with my family to Şadırvanaltı Mosque in the center of Izmir where Gülen preached. Until that time, some people used to cry in the mosque, but the preacher himself never cried—but Gülen did cry himself, and therefore he was known as "the crying preacher." He cried when he talked about the Prophet and about his Companions, and he also cried when he discussed the sad situation in the world of Islam. After his first festive [eid] prayer and sermon, people went to introduce themselves to Gülen, and they wanted to kiss his hand [a characteristic Turkish gesture of deferential honor], but Gülen withdrew his hand out of humility. Since I was only ten years old at that time, I was allowed to kiss Gülen's hand, and since I came from a village named Korucuk as well, Gülen kissed me on the head and invited me to attend the Qur'an school after I finished my elementary education.[17]

This was a memorable introduction—and İçel did in fact go on to study with Gülen.

As his student, İçel had plenty of opportunities to hear Gülen preach, and over the years he came to recognize several characteristics that made Gülen distinctive as a public speaker, along with his tears. First, Gülen was well-prepared. He would sometimes study as many as 500 pages of Qur'anic interpretation and theology for a single sermon. Second, Gülen was a hafız—one who had memorized the entire Qur'an. He could thus identify appropriate cross-references at will. Third, because he had been trained "in the Sufi way," İçel thought, Gülen was particularly attuned to the poetry of Islamic tradition. For example, while studying with Hodjaefendi, İçel once travelled with Gülen to Erzurum from Izmir—a journey of roughly 18 hours. He recalled that during the journey Gülen "was constantly reciting poems." That Gülen has a prodigious memory is a frequent observation from students and colleagues. Consequently, it should come as no surprise that, fourth, Gülen delivered his sermons "without notes." This contrasted with the common practice among Turkish preachers, who tended to read their remarks.

Even more, however, fifth, when he preached Gülen "never spoke badly of unbelievers, or the government, or anyone. He tried to talk not about how bad people are but about how good Islam is." This preaching style— to emphasize positive action, *müspet hareket*—also contrasted with the approach of many preachers who felt compelled to draw clear moral or dogmatic lines.

Another of Gülen's early students, Mehmet Küçük, used almost identical language to describe Gülen's approach to preaching and teaching. Gülen, according to Küçük, "never said anything negative about anyone."[18] The literary record does not quite support such a claim; there were clear opponents to *hizmet* in Gülen's discourse.[19] But it was also true that he urged extending charity to all, and it was equally true that he would in coming years exclude no groups *a priori* from dialogue. Even Communists, who might have been the most likely foil for him from the pulpit, given his upbringing in the Russia-scarred Erzurum region, generally were not excluded from the possibility of inclusion. Gülen, Yusuf Pekmezci offered, "used to say that we even had to love the Communists."[20] Apparently this open-minded, non-judgmental attitude also went in the other ideological direction to include nationalists or right-ists. Küçük remembered one *sohbet* by Gülen where a student associated with the "Grey Wolves," a group of right-wing ultranationalists, accused in the 1980s of dozens of political assassinations, was a participant. In the midst of this *sohbet*, the Grey Wolf-associated youth blurted out: "We should kill all Communists!" Another student attending the chat replied: "If you had done that yesterday, I wouldn't be sitting here next to you."[21] The exchange became a staple story in Gülen's teaching repertoire. His preaching and teaching was not just tears, in short, but also included a rhetorical approach that focused less on opponents, and more on pos-sibilities.

For Alaattin Kırkan, the tailor we met in Chapter Two, though, it was through Hodjaefendi's tears that people grew closer to Islam. Kırkan told the story of a conversion that could have been repeated in many variants across Turkey in the 1970s. Gülen was preaching an *Eid* sermon, Kırkan recalled (*Eid* is the name of two major Islamic festivals; one at the end of Ramadan, the other during the *Hajj*). The location was Hisar Mosque in Izmir—a sixteenth century beauty at the heart of the city. Kırkan had invited a customer who "had never prayed in his life." The customer was "scared—it was his first time in a mosque." Kırkan's rich story continues:

Hodjaefendi was at the *kürsü* [pulpit]. My friend was behind me in the second row. When Hodjaefendi started to explain about [an early Muslim conflict] there was a cry from the rear side of the mosque. My friend touched my shoulder, and said "this one in the rear must be a mystic." In the presence of Hodjaefendi we wouldn't ordinarily move, but I touched my friend's knee—meaning I understood. But then, someone from our left side started crying as well. Then my friend touched my shoulder—and said, "there's another holy one!" But the lesson was so wonderful that during the sermon there was nobody who was not crying. Even my friend was crying. At the climax of the sermon, [Hodjafendi was telling the story about] our mother Sumayra—one of the companions of the Prophet. [As Gülen related the story, Sumayra had] told her father, husband, and two sons to not come back from the war if something happened to the Prophet. And then she [heard] war news that our Prophet was a martyr. She got on her horse, went to the battlefield. There was a man lying on the ground, almost dead. Somebody said, "Sumayra, this is your father." She said, "forget about my father—where's the Prophet?" They showed her her husband as well, and she said, "This isn't the time for father or husband. Where's the Prophet?" Then they pointed to her boys, who were mortally wounded. She again said "where's the Prophet?" After this, one of the companions told Sumayra, "what's your worry—he's right there in the front!" And then she got off her horse, came close to the Prophet [and kissed] the ground. She said, "I have found you! Let time stop. Let creation stop." [While he was telling us this story], Hodjaefendi beat his breast, and said: "Ah, if this heart would stop. This heart would stop, this heart would stop!" Then he bowed down and cried for minutes. That's when I turned around and saw my friend crying as well.... Well, when we were getting out of the mosque, I put my arm around my friend and asked him: "So, are you one of those holy ones as well?" And he said: "This is such a *hodja*—not only does he cry, he makes everyone else cry!" From that day on the friend of mine who was saved by that sermon became a person who cried his whole life.[22]

Here, "crying one's whole life" was a metaphor for the *ghurba* that *Sufism* taught, and that Gülen practiced. The lesson of this particular sermon, after all, was a difficult one. Love for the Prophet might even be more profound than love of one's marital partner, or father, or son. Such love has brought many to tears.

Of course, in that release of tears in the company of others one might also find *uns*— companionship in a community of purpose. Esra Koşar's account of the impact of Gülen's preaching can help clarify how Hodjaefendi's tears led to compassionate commitment. Koşar grew up in Ankara. She learned of Gülen through audio tapes of the sermons he delivered in mosques around the Aegean. "I was wondering," she asked, "why was he crying?" It was a question many had. Over the years, Koşar worked it out. "[Eventually] it became easy for me to understand. He was crying over the situation of Islam in the world. We are behind in every subject. As humans we are failing God by not being servants of God." Hodjaefendi's tears signaled a deficit in *hizmet*. To further explain, Koşar recalled a teacher she knew in Ankara. This teacher "was filled with hatred. Unlike her," she continued, "Hodjaefendi was not angry, but [his sermons were] filled with compassion and love." Her evidence to support this assertion was that Gülen's tears stemmed from and encouraged self-critical awareness. "Look at ourselves," she paraphrased Gülen, "and rather than being angry with people around us, rather than blaming others, look at ourselves—why are we here?" That positive approach full of hope, focused on living a life of purpose, was what drew her to Gülen.[23]

It could not have been easy to find hope while in prison or being stalked by police (as Gülen was continuously from the time of his service in Edirne). Nevertheless, Gülen communicated such hope through perhaps the most durable aspect of Islamic tradition—its practices of oral communication.[24] The first message to the Prophet Muhammad from the Angel Gabriel, after all—the very beginning of the Qur'an and therefore of Islam itself—was the injunction to "Recite!" And communication through preaching in Islam was not only a means of stirring individual emotion. Preaching was also a central means of community organizing. Muslims here share much with Protestant Christians. It would be a mistake, then, to presume that it was *only* emotion that drew people to Gülen's preaching. And it was surely more than emotion that *kept* people connected to the growing Hizmet movement. Institutions do not get built on empathy alone.[25] Instead, what emerges from the reports of those who listened to Gülen's sermons during his years around the Aegean is that he promoted a balance between profound emotion and pragmatic action. Call it *engaged* empathy. Gülen's tears signified the suffering of Muslims. But his preaching also gave Muslims a positive way out of suffering through concrete action on behalf of greater justice and peace. *Ghurba* became hope through *hizmet*.

But *hizmet* was, as Gülen saw it, nothing more than authentic Islam. Consequently, it should come as no surprise that during his time in the Aegean Gülen began preaching on discrete topics—kind of an Islam 101, in series that would go on for weeks. Such multi-week sermon series were common in some Christian pulpits. They were not common among Muslim preachers. During a stretch between 1975-78, for instance, Gülen preached for 120 consecutive weeks (over two years!) on the single topic of *iman*—faith. Naturally, the Qur'anic texts and related topics that Gülen considered during this series varied widely—for example, *tawhid* (the oneness of God), and the nature of prophethood (including, of course, Jesus).[26] But Gülen also obviously considered the single theme of faith or trust in God (and in one another) important enough to dwell upon at length. Another series for 20 weeks focused on *salat*—prayer. Gülen devoted five weeks to the *hajj*, the major pilgrimage, as part of a longer series of 48 weeks on the pillars of Islam. A third sermon series—and these are simply examples, led listeners for nearly 50 weeks through the ethics of *tebliğ*—sincerity or selflessness, or encouraging good-deeds and preventing evil. Each of these sermon series included discrete addresses that Gülen communicated with emotional intensity and tears. He delivered them, again, without notes or manuscripts, yet drawing upon careful research befitting the scholar that he was. The sermons were recorded and transcribed (and, increasingly, published) later. For Mehmet Yıldız, a teacher from Bornova, what drew him to Gülen was the way the preacher balanced scholarly preparation, spirituality, pragmatism, and emotion in the pulpit. "Gülen was already famous as a preacher" when he took the post in Bornova (in 1976) where Yıldız lived and worked. "The square in front of the mosque," Yıldız recalled, "was filled with people a few hours before Hodjaefendi preached his *vaaz* [sermon] on Friday afternoon." Yıldız then offered a succinct commentary on what drew so many to

Gülen. "I must confess," Yıldız said, "that I found something in Gülen's sermons that I never experienced again: one part of knowledge; one part of *ruh* (spiritual presence); one part of action; and one part of tears."[27] Whatever the recipe, Fethullah Gülen's distinctive spiritual food quickly became very popular all over Turkey. One collection of Gülen's taped sermons and teachings eventually ran to eleven DVDs and twenty-two compact discs. Most of the sermons in those collections were from his postings around the Aegean in the 1970s.[28]

That Gülen's preaching changed people's lives is indisputable. The primary evidence is in the stories of people who found purpose in life through Hizmet. But another side of Gülen's influence, no doubt trickier to ascertain, is in the negative actions *not* taken by people inspired by him. Gülen's preaching kept some young people from radicalizing and becoming violent. One of them was Mehmet Doğan. Doğan had his academic degree in literature and film studies, and he was teaching in Antakya in the early 1970s when he became aware of Gülen. "I'd heard of Hodjaefendi," he said, "I thought he was a regular *hodja*. I didn't want to listen to him." Doğan emphasized that a "regular *hodja*" might have been as emotional in preaching as Gülen. One of them, he remembered, "screamed a lot, hit the podium—people were getting into that," he said. But Doğan was part of "an educated community; a University.... We were familiar with Western intellectuals—Sartre, Hegel, Marx, and so forth—we'd read those works, and these *hodjas* hadn't read anything. So, we wouldn't listen to them." Still, when Doğan received a transfer to Adana in 1976, he met a colleague who was a student of Hodjaefendi. Doğan saw the library of this colleague—which was impressive. "I was surprised," he went on. So, "OK, I thought—give me some [audio] tapes [of Gülen's sermons]. I started listening to the tapes. And [Gülen] knew the East, and he knew the West. He wasn't the person I thought he was going to be.... Sezai Karakoç [an influential Turkish public intellectual and poet, b. 1933] said that 'the one who knows the West and the East, he will come.' And when I heard [Hodjaefendi] preach, I thought, 'this is the one.'" That perception kept Doğan from radicalizing. "I was headed in the direction that Iran took," he said. Iran, of course, had a highly educated, secular population, but became a Revolutionary Islamic Republic in 1979. "I was a radical person," Doğan went on. "We were the *only* believers, and we'd call everyone else non-believers." Such dualism, or lack of empathy, is a widely-documented way that religions produce violence.²⁹ "I wouldn't visit my relatives at all," Doğan clarified, "because they were non-believers." But Gülen preached a different way. "Instead of fighting and war," Doğan concluded, "[Hodjaefendi] taught dialogue [and] peace ... through education [and] persuasion." Practically, this meant "Gülen made me love my father-in-law," Doğan chuckled. More abstractly, "I learned how not to put people in categories, but to embrace everyone." In fact, Doğan and his father-in-law developed a practice of listening to Gülen's taped sermons together. "My father-in-law would smoke [as we listened] and say, 'This man has two wings!'"³⁰ The image became an important one in the Hizmet movement. "Flying with Two Wings" meant holding together head and heart, Islam and science, one's own tradition and respect for others. In fact, it became a key metaphor within Hizmet for interfaith dialogue—a topic we shall explore more fully in the next chapter.³¹ As for Doğan, he went on to be one of the founding faculty members at Fatih University—a story we shall also take up in Chapter Four.

So, by the mid-1970s, despite his time in jail and regular surveillance by police, Fethullah Gülen had gained considerable fame. His commitments, however, remained unchanged: he was a preacher and a teacher, living in a dormitory as a single man, dedicated to the practice of Islam, to learning, and to service. His assertions of modesty were consistent. He generally sought to deflect attention from his person to the message he tried to communicate. On at least one occasion, this meant he stepped away from the public. In Bursa, sometime in the mid-1970s, he was preaching in a large movie theater (another innovation he began, along with visiting coffeehouses). In the middle of his talk, his words elicited applause. Gülen stopped his sermon. He asked the congregation not to clap. When applause broke out again, he abruptly said, "farewell," and left the stage. One source explained that Gülen "thought he was being praised with the applause; whereas, what he wanted was for the things he explained to be given attention and to be attempted to be understood."³² Surely, though, such adulation wasn't easy to turn away from. Fame was "a poisonous honey," Gülen once said.³³ But it was still a honey. So Gülen's commitment to the *Sufi* practice of *ghurba*—identifying with the suffering of the world—carried on. He was adored by thousands. He could not help but notice the huge crowds who thronged to hear him preach. But he was also a stranger in his own land.

Death of Ramiz Gülen

When his father, Ramiz, died on September 20, 1974, Fethullah of course returned to Erzurum to grieve. He had visited not long before, and he could have anticipated that that visit was a goodbye. Father and son were close. Fethullah had after all followed in his father's footsteps and become an *imam*. But the relationship was also a traditional one marked by hierarchical respect. Thus, before departing from Erzurum to return to his duties in the Aegean, Fethullah had requested permission from Ramiz to depart. On June 29, Fethullah had received a new appointment from the State-run Office of Religious Affairs to be a preacher in Manisa, an Izmir suburb. His visit to Erzurum was a vacation in between posts. And his father, according to at least one report, tried to delay his son's departure. Ramiz asked his son to stay for a few extra days. Eventually, the elder Gülen relented, reportedly saying to his famous son: "Go. Here one pair of eyes waits for you; there thousands are waiting."[34] It was undoubtedly a parental blessing, and these were likely the last words Fethullah heard from his dad. Ramiz died a few weeks later.

. So, Gülen's experience of *ghurba* deepened. As the oldest son, Gülen inherited responsibility for the well-being of his mother and the rest of his siblings. Because of his growing stature, he also saw that there were temptations that might divide his relations. Consequently, he gathered his family together in the wake of his father's passing, and he asked them explicitly to pledge to uphold the kind of moral integrity that Ramiz had held dear. They were not to "sell out" Islam. Gülen's brother Sıbgatullah recalled the scene:

> After my father passed away, Hodjaefendi came here to Erzurum. He told me to bring in my two aunts—and my mother was there, as the family elders, along with all the family members. He told me to bring them to my house. "I'll speak with them," he said. I got them with my car, and brought them to my house. So Hodjaefendi gave a *sohbet* about faith and religion, and about daily life. He said, "You're going to ... get together, buy some land together, make a small house for everyone, live together so that you will know where to go when you're sick," this kind of thing. Then he [asked them], "What am I to you?" We said, "You are our brother!" He asked my mom, and she said, "You are my son!" He asked my aunts, they said: "You are our nephew!"

And then he said, "I am on a path. I cannot turn back from this path. I am on the path of Allah. There's nothing I expect from this world. And I ask all of you to expect nothing worldly from me." And then he's saying to my mom, "[You think] 'he's going to work to make money, to help me eat and drink, he'll look after me.'... There should not be any such expectation from me. That's first," he said. "Second," he said, "Because of me, they could put you into prison. They will follow you. They may hurt you. You should be ready for all of this, [because] in the future all of this will happen. If you don't get ready now, you'll say, 'where did all of this come from?' Right now, it has come.... And if you want to say, 'I don't have a brother like that,' then I will go on my way, and you will go on yours."[35]

They were all in tears. It would test any family's solidarity. Refia had just lost her partner of thirty-nine years. Fethullah and Sıbgatullah and their other siblings had just buried their father. The aunts had lost their brother. Fethullah was insisting that they give up expectations of benefit from his growing fame. And yet, as Sıbgatullah recalled it, "We gave him our word. 'You are our heart, you are our soul. Whatever you say, we will put ourselves to it. Whatever comes because of you, we are ready for it.'" It had to be a powerful moment. But "this is one of his principles," Sıbgatullah went on, "'do not expect anything worldly from me.' And we have never expected anything worldly from him, with God's help. His fame, any favors in his name.... Never did we go to anyone and ask for anything for us because we were close to him. Not even a little."[36] Although it is of course impossible for me to verify this claim with certainty, from what I have been able to observe, his family was true to their word. Gülen's childhood home no longer stands. His elder sister lived in a modest apartment not far from Izmir. His younger brother, Salih, lived in a simple townhouse in Erzurum. They would appear to have kept their pledge. Sadly, Fethullah's prediction about future troubles also proved true. Hodjaefendi's tears would continue.

Why did he cry? Tears as "poetry without words"

As for why he cried, Gülen of course had his own answers. His first, not surprisingly, was theological. "I guess ... God created me like that," he simply said. A second answer was sociological. "I grew up in a place of

... domination, oppression. ... Seeing those, I can't help but feeling sad when wistfully remembering the past. It's made me soft-hearted like a child."[37] But Gülen gave perhaps his fullest answer to the question of "why does he cry?" in a *sohbet* from later in his life (2012). In it, he also displays some of the story-telling that he frequently did during sermons. The *sohbet* addressed a *hadith* which says that "sometimes God grants mercy to an entire world upon the crying of one sad heart." Misery and depravity were widespread in the society during the time the Prophet lived, Gülen began, but people had become inured to it. The same happened to people today, even in his own experience. He shared how he returned after some years to his childhood village. "After having [lived] in the city for a while," he began, "I visited my uncle who lived in the village. The moment I poked my head in through the door, I said how bad the smell was. On hearing this, my uncle's grandchildren started laughing at me.... I had stayed in the same house for about a month in my childhood and [had not felt] disturbed at all." One had to wake up to suffering, to misery and depravity. Those were not what God intended for people. Indeed, Gülen went on: "people fail to realize that there is a very distinguished position that they are supposed to take vis-à-vis their Creator, and that they stand far below this position in reality." Awakening to suffering was the first step in *remedying* it. Such awakening rarely happened without tears. Indeed, for Gülen, to awaken to suffering was "a very important invitation for Divine inspirations." God wanted people in "very different ways first to realize and then be saved from the troubled state that they are really in. For instance," Gülen went on, adapting Plato:

> If a man at the bottom of a well or a dungeon is aware of his situation and feels due suffering, he will try to get out in many different ways and will achieve his goal in the end by God's grace. Even if he does not possess any tools, he will try to climb out by using his hands like claws. He strives on and makes two small holes where he can insert his feet. After managing to stand on them, he does the same above the first ones. Continuing like this, he makes his way out of the well after a certain period of time. But a man living contentedly down there, even unaware of his situation, will never make such an effort.[38]

Hodjaefendi's tears were to awaken other Muslims to their collective suffering, and then to inspire them to claw their way out, step by patient step. That lesson, of course, was hardly limited only to Muslims. The Buddha taught, after all, that the first Noble Truth was this simple assertion: "life is suffering."

But if Gülen had stopped there, there would have been no Hizmet movement, just as if the Buddha had not taught a way out of suffering there would have been no Buddhism. Turning suffering into *engaged* purpose in the world was the challenge. Young people, who were, again, among the most prominent members of Gülen's audiences, sometimes lacked the tempering (or dampering) of years. That could lead to an exaggerated sense of their own suffering, imagining that no one had ever *possibly* experienced the agony that they currently endured. Along with his preaching, then, Gülen began another initiative during these years to reach out to young people. On Friday nights, after prayer, or sometimes on Saturdays or Sundays, when no classes were in session, Gülen would host Q-and-A sessions open to the public. Most of those who attended were students. Questions were submitted at the beginning of the meeting, and Gülen picked papers with questions from a box. Alaaddin Kırkan remembered that Hodjaefendi prefaced these sessions by saying, "I'm not Imam Ghazali [perhaps the most famous Muslim theologian]. I don't know everything. If I can answer, I will, if not, I'll do some research and answer next week. I will not answer two types of questions: political, this is a mosque, and I won't answer questions about individual persons."[39] Given the political turmoil in Turkey, the former limit was no doubt as prudent as the latter limit was principled. But because much of the suffering that young people were experiencing in Turkey had political causes, questions often touched indirectly on the troubled state of Turkish society. Gülen was scrupulous to avoid any partisan display. But Muhammed Çetin, a sociologist and Hizmet participant, who himself served a term in the Turkish Parliament between 2011 and 2015, recalled that as part of these early Q and A sessions Gülen consistently spoke out against anarchy, violence, and terror, themes that would be consistent with his later writings.[40] But the questions ranged widely. Kırkan reported that "I counted, and there were around 1200 questions over five years."[41]

Perhaps it is simply fair to say that young people in 1970s Turkey shared Gülen's *ghurba*. They felt in him a kindred spirit, even as Hodjaefendi's age crept near forty. In a later interview, journalist Nevval Sevindi asked Gülen a pointed (and more than a little leading) question about his own suffering. "You have suffered much hardship in your life," she noted. "How do you now look at those events that smothered the joy within you, that were aimed at crushing you?" Gülen replied:

> I always tried to be useful. Others before me also suffered greatly from this mission. These things can happen when you have an ideal inside you. Ever since childhood I have had the light and air of the dervish lodges … inside my soul. I have never been able to [reconcile] the smallness of a nation with such a great history. I always lived with feelings that could be regarded as utopian. I sometimes gave voice to these with tears from despair. In my view, tears are poetry without words or sound.[42]

Increasingly, in the 1970s, people who heard Gülen's "poetry without words" joined him in finding ways to climb out of whatever wells they happened to be stuck in.

In other words, a movement was growing dedicated to the service that Fethullah Gülen's sermons called for. For most of the decade, Hizmet grew largely "under the radar" of the Turkish state. That government struggled to hold itself together as anarchists, communists, nationalists, and Islamists again took to the streets. Quietly, not secretly, but also without calling attention to themselves, volunteers inspired by Fethullah Gülen across Turkey began to build institutions to turn the suffering of *ghurba* into the community of *uns*. They began the positive action of building peace through engaged empathy. Hodjaefendi's tears began to water hope. And hope began, as it often does, in initiatives with youth.

Living for a cause: engaged empathy with youth

Why were young people so socially active around the globe in the 1960s and 70s? It was not merely the baby boom that led youth into protests, street marches, and ideological clashes. There was also a subtle, and pernicious, dimension to the mobilization of youth that had been underway for decades, and that lay underneath the widespread protests. For much of history, war was generally an adult vocation. Killing and dying was the prerogative of mature individuals. Over the course of the twentieth-century this changed. By the time of the U.S. conflict in Vietnam (1955-75), the average age of a U.S. soldier killed was just over 23 years old, and 61% of those who died were under 21.[43] Turkey's situation in the 1970s was slightly different, but the sway of the military in the lives of youth no less potent. Since 1919, a term of service in the Turkish armed forces was mandatory for every young man starting at age 20—hence Fethullah Gülen's time in Ankara and İskenderun between 1961-3. Now, whether in the U.S. or in Turkey, there is much to be said on behalf of military service. Defense of one's nation can be a noble vocation. But as studies of military cultures have shown in very diverse contexts, most human beings must be trained to kill.[44] And the training associated with serving in the military has often centered on a rhetoric of sacrifice for the nation. Put bluntly, militaries train youth *to kill and to die for a cause*. That young people would in many ways protest their increased vulnerability as agents of killing and dying should, perhaps, not be surprising.

What also should not be surprising is that traditional religions like Islam could pose an alternative to sacrifice for the nation. And indeed, Fethullah Gülen and the Hizmet movement offered Turkish youth exactly such an alternative. The various initiatives begun in and around Izmir at Fethullah Gülen's encouragement engaged the empathy of young people not with glorious sacrifice for the imagined community of the Turkish nation. Instead, Hizmet engaged youth through faith and reason with service to humanity that invited them into courage in a different mode. They would not find glory through killing or dying in a battle. But neither would they be dead, nor traumatized by the experience of having to kill. They would still have to fight. There were enemies to be defeated. But the battle would be fought with weapons of the spirit, and the primary enemy was one's own ego. This was still an exciting prospect. The armies that egotism marshalled were considerable, even as they were hardly distinct to any one nation. They were ignorance, poverty, even violence itself. And yet, just as joining the Army often brought benefits to those soldiers who survived, so too did participation in the kind of struggles that Fethullah Gülen preached about bring benefits when young spiritual warriors engaged in those struggles. Islam as Gülen depicted it was not *only* an altruistic endeavor. Through Hizmet, it increasingly became clear, young Muslims could live full and meaningful lives rich with challenges and satisfactions. They could *live* for a cause.

As a metaphor, of course, the estrangement or loneliness of *ghurba* is associated with the valleys and shadows of life. So, what Fethullah Gülen and his friends offered young people in the 1970s was a series of initiatives that emphasized an alternative metaphor—light. The first initiatives were known simply as *dershanes*—student houses or dormitories. But in an influential article, Gülen once described these student houses as *ışık evler*, "houses of light."[45] If young people faced a threatening shadow of *ghurba*, and if they also faced a temptation to resolve this loneliness through participation in political or nationalist violence, then the houses of light were to be alternative centers where young people could learn to live for a cause. They would do so, of course, through Islam—one kind of light. But they would also do so through rigorous (and competitive) participation in secular learning—another kind of light. Practically, the dormitories were nothing more, initially, than subsidized apartments or rental homes, where young people lived together for mutual support. In the later years of the decade, people within Hizmet built entirely new buildings to house secondary-school, high-school, or college-age students who wanted to come to study in Izmir. Then, the idea caught on. Soon, houses of light or Hizmet *dershanes* were found in all the major urban centers in Turkey. These *dershanes* became one of the primary ways that the Hizmet movement grew. Young people lived together, and learned together, for the cause of *hizmet*.

Yusuf Pekmezci recalled that the first dormitory was built in the Bozyaka neighborhood of Izmir in 1968. It was, Pekmezci reiterated, a turbulent time. "The rich have apartments and cars, the poor are in the slums, and there's friction ... class conflict," Pekmezci set the context. "Students were coming [to Izmir] from other towns and villages—they had nowhere to stay" other than state-sponsored dorms where ideological friction was constant. "'So, let's open a dorm,'" Pekmezci recalled Gülen saying. "So, we opened the dorms. We put an elder in each dorm, [and they set strict rules]: 'you're going to leave at 8 am and come home at 5 pm'.... The first dorm in 1968 was for students going to University. We rented houses [rooms] to them. The pattern spread quickly over the country. The parents would say when students returned home, 'I didn't raise such a good child!'"[46]

These were private dormitories—sponsored and administered by *mütevelli* or trustees. Raising the money had to be done carefully. "If the soldiers caught you collecting money," one of my interviewees re-membered, "they would have thrown you in jail. So fundraising would be done cautiously not to be caught by soldiers. ... There were only 5-10 of us," he recalled. Pekmezci remembered that once he left the Board of the state-run Kestanepazarı School [in 1968], he was able to begin raising funds for all kinds of educational endeavors, including (eventu-ally) the dorm. "We opened a foundation—the Akyazılı Foundation for Secondary and Higher Education. We secured acceptance from the gov-ernment, and we went to the rich [and said to them]: 'You have a duty to educate a child.' And they helped. They put money in the bank. And we gave the students monthly stipends."[47] So while the group of volunteers had to be careful about their activities to avoid arousing the ire of local police, officially, at least, on the level of the State they were legitimate. Nevertheless, there was constant surveillance by regulators, and suspi-cion of the organizations was routine.

The structure of the group was small, Pekmezci also remembered: "We formed an administrative group; there were four of us, the fifth was Hodjaefendi." Gülen was a participant in the meetings of the *mütev-elli* only in the beginning. The small businessmen who began Hizmet weren't from among the elite. They were tailors, furniture store own-ers, factory operators. Hodjaefendi had been teaching middle school and high school students at Kestanepazarı, but this was his first venture into what was in effect community organizing and entrepreneurship. It was not an easy task to organize such a disparate group into a cohesive and functioning foundation. "Truly," Pekmezci remembered, "the four people around him were not educated."[48] Yet they managed over time to raise the funds, and the dorm was built.

As other groups of *mütevelli* sprang up in other communities, it became impossible for Gülen to meet with them regularly. Naturally, as he traveled, Gülen would meet with interested individuals to discuss their plans. And people would come to Izmir to consult with Hodjaefen-di. In Izmir itself, Tahsin Şimşek was a successful real estate developer who joined the *mütevelli* early on. He wondered whether he should quit his business and become an imam. "In 1972," he remembered,

> Hodjaefendi got into my car and looked down. I thought to myself, since Hodjaefendi was a *hafız*—"he's probably reciting to himself." But

then Hodjaefendi looked up, and said, "Tahsin bey ["*bey*" is a collo-
quial term of respect], if you put someone in a cave for two months,
made him abstain from meat ... and for those two months he never
disconnected from God, after two months that person could come out
of the cave with special abilities. Maybe he could even fly! And he
will see the stature of people outside, [but] will not be able to connect
with them. He could even fly to the stars! But people will call him
crazy, anyway, and not accept him among themselves." He went on,
"Tahsin bey, these things aren't important, to fly, to be exceptional.
But the courageous man is the one who can live with the people. He
will be happy with them. He will be sad with them. So [Hizmet] must
happen through living with the people." This was my first lesson. He
was talking about me.[49]

Şimşek stayed in business—eventually amassing a considerable
fortune—which of course did not hurt the effort to build dormitories
and (eventually) schools.

The student houses played a crucial role in forging a movement.
By the time many of them were built (roughly 1972-78), Gülen had been
teaching Qur'an students for nearly a decade. Many of his former students went on to be the "elders" in the dorms as they were established.
One historian described how

> The lighthouses play a crucial role in attracting more young people to
> join the Gülen movement. Gülen treats these lighthouses as the home
> of Ibn-i Erkam [a companion of the Prophet who turned his home
> into a retreat, study, and mentoring center], and by doing so seeks to
> give the same religiohistorical mission to them and to those who live
> in them as expressed in the original ideals of Islam. Members of the
> movement treat these houses as sacred places where private identities
> and convictions are built and put into practice.[50]

In an interview, Gülen articulated that the dormitories existed to
shelter youth from "disbelief and corruptive influences. These shelters
are the lighthouses," Gülen went on, "and I hope they help each and every young person to create their personality by living together and enlightening their environment with Islamic ideals."[51]

The metaphor of "enlightening" was important. In the Qur'an, God is described as "light" in 24:35: "God is the Light of the heavens and the earth." As Gülen interpreted this verse: "It is God Who has brought and brings everything into the Light of existence from the darkness of non-existence and has made the universe an exhibition and a book to be meditated upon, nourishing our consciences with meanings that provide light for our eyes and exhilarate our hearts." Succinctly, God is the Light, and light points to God. For human beings, to recognize God's omni-presence even in ordinary natural phenomenon was an important aspect of spiritual development. "When we consider everything," Gülen wrote, "in the light of God's Light, then everything—visible or invisible—is il-luminated and speaks about its Creator and Sustainer."[52] Lightning, for instance, was a significant phenomenon within Sufism, as a sign and metaphor. "Lightning," Gülen wrote, "hits the eye like a dazzling light and reminds one that the door of the All-Beloved is ajar." This opening to the All-Beloved takes on surprising meaning, as Gülen developed it. "We recall," he wrote, "the following couplet of Ibnu'l-Farid [a twelfth century Egyptian Sufi], a couplet full of excitement: 'Has a dazzling lightning flashed from the direction of Mount Sinai/ Or have the veils over the face of Layla been opened part way?'" Gülen is here referring to a famous figure in Islamic literature—Layla. The story of Layla's romance with a man called Majnun is, in many ways, a ninth century version of Orhan Pamuk's tale of Füsun and Kemal. Majnun loves Layla, but he is unable to marry her (she gets married to another). Majnun goes crazy (indeed, his name *means* "crazy" in Arabic) in undying devotion to her. At the same time, Layla maintains a quiet, yet unrealized, devotion to Majnun. Majnun writes copious poems to Layla, and eventually, near the end of their lives, he reads them to her. For Gülen, then, Layla was on a literal level this beloved figure in literature. But on another level, and as inter-preted in Sufism, Layla was also a representation of "The Truly Beloved One, Who is God Almighty." Layla was a *projection* of the divine in the female, always eluding one's grasp, but always loving. Gülen interpreted the "lightning" of Layla in this theological way: "So it is that while [peo-ple were] living in the dark night of corporeality and bodily desires, Layla began to show herself step by step and to send the hope of union into ... hearts, and in the end the nights changed into days in the hearts of those who had been burning for union with her."[53] Layla opened herself, and showed herself, step by step to those who sought her. Such revelation was

lightning, indeed. As developed by Gülen, then, "enlightenment" signified the desire that motivated businessmen to build "houses of light," and
it also characterized the desire that motivated young people to live and to
work in them. Both kinds of desire were also desire for God.

Now, Gülen also wrote and spoke somewhat more practically
about what he had in mind for the dormitories or student houses. "The
lighthouses are places," he offered:

> where ... people's deficiencies ... are healed. They are sacred places
> where plans and projects are produced ... and courageous and faithful
> people are being raised. Said Nursi himself said that "the [people] who
> acquire the true faith can challenge the universe.
>
> It is undoubtedly clear that today the conquest of the world can
> be realized not on the back of a horse, a sword in hand, a scimitar ...
> at the waist, a quiver on the back like the old times, but by penetrating
> into people's hearts with the Qur'an in one hand and reason in the
> other. Here, these soldiers of spirituality and truth raised in lighthous-
> es will pour the light that God has given them for inspiration into
> empty minds and help them flourish on the way to the conquest of the
> world in spirit and reality. Thus, these houses are one workbench or
> one school where these directionless and confused generations who
> have shaped themselves according to dominant fashionable ideas are
> now healed and (then) return ... to their spiritual roots with its accom-
> panying meaningful life.[54]

Gülen's military language was striking, but he used it to subvert
militarism. Youth clamoring for a cause could, through *hizmet*, conquer
the world—nonviolently. And they could do so not by killing and dying,
but by "flourishing," and by living a "meaningful life."

Such language would seem sheer idealism. In practice, however,
the student houses were early experiments in the kinds of specialized
dormitories or apartments for students that have now become common-
place on U.S. college campuses. Today on most college campuses there
are dorms for athletes, for engineers, for German studies majors—and
so on. Gülen anticipated this desire among young people to live with a
like-minded and focused group of peers. He also perceived that these
specialized dormitories could serve as a way-station to protect conservative Muslims from corrosive practices—something parents (who may

still have been footing the bill) no doubt appreciated. What Gülen may not have foreseen, but which has proven to be the case, was that these specialized dorms could also serve as a kind of hot-house for a competitive pursuit of excellence—both in academics, and in religious life. Most of the early student houses, and many down to the present, were small, with five or six same-sex students in a single house or apartment. The peer pressure to succeed was intense. They also lived under the watchful eye of an older "brother" or "sister," who both monitored troubles and encouraged aspiration. "For these reasons," as another historian put it, "conservative and religious parents encourage[d] their boys and girls to live in the lighthouses in big cities."[55] Young people flocked to them.

By 1973 there were four or five such houses around Izmir. İrfan Yılmaz encountered one of them while at university during the early '70s. At the light-house, Yılmaz first learned about Nursi's *Risale-i Nur*. Because "to read *Risale* in public made people nervous and suspicious," Yılmaz felt compelled to cover it in newspaper whenever he was in public. He was not particularly pious. He went to prayers on Friday, and fasted during Ramadan, but he had experienced hostility even for this basic level of commitment to Islam. There were, in other words, incentives in Turkish society for people *not* to practice their faith. But Yılmaz met another young man, named İbrahim, who was staying in one of the student houses. İbrahim invited İrfan to attend a *sohbet* there. The speaker was Gülen. When Hodjaefendi arrived, the crowd grew excited. İrfan was a little "intimidated" by this enthusiasm, so he "slipped out," as he recalled it later. But a year after this first brief encounter with Hizmet, he attended a conference that Gülen had organized on science and religion—and managed to stay put. "I learned then about Hodjaefendi," Yılmaz simply said. His friends invited him to Gülen's sermons in Bornova, and he attended. After receiving his degree and beginning graduate studies in zoology, he was asked to become a tutor to high school students who were connected to the houses of light. "I said, 'yes,'" he recalled. "Of course," he went on, "this was free of charge." He was one of several tutors—in physics, English, biology, and so forth. "This was in 1977," he remembered. "We were giving lessons to students; not all of us had finished [our own studies]. Some of us were still students. But it worked. We helped 90% of our students get into college. 'See,' Hodjaefendi said, 'it works!'"[56]

The student houses served, in the metaphor of Mustafa Özcan, who lived in one of the dorms for five years, as a "highway for religious families." It wasn't only that the houses became safe places away from "corrupting" influences—although that was part of it. More deeply, according to Özcan, "when these houses were opened this provided a chance for religious people to educate their children and be a part of the entire society." The intensity of leftist and nationalist factions made parents reluctant to send their children to the best universities. "So, when Hodjaefendi introduced this idea of providing accommodation for college students, this opened the way for religious families to integrate into the society," suggested Özcan. Naturally, at the same time, "this [innovation] attracted the animosity of some radical Muslim groups." Revolution, not reform or renewal, was still the preferred option for many young Muslims—as Iran would soon reveal. But the participation of religious youth in the best boarding schools and universities across Turkey "shifted the whole system," Özcan concluded.[57] A highway between Islam and scientific learning had been opened for young Muslims.

Dorms for women opened more slowly, but in coming decades multiplied rapidly. Yusuf Pekmezci offered that while equality of educational opportunity officially existed in the Republic of Turkey, in fact "in those days we didn't educate our females." Some women went to secular schools, where parents (and Muslim leaders generally) had "no control" over them, Pekmezci suggested. Other women simply didn't continue their education. Pekmezci's attitude no doubt spoke for many: "They could get into bad things," he said. "We didn't want our daughters to go into that." The solution seemed obvious. So, "we opened the girls' dorms." Young men and women would live in separate dorms, but of course "they would study together, and ... they were mixed in the universities," Pekmezci recalled. "Bad things" could still happen. But the girls' dorms generally provided a way for pious Muslim fathers (and mothers) to feel better about the risk of sending their daughters to continue their education. Esra Koşar, who grew up in a small town in Central Anatolia, was one of them. She lived in a student house in Ankara while in college. "My father was conservative," she offered, acknowledging the obvious that such conservatism was often a barrier to higher education for many girls. The problem was *mobility*, she suggested—a daughter would have to move to study, and "if you're not mobile, you can't get an education," Koşar put it. The Hizmet dorms for young women "opened that door," she said. "Many of my friends came to Ankara *only* because of the presence of Hizmet dormitories," she offered. "There was deep trust in these places," she concluded. "Hizmet has been a bridge for many, many girls."[58]

So—a "highway," an "opened door," a "bridge"—pick your metaphor. The dorms were popular. Students chose them, parents liked them, business people supported them. Naturally, there was an element of self-interest on all sides of this dynamic. "There were certain benefits," as sociologist Joshua Hendrick gently put it, that the students especially could anticipate. Hendrick tells the story, for instance, of "Osman," who moved into one of the new dormitories as a high school student [the location is uncertain] in 1978. The *dershane* had "new beds, new books, and state-of-the-art construction." Then, in 1979, at the urging of the "elder" in his house of light, Osman took a trip to Izmir. What he encountered there persuaded him to participate fully in Hizmet. He recalled:

> The *cemaat* [Gülen community] was 80 percent young, dynamic university students.... It was the first time we saw him [Gülen]. We both listened to the preaching in Izmir and we also visited the places where students stayed. We saw what kind of people they were. We were influenced by two things. The first was the person of Hocaefendi, and the other thing was the people we saw in the houses of the movement, because they were pretty good models. I mean we found their lives to be very spiritual. They were very friendly, very spiritual, the houses were rather modern ... they were unmarried people, but the houses were very modern and ... we were surprised.[59]

As the comment suggests, student housing in non-Hizmet affiliated homes could be disorderly, haphazard, and not well-maintained. Conversely, home owners, in a pattern replicated in every college town around the world, were often reluctant to rent to students. In any event, along with orderly and modern living conditions, Osman received free tutoring at his own student house, as organized by an "older brother." That led him to a high score on the national exam (the Turkish version of the SAT or ACT). And that enabled Osman to study at a university in Ankara—something he had not initially imagined for himself. Hendrick draws the conclusion: "Modern housing, free tutoring, and a focused and engaged mentor all contributed to Osman's entrance" into Hizmet.

Osman became, over time, a teacher and then an administrator in Hizmet-related agencies. If students could anticipate such a benefit from the program, parents obviously liked the idea of a safe place to send their children, and they no doubt appreciated that their offspring also had a career path to a sustainable livelihood. Donors received the benefits of stature that accrue to any donor, and (ultimately) received the blessing of Allah for their good deed, in the end.

That people had self-interested or economic motives to engage with a Hizmet student house did not rule out other motives to participate. Most people have multiple reasons for major life decisions, and economic reductionism—the assumption that people make choices *only* for economic reasons, is as deadly a simplification as any other. And in any event, the student houses were *intended* to open avenues to education for people. And education is a highway that goes two ways. People gain knowledge that can help them overcome the suffering of ignorance, thereby improving themselves. But education can also, one can hope, stoke in people the desire to share their knowledge and put it to good-use on behalf of others. Traffic went both directions on these Gülen-inspired highways. And it was the latter possibility—the *engaging* of empathy—that the Gülen-inspired student houses especially sought to foster. Students could acquire technical skills at countless boarding schools and universities across Turkey. The Gülen-inspired student houses provided students a way to orient their burgeoning skills toward alleviating the suffering of others. Young people could live *for a cause.*

Summer camps and a "golden generation"

A similar goal was evident in the summer camps that Gülen and his associates began starting in 1966. They ran throughout the following decade (1971, following the coup, was an exception). Yusuf Pekmezci was again involved. "So Hodjaefendi decided to have a summer camp," Pekmezci simply put it. "We thought he was thinking something like the Boy Scouts. 'Are we going to do Boy Scouting with kids?'" Pekmezci wondered. The idea of getting dressed up in paramilitary uniforms with a bunch of youth was not immediately appealing to the former street fighter. "And, then Hodjaefendi said," as Pekmezci remembered it, "'the youth [most of whom were middle-school aged], when they go out into summer, they forget most of the things they learned. So, let's do a summer camp.'" What Gülen had in mind, in other words, was more like summer *school* set in a natural environment than a traditional camp.

Yet the setting in nature had its rationale, too. In his 1910 essay "The Moral Equivalent of War," American philosopher William James had suggested that young people would be stronger citizens if they were tested in their youth by encountering the strenuous conditions of the natural world.[60] Youth would learn in nature, and through the hard work that living in untamed nature required, acquire key skills that would sublimate their aggressive impulses into cooperation. In the wilderness, young people could discover a beauty that transcended nation, and they could encounter challenges from which they might learn traits like self-forgetfulness and disinterestedness. It is not likely that Fethullah Gülen knew James' essay. But his instinct in starting summer camps for secondary schoolers shared similar motives. "Nature," Gülen once wrote, "is much more than a heap of materiality or an accumulation of objects: It has a certain sacredness, for it is an arena in which God's Beautiful Names are displayed." This display could motivate people to action, even to "the extent of foregoing the passion of life to enable others to live, and service to all creation." The camps thus served the goal of *hizmet*. They connected head and heart, learning and loving, through collective labor. "As stated by Bediüzzaman [Said Nursi]," Gülen went on, "there is an understanding of education that sees the illumination of the mind in science and knowledge, and the light of the heart in faith and virtue." The camps were little laboratories in scientific living, but the students in them would also study Islam. "This [combination], which makes the student soar … [with] two wings," as Gülen explained the theory, "has many things to offer. It rescues science from materialism … from being a lethal weapon." And it rescues "religion [from being] cut off from intelligence [and] life," and from being "a fanatical institution that builds walls between individuals and nations."[61] The summer camps—like all the Gülen-inspired educational activities—sought to give youth "two wings." They brought together nature and nurture, science and cultural formation. They were rites of passage, at least, if not the moral equivalent of war.

Gülen intended the camps to be more than recreational babysitting. They were one of the ways to foster what he began calling in 1977 a "golden generation." Such a lofty label was no doubt attractive to many aspiring Muslim youth. Who wouldn't want to be part of that? That golden generation would be:

> individuals of integrity who, free from external influences, can manage independently of others. ... While making the fullest use of modern facilities, they will not neglect their traditional and spiritual values.... They will be completely truth-loving and trustworthy and, in support of truth everywhere, always ready to leave their families and homes when necessary.... [They will] use the mass media and try to establish a new power balance of justice, love, respect and equality among people. They will make might subservient to right, and never discriminate on grounds of race or color. These new people will unite profound spirituality, diverse knowledge, sound thinking, a scientific temperament, and wise activism. Never content with what they know, they will continuously increase in knowledge: knowledge of self, of nature, and of God.... [They] will be altruists who embrace humanity with love and are ready to sacrifice themselves for the good of others when necessary.... [T]hey will see science and religion as two manifestations of the same truth. They will never be reactionary. They will not pursue events, for they will be the dynamism of history that initiates and shapes events.... These new people will conquer their selves, thoughts, and hearts, and those of others, and they will discover the unknown.[62]

Such inspiring language has the potential to be exploited, as terrorists would do in a few short years to rationalize their own criminal actions and to motivate suicide bombings—more killing and dying. But Gülen's focus could not be more different than that of terrorists. He sought, again, to motivate young people to *live* for a cause, not to *die* for a cause. He used dynamic language to engage youth, no doubt. And it worked. But his goal was not to have them react to any enemy, and certainly not to kill and to die. Instead, youth would "conquer their selves" by learning to love learning. They would "sacrifice themselves" not to blow people up, but to "embrace humanity." They would even "make might subservient to right," through "knowledge of self, of nature, and of God." These were lofty goals for a summer camp. Yet among the first participants were several who went on to become leaders within the Hizmet movement—where they could and did live for a cause.

Yusuf Pekmezci was, again, among them. He was not a student, but he was one of the *mütevelli* whose fundraising made the camp possible. He described the scene:

> The first camp was in a region near Izmir called Buca. There was no electricity in the camp, so Hodjaefendi would pull water from the well and then put it into containers. He wouldn't ask the students to come and help him. But the students would sometimes go anyway out of respect. Hodjaefendi would cook, clean, [do work] wherever necessary.

Most frequently, of course, Gülen taught. He reacquainted the young men with Qur'anic exegesis and theology, but they also discussed secular topics. Gülen was the inspiration behind the camps, but "I never saw him give an order to anyone." Pekmezci went on:

> He would do whatever needed to be done by himself, first. One day I asked him, "Hodjaefendi, we are normal people. We understand from verbal education, but you're teaching by doing. When there's something to be done you get up and do it first. So, tell us what we need to do. You're not telling us, and then we do it wrong!" ... Hodjaefendi responded, "Am I going to interrupt my own habits because of you? If something needs to be done, why are you waiting for an order from someone else? Just do it! If you do it wrong the first time, you'll correct it for yourself on a second try."[63]

It was a lesson an advertising agency for an athletic apparel company would in due course make its own trademark: just do it!

Mustafa Özcan joined the camps as a student in their second summer. He continued to attend every summer thereafter until 1975. He recalled that they began because Gülen "convinced a few businessmen to support children [by starting] summer camps." The natural setting mattered to Özcan. "Being in nature, on a mountain," he said, felt "like you are on holiday time, but actually you are still working—and still learning." Gülen's idea to have a summer camp that drew youth from "thirty different cities in Turkey," as Özcan remembered the make-up of the camp community, was "original" and quickly became popular:

> Parents liked the idea. After those students gained education [during the summer] they went back to their cities and created [greater inter-

est in Hizmet].... [Anyone] who had some type of religious sensitivity, at least, when they heard about these programs they were interested in these camps ... because otherwise their summertime was not spent meaningfully.[64]

Again, living for a cause meant spending your time meaningful-ly.

Mehmet Küçük attended camp at Buca for several years in the late 1960s as well. He recalled that:

Gülen brought sixty students in two big tents, while he slept in a small tent alongside them. The second year we built small sheds [cottages]. ... We did not have food, but people from the village supported us. Since we were not from well-off families, the mütevelli met the expenses for the camps. At that time, the political situation was rather tense, there were a lot of anarchists and communists around, and moreover the police did not allow religious meetings, [so] we had to be on guard in case someone would come and harm us. In the beginning, only students from the Qur'an school (Kestanepazarı) came, but later other students ... joined them.[65]

So, in addition to whatever dangers nature posed to those at camp, the young people and Hodjaefendi also had to contend with dangers from political enemies and the police. İsmail Büyükçelebi remembered that "soldiers would routinely" come to the camp to check for "clandestine activities." Students learned to hide their copies of the *Risale-i Nur*, and even to stack their bed rolls one on top of the other to make their numbers appear smaller. But the camps grew—from 60 to 120 to 275 campers in the first three years—despite the dangers of police or soldiers.[66]

More often, though, the dangers were of the natural variety. İsmail Büyükçelebi remembered that at one of the camps, a water source was a spring that would occasionally dry up. When it did so, flies became so thick as to become unbearable. Büyükçelebi remembers his friend İbrahim Kocabıyık recommending the use of a pesticide—an understandable choice under the circumstances. But Gülen, as Büyükçelebi recalled, refused even this act of killing. "We have no right to do anything to these animals," Gülen said. "But it's us or them," the students pleaded.

"Then," Büyükçelebi remembers Gülen saying, "we move the camp." So, they did. "This was not easy," Büyükçelebi recollected. "We had to build a new kitchen, toilet, septic, etc. It was hard. But through these hardships we didn't do any harm."[67] Peacebuilding for Fethullah Gülen wasn't only about Qur'an lessons. It was also, as the adage has it, about not even harming a fly.

Such a commitment to non-violence can seem like an excessively scrupulous list of prohibitions: don't do this, don't do that. But for Gülen, more often, the struggle to engage with others out of empathy on behalf of peace fell squarely under the much-contested category of *jihad*. "Derived from the [Arabic] root *j-h-d*," Gülen explained, "*jihad* means using all one's strength, as well as moving toward an objective with all one's power and strength and resisting every difficulty." More specifically,

> *Jihad* gained a special characteristic with the advent of Islam: striving in the path of God. This is the meaning that usually comes to mind today. This striving occurs on two fronts: the internal and the external. The internal one can be described as the effort to attain one's essence; the external one as the process of enabling someone else to attain his or her essence. This first is the greater *jihad*; the second is the lesser *jihad*. The first is based on overcoming obstacles between oneself and his or her essence, and the soul's reaching knowledge and eventually divine knowledge, divine love, and spiritual bliss. The second is based on removing obstacles between people and faith so that people can have a free choice to adopt a way. … In a sense, the lesser *jihad* is material. The greater *jihad*, however, is conducted on the spiritual front, for it is our struggle with our inner world and ego (*nafs*). … proclaiming war on our ego's destructive and negative emotions and thoughts (e.g., malice, hatred, envy, selfishness, pride, arrogance, and pomp) which prevent us from attaining perfection.[68]

The primary *jihad*, like the purpose of the summer camps, was not to oppose anything. Rather, the young people gathered around Gülen were being empowered in the "effort to attain one's essence" by "striving in the path of God." We shall have occasion to attend to this facet of Gülen's teaching in future chapters as well, given how the concept of *jihad* became liable both to misuse by extremists and to misrepresentation by Islamo-phobes. But, for now, it is enough to know that Gülen gathered together young people in camps, where they learned in nature to wage the greater *jihad*—a *jihad* of love, you might even call it. That police and military suspected another kind of *jihad* was their problem.

Tutoring centers and scholarships

So, the Hizmet movement that sought to invite young people to live for a cause had now spread to summer camps along with student-houses. Two other initiatives from this time-period endured as crucial elements in the movement down until the very recent past: tutoring centers and scholarship programs. The tutoring centers were also (unfortunately for future historians like me) called *dershanes*—here translated colloquially as "cram schools" or "college-prep schools." These study-centers helped prepare high school students for the Turkish college placement examinations. Unlike in the U.S., where a student can take the SAT or ACT numerous times per year, in Turkey the key test(s) can only be taken once per year. The exams have been called various things since their establishment in the late 1960s, but the earliest bore the ominous sounding name of the ÖSS—*Öğrenci Seçme Sınavı,* or "Student Selection Examination."[69] The ominous name was appropriate, for the test was a barrier to higher education for many students. It was widely perceived as biased, if not corrupt. Many thought the exams were tilted to favor the children of political and military elites (secularists), and thereby to protect privilege more than to ascertain worthiness to continue learning. The competition was fierce: there were roughly four applicants for every opening at a Turkish university in the 1970s. So, following the same pattern as with the camps and dormitories, Hizmet volunteers opened some cram schools or tutoring centers. Unlike with those other examples, it does not appear that this initiative began with Fethullah Gülen. Rather, the schools grew organically out of the successful informal tutoring efforts in the student houses. This was a historical precedent important to the future of the Hizmet movement. Gülen may well have approved of the tutoring centers, but I have found no evidence that he initiated them. Still, they worked. Students attended the schools in the evenings or weekends—usually over the course of ten months to a year, and in short order the Hizmet-connected study centers gained a reputation for results in a competition whose stakes could not have been higher for youth. "180 Minutes = A Life?" as one bumper-sticker critique of the system put it in later years. In any event, the results were reported annually in national newspapers, and the tutoring centers multiplied dramatically, numbering more than 3,500 in Turkey by 2010.[70] Not all of them were connected to Hizmet; other entrepreneurs recognized a potential revenue stream when they saw one. But the Hizmet study centers routinely placed the highest number of their graduates in universities, including among the most prestigious schools in Turkey.

Not surprisingly, given their success, the tutoring centers also became a means of recruiting gifted students for the student houses. Scholar Caroline Tee documented how a network of recruiting emerged within Hizmet, vertically integrated roughly from middle school years through adulthood, as tutoring centers also began to emerge to assist middle school students in taking the tests required for acceptance into elite high schools. The *dershanes* were often a first point of contact for recruits into the Hizmet orbit. Tee writes:

> This network of recruitment often begins before the years of university study. ... Students who have attended a Gülen School or tutoring center (*dershane*) often relate ... [how] they were directed by an *abla/abi* [older sister or brother] (most often a teacher) to a Gülen house within the same network in the city where they have gone to undertake university study. There is ... a keen concern for maintaining contact with individuals who have been exposed to the movement and to the teachings of Gülen.[71]

On one level, that concern could seem utilitarian—a way of insuring income and sustainability. On another level, it was altruistic—a way of opening opportunities for students otherwise excluded from them. Both were part of it.

Over the decades since the 1970s, similar efforts to help young people prepare for national exams spread to other regions of the world where such efforts made sense, notably Central Asia and Europe. The schools in Germany, for instance, which began among the large Turkish community in that country, were effective not only as cram centers, but also as bridges to cultural integration. Bayram Balci, in a 2014 essay for the Carnegie Endowment for International Peace, reported that:

The Gülen movement's educational network in Europe also includes hundreds of *dershane*, or private centers that tutor secondary-school students to improve their academic performance and prepare them for university entrance exams. These institutions frequently offer weekend classes to assist vulnerable children from underprivileged social backgrounds, hailing often but not only from Turkish immigrant families. The *dershane* thus make it possible for these vulnerable young people to go to college while simultaneously helping Turkish migrants integrate into their host societies.[72]

Given their importance, then, it should not be surprising that when the Turkish government began to target Gülen agencies for closure and asset-seizure in 2013, it focused quite early on the *dershanes*, which by that point served well over a million students. By then, of course, several generations had already benefited from the Hizmet initiatives. If the graduates of those programs did not necessarily constitute a "golden generation," they did constitute an intellectual elite in Turkey. They also had begun to put down roots in many places around the world. And in those places outside of Turkey where *abi*s and *abla*s had settled, it was of course difficult for the Turkish government to close down programs that served the purposes of students, their parents, and their host countries. We will track some of these stories in more detail in Chapter Five.

The scholarship programs that began in the late '60s and early '70s ran across the various initiatives. That is, students in need could receive financial assistance--subsidies or scholarships, to live in the student houses, to attend camp, or to study at the tutoring centers. The subsidies tended to be across the board—in lower than market rents or tuition. The scholarships, though, were need-based. They came from the same funding sources as the supplies and buildings: the *mütevelli*. Sociologist Helen Rose Ebaugh explained how Hizmet fundraising worked, in an example from building the first Hizmet school, Yamanlar in Izmir—a story told in more detail in the next chapter:

> A wealthy businessman [sic] in Istanbul who is a major contributor relayed a story of the first fund raising meeting to build the very first Gülen-inspired school.... "Mr. Gülen gave a motivational speech. He said it was important to help needy students and then gave historical examples from the life of the Prophet and his companions. At that

event I saw people writing checks, giving cash and some offering gold rings and bracelets. I was deeply impacted by that scene that I saw, people giving so immediately and generously. From this first impact, I thought this is something I wanted to be part of. I then saw the successes of the projects and I became part of the movement." He went on to elaborate on other examples of giving that influenced him. He saw blue collar workers with families who were making very little every month but dedicating 20% of their income to support, perhaps, half or one-fourth of a scholarship for a needy student. He realized that these people might be taking public transportation but [were] giving to help students. Later he got involved in fund raising meetings and saw what people were doing to raise money for Gülen-inspired projects, some donating keys to their cars, giving their gold watches, and women offering their jewelry to support students. A person in Izmir ... [sold *lahmacun* (Turkish meat pizza)] from a cart to raise money to build a small dorm in a neighboring small town. The more he witnessed these examples of giving, the stronger was his motivation to do his part to support the worthwhile projects. He made a commitment to donate one third of his income to further his business, one third to supporting family, and the remaining one third to Gülen projects.[73]

Such engaged empathy from across classes quickly did more than sponsor scholarships. It grew a movement centered on education. Young people could count on financial support and safe housing. Parents could relax a bit about the expenses of education and the well-being of their children. And those with means (even modest ones) could feel good about contributing to a cause.

All in all, in the Hizmet movement of the 1970s that Fethullah Gülen inspired, Turkish common people "found their voices and talked back to the elites who used to speak for them," as historian Carter Vaughn Findley aptly put it.[74] The initiatives that Gülen and his closest associates put in place—dorms, camps, tutoring centers, and scholarship programs, helped to democratize Turkey. Gülen and those close to him created opportunities for hitherto excluded groups to participate in civil society. This was the case notably for rising middle-class and devout Muslims. Not surprisingly, this populist awakening drew resistance from the secular elite. But the changes were systemic, and inexorable. Over

the course of Fethullah Gülen's life, Turkey—like most of the world—
had rapidly modernized. Technology made agriculture easier and more
efficient, freeing workers to move to cities. Education—mandatory in
Turkey since the 1920s—raised literacy rates to unprecedented levels.
And a population explosion—the baby boom was a global phenomenon—made youth in Turkey both a potential and a problem. Militaries exploited the potential, but thereby exacerbated the problem. Young
people around the world were asking, in effect, "was dying for a cause
the only option?" The burgeoning Hizmet movement suggested another
way. Young people could live for a cause that might even outlive their
own existence. Osman Şimşek, who came into Hizmet somewhat later,
but who understood this crucial dynamic, put it well: "Instead of being
a martyr, [our] desire was to *live* as a Muslim; more than desire, this
became our love."[75] And many of those young people who had learned
to *live* for love, including Fethullah Gülen himself, were now moving
into middle-age. If they were not a "golden generation" themselves, then,
perhaps they could help raise one.

*Abi*s and *abla*s: engaged empathy in brotherhood and sisterhood

Obviously, not all, or even most, of the individuals drawn to Fethullah
Gülen would share his commitment to a celibate existence. In fact, the
vast-majority of Hizmet volunteers participated while also raising families. Naturally, one of the fringe benefits of participation in any kind of
youth movement is that young people met other young people. Not surprisingly, then, some of the young people of Hizmet wound up marrying
each other. A few of them, those closest to Gülen, sought his blessing
on their union. And when they began to have children, a few of those
few even asked Gülen to help them name their children.[76] Family life, in
short, was a powerful facet of the burgeoning Hizmet movement. It was
also a frequent theme in Fethullah Gülen's teaching and preaching.

"The surest foundation for a nation," Gülen once suggested, "is a
family in which material and spiritual happiness flows, for such a family
serves as a sacred school that raises virtuous individuals." Gülen's language of the family as a "sacred school" was arresting. Many an American or European has been struck by the Turkish custom of removing

one's shoes before entering a home. This is also the practice, of course, before entering a mosque. What Gülen did was to make explicit what was implicit in everyday Turkish practice: a family home, like a mosque, was to be a sacred space. But Gülen pushed the connection even further—a family home was a sacred *school*. He no doubt reflected here on his own village upbringing, where his parents were his first teachers. But he clearly wanted formal schools for children as well, in a mutually-beneficial partnership. Thus, "if a nation can make its homes as enlightened and prosperous as its schools, and its schools as warm as its homes, it has made the greatest reform and has guaranteed the contentment and happiness of future generations." Such happiness would be based not on punishment or the removal of negative traits. "Improving a community," Gülen taught, "is possible only by elevating the younger generations to the rank of humanity, not by obliterating the bad ones." This may seem like common sense. In practice and history, however, a fear-driven, punitive, or coercive educational milieu was common in Turkey (as in many places). With psychological insight, then, Gülen encouraged emerging Hizmet families that "if children and young people are brought up in a climate where their enthusiasm is stimulated with higher feelings, they will have vigorous minds and display good morals and virtues."[77]

This was an optimistic prescription. But in his vision of the family as a "sacred school," Gülen's language of "the nation" was important. There can be little question that at this point in his life Hodjaefendi was oriented, if not limited, to efforts within Turkey. Some scholars have mistakenly generalized from passages like these to depict Gülen as a simple "nationalist."[78] Gülen has, indeed, throughout his life expressed both love and concern for his native land. In his room there is soil in dozens of small jars from many places across Turkey. They take up three shelves in a bookcase at the retreat center in Pennsylvania. So, Gülen was an advocate for a strong Turkey: "we applaud every good deed and attempt made in the name of the nation, and stand behind the fortunate people who serve it," he once wrote.[79] On other occasions, Gülen wrote or spoke about the Ottomans, and even the Seljuks (earlier rulers of Anatolia), in ways that indicated healthy amounts of national pride. He came by this honestly; in varying degrees, every Turk was, by definition, a nationalist. Nationalism was one of the explicit principles of Atatürk's twentieth century reforms. It produced its share of destructiveness. As M.

Hakan Yavuz and John L. Esposito put it, in strong but accurate terms, Atatürk's attempt to create a homogeneous Turkish nation "destroyed the multiethnic character of Turkish society by getting rid of Greeks and other Christian communities and by denying the Kurds their cultural rights."[80]

But in contrast to Atatürk's top-down and monochrome nationalism, Gülen even very early in his teaching and preaching sought to strengthen and to reform Turkish culture from the "bottom-up," starting with individuals and families. His vision of Turkey's future was thus of necessity a multi-ethnic and multicultural mix. If Hizmet began with individuals in all of their diversity, then how could Hizmet families, much less the Turkish nation, all be of one stripe? Indeed, as Gülen himself grew increasingly aware of the potential of this kind of reform from below, his vision became correspondingly more cosmopolitan and global. Not that his early vision was *inherently* parochial. He taught and practiced a model of society marked by dialogue and consultation. But that model reflected what he knew as a Turk whose only experience outside of his country was the *Hajj*. Nevertheless, what he offered to Turks was a model of society that began in the family. And the central metaphor there was not the patriarchal fatherhood of traditional Turkish culture. The central familial metaphor for Fethullah Gülen, and in the emerging Hizmet movement, was sisterhood and brotherhood. And as history and sacred texts well reveal, sisters and brothers were not always known for their unanimity. Sisters and brothers tended to differ, sometimes dramatically. So Fethullah Gülen built a movement where diverse and even competing voices between "sisters and brothers" were not only present, but welcome.

The language is ubiquitous in the literature about Hizmet. It was also widely used in everyday practice—dating from the 1970s. Sociologist Joshua Hendrick describes how the dorms were:

> organized in accordance with an age- and experience-defined system of authority, which begins with an internal authority figure, a male *ağabey* ("older brother," informally = *abi*; female = *abla*) in each student apartment. The [brother or sister's] job is to manage the affairs of students, to monitor study habits, to recommend reading material, to organize reading groups, to administer tutoring sessions for visiting

high school students, and to function as liaisons between the house and the larger ... network ... in a loosely configured hierarchy of authority.[81]

It is worth highlighting Hendrick's conclusion that this network was "loosely configured." That mirrors the pattern of relationships that emerged between Gülen's earliest associates and friends across Turkey in the 1970s. As the dorms, tutoring centers, and scholarships proved their value, sisters and brothers who were particularly skilled emerged as leaders. They then passed along what they had received to the next generation, as *abi*s and *abla*s. This was how Gülen's legacy has been promulgated and sustained; how a movement spread.

It is impossible to overestimate the importance of personal relationships as the crucial "glue" that bound people to Gülen and to Hizmet. If there was a "charismatic" leadership to the movement, in other words, it was *shared* charisma, diffused and localized as "brotherly" and "sisterly" love. One participant, identified only as Ferhat by Hendrick, captured the power of these relationships with big sisters and brothers that began to clarify themselves in the 1970s:

> Sayid [his *abi*] came from the U.S. ... Sayid was like an idol for me, you know. [From him] we learned English properly. At grade eight and nine, he attended our class ... and he was such a different person ... He had this appeal, I cannot explain it. I mean, every one of our teachers were different. They were not typical street layman. They were all different. But Sayid, for me, was like an idol. I think I even tried to make my speech like him. I tried to walk like him ... I tried to dress like him ... and I later realized that many of my friends also tried to do the same in a way [laugh].

Ferhat had planned to study business, but Sayid encouraged him instead to study English—to prepare to be a teacher or translator. "We need to have really qualified translators," Ferhat remembers his *abi* saying:

> "I recommend that you [study] English language[], [in] a foreign languages department at whatever university you want to go. ... Going into a business administration, management ... you could do certain things for your own good. But ... if you could be a really good teacher, or a good translator, then this could really could [sic] be a good service [*hizmet*]."

Such a change in his future plans was not easy for Ferhat. He re-called crying over the decision. And yet Hendrick draws the conclusion: "On the 'advice' of his [abi], Ferhat majored in English and became a translator. ... Why did Ferhat relinquish his dreams to follow his abi's advice? He did so, he explains, because [Hizmet] is about self-sacri-fice." And yet for Ferhat, as Hendrick ultimately records, the sacrifice also brought reward. "This actually made my entire life more beautiful," Ferhat put it. "I felt that I was a member of a bigger group, a bigger ... service [hizmet]."[82] Similar stories of big brothers and sisters changing lives to make them "more beautiful" began to be told across Turkey in the 1970s.

Girls and women were no exception. Cambridge University re-searcher Caroline Tee interviewed "Ayşe," who became an abla or big sister in a student house in Istanbul. It was hardly a well-rationalized or rigidly hierarchical process. "All of my housemates had left the house," probably after classes ended, Ayşe began, "and they [other people of Hizmet] didn't want me to stay in the house alone. I was doing all of the administrative tasks anyway, paying the bills, and so on ... So, they called me and said, 'Congratulations! You've been chosen to be an abla.' ... I was unaware this selection process was going on!" Ayşe's life gained direction after she was selected-by-default to be a big sister. She was initially assigned two students to care for. When that went well, she was then assigned larger groups of students, moving to different dorms across Istanbul. Throughout, she herself always had access to a more se-nior abla. About one of them she recalled: "She is always immediately ready to help—to talk to my students, to warn them about how they are speaking to me, or how they are behaving. ... Also, financially, if there is a need, she will help. She is a student, too, of literature. You can go wherever and there is an abla to help you. I am rather lucky because I really love my abla."[83] Again, these relationships grew organically. Their characteristics—trust, increasing accountability, and mutual support—began with the ways Gülen related to his own students. That spirit spread to those to whom he preached. It then worked its way through busi-nessmen and trustees. And these trusting relationships expanded in the dormitories and tutoring centers through the efforts of abis and ablas.

Interestingly, as these networks grew, along with Gülen's fame, they actually rendered Gülen less directly involved with the activities of the movement he had inspired. Those inclined to imagine a "*sheikh*" model of hierarchical leadership within Hizmet, connecting everything to Fethullah Gülen, will not find much evidence in the historical record. Hizmet took on a life of its own as the brothers and sisters took care of each other. The networks they perpetuated did not need much, if any, input from "the top." One woman who both benefited from an *abla* and then became one herself put it like this: "The older *abla*s [I encountered in Hizmet] practiced *ihlas*—selflessness [sincerity]." By being sincere—*integrity* might be another word for it—they did not wait for orders from headquarters. Their motivation was from elsewhere. "They did things," this woman put it, "only for God's sake, for God's pleasure. They were role models, devoted, selfless." Recalling one of her older sisters in particular, who was her mentor while she was a university student in Trabzon, she remembered how this role model "embraced the world with compassion ... she removed herself from the equation: no ego." An egoless role model obviously set a high bar. But the pattern repeated itself. This woman remembered another *abla*, who worked with her in Eskişehir, who was "also devoted, selfless. She [also] worked for God's pleasure. But at the same time, she was knowledgable. An intellectual. She was scholarly. She was the [one] to connect me so passionately to *Risale-i Nur* ... We studied together." So, ego-less, working for God's pleasure, and intellectually-engaged: that described the ideal for a big brother or big sister. And in varying degrees, of course, people matched it. When this young woman matured and became an *abla* herself, she discovered just how widespread the pattern was. There was a "method—the Hodjaefendi method," she called it:

> You offered them some duties. You put them in charge—and by doing so, you learn. You learn by doing. That's [how] I learned. As you are concerned about others' inner struggles, you learn about your own. As you're fixing their spiritual houses, you discover how to fix your own. As Mevlana [Rumi] said: "Care for others paves the way for you."[84]

A network of brothers and sisters, locally-generated, self-sustaining, engaging empathy, inspired by Gülen but hardly dependent upon his direction, was operating. And it was this network of sisterhood and brotherhood, the "Hodjaefendi Model," that Fethullah Gülen sought to institute between people of Hizmet across Turkey in the 1970s. It was also a model that would be implemented to protect Gülen himself, in the coming decade.

Engaged empathy bridging science and religion

For the fact is that it was not easy to be an observant Muslim sister or brother in 1970s Turkey. One dramatic social location where this difficulty manifested itself was in the relationship between religion and science. Just as some Christians encountered trouble reconciling Charles Darwin with their faith, so did some Muslims. There was not exactly a war between science and religion in Turkey, as some declared in the West, but there was surely misunderstanding on both sides. The most secularist of scientists dismissed religion as sheer superstition. The most rigid people of faith buried their heads in the sand about the truths of science. In Turkey, the official position was secularist. It could produce more heat than light. For example, İrfan Yılmaz, who was studying zoology in 1970s Izmir, recalled an incident from his school days that can set the context to understand how Fethullah Gülen addressed this problem. İrfan was a pious boy. His grandmother, he recalled, liked to remind him that God was the Creator of everything. "But in middle school," Yılmaz goes on

my physics teacher said "nature makes it rain. The sun heats up the waters and condensation occurs." He made an experiment in class and said: "I made it rain." He heated up a teapot, put a cover on it, and he said: "Do you see, children? I made it rain. There is no God here." I interjected. I said: "Everything is done by Allah." And then my teacher came back and said: "Look, son, that's not how it is." Then I interjected again. I became stubborn. I interrupted every time to say, "God made that." He then said, "This is a bigot of the future. Probably his mother wears a headscarf." So that was the context in which we grew up. And then the whole class gave me the name of *Yobaz*—the bigot.[85]

Such pain, alienation from peers and teachers, was a common part of the experience for many observant Muslim youth under a secularist regime. The relationship between faith and science was often a flashpoint.

So, in 1975, while serving in the university neighborhood of Bornova in Izmir, Gülen organized a series of conferences on science and religion. They focused especially on the topic of Darwinism. Over the course of the year, the conferences were repeated at sites across Turkey: in Ankara, Çorum, Malatya, Diyarbakır, and Konya, among others. Yılmaz remembered attending the first conference, in Izmir. He recalled that:

> My friends invited me to this conference, but some of my other friends were saying, "Forget about this *hodja*; he only finished primary school. How can he explain anything?" Thankfully, we went … [and] I sat in the first row. It was really interesting. There was a different perspective…. The points he was making were so vital; he was getting the topic right at its crux. Even sometimes this becomes a joke between me and Hodjaefendi; this was 40 years ago. I ask him; where did you learn all that? During that time, there were no books against Darwinism. … [So] Hodjaefendi read books about Darwinism [and] from the books that supported Darwinism he was able to discredit those arguments. He read the arguments at their deepest points. That day I took Darwinism from my heart.[86]

By rejecting "Darwinism," however, Yılmaz did not embrace an anti-scientific point of view. Indeed, as we shall see, he went on to become editor of a magazine explicitly intended to explore the interface between faith and science.

Instead, the 1975 conference rejected a *particular* kind of science, summarized by the term "Darwinism." The conference also, by its very existence, rejected a particular kind of religion, which might be summarized by the term "Islamism." Gülen, characteristically, sought a middle way. He critiqued materialist or positivist science, but also critiqued an anti-scientific religion. For Gülen, as Georgetown's Osman Bakar clarified in a helpful article, the truths of religion were in one category, and the truths of science in another, but both were forms of *theological* truth. When the two intersected, it was to reveal God's glory. When they conflicted, we had more to learn. Such an approach ruled out, in effect, philosophical speculation that reduced all phenomena to materialist interactions. It's not that one didn't *study* those materialist interactions in all their specificity and detail. It's just that one didn't *reduce* all of life to those materialist interactions. In day to day practice, Gülen suggested, a Muslim scientist and a secular scientist might do identical experiments.

Physics and biology and genetics didn't change because you were a faithful Muslim. But being a faithful Muslim gave you a different place to *start* in doing that experiment. And being a faithful Muslim also gave you a different *goal* or purpose in applying what you learned in the experiment (and, perhaps, some limits on how you might apply what you learned in the experiment, for instance, in not developing any technology, whether weapons or other machines, to harm humanity or the environment).

Gülen put it this way in a writing that probably reflects some of what he shared at the 1975 conference:

> The universe, the subject matter of the sciences, is the realm where God's names are manifested, and therefore has some sort of sanctity. Everything in the universe is a letter from God Almighty inviting us to study it to have knowledge of Him. Thus, the universe is the collection of those letters or, as Muslim sages call it, the Divine Book of Creation issuing primarily from the Divine Attributes of Will and Power. The Qur'an, issuing from the Divine Will of Speech is the counterpart of the universe in verbal form. Just as there can be no conflict between a palace and the paper written to describe it, there can also be no conflict between the universe and the Qur'an, which are two expressions of the same truth.[87]

This was, to be clear, a sharp critique of the kind of dismissal of God that Yılmaz experienced at the hands of a cruel teacher. As Bakar put it, "Gülen contends ... that the modern scientific methodology is simply incapable of penetrating and knowing 'the essence of existence.' There are simply domains of reality that are beyond its competence."[88]

But if this turned the table on materialist science, or on "scientism," it also opened a critique of Muslims who *refused* to study the sciences. Indeed, Muslims should, in principle, make the best scientists. This was so because "it is the love of truth which gives the true direction to scientific studies," and Muslims were mandated to love truth. At one time—in the age of Avicenna (Ibn Sina) and Averroes (Ibn Rushd)—Gülen pointed out, Muslims *were* the world's foremost scientists. Modern science might not exist were it not for medieval Muslim thinkers. Recalling this heritage, Gülen suggested that faith in God could actually be motive and goal for the most rigorous scientific study. To be sure, such rigor required recognizing that "while the Qur'an contains allusions to many scientific truths, it is not to be read as a book of science or scientific explanations."[89] The world was large. Understanding it required many methods. In the end, all those methods originated in and would lead back to God. But it took faith along the way to recognize this truth, just as it took faith in the reliability of an experiment to undertake science. For İrfan Yılmaz, and no doubt for many others who attended those 1975 conferences, this was refreshing. Put differently, then, what Yılmaz learned was not only to "take Darwinism from" his heart. More profoundly, he learned, as he also put it, that "science and the Qur'an ... were not contradictory. The problem is us."[90] It was human interpretation that set up conflict between two of God's revelations. Gülen had suggested for Yılmaz a more peaceful way than he had experienced from either his dogmatic grandmother or his equally dogmatic teacher.

Having been inspired at the Izmir conference, Yılmaz made it a point to seek out Gülen and to meet with him personally. He remembered that Gülen told him to: "Look for a way to stay at the university. Stay a man of science.... Believers must be in these fields. In our society, the conflict between religion and science has been constant. You must show that religion and science don't conflict."[91] Four years later, in 1979, Yılmaz began to edit Sızıntı. It was the first major publication, of what would eventually be many media projects, produced by people of Hizmet. Sızıntı means literally to "leak," "seep," or "ooze." But the metaphor was designed to suggest how the subtle power of nature reflected God's magnificence. "Those who belittled you," Gülen once wrote about a single drop of water, "never thought that one day you would grow into such a waterfall."[92] Less poetically, Sızıntı aimed to bring cutting-edge science to a popular audience in ways that also revealed the compatibility of science and religion. It was modeled after Scientific American, Yılmaz explained, "without the materialism." Sızıntı's first issue, in Februrary, 1979, featured on the cover a painting by Italian Bruno Amadio, entitled "Crying Boy." Along with the painting were words from a poem by Mehmet Akif Ersoy: "You may not have compassion for yourself, but won't you have compassion for your child?" The initial press run was 6,000. Gülen anticipated more. "Inshallah [God-willing]," he told Yılmaz, "this will go into the 100,000s."[93] By the time the Turkish government shuttered the publication, in July 2016, its circulation was over 800,000.[94] Looking back after 30 years, then Editor-in-Chief Arif Sarsılmaz (pen-name for İrfan Yılmaz) recalled: "Turkey was suffering from a calamity of anarchy 30 years ago and ... we had the idea that exaggerated positivist and materialist thoughts lay behind the youth problems which were the result of misunderstanding the way the world works. There was a depression of faith and belief at the root. As time has gone by, we have come to see that the way we approach science creates a positive influence on youth."[95] *Sızıntı's* growth, and contents, will also appear in Chapter Four.

1977 preaching tours—across Turkey, and to Germany

So, while it was difficult to be an observant Islamic brother or sister in the mid-1970s in Turkey, it was not impossible. In fact, Gülen's growing stature led him to speaking opportunities across the country, and beyond. 1977 was a particularly good year. He preached at Sultanahmet mosque in Istanbul on September 9, 1977. The mosque was packed. The audience included Prime Minister Süleyman Demirel, and Secretary of State İhsan Sabri Çağlayangil. Gülen preached on "Altruistic Spirits." Altruism was rooted, he suggested, in a "sense of responsibility." Unless one truly listened to others, including of course to God, one could not truly be altruistic. And it was only through altruism that one could realize "the obligations of a person." No one existed for themselves. Islam required existence for others, and existence for others was, finally, the cause that made life worth living.[96] Gülen repeated the sermon, with some variations, in Ankara on September 30, again in the presence of dignitaries. But this single sermon was only one of many that year. He continued his practice of preaching for weeks on a topic. A series of sermons in January and February, all of them delivered at Bornova Central Mosque, focused on the positive sciences and the Qur'an. That series also attended to moral living and character development, and it concluded with a sermon about the Qur'an and European civilizations. Then, in March and April, also in Bornova, Gülen gave a multi-week series on the family and child-rearing. The themes repeated those we saw above: the family was a sacred school, and the example of the Prophet suggested mutuality and diversity, not patriarchy, as a model for family life. During summer and into the fall, Gülen preached on the topic of "Women in Islam." He interrupted the series during Ramadan in September for his trips to Istanbul and Ankara, but otherwise he continued to develop in these sermons the thesis that his family-sermons had developed: there should be no barriers to women's full inclusion in Turkish society. Islam was not an obstacle to, but a vehicle for, women's empowerment.

In December, then, Gülen traveled to Germany. He preached on the Prophet Muhammad (pbuh) in Berlin on December 9, and on moral accountability in the same city on December 10. He then traveled to Bremen, Frankfurt, Hamburg, Cologne, and Munich, where he also preached and/or gave *sohbets*. At each site, he interacted with people who had been inspired by him, and with some who were simply curious about the Turkish "celebrity" who was in town. Gülen flew back to Izmir on December 16. This was earlier than his original itinerary had anticipated. The trip did not go as expected. Some Turks connected to political Islamist currents in Turkey raised objections to Gülen's presence in Germany, and Gülen did not relish confrontation. The preacher from Erzurum was also homesick. As he put it, "I had never been apart from Turkey and my friends for so long." Twenty or so of those friends were waiting for him at the airport in Izmir. "I will never forget that warm greeting," he recalled. "We all embraced. When I returned to Izmir, I was as happy as a bird who'd found its nest. I was with my friends now."[97] Among those who were his closest friends during these years were Kemal Erimez, Mustafa Birlik, İlhan İşbilen, Cahit Erdoğan, Bekir Akgün, and Mustafa Asutay.[98]

Despite having been homesick, Gülen had enjoyed the tour to Germany, and it bore fruit with long-ranging significance for the Hizmet movement. Despite some friction, there were also ready audiences in every city for his orthodox-yet-modern Islam; a hybrid that matched the experience of the many Turks who had migrated to Germany since the 1960s. As historians Rainer Münz and Ralf E. Ulrich make plain, between 1961 and 1977 hundreds of thousands of Turks had emigrated to Germany at the invitation of the German government. The Turks were drawn by jobs, and by an agreement signed between Germany and the Republic of Turkey in 1961. By 1973, "employment of so-called guest workers reached its peak: 2.6 million, or 12 percent of all gainfully employed people in West Germany." Turks made the largest single group—605,000.[99] Word of the "crying *hodja*" had circulated among these Turkish ex-pats, so Gülen had been welcomed with crowds, if not with friends, wherever he spoke. He encouraged these Turks to take a middle way: to integrate into German society, and to practice their Islamic faith robustly and peacefully. Reflecting in later years on the opportunities he had to travel abroad— several more trips were coming in the 1980s and 90s—including a definitive one to the U.S. in 1999, Gülen observed that:

> By visiting the States and many other European countries, I realized the virtues and the role of religion in these societies. Islam flourishes in America and Europe much better than in many Muslim countries. This means freedom and the rule of law are necessary for personal Islam. Moreover, Islam does not need the state to survive, but rather needs educated and financially rich communities to flourish. In a way, not the state but rather community is needed under a fully democratic system.[100]

No doubt this was a gradual insight for Fethullah Gülen. He did not, alas, yet live in 1977 under "a fully democratic system."

Political turmoil in Turkey, another coup, and a Gandhi-like meal

Nevertheless, he carried on with his everyday activities. In that way, he was like the fictional Kemal and Füsun, and even more he was like the millions of other Turks who lived under oppression but found ways to get by. Meanwhile, the society was once again torn by overt violence. In 1977, according to one historian's recording, politically-motivated killings accounted for 230 deaths. The same year saw 39 die in a single gunman's attack on a May Day rally in Taksim square. As that event might suggest, much of the violence was from right-wing nationalist groups. The most notorious were the "Grey Wolves," who targeted Communists or suspected Communists, but the Communists were hardly innocent, either. By 1978, the number of assassinations or massacres over the course of the year reached 1,200. The worst incident was a cold-blooded massacre in December of nearly 100 Turkish Alevis, who generally leaned to the left politically.[101]

In that context, then, it surely had to be tempting for the preacher from Erzurum to step directly into politics by declaring an allegiance. Doing so would have mobilized the thousands who had come to hear him preach. Doğu Ergil puts the matter dramatically:

Fethullah Gülen moved to the United States in 1999. Since then, he lives at Golden Generation Worship and Retreat Center (also known as Camp Chestnut) in Saylorsburg, PA, where he leads a life of prayer, study, and teaching.

Gülen's mentors - ABOVE Refia Hanım, his mother (d. 1993), Ramiz, his father (d. 1974), Muhammed Lütfi (far right) (d. 1956), and Belma Özbatur, his elementary school teacher. Also known as Alvarlı Efe, Lütfi was a renowned scholar, mystic, and poet. His deep spirituality had a lasting influence on Gülen.
BELOW Belma Özbatur, Gülen's teacher, with her students in Korucuk, Erzurum.
BOTTOM Gülen's home in Korucuk.

ABOVE   Gülen (second from left) at People's House (Halk Evi) in Erzurum, where he lectured on Rumi (1963).
RIGHT   Gülen's older sister Nurhayat.
BELOW   Gülen (left) with other clergy members in Edirne (circa 1959).

FACING PAGE, TOP RIGHT AND MIDDLE   Gülen did not only deliver sermons at the mosque, but also lectured at symposiums and coffeehouses.   FACING PAGE, TOP LEFT   He keynoted at the Ebedi Risalet Symposium on the life of the Prophet Muhammad in 1991.

FACING PAGE, BOTTOM   Becoming a renowned figure made Gülen a target and he was put on trial in the aftermath of the memorandum by the military in 1971. Mustafa Birlik (d. 2012) (second from right) and many students of *Risale-i Nur* were also being tried. Their lawyer, Bekir Berk (d. 1992) (far left), was known for his strong cases against the oppressive regime.

ABOVE   Gülen speaking at an event by Journalists and Writers Foundation (JWF) in 1996. JWF, founded in 1994, was the pioneer of interfaith and intercultural dialogue in Turkey until 2016 when they had to move their offices to New York. JWF was exceptionally successful in bringing community leaders of different ethnic and religious groups (Kurds, Armenians, Alevites, Sunni-Shia Muslims, Jews, and Christians) around the same table to seek solutions for pressing social problems and celebrate differences.

BELOW   Gülen is together with former members of parliament, Kasım Gülek (to Gülen's right) and Hasan Celal Güzel (to Gülen's left).

ABOVE World-famous soccer player Diego Maradona came to Istanbul to support the friendly game organized by the JWF in 1995 for the benefit of the Bosnian children.

Gülen personally met with leaders of world religions and exchanged messages of good will and cooperation:

LEFT Bartholomew I, the Patriarch of Eastern Orthodox Church.

BELOW Eliyahu Bakshi-Doron, Chief Sephardic Rabbi of Israel.

RIGHT   Pope John Paul II in the Vatican (1998) with Msgr. Georges Marovitch, the Vatican's Istanbul representative, and Rüştü Kalyoncu, Gülen's friend.

BELOW   Msgr. Marovitch with a Christian delegation visiting Gülen.

The path of Gülen has crossed with the leaders of Turkey many times over the decades regardless of their ideological position in the political spectrum.

TOP LEFT Gülen met with the former Prime Minister Bülent Ecevit a few times. Ecevit was a principled secularist, and yet he stood in defense of Gülen, especially when Gülen and many prominent religious figures were under pressure by the military which forced the government to resign with "postmodern coup" in 1997.

LEFT, SECOND FROM TOP Former President Süleyman Demirel at a JWF event with Gülen. He wrote letters of reference to facilitate opening of schools abroad.

LEFT, SECOND FROM BOTTOM Gülen visited former President Turgut Özal in Dallas where Mr. Özal had an operation in 1992. Mr. Özal was very supportive of Hizmet; he spoke with presidents of other countries in favor of Hizmet schools and visited them when he had the opportunity.

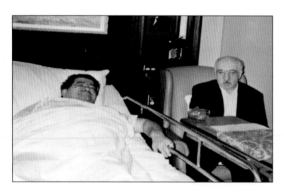

LEFT BOTTOM Former Prime Minister Tansu Çiller is with Gülen at the opening ceremony of Bank Asya (1996), an interest-free bank that was founded by Hizmet-affiliated businessmen. Mrs. Çiller cut the ribbon with former President Abdullah Gül (who was then Minister of State), and Recep Tayyip Erdoğan (who was then Istanbul Mayor). Ironically, the same Erdoğan took over the management of the bank and then shut it down completely in the aftermath of the coup attempt in 2016).

The 1990s were very active years for Gülen and Hizmet participants. While reaching out to different communities and individuals to promote dialogue, Hizmet participants were also opening schools all around Turkey and abroad.

ABOVE   Serhat Secondary School in Edirne, Turkey's northwestern province bordering with Greece and Bulgaria.

ABOVE RIGHT   Mehmet Döğme Dormitory in Kilis, near the Turkish border with Syria (1990). Whenever he could, he would get together with his family (below with brother Sıbgatullah). He sometimes helped the staff at the dorm in Altunizade where he was staying on "the 5th Floor."

FACING PAGE, RIGHT COLUMN, TOP   Famous Turkish singer Barış Manço (d. 1999) visiting Fethullah Gülen in Altunizade, Istanbul. Manço's appreciation of Hizmet schools is told in Chapter 4, including a fascinating story set in Chiang Mai, Thailand. (second from top) Gülen is with film director Halit Refiğ and actor Tanju Gürsu at the set for *Köpekler Adası* (The Island of Dogs) (1997).

BELOW   Gülen delivering one of his latest sermons in the mosque in early '90s.

ABOVE   Jon Pahl with Fethullah Gülen at his home in Saylorsburg, PA (Feb. 8, 2018)

Since the 1970s, Gülen has written for a number of periodicals like *Sızıntı*, (now *Çağlayan*). His essays are also translated for *The Fountain* (English), *Die Fontaene* (German), *Hira* (Arabic), *Mata Air* (Indonesian), and *Grani Misli* (Russian). When he is available, Gülen reviews proposed articles and consults with editors about the content of these publications.

On an ordinary day, unless there is a hospital visit (next page) or interview (left, with BBC), Gülen is busy with readings of classical Islamic texts with his students in the morning (next page), having conversations with guests, and attending group prayers before the evening prayer (bottom). He delivers lectures once or twice a week, which are published online at www.herkul.org (above).

Gülen, who was drawing larger and larger crowds, was forced to make a critical decision. Would he be a civic leader? Was he going to govern daily lives of people? And probably most important of all, was he going to play a political role in his community? Or, would he take another path and preach solely a message of spirituality and inspire others to make their own choices in the religious and ethical fields of daily life? Gülen chose the second option. He committed his life to addressing the problem of how people were to establish a direct relationship with their Creator and based his philosophy on that foundation. He taught that true faith was the key to discovering one's true self in interpersonal relationships. When he said that loving your fellow human being was the other side of the coin of loving the Creator, he was suggesting that through the bridge of love, it is possible to reach other human beings. He emphasized that by using tolerance and dialog it was possible to make the "other" closer. He believed that anyone who could achieve this was the beloved servant of God.[102]

Less dramatically, but more personally, İrfan Yılmaz simply recalled that: "I'm lucky I didn't become a militant. We were all afraid the Communists were coming. Many of us were close to the nationalist (rightist) movements." Such an alliance between Islamists and right-wing politics exploded into revolution in Turkey's next-door neighbor, Iran, in 1979. In contrast, "Hodjaefendi always told us," Yılmaz recalled, "never go into the streets. Never anarchy. Anarchy is only fueled by powers that do not want anything good for this country. If you want to help your people, you are going to study."[103]

Said Nursi had once said, "I take refuge in God from Satan and politics."[104] Gülen took a similar approach. Looking back on these years, Gülen recalled that:

many people were killed in Turkey. This group killed that person, another group killed another person. ... Some people were trying to reach a goal by killing others. Everybody was a terrorist. The people on that side were terrorists; the people on this side were terrorists. But everybody was labeling the same action differently. One person would say, "I am doing this in the name of Islam." Another would say, "I am doing it for my land and people." A third would say, "I am fighting against capitalism and exploitation." These all were just words. The

Qur'an talks about such "labels." They are things of no value. But people just kept on killing. Everyone was killing in the name of an ideal.[105]

In contrast, Gülen sought to build a society of sisters and brothers who *lived* for ideals. And those individuals who were committed to Hizmet knew, as he put it in a later interview, that:

> when anarchy was everywhere in our country, I called for calmness and controlling of anger. I had received death threats, yet, I called upon my admirers to continue working for peace. 'If I am assassinated, despite all your anger, I ask you to bury my body and seek order, peace and love in our society. Regardless of what happens, we believers should be representatives of love and security.'[106]

That was Hodjaefendi's consistent message throughout the turbulent 1970s. It was a worst-of-times and best-of-times scenario. It is hard to get worse than facing death threats. And yet in everyday life Gülen had never had more friends. So, despite whatever threats swirled around them, Kemal and Füsun, the millions of Turks like them, and the one preacher from Erzurum kept struggling between *ghurba* and *uns*, between loneliness and community. Hizmet kept growing. The Secondary and Higher Education Foundation gave rise to others. A Foundation for medical doctors began in 1979. Another one for teachers got underway in the same year. Businesses were sprouting up in support of Hizmet. Notable among them was what was later going to become Kaynak Holding—a conglomerate that would eventually incorporate over twenty different companies.[107]

And in the midst of it all, there were the simple pleasures of being with sisters and brothers and praying, studying, talking, and eating. İrfan Yılmaz remembers how in 1978 "we used to meet every week and read *Risale* with academicians." One time, Hodjaefendi came to the session, which was held in Yılmaz' house. He suggested that the following week the brothers set aside two hours, rather than just the customary hour. "That day," Yılmaz recalled:

> Hodjaefendi cooked everything for all of us. We sat down, there was potato soup. Then meat with potato. Then potato salad, potato *köfte*, potato pastry—and one more potato course—and then there came a dessert, and I suspected from the courses before that it had to be a po-

tato, but I couldn't taste it. One of our friends asked Hodjaefendi, "this dessert is really nice, what is it?" And then I jumped in and asked, "is this a potato dessert?" And Hodjaefendi said, "yes it is. ... We peeled one big sack of potatoes! ... Today is the meal of Gandhi." Gandhi, [Yılmaz explained], used to cook in one type.[108]

The reference to Gandhi was no coincidence. The similarity went well beyond cooking style. Like Gandhi, Gülen was committed to non-violence. And like Gandhi, he was threatened with death for it.

Death did not come for Gülen as the decade of the 1970s passed. Another military coup did. The instability in Turkey's government had exacerbated economic problems. Unemployment was as high as 15%. Inflation ran into triple digits. There were shortages of food in some locales.[109] In December 1979, a group of Generals again issued a memorandum to Bülent Ecevit and Süleyman Demirel (yes, that Süleyman Demirel), who were the leaders of Turkey's two largest political parties— respectively, the conservative Justice Party (*Adalet Partisi*, AP) and the social-democratic Republican People's Party (*Cumhuriyet Halk Partisi*, CHP). Ecevit and Demirel had traded being Prime Minister for most of the decade. Given prior history, especially Demirel's, this memo could not have been regarded as anything other than the warning of a coup. The two politicians managed to forestall the crisis for several months. But on September 12, 1980, General Kenan Evren ordered the tanks into Turkish streets at 4 am, and he then took over the state-run media to declare a coup. The rationale was the usual—to preserve national unity and to restore Atatürk's secularism. Events then followed what was becoming a familiar pattern in Turkey. Imprisonments marked by torture led to military tribunals that resulted in hangings—fifty in all. Evren allegedly boasted that "we hanged one from the left, one from the right, to show that we didn't take sides."[110]

By now, Fethullah Gülen had, if not friends, at least contacts in high places. Signs of an upcoming military intervention were widely recognizable. Gülen last preached on September 5, 1980, a week before the coup. He then requested, due to illness, and was granted, a leave of absence for twenty days. The timing was propitious. Nevertheless, on the day of the coup, his home was raided—but he wasn't present. Gülen then requested another leave of absence—for forty-five days. It was not enough. With an arrest warrant in his name, it was only a matter of time when he would be put behind bars by the military junta. He went off the radar for the next six years—six long years away from the pulpit and any public scene.

***

It had been a very full decade, in between the military interventions. Gülen had lost his father, but he had gained a growing reputation for preaching and teaching excellence. He had experienced the *ghurba* of imprisonment and the *uns* of companionship, with a growing circle of friends. He had cried tears that led many to identify with him, and he had inspired those closest to him to establish a range of institutions that put *hizmet* into action—foundations, dorms, tutoring centers, scholarships, and a publication. These institutions served especially youth, who were to be "brothers" and "sisters" to each other in living for a cause. Running throughout the various initiatives was what we have called "engaged empathy." Identifying with the suffering of others, and using science and Islam to alleviate that suffering, might grow a "golden generation." It seemed possible. And yet for all these successes, resistance within Turkey had also increased. "My objective," Gülen explained in an interview, was "the establishment of harmony, reconciliation, and stability in society." Even though things went awry in the country, Gülen still maintained hope for a future of collective positive action:

> If we seek brotherhood in shaking someone's hand, if we seek friendship and tolerance and take that as our aim for ourselves, then we need to carefully identify what needs to be said and done and act appropriately. Otherwise we will receive a slap in the face rather than attaining our objective. For a long time we suffered the pains of being different; we've experienced cruelty. … [But] Allah's greatest gift to an individual or society comes in the form of togetherness. If people come together and are united, I hope that Allah will give them extra, extraordinary gifts.[111]

The next several decades would, despite ongoing troubles, become years of togetherness and of extraordinary gifts. Peacebuilding would proceed. But they would also be years of pains and cruelty, alas.

In a society riddled with distrust, Gülen preached that the foundation of all good was trusting relations in engaged empathy—in a word, compassion:

Compassion is the beginning of being; without it everything is cha-os. Everything has come into existence through compassion and by compassion it continues to exist in harmony. ... Everything speaks of compassion and promises compassion. Because of this, the universe can be considered a symphony of compassion. All kinds of voices pro-claim compassion so that it is impossible not to be aware of it, and impossible not to feel the wide mercy encircling everything. How unfortunate are the souls who don't perceive this. ... [Human beings have] a responsibility to show compassion to all living beings, as a requirement of being human. The more one displays compassion, the more exalted one becomes, while the more one resorts to wrongdoing, oppression and cruelty, the more one is disgraced and humiliated, be-coming a shame to humanity.[112]

This would be a hypothesis tested in the coming decades. Could something as apparently simple as compassion produce the togetherness that Fethullah Gülen sought? Or would oppressors prevail?

CHAPTER FOUR

MELANCHOLY AND DIALOGUE - ISTANBUL, 1980–1999

For centuries, it was known simply as "The City."[1] By 1980, when Fethullah Gülen made Istanbul his primary residence, The City's sky—sun-kissed, foggy, smoky, snow-squalled, and star-studded—had seen millennia of military conflict, of worship in Greek, Latin, Arabic, Ottoman and modern Turkish, of child-bearing, of family strife, of buying and selling, of poetry and the lilting music of the ney-flute, of tea-drinking, of kebab-eating, and of hookah-smoking. Its hills, dotted with the majesty of countless mosques—undulated down to the Bosphorus: a swirling vein of deep grey-green-black-blue water through which flowed the lifeblood of two continents. Istanbul's streets and sidewalks—in neighborhoods like Üsküdar, Beşiktaş and Eminönü, among so many others—were ribbons of cobblestone, asphalt and concrete that climbed and descended through alleyways and around tight corners packed with parked cars and pedestrians, and up and down wide-boulevards lined with tulips, while busses and trams bustled down the center. And then there were the ruins—a stone aqueduct that appeared out of nowhere and went nowhere; an obelisk, cistern, or Roman bath—now dry with dust and overgrown with weeds; and the Byzantine city wall, wrapped beside highways and side streets, covered with moss and dirt accumulated over centuries, looming like a sentinel over the bustling and sprawling city.

In his memoir of becoming a writer, *Istanbul*, Orhan Pamuk suggests that what was distinctive about The City, its essence—is *hüzün*. *Hüzün*, like *ghurba*, is an Arabic word. It evokes not only loneliness and exile, but the even stronger emotion of melancholy—the looming dread on the edge of despair. "On cold winter mornings," Pamuk writes, "when the sun suddenly falls on the Bosphorus and that faint vapor begins to rise from the surface, the *hüzün* is so dense you can almost touch it, almost see it spread like a film over its people and its landscapes." When one lives among such ruins, as Fethullah Gülen did for his last years in Turkey, one experiences not only the nostalgia that every tourist can feel, but also a ceaseless yet resigned longing; in a word, one feels heartache: "In Istanbul the remains of a glorious past civilization are everywhere visible. No matter how ill-kept, no matter how neglected or hemmed in they are by concrete monstrosities, the great mosques and other monuments of the city, as well as the lesser detritus of empire in every side street and corner—the little arches, fountains, and neighborhood mosques—inflict heartache on all who live among them."[2] Yet like *ghurba*—which can resolve through Islamic practice into *uns,* into companionship, so too can the heartache of *hüzün,* Pamuk suggests, open into depth, imagination, creativity, and what he identifies with the Turkish word *cemaat*—community. "Istanbul," Pamuk conveys, "does not bear its *hüzün* as an incurable illness … as an immutable poverty to be endured like grief, or even as an awkward and perplexing failure to be viewed and judged in black and white; it bears its *hüzün* with honor," as people dwell together in *cemaat.*[3] Shared *hüzün* forges solidarity. But this solidarity is not merely contiguity. Paradoxically, one must embrace interiority in Istanbul, one must resign oneself to the heartache, to find oneself embraced by others. And the bridges of this kind of community between Istanbul residents are as real as those steel and concrete monstrosities that span the Bosphorus. "It is when the heroes have withdrawn into themselves," Pamuk writes, "submitting … to the conditions imposed on them by history and society, that we embrace them, and at that same moment so does the whole city."[4]

Following the 1980 coup, Fethullah Gülen withdrew into himself for nearly six years. After this period, he was embraced in unprecedented ways by what must have seemed to him to be nearly the whole city. His withdrawal was forced. There were "conditions imposed upon" him by history and society. More accurately, his withdrawal was due to the military regime and its political repression. The embrace that followed also was helped along by a regime—the relatively friendly rule of Turgut Özal, who served as Prime Minister from 1983-89 and as President from 1989 until his untimely death in 1993. But the growth in Hizmet that followed

Gülen's return to public life in 1986 also had causes beyond the realm of politics. It was Gülen's capacity to turn *hüzün* into community that helped the Hizmet movement expand. And expand it did, dramatically—as people inspired by Fethullah Gülen built schools, started social businesses, and held intentional interfaith public dialogues that were unprecedented in the history of the Turkish Republic. Through these endeavors, Gülen's teaching, and his person, was engaged and tested in the court of public opinion. That testing took its toll on the boy from Erzurum. He exacerbated some chronic illnesses—heart disease and diabetes—during his time in The City. For six-years he lived out a melodrama of political theater: hiding-in-plain-sight, and pursued by police—while at the same time he taught regularly, consulted with *abi*s and *abla*s, and urged those inspired by him to grow the institutions and agencies they had started. And then for over a decade, from 1986-1996, he was a very prominent if not omnipresent figure in Istanbul high society. He was not merely a preacher and teacher. He was a public intellectual who promoted an Islam that helped many Muslims bridge secular and sacred community. It could have been dizzying. Gülen experienced over two-decades a bad-cop, good-cop psychological yo-yo. By the time he emigrated to America in 1999—following yet another round of political persecution that began in 1997—he was in many ways not a healthy man. And yet he was also in many ways on the verge of the most productive, and surely the most peaceful, period in his life.

One of the residences Gülen lived in for the six years of his withdrawal—known to close associates and friends—was a small apartment in a modest concrete flat in the Altunizade neighborhood of the Üsküdar district, on the Asian side of The City. It was a Hizmet dormitory, built with rooms for teaching along with rooms for students. Gülen's room was on the 5th Floor. And that designation, "the 5th Floor," soon became a metaphor for how in Gülen's life and work the melancholy of Istanbul turned into both a deep personal peace and an expanding network of people that came to be called throughout Turkey, in fact, the *cemaat*—the community.[5] That community was dedicated, as previous chapters have documented, to literacy, to nonviolence, and to engaged empathy. But during Gülen's years in Istanbul he also became known for a commitment to interfaith dialogue and to a Turkish word found often in his preaching and teaching that has generally been translated as "tolerance," but that really means more than that tepid term can convey. That word is *hoşgörü*. My understanding of *hoşgörü* is something like "principled pluralism." A person committed to *hoşgörü* lives with integrity in one's own tradition (hence "principled"), but also lets others live out their deepest commitments that might differ dramatically from one's own (hence "pluralism.")[6] But principled pluralism or *hoşgörü* as preached by Gülen and lived out in Hizmet was not mere relativism, where every opinion was equally likely to be as true as any other. Instead, principled pluralism or *hoşgörü* in Hizmet wagered that Islam provided a foundation from which differences could be engaged and turned to productive cooperation through dialogue. A quote that Gülen often cited from Said Nursi made the point: "Victory among civilized persons is won through persuasion." That is, when people of Hizmet met across differences they did so on a basis of mutual respect. Knowing where one stood as a Muslim made it possible to accept differences without judgment, and surely without violence. Differences then created conditions for dialogue. And dialogue helped people learn to live together with greater peace and justice than before. That's an academic definition of *hoşgörü*, then: as principled pluralism. But *hoşgörü* also meant, theologically, to *see another as God sees them*. And God sees above all with eyes of mercy and compassion, as the *Bismillah-ir Rahman-ir Rahim* with which Muslims begin many public events proclaimed. It was this God's-eye aspect of *hoşgörü*, as articulated by Fethullah Gülen, that led so many people of Hizmet in the 1990s to invite people from diverse cultures and customs into community. During his years in Istanbul, then, Fethullah Gülen turned *hüzün* into *hoşgörü* through Hizmet. Melancholy through dialogue became a community of service.

Hiding in plain sight

Shortly before the 1980 military coup, Gülen's lead article in *Sızıntı* took up the topic of "peace." "Throughout our history," it began, "peace has been like the distant beloved whom we mention at every opportunity, but with whom we never reunite." Despite, or perhaps because of, this absence, "we should direct all our efforts toward helping people build a society of peace, on both a national and global scale." This sounds like a platitude. But in the context of a Turkish political culture that was constantly on the verge of coming apart, what Gülen meant by "a society of peace" was quite comprehensive if not radical. Peace, as he described it in 1979, encompassed the state, businesses, educational institutions, and the judiciary. Peace was not merely the absence of conflict. More profoundly, peace was the presence of a trusting community that infused and transformed every aspect of life. Peace as Gülen envisioned it "begins in the individual, resonates in the family, and from there pervades all parts of the society." The method was straightforward: Islam would inspire individuals, who would develop strong families, who would contribute to civil society. That sounds innocuous enough. To some in 1970s Turkey, however, it seemed to be a profound threat to the secular State. It started with an Islam that was not under State control. "We must keep in mind," Gülen reiterated, that "if our aim is to attain peace through goodness and beauty, hope and security, our work must begin with the individual."[7] This seemed subversive. And yet, in the first years after the coup, as he withdrew from public life, Gülen had plenty of opportunities to hone this method of peacebuilding. He deepened his relationships with individuals that fostered the trust that grew community: call it deep peace.

The military government of General Kenan Evren followed the pattern of previous martial law regimes in the Republic of Turkey: Communists, anti-Communists, religious leaders, journalists, academics, and other intellectuals were arrested on charges of threatening national security. Some estimates put the number jailed or detained at 100,000. Most were arrested within a few days of the coup. Most were also eventually released. Nevertheless, in the ensuing years as cases worked their way through military tribunals, nearly two-thousand faced the death penalty and fifty were eventually executed.[8] Gülen himself was under surveillance and regularly hunted as a person on a watch-list. He strategically avoided capture, for the most part. His late brother Sıbgatullah recalled that:

> After the 1980 coup he was on the wanted list. They put his pictures up everywhere with anarchists. They said he was going to create a government of Sharia. They said he was an enemy of the Republic. But in his sermons he had always said a Republic was the best form of government. … We learned later on that when the list of anarchists was set up … they said 'put Hodjaefendi on the list, too' to 'make them [leftists] happy.' That's what I heard. … But they weren't able to catch

him. ... He came to Erzurum and stayed here [sometimes]. I went to Istanbul and was his cook for three months. Nobody knew where he was staying.[9]

Nobody may have known where he was staying, but plenty of people managed to visit him nonetheless.

Among them was Zafer Kesmez. "In the 1980s nobody knew where Hodjaefendi was staying," this businessman recalled, "although I saw him regularly. He was in Istanbul. My friends here were not able to see Hodjaefendi. They said, 'we know you are seeing him regularly—take us there! We miss him!'" In fact, he recalled one trip when Gülen offered a *sohbet* that was attended by one-hundred. Kesmez was among them. When they arrived, Gülen greeted him by saying "you have been a mercy to me!" After hearing this compliment, he recalled thinking, modestly, that: "I know I'm not a mercy, but if anyone was a mercy, that would be Hodjaefendi." Gülen called him to sit closer to him during the sohbet. He then suggested that he might provide some support for the family of another brother who had been imprisoned. And because he could be a mercy to another, "that's why he had said, 'you're a mercy to me,'" he concluded. He also recalled that while driving to Istanbul, he had sung a song in the car, "The Wind Broke My Branch—What's the Sin of My People?" He had sung it five times, in fact, and then stopped, after which a friend traveling with him asked him to sing it once more. Then, during the *sohbet*, as he remembered it, Gülen himself began to sing the same song. "I don't know how he did it," he recalled. "None of us who had been in the car had ever left [each other]," he marveled. In other words, Hodjaefendi somehow echoed his favorite song. Such coincidences, among other more explicit teachings, cemented trust in Gülen's spiritual stature. And as the presence of one-hundred students in attendance suggests, although Gülen was supposedly in hiding from the police, he was also "teaching openly in his own place," as Kesmez put it.[10]

That tension in Fethullah Gülen's life—between private practice and public oppression—lasted from September 1980 to April 1986. In a 1995 interview with *Sabah*, Gülen was asked "Why did they pursue you after the September 12th coup?" His answer explained a great deal about how tone-deaf (intentionally or otherwise) some could be to the nuances in Islamic theology and practice:

A newspaper columnist instigated action against me. It was one of my last sermons in Bornova. I talked about the *Sharia al-Fitriya*. God has two collections of laws: one, issuing from His Attribute of Speech, is the principles of religion, also called *Sharia*. However, in the narrow sense they mean the political laws of Islam. The other, issuing from His Attributes of Will and Power, is the principles to govern the universe and life, the [natural laws] that are the subject matter of sciences. In Islamic terminology, this is called *Sharia al-Fitriya*. Respecting these two collections of laws will make us prosperous in this world and the next, while opposing them will lead us to ruin. The Muslim world remained behind the West because it opposed *Sharia al-Fitriya*.

I explained this matter to the congregation. I encouraged them to undertake scientific research and advancement. However, the next day a columnist wrote about this and claimed I had made propaganda for *Sharia*, meaning the political laws of Islam.

This matter was investigated officially by the public prosecutor's office. Later, this office understood its mistake and referred the case to the head office of the religious affairs department. This office said that no action was needed. But I guess, just as today some people are allergic to the word *sharia*, the martial law commander in Izmir was bothered by that word. He put me under surveillance. The situation was very difficult. Of course, some people supported me, but it was very hard to make the military regime listen.[11]

When they weren't listening, they would send the police to raid the 5th Floor. And Gülen would have to pack a bag, sneak out the back steps, and get in a car to escape capture. He was on the run.

Sometimes he would go to Erzurum. He was always welcome there, where he could hunker down with family or friends in the lower-profile culture of Northeast Anatolia. "I had built a house in Erzurum that nobody knew about," Sıbgatullah recalled. That was a safe house for his brother, Fethullah. On one of these trips "Hodjaefendi stayed here for a long time," Sıbgatullah recalled. "We would go out in the morning in my car, visit surrounding towns, and we were getting news from soldiers that we knew" to help avoid patrols. On one of these off-the-radar excursions, Sıbgatullah went on, "we visited Van and historical places and other communities from the Seljuks. One time we went to Erek mountain where Said Nursi had stayed. Hodjaefendi really wanted to go there. To get to that place in the mountain, we needed to cross a river. Hodjaefendi fell in. He got all wet. And he said, 'When you try to attain something too much, you're taking away from it.'"[12] On another excursion, Fethullah and his brother visited a military base in Erzincan. Several of Gülen's students were at the base completing their mandatory service. "I went there," Sıbgatullah recalled, "and Hojaefendi was standing behind me. And I requested the two students. But somebody saw him, and said, 'Oh, Hodjaefendi—he's here! I heard him! He's here!' And I said, 'Shhh! He's being sought, keep quiet!'"[13] Keeping quiet was important, but Gülen was obviously willing to take the risk of visiting students, even on a military base.[14]

While he was on the run, then, he continued to keep in touch with *abi*s and *abla*s around the country. Şerif Ali Tekalan was one of them. Tekalan was a medical doctor who would become Rector at Fatih University in Istanbul, which was opened by people of Hizmet in 1996—a story we'll recount in a bit more detail shortly. In these travels, Gülen would meet "with small groups" of people, Tekalan reported, some of whom would then harbor Hodjaefendi for a night, or longer. One of these trips of which Tekalan was aware was to Ankara, another to Kayseri—where Tekalan was assistant professor in the mid-80s. On his visit to Kayseri, either in 1984 or 85, as Tekalan recalled, Gülen encouraged setting up more dormitories and tutoring centers. Tekalan himself then saw that those projects were realized. Hizmet began to grow even in that religiously conservative city.[15] On another one of his flights away from Istanbul, this time to Izmir, Abdullah Birlik remembered that Gülen arrived at his family's home "around midnight." "For those five or six years it was very difficult," Birlik remembered. Some people were tortured by "rough police," and Gülen was "on the run." "Who took care of him?" Birlik asked rhetorically. "Hizmet had expanded [by then]," he explained, so as needed Hodjaefendi "stayed at friends' houses."[16] On at least one occasion in the mid-80s, in an incident I have not been able to verify independently, the authorities may have caught up with Gülen. Haluk Ercan was a police officer who at various times served different municipalities in the Aegean. He was friendly to Hizmet, and upon receiving an assignment to Burdur (a city in southwestern Turkey), he was surprised to discover that Hodjaefendi "was in detention at the station. He was detained before I came," Ercan recalled. "He had been in jail one day, one night. When I saw him, he was in bad shape due to prison conditions. I got him cleaned and got his medicine."[17] Gülen's release came a day later at the instigation of Prime Minister Turgut Özal through Galip Demirel, Deputy Minister of the Interior. Özal was, like Gülen, a Sufi, and over the course of his time in power he lent quiet support to Hizmet (insofar as he could support it, given military opposition. When he wasn't on the run, Gülen was often on the 5th Floor, where he was visited by former and current students, *abis* and *ablas* from the dormitories, tutors from the *dershanes*, and *mütevelli* from the various foundations. These individuals now formed an expanding network covering every major city, and some smaller ones, in Turkey. One of them was Nurten Kutlu. She recalled being among a group of other students visiting Gülen on the 5th Floor. Although the meeting probably happened in the 1990s, it reflected the patterns of earlier years, too: "I was working as a volunteer at FEM [one of the tutoring centers]. I was studying history as a student. I had just been accepted into university. I was nervous" to be invited to meet with Hodjaefendi, she remembered feeling. She had been raised in a secular household, and her impression of *hodjas* [she refers to clerics] was that "they are so holy." But "Hodjaefendi was different," she recalled. "He was kind, nice, gentle—not an ordinary *hodja*. ... He asked me what I was doing, but I couldn't talk—I was in awe! But that meeting changed my mind. I have to read about him," she thought. "So, I started reading his books. After I met with him I was more motivated to learn more about him and his ideas."[18] That story was repeated countless times over these two decades. A simple meeting could change an individual's life.

Gülen spent most of his time while on the 5th Floor in the practices that had occupied him since his youth—prayer five times per day, of course, but also regular reading. As he explained in another 1995 interview, "I try and read as much as time permits. Regardless of whether the subject is religion or not, I try and read not less than two hundred pages a day."[19] He traced his love of reading to his family:

> In my childhood, accounts of the heroic deeds of the Companions [of the Prophet] were read at home. I read many books like the one about Abu Muslim al-Khorasani, which can be considered as legends

from Islam's early period. In later years, around the age of 18-20, I inclined more toward books on jurisprudence and philosophy. ... Some books led to other books, and it continued like this. When I was in the military, I had a very wise commander. He had a deep knowledge of Sufism. He had read both Eastern Islamic and Western classics. He advised me to read Western classics. This caused me to read many famous Western writers such as Rousseau, Balzac, Dostoyevsk[y], Pushkin, Tolstoy, the Existentialists, and others.[20]

Although that list leaned heavily toward the French and Russians, it was in fact a German that Gülen found particularly important, and about whom he remembered an amusing anecdote. "It's impossible not to admire Kant," he suggested:

Although Russell criticized Kant bitterly and described him as one who turned the history of philosophy upside down, Kant was an important philosopher. Kant was well-known among theologians in Turkish theology schools. ... [In fact], in the examination for preachers and muftis that I took, they asked "In his book, A Critique of Pure Reason, the philosopher Kant separated intelligence into two types—practical and theoretical. He said that theoretical intelligence could not know God and that practical intelligence could. What do you understand from this view, and how do you evaluate it?" Those who had not studied philosophy couldn't answer this question. In fact, one of my friends who was entering the exam apparently didn't understand the question. He asked me jokingly, "What is this Kant?" I told him in jest, "put some sugar in hot water, stir it well, squeeze a little lemon in it, and you'll have a kant." [In Turkey, this kind of beverage is called kant].[21]

Humor aside, the imposed solitude of the 5th Floor was at least tolerable for Gülen, so long as he had access to books. And one can find more than an echo of Kant's idealism in Gülen's thought.

Gülen also wrote and read poetry and other literature during his time in Istanbul. He is not a literary figure of the stature of a Pamuk, but he could readily identify in a 1997 interview a range of his own favorite writers. "I like the works of all talented people and artists," he generously suggested, but there are definitely people I prefer due to their weight on the horizon of thought. ... Shakespeare, Dostoyevsk[y], and Pushkin amazed me. In Turkey, there are several literary men whose poetry and prose I appreciate. However, I admire Yahya Kemal, Mehmet Akif and Necip Fazıl in poetry. In both prose and poetry, Sezai Karakoç should also be mentioned. Among the Tanzimat [a nineteenth century Ottoman reform era] and the succeeding generations, Namık Kemal, Şinasi, Recaizade Mahmut Ekrem, and Refik Halid were good. Tevfik Fikret wasn't difficult to read. Among Western writers I also like Balzac. Although he's considered a realist, his *Lily of the Valley* shows his romanticism. There might be parallels between Iranian poetry and French literature. Among those I read from Persian literature, I can mention Sa'di, Hafiz, Nizami, and Anwar.[22]

Other arts, too—could enliven Gülen's days on the 5th Floor. Unlike some Muslims, Hodjaefendi appreciated music. "Until I was 16 years old, I was in contact with some players of *Sufi* music while I lived in Erzurum. As is known, *Sufi* or our classical music was born in the dervish lodges and hostels. Hymns and similar poetry attracted me to classical music. For example, I liked and listened to Itri and Dede Efendi. I also admired Haji Arif Bey as if he were a saint." Gülen also had some familiarity with Western classical music. He identified Mozart and Beethoven symphonies and concertos as particular favorites, which could be "really serious, dignified, and rich."[23] So, the arts made solitude less lonely, and brought dignity to even a melancholy mood.

The 5th Floor—sources and methods in Gülen's teaching

But most of Gülen's time on the 5th Floor was spent in teaching. A very helpful article by Ergün Çapan listed the range of texts and methods that Gülen honed during these years in Istanbul.[24] Not surprisingly, Gülen's teaching followed the six classical disciplines of Islamic inquiry: Arabic grammar, Qur'anic exegesis (*tafsir*), Hadith study (which included attention to stories about the Prophet's life, his companions, and his relations with non-Muslims), jurisprudence (*fiqh*), systematic theology (*kalam*), and Islamic mysticism (*tasawwuf*). A few words about how Hodjaefendi approached each of these disciplines can clarify how Gülen interacted with students during his days on the 5th Floor. Understanding those interactions can also help make manifest how Gülen's withdrawal from public life paved the way for his embrace by The City. Lessons with Gülen ran from two to four hours. They were generally held between morning (dawn) and noon prayers. Sometimes students would gather before breakfast, start a lesson, take a break to eat, and then resume for the remainder of the morning. Sometimes lessons would start after breakfast and run longer into the morning. On occasion, lessons would happen in the afternoon, and sometimes they would even begin an hour before the dawn prayer. That Gülen slept little is a well-attributed fact about him.

Gülen himself once described his general teaching method with the modest sentence: "I discuss books with my friends." In fact, Gülen tailored his teaching to the needs of students. He lectured frequently early in a student's progression, then engaged in greater dialogue over questions as a student matured. Throughout, Gülen taught with what Çapan identified as a "culture of presence," where "his students personally experience and benefit from his presence; they witness the vastness of his horizons and enthusiasm and are colored by his influence. The degree to which one benefits from that atmosphere depends on a person's capacity, intention, concentration, and abilities." It is no doubt the case, on the one hand, that learning of any kind depended on an individual's intention, concentration, and capacity. Exactly what a "culture of presence" meant, on the other hand, was less quantifiable. It might convey charisma, *gravitas*, energy, even *hüzün*, perhaps. In any event, lessons with Gülen began "with mentioning the name of God, praising and glorifying Him, and praying for and sending greetings to the Prophet." For instance, one of these opening prayers began sensibly with "Our Lord, increase our knowledge." But it then went on to ask also for increase in a long list of attributes: "faith, certainty, trust, surrender, entrustment, reliability, tranquility, sincerity, loyalty, faithfulness, ingenuity, affection, decency, chastity, intelligence, wisdom, memory, and our trust in You and our love and desire for meeting You. My God," it then went on, "we ask You for perfect and permanent health and well-being and a [tranquil] heart. Bestow your power and might on us, O most compassionate of the merciful."[25] Although God was merciful, Gülen expected students to come to lessons prepared. That meant students would have read assigned passages (usually 40-50 pages), and that they would have consulted dictionaries and commentaries as required or necessary. They would then bring prepared questions to contribute to the discussion. "Analytical reading" was encouraged.

A considerable portion of any lesson with Fethullah Gülen in Istanbul (and elsewhere) involved recitation. Students would read out loud a Qur'anic verse or required text. Sometimes this recitation was from memory. According to Çapan, Gülen was "very sensitive to reading correctly, especially with verses from the Qur'an and *hadith* texts." He stressed proper pronunciation: "One may read Arabic incorrectly," Gülen once said, "but do not read Qur'anic verses inaccurately." During recitation, Gülen would listen and, if a student erred or halted, quietly interject with a correction or encouragement. As any teacher knows, such an ability—to critique and yet to encourage, is no small skill. As recitation went on, Gülen would occasionally interrupt to mention important commentators or references—some of which were then assigned for a subsequent session. Questions were welcomed. As Çapan put it, in a statement that Gülen often echoed, the Prophet once said that "a good question is half of knowledge."[26] When students did raise a question, Gülen would summarize "the general view of scholars on the subject," and then express "his own interpretations particularly addressing the present conditions. Some of the most attractive aspects of the lessons," Çapan opined, were "these explanations and interpretations of Fethullah Gülen." Given how much Islam looks to the past, it is a tricky art for Muslim thinkers to generate independent or innovative interpretations—called *ijtihad*. The one who performs *ijtihad* is called, in a term of honor: a *mujtahid*. Gülen, typically, disavowed this honor for himself. But in fact *ijtihad* characterized his practice, and he possessed the qualifications to be a *mujtahid*.[27] So, it is not surprising that students on the 5th Floor would lean in when, after tracing the long-line of precedents on a question, Gülen would then venture his own interpretations.[28] Each such dialogue was another bridge of words between ancient truth and modern contexts. Throughout his teaching, in short, Gülen "tried to keep his students engaged with the class and actively participating." He encouraged them "to read more, to develop skills in dealing with challenges posed by intense texts and concepts, to introduce them to varying ideas, methods, disputes, and debates, to help them adopt a holistic approach to all sciences, and to teach them not to limit themselves to one field of expertise but to be familiar with other sciences" as well.[29]

Scholars may appreciate some details, and general readers may benefit from some awareness, of the range of literature and pedagogical methods upon which Hodjaefendi drew. In grammar, Çapan notes that "Fethullah Gülen has taught almost every group of students a book related to the structure of Arabic grammar." Gülen required students to memorize some of these texts—for instance the *Amthila, Bina*, and *Maqsud*—the three most prominent Arabic grammar books used during Ottoman times. Two grammars by Imam Birgiwi (d. 1573) were, among others, the subjects of lectures by Gülen. Çapan reports that students struggled to memorize a grammar of Baha al-Din Abd Alla b. Aquil (d. 729) that ran to one thousand verses. "After they had memorized 30-40 verses," Çapan narrates the failure, "memorization was put aside at the students' request because they were having difficulty with it. 'Memories are blown,' Fethullah Gülen regretfully said." Regrets or not, such an adjustment suggests a teacher actively listening to his students, and a teacher being willing to tailor lessons to their capacities. Still, these were only a few of the seventeen different grammars that Gülen used over the years. Dictionaries were also often close at hand when Gülen was leading a study session. "I don't know about you," Gülen reportedly said, "but I look up several words in the dictionary every day."[30]

As for Qur'anic exegesis and *hadith* study, the list that Çapan collected ran to over twenty volumes. Among them were of course Bediüzzaman Said Nursi's commentary on the Qur'an, but also the two volumes of what is known as Baydawi's *tafsir*—a "famous, short, to-the-point exegesis" penned by Nasir al-Din Abd Alla b. Umar al-Baydawi (d. 1286). Gülen also taught the three volumes of Abu al-Fida Ibn Kathir (d. 1341), "one of the most important *tafsir* works, explaining the Qur'an by referring to the Qur'an and *hadith* and to what the Companions (*Sahaba*) and Successors (*Tabi'un*) were recorded to have said." Particularly interesting to some readers will be the fact that Gülen taught Sayyid Qutb's six-volume *Fi Zilal al-Qur'an* [*In the Shade of the Qur'an*], but he made himself clear that he disagreed with Qutb's political ideology. Finally, in the category of exegesis, from among many others Gülen often taught the 9 volumes (in Turkish) of M. Elmalılı Hamdi Yazır (d. 1942), *Hak Dini Kur'an Dili*. "No commentary equal to [Yazır's], including the ones in Arabic, has been written," Gülen once said.[31]

Among *hadith* collections, Gülen repeatedly taught the famous six collections, along with commentaries on them; the two collections of *Sahih Bukhari* and *Sahih Muslim*; and the four collections called *Sunan*. The work was rigorous; the sixteen volumes of the collection by Ali al-Muttaqi (d. 1567), *Kanzu'l ummal*, ran to 46,000 discrete sayings. Gülen did not avoid the challenge. He "once taught his students ten volumes of this work during the month of Ramadan and the remaining six volumes in the following 6 months." 46,000 sayings in seven months was plenty of reading in its own right, but Gülen also stressed knowing the chain of transmission of these stories about the Prophet. This included being able to identify and to pronounce accurately the name of the transmitters, as well as to communicate details about their biographies and thought—something of a lost art in Islamic cultures.[32] As we shall see, this emphasis on the Companions of the Prophet would become an important part of Fethullah Gülen's years in Istanbul—and a distinctive aspect of his legacy as an Islamic scholar.

"In every study group," and hence among those who joined him on the 5th Floor in Istanbul, Gülen also taught at least one book related to jurisprudence (*fiqh*). "'One cannot become a scholar without knowing jurisprudence,'" Gülen simply put it. That mentality is accurate enough—given Islam's emphasis on ethics and morality. But studying *fiqh* could also get a student into trouble. After all, it was an attempt to draw upon a distinction in *fiqh* between two types of *Shari'a* that led to Gülen's extended leave of absence from the pulpit during this time-period. Still, Gülen worked through more than a dozen different works of *fiqh* over the years, including the *Diyanet İslam İlmihali* (also known as "the Turkish Islamic Catechism"). That work was prepared by a committee from the Turkish Presidency of Religious Affairs. It codified the current understanding of Islamic jurisprudence for the Hanafi school of thought. Several of the other works of *fiqh* that Gülen studied with his students were in Arabic. They were, ordinarily, read in that language and then translated into Turkish by students—although sometimes Arabic alone sufficed for those with capacity. While Gülen clearly identified throughout his life with the mainstream Hanafi school of jurisprudence, as we saw in Chapter One, at times he also drew "respectfully," Çapan editorialized, on the works of scholars in other schools. Among the topics in *fiqh* that Gülen stressed among his students were the *fatwas*—those authorized declarations on a legal matter given by a recognized Muslim scholar or scholars. This topic became important after September 11, 2001, when Gülen responded by condemning the so-called *fatwa*s of Osama bin Laden and other Muslims that justified suicide attacks.

Now, much of the above teaching that Gülen was doing in Istanbul would fall under the broad category of "theology" as generally used in the Western academy. *Kalam* or "theology" as understood within Islam, however, denotes a "sub-discipline" which Gülen once described as articulating "the Islamic system of faith with reason and narrative proofs." This sub-discipline also has several recognized streams that have developed over the centuries (not to be confused with the different schools of jurisprudence discussed in Chapter One). These streams become particularly important because there is no central hierarchy within Islam comparable, for instance, to Roman Catholic ecclesiology with its priests, bishops, cardinals, and the Pope. Islam also does not have institutional differentiation between groups of Muslim believers comparable to Christian denominations with their related bureaucracies, headquarters, and regular assemblies. Muslim differentiations tend, then, to be *kalam*-based. To extend the comparison with Christianity, with perhaps greater precision, just as some Christians identified with the fourth-century Nicene-Constantinopolitan Creed, some did not, and just as some Christians identified with the Lutheran Confessions of the sixteenth century, most did not. Similar fluid differentiations along the lines of *kalam* or creed exist among Muslims. Within that arena, then, Gülen taught most frequently and generally what is known as Maturidi theology—which is the most widely-adhered to variety of *kalam* associated with the broad Sunni tradition. One of the several Maturidi theologians whose works Gülen favored in his teaching was Saad al-Din al-Taftazani (d. 1390) and his *Sharh Aqa-id al-Nasafiyyah*, translated as *A Commentary on the Creed of Islam.*[33]

Finally, within the arena of mysticism, at least one *Sufi* text was a part of every class Fethullah Gülen taught in Istanbul. Because of his education by *Sufi* masters such as the Imam of Alvar, whom we met in Chapter One, Gülen could draw on an impressive range of sources. They included most notably al-Qushayri (d. 1120), whose work *al-Risala al-Qushayriyyah fi Ulum al-Tasawwuf* [translated as "*Epistle on Sufism*"] linked *Sufi* practice to the Qur'an and to the tradition of the

Prophet.[34] Gülen also taught, from among many other *Sufi* classics: the two volumes of Indian Imam Rabbani (also known al-Sirhindi, d. 1624), entitled *Maktubat* ["Letters"]; the work of Harith al-Muhasibi (d. 857), *al-Ri'aya li Huquq Allah* [*"Obeying What God Permits"*], and Abd al-Rahman al-Jami (d. 1492), *Nafahat al-Uns* [*"Lives of the Saints"*]. Sufism is "Islam's heart and spiritual life," Gülen has claimed, and no description of his teaching would be complete without mentioning it. It's also worth noting that the version of Sufism that Gülen practiced and taught was in keeping with the orthodox disciplines of Islam, and not some of the more exotic or esoteric practices and doctrines judged by many Muslims to be heretical.[35] He has his own four-volume work on Sufism (*Emerald Hills of the Heart: Key Concepts in the Practice of Sufism*).

The 5th Floor—deep peace through knowing the tradition, and knowing one's self

So, while on the 5th Floor, and withdrawn from public life, Fethullah Gülen was also intensifying his study with selected students. His withdrawal from public life allowed him to dig ever more deeply into the breadth and depth of Islamic scholarship. As Çapan puts it:

> While teaching his students, Fethullah Gülen is extremely respectful toward the interpretations and approaches of scholars from the time of the Age of Happiness [the origins of Islam] to the present. He shows great respect toward the Companions, their Followers, those coming after the Followers, the imams of the schools of thought, and great men of spirit like Abd al-Qadir Jilani, Hasan Shazili, Ahmad Rifai, Shah-i Naqshiband, Imam Rabbani, and Bediüzzaman Said Nursi and to their interpretations and approaches. He frequently emphasizes that the interpretations and approaches must be very respectfully taken into consideration regardless of which Islamic discipline the scholars are from. Furthermore, paying utmost attention to the essentials of faith, he humbly voices his own views saying, "*Ibn Kathir* ('the son of abundance') had this view, but *Ibn Qalil* ('the son of little' referring to himself) has this approach," or "This poor soul has this interpretation or view."[36]

This was how Gülen enjoined *ijtihad* or independent reasoning.

Independent reasoning was neither something he claimed as a right, nor was it his duty to generate some new knowledge. Rather, *ijtihad* was about the possibility of extending the tradition into the present. If *hoşgörü* or hospitality was a central aspect of Gülen's life and work during his time in Istanbul, then it included respect for those who went before him as *mujtahids*. Gülen also expected a similar respect for the past among his students, while at the same time he encouraged them to think in terms appropriate for the present. He held

> that students in [his] class may have/should have interpretations and approaches towards scholars on an axis of respect and in a way that does not contradict the basic disciplines of religion, for everyone in a sense is an "*ibn al-zaman*" (child of his or her own time). Every era has assets which are open to interpretation and which can be interpreted according to the conditions of the current period. It is the responsibility of every Muslim to read the signs of the time well and, taking that asset, to put the values he [or she] believes in into practice. Meanwhile, it is very important not to take scholars lightly and disrespectfully ridicule them saying things like, "They did not understand this matter."[37]

Like a good historian, in short, Gülen sought through his teaching with his students to engage them in a dialogue, not a monologue, with the past.

Since all the faithful dead were thus among his conversation partners, Gülen never lacked for a community of conversation. No matter how constrained he might be by political oppression, he could always "discuss books with his friends." Put even more generally, his *cemaat* or community was practically unlimited, and it extended *across centuries*. Consequently, Gülen's forced turn inward wound up being a profound opportunity for him to deepen the foundations of Hizmet. That happened when Gülen turned the movement back, as he himself had been forced to turn, to the individual. Hizmet was thus wrapped in the mantle of Socrates:

> The self-control that comes from self-[awareness] is one of our most significant characteristics as human beings. But this, ironically, is what too many of us neglect. How many people can you point to who have

made a habit of self-awareness? How many people can you name who explore their inner depths, rediscovering themselves every day? How many who recognize their frailties and their strengths, their failures and their achievements? ... Socrates often repeated the imperative inscribed at the Temple of Apollo: "Know thyself." This ancient maxim, proclaimed in countless schools of wisdom, acquired a divine dimension in the *Sufi* tradition: "He who knows himself knows his Lord." I wonder how many people have lived up to this lofty formation? I doubt the number is large. ...

Although society, reason, and the subconscious are each important aspects of human life, we are not reducible to any one of these aspects. Our potential is such that, when destiny paves the way for our will, we are able to transcend everything in the world. History has demonstrated this to be the case. Each of us possesses an inner dynamism that can propel us beyond our own selves, even beyond all creation. And if we direct this mysterious potential toward its origin, we can transcend finitude and give meaning to our decaying mortality.

Today, we are able to harness thunderbolts, view subatomic particles, observe phenomenon millions of light years away. ... [But] despite the all-encompassing genius of modern humanity, we are cursed because we have misinterpreted ourselves.[38]

Deep peace depended upon self-aware individuals. Such individuals knew their personal failings, and knew their infinite potential—their Lord, if you will. Knowing anything less would be likely to continue the chaos and suffering.

So Gülen withdrew to "the 5th Floor" in the heart of The City for nearly six years.[39] It is an axiom of contemporary cultural studies that place matters. So it should be no surprise that over time the 5th Floor became to people of Hizmet much more than just an apartment. As Farid al-Ansari put it, in his hagiographical historical novel about the life of Gülen:

The 5th Floor ... was the treasury and the depository of Fethullah's secret invitation to the spiritual realm. It was a social and communal center of his Hizmet, or benevolent services. ... The man would never leave the 5th Floor except for the necessity of safety. To him, the 5th Floor was like the Cave of Hira [where Muhammad received his first revelations from God] or the House of ibn Arqam [a sanctuary for the early Muslim community under persecution] or the valley of Abu Talib—a refugee camp of sorts outside of Mecca where the Noble Prophet's uncle Abu Talib provided what protection he could during the three-year tribulation. Therein [Gülen] found retreat and revelation, his exile and prison, his companions and gatherings. Month after month he would stay there in his sacred space and not leave it except to go to one of his other small rooms if he received a sign, an indication or warning that it was necessary for him to leave [and] go to another place. Out of the 5th Floor, Fethullah served to revive religion in Turkey.[40]

Although it can be argued at what scale Gülen revived religion in Turkey, there can be little doubt—as we shall see, that even while Hodjaefendi was ensconced in his "sacred space," Hizmet was growing around the country.

Somewhat more prosaically, but confirming the general contours of the above, scholar of Islam Marcia Hermansen saw the "5th Floor" as more than a literal place. It was, yes, the top floor of a dormitory. But "the number five in itself was not the idea; it could have been the fifteenth or the fiftieth floor," Gülen opined. Rather, it was "the concept of height or sublimity" that mattered, and it was that awareness of the sublime that made this period, for all of its difficulties, one that was "remembered fondly by senior students." The 5th Floor thus represented "an experience of a spiritual retreat, and a vantage point at which [Gülen] received inspiration of future projects as seen on the horizons. ... It is also remembered as a time of his deepest contemplations and self-accountings, a formative and inspired period in the development of the movement."[41] As Hermansen goes on to suggest further, among people of Hizmet a "sacred space" also gave birth to "sacred time." Out of Gülen's withdrawal developed a growing sense of shared (if not mythic) history. That collective history centered on a narrative of struggle associated with Gülen himself. Of course, not all of those inspired by Gülen shared this metaphorical attachment to myth. To many, "the 5th Floor" was simply a way to talk in code about Hodjaefendi without getting into trouble with State security services.

The 5th Floor—deep peace as trust

Even less poetically, but crucially, during his years in Istanbul people's trust in Gülen grew. They saw him respond to oppression not with fear or reaction, but with patient commitment to the principles and practices that had defined his life from the beginning. On one level, this was sheer consistency—practicing what he preached. But on another level, it was pragmatic—it produced results. Thus, one Istanbul businessman reported in an interview with sociologist Helen Rose Ebaugh that: "People in the Gülen movement turn their ideas into projects; they tell how they accomplished their success. People trust them, if they ask for a project, they expect it from the Creator, not from creatures, and that's why I believe they reach success."[42] Such trust in one's Creator can be naiveté—when not linked to practical action. But "in every local circle in which I interviewed," Ebaugh reported, "members expressed their trust" in Gülen, and in each other. That trust was the foundation of deep peace—and the principled side of the principled pluralism of hoşgörü. Trust in God, inner peace, translated to trust in people in practical action on behalf of the community. Or, as Orhan Pamuk put it, again, "it is when the heroes have withdrawn into themselves … that we embrace them."

That embrace happened gradually during the decades of the 1980s and 1990s, and not first of all in The City. "In those hard days (on the run)," Tahsin Şimşek explained, "he was constantly going. There was a reason for this. This allowed Hodjaefendi to visit everyone across the country. This may have been a vehicle for Hizmet to expand."[43] So what had been a set-back—detainment and surveillance—turned into a positive: building community across an entire nation. Gülen's biography here mirrored broad social and demographic changes across Turkish society. What had happened to Hodjaefendi over the course of his life, moving from the provincial town of Erzurum to Edirne to Izmir and finally to Istanbul, was happening in similar ways for many other Turks. And Gülen's example, and explicit teachings, helped them to navigate these changes. People inspired by Gülen were "internally mobilized people," said journalist Kerim Balcı. They were moving "from the periphery to the center." It was a "shocking experience," Balcı contended, for some Turks to "see a different world in their own country." They began to realize that as rural residents or villagers they had by and large been "left out" of Turkey's modernization.[44] For some—and Gülen urged people in this direction, such alienation produced a profound motivation to improve their lot. For others, and again Gülen served as a goad, they took their alienation and turned their attention toward improving the lot of their fellow human beings.

Balcı's own story is illustrative. He grew up in a "mountain village" near the Black Sea—"totally cut off from city life," as he put it. Yet, at the age of 12, he enrolled in Samsun Anatolian High School—a prestigious boarding school in the Black Sea resort city. There, he "started to hear the term 'Hodjaefendi,'" he recalled, and he began to read *Sızıntı*. He found the journal marked by what he called "high Turkish" style. It had strong lead articles, as he remembered them, that were always written by Gülen, even while he was on the run. Balcı had grown up in a "nationalist" household, but he had begun praying as a young teenager, so he would have been recognized at prayer on Fridays in Samsun mosques. He began receiving invitations to *sohbet*s at area houses of light. After he attended a few times, *abi*s began to visit him, asking him if he needed anything. He then began to listen to tapes of Hodjaefendi's sermons, which were in wide circulation. Balcı also benefited from tutoring at Hizmet *dershane*s. After a few years, he gained acceptance to Istanbul's Boğaziçi University in 1986—no doubt one of the best schools in Turkey. It specialized in educating "the secular elite," Balcı said.

About people of Hizmet, Balcı simply said: "I learned to trust them." "I started to feel as if I were a member of a new family," he went on, "that sense of belonging I'd been missing was now there ... I felt tranquility, peace." Alienation gave way to community. Such a sense of peace—of belonging—motivated him to try to give back: "I found myself doing the same [things] that the *abi*s had done for me. I started asking [other students] whether they were having problems. I chose students from village backgrounds." This, Balcı opined, shows how Hizmet "doesn't teach theory, it teaches practice." By 1992 Balcı was volunteering at the public events where Gülen spoke. He acted as a gatekeeper during the entry and exit of Gülen, in part to prevent some people from exhibiting extreme acts of veneration which bothered Gülen. "This gave me a chance to have encounters with the older *abi*s," Balcı said. "Not recognizing all of them initially, I physically prevented some of them from following Hodjaefendi." Despite these missteps, Balcı was gradually accepted as a trusted volunteer within Hizmet. After graduation, he began preparing leaflets on behalf of various Hizmet initiatives and events—sometimes in ways that led to debate and even disputes. But that was his introduction to the world of publishing. He would remain in that business until 2016, when he had to flee Turkey after the failed coup. He eventually landed in Great Britain, where he continues active in various Hizmet initiatives there. In general, "we were the people of the periphery moving to the center," Balcı concluded. Those people had been "internally mobilized" by Gülen's teaching, and then both "horizontally mobilized" to move to new places, and "vertically mobilized" by being connected with various Hizmet agencies and institutions.[45] Such mobilization was the kind of peacebuilding that Gülen had envisioned very early in his teaching career. He had anticipated and encouraged an emerging "golden generation." These individuals would be nonviolent and literate advocates for a more empathetic and just Turkey. People like Kerim Balcı, mobilized from periphery to center, would be among them.

Founding schools—Yamanlar and Fatih

The emergence of the Hizmet movement from the inspiration of Fethullah Gülen was actually much less hierarchical than the word "mobilization" suggested in this single story. "Trust" is another word that Balcı used. And it was trust that was the crucial, albeit difficult to quantify, factor. Throughout the 1980s and '90s, associations between Gülen, students, and the wider Hizmet movement were loose. People came and went. Gülen was no longer, or rarely, preaching. There was no organizational flow-chart. Somewhat astonishingly, nevertheless, friends of Gülen managed in 1982 to turn the dormitory in the Bozyaka neighborhood of Izmir, founded in 1976, into a high school. It was called Yamanlar. Tahsin Şimşek was one of the organizers, and according to him Gülen played a key role as goad, if not pest, to motivate the project. "One day," Şimşek remembered, in a meeting with other business leaders held in Bozyaka, Gülen said, "'Let's make this building a high school.' That sent a chill through the room," Şimşek recalled. The room became chilly because such a plan was, at the time, not embraced by some of the board members, not to mention expensive. Yet Gülen "kept it up for three months. Finally," Şimşek recounted, "I said to my friends, 'I love you all, but Hodjaefendi … [keeps] asking about this school. Can't we hurry this up?' Then after an hour Hodjaefendi came to the room. He looked in our faces. And I said to my friend, Halit: 'go to Ankara. Get a license for a school.' And that's how the process started."[46]

There was a back story or context to this personal pestering by the fugitive Gülen. A new Constitution for the Republic of Turkey had been ratified on 5 November of 1982. Turgut Özal's Motherland Party was in political ascendance, and it would win a surprising Parliamentary majority in 1983 elections. With Özal and his party in power, people of Hizmet had reason to believe that the strictures on their contributions to public life were likely to ease. Sociologist Muhammed Çetin explained: "An aspect of Özal's liberalization was his encouragement of a role for Islam in public life. Özal understood that Islam was the source of the belief system and values for most Turkish citizens, and that it was excluded from the public sphere only with increasing awkwardness and artificiality. He said in 1986: 'Restrictions on freedom of conscience breed fanaticism, not the other way around.'"[47] With that attitude as their milieu, Hizmet *mütevelli* like Şimşek could imagine realizing an initiative like a high school at Yamanlar. It was not that repression had ended; the military was still very much on the scene. But a new opening was on the horizon.

Gülen's own vision for the school was typically exalted. It would foster students who would be "disciplined like soldiers, knowledgeable like doctors, spiritual like members of a *tekke* (*Sufi* lodge), and healthy like athletes."[48] His lofty ambition was realized more fully than even he might have imagined. Within a few years, Yamanlar was drawing elite students from all over Turkey. Those students were performing well at Science Olympiads and athletic competitions. They also were gaining admission to Turkey's most prestigious universities. By 2008, Yamanlar had expanded educational initiatives across age groups on ten campuses, and, according to sociologist Joshua D. Hendrick, "collectively, its graduating middle school students earned more points on the [selective high school admissions] exam than did any other … school in Turkey. Two students scored a perfect 100."[49] Dr. Ali Yurtsever, an Administrator at the school in the 1990s, remembered that "Hocaefendi personally assisted in building the school." Whether Gülen wore a hard hat isn't clear, but Yurtsever did remember that Gülen "refused money from [a donor in] Saudi Arabia since he wanted the school to be an entirely local initiative.

He even brought in benefactors to guard the buildings during the night, so that they would remain connected to the project."[50]

A similar connection was underway in Istanbul, and that led to the founding of Fatih High School in The City. Hendrick describes the trajectory, in what sounds like a puff-piece, but isn't:

> In a conservative Istanbul neighborhood called Fatih, followers of Fethullah Gülen incorporated a pre-existing private dormitory into a new private educational institution. In 1982, just after the opening of Yamanlar, Çag Öğretim İşletmeleri (Era/Age Educational Enterprises) opened Fatih Koleji. In its first year, Fatih sent over 85 percent of its senior class to prestigious universities in Turkey. By the late 1980s, Fatih graduated some of Turkey's highest-performing students on the [college entrance exam]. By 2007, Fatih College was known as one of the most reputable private education institutions in Turkey, managing six primary schools, three high schools, and five dormitories. Like their counterparts at Yamanlar, students at Fatih College in Istanbul (as well as students at numerous [Hizmet-related] private high schools throughout Anatolia) spent the 1990s and 2000s continuously winning national and international science and math competitions.[51]

Hendrick asks the obvious question—how did they do it? Students tended to credit faculty, but Hendrick's answer was that "Fatih College, Yamanlar College, and numerous other schools and companies in Turkey were connected via social networks to dozens of supplemental education institutions." These supplemental education institutions—tutoring centers, "offered students coming from [these schools] ... special services, discounts, and added attention because they were 'in the community' (cemaatın içinde)."[52] Hendrick speculated somewhat cynically that these "professional incentives" predominated over students' desires to "participate in a national revival of faith." And, for a few, that was probably true. Incentives to talented students bred success. But for many others, probably most, they had intentions that were beyond economic calculation. If they were not motivated to participate in a "national revival of faith," they were at least in sync with Gülen's own life and thought. Such students wanted to be part of that Golden Generation. They bought into the stated rationales for which "the community" existed. And the schools associated with the community multiplied quickly. Joining Yamanlar and Fatih, in short order, were Hizmet-related school networks such as Samanyolu in Ankara, Aziziye in Erzurum and Serhat in Van, among others.

Succeeding "for the pleasure of God"

Whatever the motives for students (and their parents) to support these schools, the rationales of those who founded them were theological. Educating children was serving God. The community gathering around Gülen was a theological community, even while its educational aims and accomplishments were secular by law and intention. Of course, students were motivated to succeed (few have actively sought failure, after all), and of course students sought to accrue awards or to win competitions that reflected well on themselves and their parents. But the *community* mattered too. That's why students routinely deferred recognition of their accomplishments to the work of their teachers: it was relationship, community, that mattered more than one's ego-accomplishments. This may be difficult for Western readers, and particularly Americans raised with both individualism and striving privilege as our lifeblood, to comprehend. But in students' own words—which it would be good for a historian, at least, to credit—they were striving not just for secular success, but to realize something encompassed by an Arabic term that was central in the practice of Sufism: *rıza-i İlahi*—succeeding for the "pleasure of God."[53] Yusuf Pekmezci—present for the founding of Yamanlar—said this about Gülen, and why people were attracted to him: "He did not care for money or possessions; he only cared about *rıza-i İlahi.*"[54]

As theologian Pim Valkenberg first pointed out, the entry on *rıza* is the longest in the first volume of Gülen's book on Sufism. Technically, the term translates as "resignation." But as with so many concepts within Sufism, this one contains a paradox. "Giving up" of the ego and its desire for control—which is one way to describe *rıza,* can open a person into greater depth, creativity, even joy. Thus, as Gülen defined it, "*Rıza* (resignation) means showing no rancor or rebellion against misfortune, and accepting all manifestations of Destiny without complaint and even peacefully." This was the deep peace that Gülen found on the 5th Floor, and that he soon turned into deep dialogue across Turkey, as we shall see. Just as he did in his teaching in Istanbul, Gülen in his description of rıza patiently walked the reader through a variety of Muslim authorities on the concept. Then he added his own interpretation of the key Qur'anic passage:

> One can have no greater reward or higher rank than God's being pleased with him or her, which is only attainable by personal resignation to what [God] has decreed. *"God has promised the believers, men and women, Gardens through which rivers flow, therein to abide, and blessed dwellings in Gardens of perpetual bliss, and greater is God's being pleased with them. That indeed is the supreme triumph"* (9:72).
> ... As the greatest rank in God's sight, resignation or God's pleasure is a final target that has been sought by the greatest members of humanity, from the glory of creation [Muhammad], upon him be peace and blessings, to all the other Prophets, saints, and purified scholars who have passed the final test through sincerity, certainty, reliance, surrender, and confidence. They have surmounted many difficulties and obstacles, and bore many unendurable sufferings and torments."[55]

Clearly, a life dedicated to "God's pleasure" was not necessarily a life of personal ease.

Of course, such idealism (recall Gülen's admiration for Kant) would be nothing but rhetoric without action to back it up. Hence, along with the schools that were founded in the 1980s came a dramatic expansion in tutoring centers and other social businesses. Turgut Özal had studied engineering and economics, had spent a year in the U.S., and had worked for the World Bank. He was influenced by and had studied *Nakşibendi* Sufism from the 1960s. He was probably prepared to understand Gülen better than any prior leader of the Republic. The two grew, if not close, certainly cordial: in fact, Gülen visited Özal in the U.S. in 1992. At that time, Gülen was on his first (and only) world tour, of sorts, and Özal was hospitalized in Houston, where he was receiving specialized medical care not available in Turkey. In any event, during his years in power, from 1983-93, Özal "reoriented Turkish politics more significantly than anyone since Atatürk," according to historian Carter Vaughn Findley. "Economically," Findley continued, Özal "replaced the inward-oriented, import-substitution policy pioneered in the 1930s with an export-led growth strategy, so adjusting to the global trend toward privatization."[56] Put more succinctly, Özal adjusted Turkey to neo-liberal economics. More crassly, he opened the way to crony capitalism. Recep Tayyip Erdoğan—the next leader who would dramatically transform the Republic—certainly followed those models. Perhaps most accurately, though, Özal shaped Turkey in the direction that Muhammad Yunus would later define as social business. That is, Özal sought to promote businesses that both served private ends and the public good. People could do well and do good, he thought, by merging Islamic ethics and modern capitalism. In those efforts, Özal found Fethullah Gülen and the people of Hizmet to be decided allies.

We shall explore more fully the business side of Gülen's biography and Hizmet's growth in Chapter 5, but several of the initiatives that took root in the Özal era deserve at least mention here. We've already seen the founding of Yamanlar, Fatih, and other schools from pre-school through secondary. Özal generally loosened (while hardly ending) the State's stranglehold on education. He allowed private educational enterprises to develop—from preschools to universities. Over the decade of the 1980s, for example, the number of universities in Turkey went from 19 to 29.[57] Obviously, such policies coincided nicely with the efforts begun by Hodjaefendi and Hizmet. Admissions standards to colleges and elite high schools—previously skewed to favor the secular elite, were changed to incorporate more objective criteria (hence examinations). Along with these structural changes came an opening to education in Islam itself— which of course had been officially curtailed since Atatürk. In fact, *mandatory* instruction of basics of Islam was approved by the government as a component within the secular educational curriculum. It is difficult to overestimate how strong a break this was with the legacy of modern Turkey's founder. As a result, in 1984, 34 new *Imam-Hatip* middle and high schools, which were designed to train ministers and preachers, opened across the country. Many of the graduates of these schools—both boys and girls, then went on to secondary education, often in secular topics. Although girls could not anticipate being prayer leaders (except for in womens' only prayer meetings), they could serve the faith in many other ways, and many parents liked the security of sending their daughters to a "faith-based" school, where along with the standard secular curriculum the girls would receive a strong dose of Qur'anic and other Islamic studies. Some students associated with Hizmet attended these *Imam-Hatip* schools, and dormitories were built to support these new initiatives.

Generally, though, Hizmet-related schools were secular in curriculum and operation. They were tuition-driven, but also subsidized by charitable donors.[58]

Along with the dramatic increase in schools across Turkey came a corresponding expansion in the number of test-prep centers—*dershanes*. Between 1984, when the tutoring centers were incorporated into Turkey's education system as "supplementary" institutions, to 2002, the number of such agencies grew from 174 to 2,100.[59] Gradually, the dozens of these agencies connected to people of Hizmet took shape in a kind of franchise operation, often under the umbrella brand of FEM [Fırat Eğitim Merkezi—Fırat Educational Center—named for a major donor.] FEM was soon joined by a "sister organization," called "'Sevgi Çiçeği' Anafen (Flower of Love)," which is a combination of Ana (short for Anadolu, schools specialized for humanities) and Fen (schools with intense curriculum with science)." This latter organization focused on tutoring adolescents and young teenagers. By 2007, "FEM ... was the most highly acclaimed supplemental education company in Istanbul with forty-seven branches" in The City alone, and hundreds in cities and towns across Turkey. Not all the students at these test-prep centers were directly connected to the community or to Gülen. Hendrick tells the story of one, Lale, who at first wanted "nothing to do with" the Gülen-associated *dershane* in her hometown of Ankara. In Turkey's capital, anti-Gülen hostility was often high. Yet after disappointing experiences at another tutoring center, Lale eventually found herself in a Gülen associated study program. She found there serious peers, and extra help (including one-on-one tutoring) from university students who lived in a nearby *dershane* or "house of light." Eventually, she scored well on the exam, and went on to study at prestigious Boğaziçi University.[60] Her personal success was fostered by dozens of people committed to success "for the pleasure of God."

New media efforts

Along with educational initiatives, the 1980s and '90s also saw people inspired by Gülen forge new media-initiatives. The first was a daily newspaper—*Zaman*. The name means "Time" in English. The first issue appeared on November 3, 1986. According to one source, before then there were ... attempts [by] other Muslim entrepreneurs but they couldn't survive. In that period, the [Hizmet] schools, dorms, and *dershanes* continued to be developed. And there were supporters of these institutions and there were enemies. In Turkey, media was a monopoly. Journalists [were] raised by the paper *Cumhuriyet*. They are totally leftist, atheist people. ... So, there were aspirations to do something about this. ... Then what happened? The other papers could not write fake news, because now, our correspondents were everywhere and by then we had a newspaper and a television channel [Samanyolu TV—founded in 1993]. You must think of *Zaman* as a tool to correct fake news.[61]

No news, of course, is neutral. But Turkish journalism was particularly suspect. There were stories that had circulated in the Turkish press that directly contradicted widely-known facts about cases, especially in religious matters. So "fake news" meant, by and large, ideologically biased reporting. *Zaman* arose, then, to present an alternative perspective on current events to that presented by the traditional print media. One editor with whom I spoke described *Zaman*'s political orientation in 2009 as "center-right," and that is probably an accurate description of its political orientation throughout its existence (it was confiscated by the government and closed in 2016). Not surprisingly, *Zaman* was generally friendly to Islam. It featured stories and columns that highlighted Gülen and Hizmet, including some written by Hodjaefendi. But it would be too strong to label even the early efforts of the paper in the 1980s "Islamist." In the 1990s, furthermore, the newspaper dramatically increased its professionalism—for instance, using fact-checkers. *Zaman* also boasted the first online presence for any Turkish newspaper, in 1995. These initiatives were begun by several students of Gülen who had graduated from professional journalism programs in the U.S. and in Turkey. They had undertaken that study at Gülen's recommendation. Increased professionalism led to increased subscriptions. Between 1986 and 2007 the paper grew tenfold to become Turkey's most widely circulated newspaper, with stated subscriptions of over a million.[62]

Gülen's own role in the founding of *Zaman* was, typically, opaque. When asked in an interview about the start-up, Gülen obliquely offered that whenever Hizmet grew it was "all up to people being able to get together and talk and enlighten themselves and view each other with tolerance."[63] The word translated as "tolerance" here was *hoşgörü*. *Zaman* was to be one means to promote *hoşgörü*. The newspaper was thus part of the broader peacebuilding effort of the "golden generation." About that generation, Gülen wrote, generally, that in an effort to "stay in touch and communicate with people's minds, hearts, and feelings, these new men and women will use the mass media and try to establish a new power balance of justice, love, respect, and equality among people. They will make might subservient to right, and never discriminate on grounds of color or race."[64] These were not modest aims for a newspaper. The history of mass media, with its occasionally crass commercialism and more frequent tendency (in Turkey) to veer into propaganda, might have suggested that such aims were not likely to be entirely realized. Yet the hope for a free and critical press dies hard. When the newspaper was closed in 2016, supporters carried signs with the slogan "Free Media Cannot Be Silenced." Time will tell.

From 1986 on, back in Istanbul, other media initiatives followed rapidly. Since the 1960s, Gülen's sermons had been audiotaped and videotaped and circulated widely. An expansion of those forms of media could solve the problem of crowd control that was vexing people of Hizmet, once Gülen returned to public life in 1989. According to one source, who was also a participant in the events: "People over-crowded the mosques and not everybody could listen to him. And there was a need to inform people correctly." Stereotypes about Gülen were circulating, so a range of options was needed both to provide friends with the latest news and to broadcast accurate information to others. Conveniently, though, the market also required this move: you could "address many more people from the TV through several different kinds of productions." And so began Cihan News Agency—a sort of "associated press" of Gülen-inspired television, radio, and print journalists. Most of these journalists wrote for or worked in production capacities for what eventually became a conglomerate of Gülen-related media businesses—Feza Publications. Feza, like *Zaman*, was incorporated in 1986; in fact, *Zaman* was one of its companies. Cihan News Agency was founded in 1994. Before it was shut down by the government in July 2016, it had employed over 500 men and women, and had branch offices or correspondents in Central Asia, the Middle East, the Balkan States, Europe, South America, Africa and the Far East, including global hotspots like Gaza and Kabul.[65]

Truly, within a few years, people of Hizmet formed a rather astonishing array of private media initiatives. One observer sketched the multiplication in a succinct compression:

> In addition to the newspaper *Zaman*, the Gülen movement ... launched
> a national television channel, known as Samanyolu, and popular radio
> stations such as Dünya (World), and Burç (Tower). The movement
> also [published] *Sızıntı* (a scientific monthly), *Ekoloji* (an environ-
> ment-related magazine), *Yeni Ümit* (a theological journal), *Aksiyon*
> (a weekly magazine), and *The Fountain* (English language religious
> publication). Gülen's activities [were] aimed at molding a cohesive
> and disciplined community through education, mass media, and fi-
> nancial networks. In the United States, the movement ... established
> Blue Dome Press and has been active in the book publishing business.

All these agencies were related to the Hizmet movement, but none of them was technically owned by the movement. More accurately, these media companies were owned and operated by individuals inspired by Gülen. Gülen himself played no direct role in their operation. Naturally, he was aware of them, frequently appeared in or on them, and he approved generally of their work as professional media enterprises, in an Islamic-friendly mode, in the public sphere. But the success of these initiatives pointed toward a momentum in Hizmet to move well beyond the 5th Floor. The City was starting its embrace of Fethullah Gülen. It must be noted here that all these publications were shut down in Turkey by the Erdoğan regime in 2016. Some of them continued publication abroad. For example, Blue Dome Press started *Çağlayan* magazine [Waterfall].

Return to preaching, and a refuge in Mecca?

But Gülen also experienced other events in 1986 that made it possible to establish these media initiatives. Most notably, Turgut Özal arranged to have dropped or overturned the military charges against Gülen. Those charges had kept him on the run and out of public life for six years. His first public appearance after being so exonerated was as preacher at the opening of the Büyük Çamlıca Mosque in Istanbul on 6 April 1986. His sermon developed a theme that would dominate his public addresses for the next decade: the importance for Muslim faith and life of the Prophet Muhammad (peace be upon him). More specifically, the sermon concentrated on Muhammad's *Mi'raj*—or "Ascension."[66] The "Ascension" is the story told in the Qur'an (Chapter 17, al-Isra, which means "night journey"), and elaborated considerably in the *hadith* literature, of Muhammad's spiritual and physical journey in one night first to Jerusalem, and then to heaven. It was during this visit to heaven where Muhammad received the rule from God mandating prayer five times per day. Gülen's topic was hardly a coincidence. *Lailat al Mi'raj*—the festival to celebrate the Ascension—is one of the most important in Islam, and it coincided in 1986 with Gülen's address. One source reports, with a touch of melodrama, but probably in a way accurate to the spirit of the night, that Gülen "was at the pulpit with tears in his eyes as he usually was. He was excited, on the one hand, to talk about God and His beloved Messenger and, on the other hand, to be before the people [from] whom he had been separated for years. There was a spiritually heavy atmosphere at the mosque."[67] Spiritually heavy, or not, it was surely a historic occasion. That it also set the theme and tone for Gülen's next decade and more of preaching and teaching made it both a dramatic return to public life and an indication of a new or deepened trajectory in his thought and influence. The example of the Prophet would become Gülen's chief inspiration to advance *hoşgörü*.

Also, in 1986 Gülen made his third, and what would probably be his final, pilgrimage to Mecca. That Gülen's public profile had improved was evident in his travel partners. He was accompanied not only by students and businessmen close to him, but also by a member of the Turkish Parliament, Arif Hikmet. Gülen on at least one occasion told the story of how he and this politician interacted. "Let me narrate an incident that occurred during a visit to the Prophet's holy city," he began.

> The atmosphere was overpowering. Something occurred to me: I pray to God every morning, saying seven times: "O my God, save me from Hellfire and make me enter paradise among the company of the godly people." There can be no believer who does not wish to enter Paradise. However, in this environment I asked myself: "If they were to invite you to Paradise through any of its seven gates, which would you prefer,

entering in the *rawdah* (the area in the mosque next to the Prophet's tomb) or entering Paradise? Believe me, I swear by God that I said to myself: "This place [that is, staying in proximity to the Prophet's tomb] is more dear to me. I have had the chance to rub my face against the soil of my master, at whose door I prefer to be a chained slave rather than anything else in the world. I do not want to miss this chance."

I believe this is the desire of every believer. When I was blessed with this great opportunity, I was with Mr. Arif Hikmet, who was then a member of the Turkish Parliament. He told me he had promised himself that he would roll in the soil like a donkey when he stepped across the border and entered the land of Medina. This great man kept his promise. When I remember this incident, I cannot prevent my eyes from watering.[68]

Now, there is a lot going on in this narration. On one level, it pointed to Gülen's intense devotion to the Prophet and to the sacred places associated with him. He was willing to forego paradise to be in proximity to those places. On another level, it indicated that Gülen's travel companion was a person of stature, even a "great man," who in the presence of the sacred places of the Prophet humbled himself in a demonstrative ritual. Finally, it made a theological point: to be a "slave" to the Prophet, or even to make an "ass" out of oneself, was paradoxically to be free. This deep freedom, if you will, came about through community with the Prophet. After all, the Prophet's way opened-up to all people nothing less than Islam itself—a way of truth, goodness, and peace that included (of course) paradise.

While on *Hajj*, Gülen would have needed this deep notion of freedom, for his legal troubles back in Turkey were hardly over, despite Turgut Özal's intervention. News made it to Gülen while in Saudi Arabia—perhaps through his Parliamentary contact—that a new case had been opened against him. This case, not surprisingly, involved accusations of "eroding secularism." It centered around the actions of a man named Mehmet Özyurt, who was at the time an *imam* in Diyarbakır in Southeastern Turkey. Özyurt had been the *imam* at Bornova in 1976 where Gülen had served as preacher, and the two were close (Gülen wrote a eulogy when Özyurt died in a traffic accident in 1988). Özyurt, like Gülen, also had a record of run-ins with the authorities; he had previously been arrested in

1983. But in July 1986 Özyurt was working in Diyarbakır, where he was arrested again, along with two other Gülen associates—Yahya Kaçmaz and Ahmet Kuş. A journalist had reported that the three planned to establish a "United Islamic Republic" in Turkey—a ludicrous charge. But Gülen, in an unfortunately all-too-common Turkish mode that ascribed guilt-by-even-the-most-tenuous-association, was linked to the three and a warrant was issued for his arrest.[69] Such a warrant of course would have made his re-entry into his native land challenging, if not impossible.

As this news reached Gülen in Saudi Arabia, he discussed it with his travel companions and his hosts. He could not return to Turkey without facing arrest. He had been avoiding exactly this prospect for six years, and he had thought that the Özal intervention had put this fear behind him. According to one source, Gülen was then offered the opportunity to stay in Saudi Arabia. It is interesting to speculate about how different the future of Hizmet might have been had he accepted the invitation to become a permanent resident scholar in Mecca or Medina. It is possible to imagine that he would have had a comfortable life. And surely a preacher of Muslim tolerance in the heart of hard-line Saudi Arabia could have done a lot of good. But another possibility emerges. Perhaps this invitation was also a temptation. Perhaps Gülen would have been swallowed up by the Saudi regime—either co-opted or coerced, and rendered useless. In any event, it is doubtful that the global initiatives associated with Hizmet to emerge after 1986, as we shall see, would have begun had Hodjaefendi stayed in his beloved land of the Prophet. Thus, as a source recalled it, Gülen replied to the offer to house him in the holiest lands of Islam with the following words, more or less: "No, thank you very much for your offer, but if I don't return it could be taken to mean that I am accepting the crime I am accused of. In addition, I set out on this path to serve others. The people of Anatolia are waiting for me. I have to go back." So, he went. He traveled by land, through Syria—on foot some accounts have it, crossing over into Turkey via Kilis on the Syrian border, and traveling incognito to the relatively friendly (or at least familiar) city of Izmir—where he surrendered to the police. In Izmir, after a brief statement was taken, he was released. Shortly thereafter, those charges against him were dismissed. It would be December before Özyurt and the others were also exonerated.[70]

So, on one level, by 1986 things were looking up for Gülen and people of Hizmet. Turgut Özal was still the Prime Minister, and Hizmet was growing throughout the country. But on another level troubles endured—charges of sedition could come from anywhere, and there would always be someone who believed them. Consequently, Hodjaefendi once again felt it prudent to fall silent and to retreat to the 5th Floor (along with various other safe houses throughout Turkey). He would not resume his public preaching until 1989. Yet the decade had given Gülen a ground of trust with many individuals in Turkey; a foundation of deep peace. It was on that foundation that Fethullah Gülen would turn *hüzün* into *hoşgörü* through Hizmet.

Final years of preaching—dialogue with the Prophet

When Gülen came back to public preaching—for the last time—it was with a schedule that eventually took its toll on the fifty-one-year-old. For over two years, from January 13, 1989 to June 16, 1991, he preached at least weekly, and often twice per week, in mosques in three major cities of Turkey. His most frequent pulpit was Üsküdar's Valide Sultan Mosque, on the Asian side of Istanbul—not far from the 5th Floor. But over the next months, he would also preach at Sinan's sixteenth-century masterpiece, Süleymaniye, Fatih Mosque, and at the gorgeous seventeenth-century mosque at the heart of The City, Sultanahmet (the Blue Mosque). His sermons at the latter sites became increasingly common in the early 1990s, as did a pattern of preaching in Istanbul on Fridays, and Izmir on Sundays. In Izmir, he usually preached at two famous mosques—Hisar and Şadırvanaltı. Among the other sites Gülen visited to speak at were Istanbul's Fatih (several times), Ankara's Kocatepe, in March, 1990, and Erzurum's Ulu Mosque, in June, 1990. The latter was surely a pleasant homecoming—now as an invited and honored guest, rather than on the run.[71]

These were the most famous mosques in Turkey. Kocatepe alone could fit 24,000 people. At each site, whenever Gülen preached, crowds packed the mosques. People spilled out into the streets surrounding the venues; at Hisar Mosque in Izmir, and perhaps at other sites, video screens and loudspeakers were set up outside for people to see and to hear Gülen preach. Despite all of this enthusiasm, and in part because of it, the situations were becoming unsafe. Bomb threats were not uncommon. Gülen had been targeted by death threats repeatedly. According to sociologist Muhammed Çetin, "at the beginning of the 1990s, the police uncovered a number of conspiracies by marginal militant Islamists and other small ideological groups to assassinate Gülen," and these same groups also placed "agents provocateurs" to cause "disorder" among the massive crowds gathered to hear him.[72]

That dynamic hastened Gülen's permanent retirement from public preaching in 1991. But over an intense eighteen-month period of preaching and teaching activity Gülen concentrated the attention of the many who followed him on the Prophet Muhammad (pbuh). For sixty-one weeks, from January 13, 1989 to March 16, 1990, Gülen preached on themes related to Prophet Muhammad and his Companions (the *Sahaba*). Then, in June 1991, Gülen keynoted a symposium in Istanbul on the Prophet (Ebedi Risalet Sempozyumu). The focus was impossible to miss for anyone paying attention. Gülen had concentrated on particular topics in his preaching before. But this was unprecedented. Fethullah Gülen obviously thought Muslims in the 1980s and 1990s would benefit from a careful study of the life of the Prophet.

Now, Prophet Muhammad was hardly a controversial choice for a sermon series, or for a symposium. But, the 1979 Iranian revolution had showed one of the ways that Islam and the legacy of the Prophet could be applied in public life—by narrowing choices for people and by imposing theocracy (or mullah-ocracy). As interpreted by Gülen, however, following the Prophet Muhammad was not primarily a means to revel in Islam's glory days; it meant in fact that Muslims should be leaders in the practices of *hoşgörü*. That meant, again, to see all others as God saw them, with eyes of mercy and compassion. And that meant opening-up options for people, not narrowing them. And that meant advancing democracy. It was through *hoşgörü*, Gülen contended, that the Prophet had persuaded his closest Companions to join him in positive action in the early years of the Muslim *ummah* or community. It was through *hoşgörü*, Gülen preached, that Islam grew as rapidly as it did in the first glorious years of the tradition. And it was through *hoşgörü*, Gülen helped other Muslims to see, that *hizmet* could be activated in the modern world on behalf of a more just and peaceful planet. What followed from this sermon series was a dizzying array of new partnerships over the decade of the 1990s in Turkey and (increasingly) around the world: dozens of new educational initiatives and institutions, handfuls of new social business start-ups, and (especially) large public interreligious dialogue events. Gülen's focus on the Prophet produced an outpouring of energy that made it seem as if The City in its entirety had embraced him. The truth, of course, was more complex, as Gülen's self-imposed exile to the U.S. by the end of the decade suggested. But by then, both scholars and diplomats around the world had taken notice of the collective energy that began to be called, primarily in the West, "the Gülen movement."

It was a name that the man himself rejected. For Gülen, *hoşgörü* was hardly his idea. Instead, *hoşgörü* was living out what the Prophet Muhammad had practiced. *Hoşgörü* was at the heart of the peacebuilding that was at the heart of Islam. Although the emphasis that Gülen placed on the life and example of Muhammad in the 1990s was a new focus in his preaching, devotion to the Prophet and Companions was not new in his life. One of his oldest associates, Hatem Bilgili, reported that as a young man living in Erzurum, Gülen would pay night visits to the graves of departed scholars and saints who were identified with the Prophet and his Companions. "A year before he left Erzurum [1958]," Bilgili recounted, "I saw [Hodjaefendi] start visiting the surrounding cemeteries. He'd go to the known and unknown [scholars and saints] that were buried there. He'd pray for them. This was at night. He wore thin clothing—it was really cold. I was afraid for him. There were wolves in the region. One day I saw him put his head on a rock at a mausoleum. ... It was as if he was saying 'get up!' He seemed to form a connection. ... He'd go all over Erzurum to visit the buried scholars."[73]

One of those saints was Gazi Abdurrahman. The story has it that Gazi Abdurrahman ibn Abu Bakr, the son of Prophet Muhammad's friend, lived during the reign of Yazid (d. 683), who was the second caliph of the Umayyad Dynasty (centered in Syria). Although a Muslim, Yazid is remembered with the brutal murder of the Prophet's grandson, Husayn, and his family at Kerbela. Many of the Prophet's extended family members, and the families of his Companions, thus fled the Arabian Peninsula for distant lands, including Anatolia. Gazi was among them. His tomb, high atop a mountain on the outskirts of Erzurum, remains an important site of devotional visits down to today. It was one of the sites that Gülen visited on his youthful night-time excursions. It is also, it's worth pointing out, a location that wolves would no doubt have found congenial.

These details about Gülen's devotion to the Prophet and his Companions are not merely amusing anecdotes; they point to several important aspects of Gülen's understanding of the Prophet's role in Islam that are worth highlighting. One is that while Prophet Muhammad historically had to engage in battle, and thus was a military leader, whose expeditions Gülen narrated with vivid and dramatic detail in his sermons, those sermons also emphasized far more frequently the *nonviolent* and peacebuilding practices of the Prophet and Companions. Thus, "God's Messenger never sought a worldly kingdom," Gülen suggested, "[because] he was sent to guide humanity to salvation in both worlds. His goal was to revive people, not to kill them."[74] This common-sense maxim—"revive people, don't kill them"—coexisted with another aspect of Gülen's devotion to the Prophet and Companions that was (and is) somewhat controversial to some literalists.

For the fact of the matter is that to these literalists, paying attention to the Companions and saints in Islam can raise the danger of associating (the Arabic word is *shirk*) some material entity or individual human with God. As scholar of Islam Annemarie Schimmel noted decades ago, veneration of saints has been viewed with suspicion by some Muslims, although of course regard for Prophet Muhammad is high across the Muslim world.[75] Night-time visits to saints' graves and putting one's head down on their tombstones would not ordinarily excite, except to umbrage, some orthodox Muslim scholars, for whom such devotion would veer perilously close to idolatry. Those voices who are critical of saint-veneration are minorities. They are associated especially with hard-line Wahhabism and the Salafi mentality. But those voices are loud and (sometimes) violent, and they could (and did) threaten Gülen's safety and the safety of people close to him. Death threats were nothing new for Gülen. But just as Americans and Europeans began to discover that there were Muslims willing to kill "infidels" in the 1980s and 90s, so did Gülen and the rest of Turkey.[76]

Another risk Gülen faced in turning attention to Prophet Muhammad was the inverse relationship between nostalgia and progress. To a critical Western reader, some of Gülen's words about the Prophet and his Companions may sound like nostalgic exaggeration. He said, for instance, that "the time of the Companions and the two succeeding generations was the time of truthfulness. People of great righteousness ... appeared during these first three generations."⁷⁷ Now, this may be true, but God-willing the seventh century CE was not the only time when people of great righteousness lived. Along the same lines, Gülen also quoted a widely attested *hadith* that reads: "The best of words is the Book of God; the best way to follow is that of Muhammad. The worst affair is innovations (against my *Sunnah*). Each innovation is a deviation."⁷⁸ The Arabic word used here for "innovation" is *bid'ah* and it implies erroneous, heretical, or false associations, not any new ideas. But when this *theological* point is missed and such passages are interpreted narrowly, they might impede progress in *hoşgörü*.

One final risk inherent in Gülen's intense focus on the Prophet also reflected a tendency he did not intend, but that was widespread across modern Islam and in the secular Republic, of deference to individual authority. An authoritarian temptation existed. Thus, Gülen once preached: "the Messenger ordered his Companions to obey his *Sunna* absolutely." Even more dramatically, he went on: "The way of the Prophet is the way of God. As the *Sunna* is the way of the Prophet, those who reject it are, in essence, rejecting (and disobeying) God. As the Prophet stated: 'Whoever obeys me, obeys God; whoever disobeys me, disobeys God.'"⁷⁹ By 1990, Gülen's influence within Turkey had reached unprecedented heights. He did not himself demand obedience from his students or from those inspired by him: they were always free to disagree with him, and they were always free to go their own ways. Many did. But in another vein, the adulation directed toward the leader and an emphasis on obedience could be co-opted and marshaled by unscrupulous political leaders to secure devotion for their own claims of absolute obedience. A future Prime Minister and President of the Turkish Republic would, in the second decade of the twenty-first century, succumb to that authoritarian temptation, with tragic results.

Prophet Muhammad as an advocate of *hoşgörü*—as a uniter

Still, in his public preaching and teaching about the Prophet between 1989 and 1991—much of which is collected in a single large volume translated by Ali Ünal—Gülen did *not* amplify the notes that stressed nostalgia and obedience. Much louder were many other notes that stressed the peacebuilding potential of Islam, as we shall shortly see. And there can be little doubt that far from stymying action by nostalgia or thoughtless obedience, his sermons engaged people in active service across Turkey and around the globe. At the center of what Gülen preached about the life of the Prophet, again, was that the Prophet provided an example for Muslims of *hoşgörü*—of principled pluralism. Gülen developed this thesis in two broad trajectories. The first showed how *hoşgörü* as evident in the life of Muhammad could help Muslims build what sociologists have come to call "bonding social capital." Across the social sciences, as we saw in Chapter One, the concept of "social capital" has been widely used in recent decades to highlight how social relations can have productive benefits for individuals and society.[80] Bonding social capital, as the title suggests, produces stronger ties *within* a group by deepening understanding, trust, unity, and so forth. Gülen fostered and strengthened this adhesive potential of religion in his preaching about Muhammad in the 1990s. He invited Muslims in Turkey to invest in and to benefit from the way the Prophet and Companions had discovered unity. Succinctly, the Prophet's *hoşgörü* could encourage Muslims to trust each other and to work together. The second trajectory of *hoşgörü* as evident in Gülen's sermons about Muhammad, then, was in the arena of "bridging social capital." This type of social relation invites people to reach *outside* of their normal relations to forge new partnerships and new networks among people of apparently diverse backgrounds and interests. As elucidated by Gülen, the life of Muhammad clearly impelled Muslims to build such bridges across many common divides. Succinctly, the Prophet's *hoşgörü* could encourage Muslims to trust and to work together with non-Muslims. And as we shall see shortly, people of Hizmet clearly heard these messages and acted on them. Over the last years of the twentieth century and first decades of the twenty-first century, people inspired by Fethullah Gülen bonded and bridged with remarkable energy and effectiveness.

Gülen developed his teaching about Muhammad as a uniter in seven themes. The Prophet was truthful, trustworthy, a communicator, persistent, a diplomat, intelligent, and an educator. These seven themes each deserve some more detailed attention. They were aspects of Muhammad's life worth understanding. And they reveal nuances in Gülen's own thought and life in relation to the growing Hizmet movement in the 1990s; a blueprint, if you will, of how to grow a movement. Thus, "truthfulness is the cornerstone of Prophethood," Gülen contended. The Qur'an put it directly, Hodjaefendi made plain: "O you who believe, fear God and be with the company of the truthful!" (9:119). Such a company included the Companions who fought (and in some cases died) with Muhammad. It also included those who recorded the sayings and actions (*hadith*) of the Prophet that constituted the broad truth of God's message as conveyed through him—the *Sunnah*. To Western readers, some of this "truth" seems to stretch credibility. For example, many of the *hadith* describe "predictions" by the Prophet that either appear to be coincidences or very creative interpretations of historical developments. Within the worldview of Islam, however, these texts operated as stories that bonded Muslims together. They communicated a simple social truth as strong as any factual account: "Truthfulness always brings salvation, even if it causes one's death. We die through truthfulness only once, whereas each lie is a different kind of death." More succinctly, with only a slightly different nuance, "truthfulness is the pivot of Prophethood."[81] And if the Prophet was truthful, that meant Muslims were to be truth-tellers as well. Gandhi, years before Gülen, had described his own movement in India as one driven by *satyagraha*—truth-force. Intentionally, or not, Gülen was inviting people of Hizmet to act on a similar platform.

Truth-tellers, second, are trustworthy, and Muhammad forged Islam on a foundation of trust. "The second attribute of Prophethood," Gülen taught, "is *amana*, an Arabic word meaning *trustworthiness* and derived from the same root as *mu'min* (believer). Being a believer implies being a trustworthy person." In a culture torn by ideological conflict, this practical wisdom was imperative. "Prophet Muhammad," Gülen made the case, "was completely trustworthy toward all of God's creatures. He was loyal and never cheated anyone." This trustworthiness started, of course, with the recitation of the words of the Qur'an. Muhammad was *ummi*, unschooled, yet "as the Qur'an was given to him as a trust, he conveyed it to people in the best way possible." Gülen's examples of the Prophet's trustworthiness made clear that people's trust in him grew from Muhammad's scrupulous attention to what Gandhi called *ahimsa*—nonviolence to all living creatures. For example, Hodjaefendi told a story from the *hadith* literature about how some of the Companions, while returning from a military campaign, found baby birds in a nest and took them out to pet them. The mother bird, returning to the nest to find it empty, began to fly around in distress. Muhammad, coming to the rescue, ordered the birds returned to the nest immediately, where the mother bird attended to them. "Such an order," Gülen concluded, "was meant to show that representatives of trustworthiness should harm no living creatures."[82]

For Gülen, to be clear, *ahimsa* could in fact coincide with defensive war. After all, even Gandhi had counseled the people of India that taking arms to defend oneself was more virtuous than cowardice and dishonor.[83] In a similar fashion, Hodjaefendi narrated the story of Abu 'Ubayda, the commander of Muslim armies in Syria:

> When the Byzantine Emperor set out to recapture [Homs], Abu 'Ubayda decided to evacuate the city, for his forces were vastly outnumbered. He had the non-Muslim population assembled and announced: "We collected the protection tax from you because we had to defend you. Since we can't defend you against the coming Byzantine assault, we are returning the tax collected." This was done. Pleased with the Muslim administration, Christian priests and Jewish rabbis flocked to the churches and synagogues to pray that God would cause the Muslim army to be successful.

This seems unbelievable, but in fact the Byzantines were not friends of the Christians in Syria, whom the Byzantines considered heretics. And Jews had plenty of reasons to be wary of Christian rulers, as centuries to follow would make plain. But Gülen's point was broader than historical. It was about how Muslims treated others. "Muslim rulers did not interfere with a conquered people's religion, language, or culture. If they had done so, there would have been no followers of other religions in the lands they [ruled]." Gülen was here making what amounted to a radical statement in Turkey—which had established itself as a Republic largely by *reducing* the religious diversity that had existed under the Ottomans. In contrast, the trustworthiness of the Prophet had made Muslim rulers in the first centuries of Islam trustworthy patrons of religious and cultural diversity. Thus, "believers see the whole universe as a cradle of brotherhood and sisterhood, and feel connected to everything. ...Trustworthiness is a cornerstone of belief."[84] Trustworthiness was also, Gülen implied, the foundation for all good politics. Gülen would soon have occasion to put this rhetoric into practice—fostering trust with both Jews and Christians—as we shall see. But by linking this bridge-building to the example of the Prophet, Gülen made his progressive initiatives seem like a matter of bonding with the historic tradition.

A third way that the life of Muhammad promoted unity, according to Gülen, was his work as a communicator. "Just as God manifests [God's] Mercifulness through the sun's warmth and light, He manifested His Mercy and Compassion for humanity through the Prophets. He chose Muhammad, whom he sent as a mercy for all worlds, to establish eternally the Message of compassion and mercy." Muhammad, in short, was to communicate *hoşgörü*. *Hoşgörü* was mercy and compassion in practice; in relationship. This meant forgiveness, above all. Thus "when the Prophet was severely wounded at [Battle of] Uhud," Gülen related, "some Companions asked him to invoke God's curse on the enemy. Instead, he prayed for them, saying: 'O God, forgive my people, because they don't know.' He did this while his face was covered with blood." Such vivid story-telling was a regular feature of Gülen's preaching. The theme of forgiveness was also a regular one for Hodjaefendi. He related, for instance, the story of Muhammad and Wahshi—an Ethiopian slave of an Arab warlord. Wahshi had killed Muhammad's uncle Hamza in the battle of Uhud in 625. His conversion to Islam came through forgiveness. As Gülen spun out the story, Muhammad initiated correspondence with Wahshi (now freed in exchange for his murder of Hamza), and Wahshi replied by saying that he had committed every sin in the book—idolatry, sexual immorality, and murder. Gülen put the question in Wahshi's mouth: "Can such a person really be forgiven and become a Muslim?" The answer, of course, was yes. And this answer was communicated to Wahshi in another letter from the Prophet that contained this verse from the Qur'an, as Gülen taught his listeners: "Say: 'O My servants who have transgressed against their souls! Don't despair of the Mercy of God. God forgives all sins. He is the Oft-Forgiving, the Most Compassionate'"(39:53).[85] The Prophet communicated *hoşgörü*.

Forgiveness as a feature of Muhammad's prophetic communication went along with another aspect of his life that Hodjaefendi felt it important to emphasize: persistence. As is well known, Muhammad faced considerable obstacles as he began preaching Islam. Entrenched tribal loyalties inhibited his efforts to unify Arabs under one God. He faced scorn and much worse. And yet, as Gülen described his life, "insults, derision, and torture did not deter him even once." Some of Gülen's listeners might have faced all the above. Gülen himself had experienced insults, derision, and rough treatment at the hands of police. Yet, "the Messenger persevered," Gülen succinctly put it, despite "enduring relentless and increasingly harsh derision, degradation, beatings, and expulsion." If Muhammad persisted, so should people of Hizmet. And Muhammad did not only demonstrate physical courage. More profoundly, he evidenced *integrity*. "Those who want their words to influence people," Gülen drew out the moral, "must practice what they preach." Consequently, *principled action* was necessary to enact *hoşgörü*. "Human beings are active," Gülen preached. "Therefore, they should be led to those activities that form the real purpose of their lives, as determined by God and communicated by the Prophet. God did not create people only to have them to become passive recluses, [or] activists without reason and spirit, or rationalists without spiritual reflection and action." [86] Islam as practiced by the Prophet was a "middle way," consistently avoiding extremes. And a Muslim who followed the Prophet would persist, no matter what.

Fifth, Muhammad was a diplomat. What Gülen meant by this was that Muhammad tailored what he communicated to the circumstances of the people hearing him. Messages, as Gülen put it, "must be used to reach people on their own level."[87] All of the diverse media efforts of Hizmet are embedded in that brief maxim from the Prophet. Thus, as Hodjaefendi told the story, after having solidified the peace of Islam in Arabia with the Treaty of Hudaybiya, Muhammad reached out in correspondence to the Christian King of Abyssinia—in present day Ethiopia and Eritrea. He did so by first offering him "peace," as Muslims of course do whenever they meet or correspond. The Prophet then identified that "'Jesus is a spirit from God, a word from Him.'" This was, Gülen made it plain, a way of "emphasizing the point of agreement" between the two men. That Jesus was the Word of God was of course a central Christian affirmation. What followed in this relationship between the Prophet and the King of Abyssinia, as Gülen related the tradition, was that the King accepted Islam, although with the caveat that he was "not in a position to make [his] subjects Muslim." The Prophet accepted this compromise, and Ethiopia remains a majority Christian nation down to today. If people were not *against* Islam, they could be taken to be *for* Islam. A good Muslim who practiced *hoşgörü* was a good diplomat—internally, as well as externally.[88]

A sixth feature of the Prophet's *hoşgörü* was intelligence. Gülen did not mean by this narrow rational ability. Rather, intelligence had "a specific meaning" as applied to the Prophet, namely "a composite of reasoning power, sagacity, intelligence, sound judgment, and wisdom." Such a daunting list highlighted how intelligence was a feature of Prophethood that reflected Divine intelligence: "God manifests His Names through veils," as Gülen put it, which meant that we needed Prophets to "unveil" or to reveal to us God's intentions. This kind of intelligence, Gülen preached, was evident primarily in Muhammad's "concise speech." By this phrase Gülen meant to refer less to brevity than to the poetic beauty of the Qur'an. The Prophet spoke appropriately for any circumstance, in short. Gülen could wax poetic about this kind of intelligence as evident in the life of the Prophet: "The nightingale is said to convey the gratitude of plants and flowers to the All-Provider. Likewise, God's Messenger came to 'sing' the praises of God in the 'garden' of humanity and announce His Commandments with his enchanting 'songs.' His words opened ever-fresh flowers in all human hearts."[89] What Gülen saw in the Prophet, and recommended to his listeners, in short, was something like a moral intelligence or even aesthetic intelligence that could unite a community.

Practically, to stay with this topic for a bit—to follow Muhammad's example of "concise speech" meant that a Muslim could give up anything useless to concentrate on things that mattered. *Hoşgörü* may have meant seeing others as God saw them, but that didn't mean that one needed to continue in practices that were unproductive, even if they were lawful and moral. This was especially true if those practices happened to be popular. If humans were to see as God saw, then a corollary was that God *saw* humans, and the Merciful and Compassionate One did not want to see people expelling energy in useless pursuits. "God's Messenger says," Gülen related, "that: 'It is a sign of one's being a good Muslim that he [or she] abandons what is of no use.'" Gülen's exegesis explained: "Such people practice *ihsan*, a term denoting that we worship God as if we see Him, fully aware that even if we cannot see God, [God] sees us all the time."[90] *Ihsan* was an important concept in Sufism. Gülen defined "*ihsan* (perfect goodness) [as] an action of the heart that involves thinking according to the standards of truth; forming the intention to do good, useful things and then doing them; and performing acts of worship as best as possible and in the consciousness that God sees them."[91] From among the many examples that Gülen offered listeners of this kind of intelligence as *ihsan*, one involved, interestingly, the habit of visiting the graves of saints. "Both Bukhari and Muslim relate," Gülen noted to establish the lineage of his teaching in the appropriate *hadith* collections, "that God's Messenger said: 'Patience is shown at the moment of misfortune.'" Gülen then told the story:

> In the early days of his mission, God's messenger forbade people to visit graves, as some un-Islamic practices were still observed. After such practices vanished, he encouraged his Companions to visit graves, and did so himself, for this encourages people to improve their moral conduct and strive for the next life.
>
> During a visit to Medina's graveyard, God's Messenger saw a woman weeping bitterly and complaining about Destiny. When he sought to console her, the woman, who did not recognize him, angrily told him to go away, for: 'You don't know what misfortune has befallen me!' When she later learned his identity, she hurried after him and, finding him at home, begged his pardon. God's Messenger told her: 'Patience is shown at the moment of misfortune.'[92]

A pithy proverb like this pointed to a practical kind of intelligence, indeed. Injuries, slights, or misfortunes could seem overwhelming if one obsessed about them in self-laceration, much more if one plotted revenge: "woe is me," or "woe unto others." Through *ihsan*, however, one could realize that letting go of troubles, not reacting to them, and maintaining focus on what was important was a more intelligent path to peace than wallowing in offense or plotting pay-back.

And it was peace that was the ultimate horizon of the kind of intelligence evident in the life of the Prophet, as interpreted by Gülen:

> Bukhari records that God's Messenger said: "The Muslim is one from whose tongue and hand Muslims are safe. ... " This short *hadith* expressed many truths. First of all, it describes the ideas or norm by beginning with *the Muslim*, as opposed to a Muslim. In this way, our Prophet draws attention to the qualities of perfect Muslims, not to those who are only nominal Muslims.
>
> The word Muslim, derived from the infinitive *silm* (security, peace, and salvation), comes to mean one who desires and gives peace, secu-

rity and salvation. So, the Muslims are believers who embody peace, cause no trouble for anyone, from whom all are safe, and who are the most reliable representatives of peace and security. They strive to bring peace, security and salvation to others, and dedicate themselves to disseminating their inner peace and happiness.

Our Prophet mentions the tongue before the hand, for slander, gossip, and insult often do far more damage than physical violence. If people can refrain from verbal assault, they can more easily refrain from physical assault. Moreover, self-defense against physical violence is often easier than that against gossip and slander. So, true Muslims always restrain their tongues and hands so that others will be safe from them.[93]

Importantly, Gülen here extended the *hadith* not only to Muslims, but to all "others." The unity he had in mind would not be at the expense of some scapegoat or enemy.

Muhammad's role as educator was the final unifying feature of the Prophet's life that Gülen highlighted. This should hardly be surprising, given the long-standing emphasis on education within Hizmet. Still, by emphasizing the example of the Prophet as educator, Gülen sought to unite his listeners in productive action. "An educator's perfection," Gülen suggested,

> depends on the greatness of his or her ideal and the quantitative and qualitative dimensions of his or her listeners. Even before Prophet Muhammad's death, the instructors and spiritual guides he dispatched were traveling from Egypt to Iran and from Yemen to Caucasia to spread what they had learned from him. In succeeding centuries, people of different traditions, conventions, and cultures ... rushed to Islam. An educator's greatness also depends on the continuation of his or her principles. No one can deny that people all over the world accept Islam and adopt [the Prophet's] principles.[94]

This description of the Prophet's educational mission was a virtual blueprint for what people of Hizmet would accomplish in the next few decades. Individuals inspired by Gülen, and in some cases sent directly by him, would build schools in a network dispatched from Turkey to the rest of the world.

Of course, in the many sermons he gave on the Prophet over the course of the years 1989-1991, Gülen emphasized other aspects of Muhammad's life that could bind Muslims together. The Prophet was generous—no doubt a helpful point to make in encouraging financial support of service activities. The Prophet practiced modesty. "He never regarded himself as greater than anybody else," Gülen said. In a provocative story reinforcing this theme, from yet another *hadith*, Gülen recalled for listeners how: "Once a woman saw [Muhammad] eating and remarked: 'He eats like a slave.' The Messenger replied: 'Could there be a better slave than me? I am a slave of God.'"[95] This is the kind of self-deprecation that interviewer after interviewer, and student after student, has also reported about Gülen. The Prophet also practiced "mildness and forbearance," attributes hard for anyone to question. And, perhaps most controversially, the Prophet was infallible. Infallibility was an attribute ascribed to all Prophets in Islam—from Adam to Jesus. But what it meant, according to Gülen, was not mere consistency with some arbitrary external standard. Rather, infallibility (in Arabic, *'isma*) primarily meant "protecting, saving, or defending."[96] To say that Muhammad was infallible was to say that he protected, saved, and defended Islam—that is, that he protected, saved, and defended the message he had received from God. It could be trusted, as he could be trusted.

Prophet Muhammad as an advocate of *hoşgörü*—as peacebuilder

Still, if his sermons on the Prophet's *hoşgörü* bound Muslims together in trust, what was perhaps most startling about Gülen's sermons is how they also subtly harnessed *bridging* social capital. Gülen's interpretation of the Prophet's life impelled Muslims to try to forge new and more just and peaceful relations with their neighbors. They did so neither out of ideological allegiance to a "Western" project—as Atatürk had of course attempted—nor out of duplicitous lip-service to human rights embedded in a neo-liberal economic plan, as more recent leaders in Turkey have attempted. Rather, Gülen's project to persuade Turkish Muslims to live lives of *hizmet* grew organically out of his interpretation of the life of Muhammad. That it succeeded almost as rapidly as Islam itself says something important about how religion might be a foundation for peacebuilding. The kinds of initiatives that Gülen proposed bore many if

not most of the hallmarks of classical progressive social change: religious
freedom and respect for diversity; equality for women; and ending racism. But they were forged on an undeniably Islamic foundation.

It is crucial to recall that Istanbul was the context for most of these
sermons. The boy from Erzurum was now on Turkey's largest stage. And
The City had attained its lofty status not through some narrow interpretation of Islam, Gülen preached. Instead, Istanbul under the Ottomans
had embraced the Prophet's own *hoşgörü*. And the Prophet's *hoşgörü*
included religious freedom and diversity. Naturally, Gülen made clear,
Muhammad wanted all people to be Muslims—and he did his best to
persuade them to do so. But the Prophet was also respectful of differences, Gülen stressed. The Prophet sought to respect especially Jews and
Christians—the People of the Book. It is fascinating to see how Gülen
subtly invited his listeners to recognize the broad and deep relationships
between Muslims and Jews. He did this in a context when for some Muslims—under the influence of Wahhabi rigorism and Iranian revolutionary zeal—both Jews and Christians were infidels. And yet from the most
foundational Islamic sources—the Qur'an and the *Sunnah*, Gülen identified an irrefutable common lineage of Prophets who came before Muhammad that linked Muhammad to both Jewish and Christian forbears.
"A Companion once asked God's Messenger to talk about himself," Gülen
introduced the matter. "He said, I am the one for whose coming Abraham prayed and of whom Jesus gave glad tidings."[97] Now, Gülen here
argued that Muhammad was anticipated in both the Torah and Gospels.
That bit of exegesis most Jewish and Christian scholars would struggle
to accept. But in the context of his preaching, Gülen's effort conveyed a
matter far more serious than some literal correspondence between text
and historical causality. Gülen sought to clarify the point, as he put it in
another of his publications, that "more than anything else ... the Pride of
Humankind [i.e., the Prophet] gave value to every human being, regardless of whether that person was a Muslim, Christian, or Jew."[98]

Dialogue with Jews

In the 1990s, Fethullah Gülen put this prophetic bridge-building into
practice. He actively sought out relationships with Jews and Christians.
He had done so his entire professional life, having met with Jews and

Christians even in his earliest appointments in Edirne and Izmir.[99] But it was in the 1990s that these efforts at dialogue became widespread and gained publicity. For instance, in 1997, while on a trip to the U.S. for medical treatment, Gülen met in New Jersey with Abraham Foxman—President of the Anti-Defamation League, and Kenneth Jacobson, National Deputy Director of the ADL. The ADL was of course the most prominent agency to prevent and combat anti-Semitism. At the meeting, according to Jacobson's report, "Gülen talked about his moderation regarding Islam, the Jews, Israel, and expressed reasonable and non-extremist views.... It was a very good meeting, very friendly." A few months later, Jacobson again met with Gülen, this time in Istanbul, and accompanied by some representatives from the Conference of Presidents of Major American Jewish Organizations. It was a meeting opposed by some Jewish leaders in Turkey, and by some Turkish Muslim leaders. Yet Jacobson again recalled that "I remember it like it was yesterday. There were all sorts of television cameras there ... as if it were a high-profile meeting. We met, and it was another pleasant encounter. We were given gifts.... Again Gülen spoke in terms of moderation. He presented himself as someone that cares about ... good relations with Israel and the Jews."[100] That set the foundation for broader dialogue between people of Hizmet and the Jewish community.

An even more important meeting happened in January, 1998, when Gülen met publicly during Ramadan to break the fast with Jewish businessmen Üzeyir Garih and İshak Alaton.[101] The two were partners in Alarko Holdings—a Turkish business conglomerate with ventures in contracting, energy, industry, trade, tourism, and real estate development.[102] According to a biography of Alaton by journalist Mehmet Gündem, Garih and Alaton supported Hizmet activities after the two were convinced of Gülen's sincerity and commitment to dialogue and democracy.[103] Even more, as discovered by scholar Efrat E. Aviv of Bar-Ilan University in Israel, and reported in 2010, Alaton

> met with Gülen several times in Istanbul and they regularly keep in touch on the telephone. Alaton helps Gülen, thanks to his plentiful contacts worldwide. According to him, the first meeting with Gülen was mediated by his business partner, Üzeyir Garih, and the nature of the meeting did not cover business matters [reportedly they talked

about philosophy and theology]. In any case, Gülen turned to Alaton asking for help, because Alarko built the airport in [Ashgabat], Turkmenistan, where Gülen wanted to establish a school. The second instance where the two helped Gülen was in Moscow in the early 1990s. The third instance was Cape Town, a request that stemmed from Alaton being an honorary General Consul of South Africa.[104]

As this paragraph suggests, by the 1990s Gülen's vision had expanded well beyond the borders of the Republic of Turkey, as had his contacts and supporters. Gülen would maintain a friendly relationship with Alaton until the latter's death, at age 89, in 2016.

Shortly after his *iftar* with Garih and Alaton, Gülen would have a very public meeting with the chief Sephardic Rabbi of Israel, Eliyahu Bakshi-Doron. It had not been easy to arrange such a historic dialogue. It was the first official visit by a chief rabbi of Israel to Turkey, and only the second visit by a chief rabbi of Israel to any Muslim country. Kerim Balcı, who at the time was serving as *Zaman* correspondent in Israel, had made an effort in the early '90s to bring the two religious leaders together. It failed. It was only when Zali De Toledo, cultural attaché in the Israeli embassy, sought to secure an invitation that things began to move forward. Even then, Mehmet Nuri Yılmaz, at the time President of Religious Affairs in Turkey, initially balked at the meeting because Gülen had no official title. He eventually relented, and Bakshi-Doron met with Gülen on February 25, 1998. The various parties of course had different interests. The Israeli Foreign Ministry hoped that Gülen could be a Muslim voice in Turkey to quiet rampant anti-Semitism. Bakshi-Doron and Gülen also had interests, as Zali De Toledo recalled in his report on the meeting:

> At first, I translated for Rabbi Bakshi-Doron and Fethullah Gülen, in front of approximately 15 television microphones. The meeting took place in Gülen's building in Istanbul [the 5th Floor]. ...The Rabbi and Gülen quoted excerpts from the Torah and the Koran, and I translated. Afterwards, we adjourned to a quiet meeting, with the attendance of Rabbi Bakshi-Doron, Fethullah Gülen, his assistants, Rabbi Bakshi-Doron's assistant Rafi Dayan, Eli Shaked, who was then the General Consul, and me. Rabbi Bakshi-Doron requested assistance for Iranian Jews, saying that there are widows and 'agunot' (literally 'anchored

or chained', a Halachic term for a Jewish woman who is "chained" to her marriage) left there and that there is no Rabbi there to help them. Gülen said that he had no ties with Iran and that's where the matter ended... Gülen was interested in opening one of his schools in Israel and that was the reason for his meeting with the Chief Rabbi.[105]

In fact, Gülen apparently proposed building two schools—one in East Jerusalem, and one in the West Bank. The Israeli government, however, wasn't interested—and it would be many more years before the prospect of a "Gülen-inspired" school in the West Bank would move closer to realization.[106]

Nevertheless, a historic bridge had been built. Gülen continued throughout his time in Istanbul to foster good relations with the Jewish community around the globe and in Turkey. He met several times throughout the decade with Turkey's Chief Rabbi at the time, David Asseo, and with his deputy, Rabbi Ishak Haleva. Haleva, in particular, came to appreciate Gülen's initiatives to promote hoşgörü. Haleva gave Gülen credit for mediating between the Jewish community and various Turkish media outlets that "published inflammatory content against the Jews."[107] It was, and is, possible for demagogues in Turkey to stoke anti-Semitism to solidify support against a scapegoat—a pattern that ought to have ended in 1945. Nevertheless, within 1990s Turkey, Haleva also credited Gülen for having given a unified voice to the various religious minorities in Turkey. Jewish, Christian, and Muslim minorities (notably the Alevis), all shared a desire to be free to practice their faith traditions without interference or hostility. That would be an uphill struggle.

Still, Gülen's rationale for these meetings with the Turkish and global Jewish community was not simply the practical one of generating benefactors. It was, instead, grounded in principle—and, more specifically, in the life of the Prophet. In a hadith that he cited many times, Gülen recalled that:

the Pride of Humanity . . . one day stood up as a Jewish funeral was passing by. One of the Companions at his side said, "O Messenger of God, that's a Jew." Without any change in attitude or alteration of the lines on his face, the Prince of Prophets gave this answer: "But he is a human being!" May the ears ring of those followers who do not know him in these dimensions and those human rights advocates who are ignorant of the universal message he brought in the name of human-kind![108]

Gülen here directed critique in two directions. He criticized Muslims who did not follow the Prophet in respecting Jews. And he criticized secularists who did not recognize Islam as a ground for advancing human rights. But Gülen offered the clearest admonition to his fellow Muslims: "There is nothing I can add to these words," he claimed, before in fact adding something more anyway: "but if we are disciples of the glorious Prophet who spoke these words, it is not possible for us to think any differently. Thus, it would be beneficial for those who oppose the recent activities made in the name of dialogue and tolerance [hoşgörü] to review their situations in respect to their heedlessness or their obstinacy."[109]

There were quite real targets for these critiques. Despite his practical and principled advocacy for dialogue and cooperation between Muslims and Jews, Gülen was charged with being anti-Semitic, by a few, and with being a tool of Israel, by many others. Regarding the charge of anti-Semitism, Hodjaefendi admitted that his thinking had evolved, and that some of the statements from early in his career could unwittingly have stoked hostility to Jews. "During the interfaith dialogue process of the 1990s," he said in an interview in The Atlantic in 2013, "I had a chance to get to know practitioners of non-Muslim faiths better, and I felt a need to revise my expressions from earlier periods," he said. "I sincerely admit that I might have misunderstood some verses and prophetic sayings," Gülen went on:

> I realized and then stated that the critiques and condemnations that are found in the Koran or prophetic tradition are not targeted against people who belong to a religious group, but at characteristics that can be found in any person.[110] In some cases my words have been taken out of context. Sometimes people with questionable intentions selectively extract statements from my speeches and writings without regard to the context or circumstances. My efforts for interfaith dialogue were criticized as softening Muslims' perspectives on Jews and Christians. I have not done anything that I did not believe to be in the footsteps of the Prophet Mohammed. He was the one who stood for a funeral procession of a Jewish resident of Medina, showing respect for a deceased fellow human being.[111]

Characteristically, Gülen here identified the problem with himself, not with the tradition, while also defending himself from those who chose to highlight some inflammatory passages while ignoring his other statements and practical actions on behalf of interreligious dialogue with Jews. Simply put, if the Prophet was the model for *hoşgörü*, as he was for Gülen, then good relations with Jews were both possible and necessary.

For instance, in a discussion of prophetic "infallibility," Gülen spent as much time preaching about *Jewish* prophets as he did preaching about Muhammad. Prophets Adam, Noah, Abraham and Joseph were all "infallible," as Gülen defined it, that is as capable to "protect, save, and defend" believers. Gülen's mature thought on relations between Muslims and "People of the Book," then, can best be clarified by his own words, quoted here at some length, as found in a 1996 column:

> Some assert that expressions in the Qur'an regarding Christianity and Judaism are very sharp. Great care should be taken when approaching this subject. There is a rule in *tafsir* (Qur'anic commentary): In order to conclude that a verse refers to a particular people, it must be established both clear and historically that the verse in question refers to them exclusively.
>
> Approaching the matter from this angle, the verses condemning and rebuking the Jews and Christians are either about *some* Jews and Christians ... or those who deserved such condemnation because of their wrong beliefs or practices. For example, at the beginning of Surat al-Baqara, after praising the believers for some of their praiseworthy attributes and acts, the Qur'an says: "Surely, the unbelievers: it is the same whether you warn them or not, they will not believe. God put a seal on their hearts and ears, and over their sight is a veil. For them is a mighty torment." (2:6) This verse is about ... stubborn unbelievers who lived during the Prophet's lifetime. ... [and then] it includes all unbelievers, regardless of time or place, who show the same type of resistance against the enlightening rays of the Qur'an. So, the sharp criticism of the Jews and Christians is, first of all, about those whom the relevant verses refer to directly, and others of the same attitude. It is not definite that they pertain to all Jews and Christians from that time until now.

Second, that [harshness] ... was used in the Qur'an because [some so-called Jews and Christians] used religious thought and belief as a cause and material for hostility. Rather than individual Christian and Jews, the Qur'an goes after wrong behavior, incorrect thought, resistance to the truth, creation of hostility, and non-commendable characteristics. The Bible contains even stronger statements against the same attributes. Even if the expression seems sharp to some, immediately after appropriate warnings and threats come very gentle words to awaken hearts to the truth and to plant hope in them. In addition, the Qur'an's criticism and warning regarding some of these attitudes and behaviors of non-Muslims also were made about Muslims whose faith did not prevent them from engaging in the same behavior. Both the Companions and expounders of the Qur'an agree on this matter.

Religions are meant to unite people separated by misunderstandings. Islam and Orthodox Christianity have many common aspects and few differences. Both believe in God, Prophets, angels, the afterlife, and holy books. All Muslims believe in Jesus and the Virgin Mary. Many moral and legal principles are the same. Thus, any conflict between these two religions is due to misunderstanding or exploitation for political or other purposes. The Qur'an states: "Come, let's unite on a common word: worshipping God, not assign Him any partners. Abandoning Him, some of us should not make Lords some among us over others." In this call, a matter that causes division is mentioned and a warning is given: Don't leave God due to misunderstandings or other reasons, and be wary of those who use religion to divide people. When there are hundreds of common bridges between us, it is a mistake to emphasize a few differences. When people really understand such things, Islam and Orthodox Christianity will contribute positively to relations between [people].[112]

Such expressions and actions that linked religion to peacebuilding were startling and refreshing in 1990s Turkey.

Secularists in Turkey had committed all religions to the dustbin of violent superstition. Islamic extremists in Turkey were replicating the worst tropes of violent anti-Semitism and anti-Christian bias. Gülen sought to show that the way of the Prophet was a middle-way. Islam opened up a principled peace that granted religious freedom to others to practice their faith: "When dealing with People of the Book who are not oppressors, we have no right to behave violently or to think about how to eliminate them. Such behavior is non-Islamic, contrary to Islamic rules and principles, and even anti-Islamic," he preached. Pluralism was compatible with the Prophet's *hoşgörü*. Thus, Gülen went on, in the Qur'an it is stated:

> *God forbids you not, with regard to those who fight you not for (your) faith nor drive you out of your homes, from dealing kindly and justly with them: for God loves those who are just* (60:8). This verse was revealed when Esma asked the Prophet if she should meet with her polytheistic mother, who wanted to come from Makka to Madina to see her daughter. The verse suggests that such a meeting was perfectly acceptable, and that she can do good for her as well. I leave it to your understanding as to what approach should be used towards those who believe in God, Judgment Day and the Prophets. Hundreds of Qur'anic verses deal with social dialogue and tolerance. But care must be taken to establish balance in forbearance and tolerance. Being merciful to a cobra means being unjust to the people the cobra has bitten.[113]

Islam was a middle-way that protected believers, but also recognized diversity.

Dialogue with Christians

Christians, of course, had for many centuries been cobras to Muslims—most notably in the Crusades. And yet in the 1990s, Gülen sought out meetings with Christian leaders that, if anything, surpassed in historic significance those he arranged with the Jewish community. The meetings were dramatic, and they culminated in a meeting with Pope John Paul II on February 9, 1998. Informal meetings between Christians and Muslims had been going on for years, but they gained momentum in Turkey following the founding of the Journalists and Writers Foundation (JWF) in 1994. That organization sponsored an interreligious *iftar* dinner to break the Ramadan fast on the evening of February 11, 1995. The event was held at the Polat Renaissance Hotel, a posh five-star hotel on the Sea of Marmara. More than 1,000 attended from among the elites of The City. They came regardless of ideology or religious affiliation. Journalist

Ayşe Önal reported for *Akşam*, "When I was invited to the Ramadan dinner given by the Foundation of Writers and Journalists ... I thought it would be for fifty or sixty people. However, from the moment I entered the Polat Renaissance Hotel, it was clear that ... this type of dinner had not been seen before in Turkey." What made the dinner different was its diversity. Jews, Christians, and Muslims all mixed together. Secularists dined with Sunni and Alevi Muslims, and Greek and Armenian Christians broke the fast together with representatives of Turkish Islam. "Several women had been invited to this event," Önal reported. "Some were strikingly dressed; others were covered." Professor Ayhan Songar also recalled that the event featured "more than 1,000 writers, members of the arts, and scholars. ... As the time to break the fast drew closer," Songar reported, "everyone was very quiet, as if not to disturb the moment's sanctity. Talking was done in whispered tones. Only the sweet sound of a nay (flute) from the loudspeakers filled the hall and added exhilaration to our hearts. It was as if Rumi was there, and the nay was 'complaining of separation.'" Professor Mehmet Altan, a university lecturer and journalist who used to write for the newspaper *Sabah*, reported that he was "amazed when I saw this meeting. It can be seen as a model of a multicolor, multivoice, pluralistic Turkey that we all desire."[114] The event was, in many ways, an introduction of the real Fethullah Gülen—the one who tried to practice the Prophet's *hoşgörü*, to many individuals who had hitherto only heard scandal or propaganda about him.

Gülen spoke for about a half hour as the keynote speaker. He first shared that he had tried to beg off the obligation. As he put it, while most Muslims hold to the fast, as a diabetic, "the fast holds me." It took him several hours after breaking the fast for his blood sugar to stabilize and for him to return to feeling normal. Nevertheless, he offered his respects to the "honorable ministers and parliamentarians, enlightened people of the world of art, members of various religions," among others, and then gave thanks for the work of the Journalists and Writers Foundation. Through their activities, such as the dinner at which he was speaking, "we have seen with our own eyes that there's no reason to fear one another, and that all people can meet with whomever they want. If we have not come together until today, it means that we have been hung up on our mistaken conjectures and neglected an important human responsibility." That responsibility—manifest in the work of the JWF, was to practice *hoşgörü.* "The foundation is known in Turkey mainly as a representative of tolerance [*hoşgörü*]. In fact, it has identified itself with tolerance. Whenever it is mentioned, immediately after that tolerance is mentioned as well." In fact, Gülen went on, "envy" had led other organizations dedicated to *hoşgörü* to arise in Turkey—a development for which he gave thanks. But he also clarified that *hoşgörü* was not merely a secular virtue; it arose from the example of the Prophet, and at the heart of Islam: "When the Prophet was dying and about to pass on to the next world," Gülen spoke to his audience in the hotel ballroom, "he stated: 'I place in your trust the People of the Book, the Christians and Jews.'" Gülen then went on to give other examples of Muslims who practiced *hoşgörü*—including Salah-al-din, who according to Gülen personally attended to the wounds of Crusader Richard I—in what may be apocryphal tale but served to secure Gülen's point in any event: "We are the children of a culture that produced such people."

This was the high-road—an appeal to Turkish and Muslim pride to inspire "the better angels" of Muslim nature. But Gülen also concluded his keynote to the gathered elites of The City with a warning—and a challenge. "Turkish society," he began:

> which has been wrung by internal conflict, was awaiting tolerance just at this time. Upon finding it, when one step toward it was made with this view, it responded with three steps. But it also is obvious that certain weak and marginal persons, who by ranting and raving demonstrate their own weaknesses and try to show themselves as strong by being destructive, will lie in ambush to attack tolerance and attempt to destroy the bridges to dialogue.

Gülen here made explicit that *hoşgörü was* a bridge—and that it would accumulate a kind of capital that would stoke enmity. But no matter the "future tests," no matter the "cost," no matter the "trials": "We must be as if 'handless to those who hit us and tongueless to those who curse us.' If they try to fracture us into pieces even fifty times, still we are going to remain unbroken and embrace everyone with love and compassion. And, with love toward one another, we will walk toward tomorrow."[115] Nonviolence was the practical expression of *hoşgörü.*

Professor Songar was right to see Rumi behind such an event. In a later interview, Gülen evoked the legacy of Rumi to ground his dialogue activities in what is a clear articulation of principled pluralism. "Using Rumi's expression," Gülen put it, "such a person [practicing *hoşgörü*] is like a compass with one foot well-established in the center of belief and Islam, and the other foot with people of many nations." Such a person was "deep in his or her own inner world, so full of love ... so much in touch with God; but at the same time an active member of society."[116] It is that paradigm—like the whirling dervishes, of course, that inspired so many to *hoşgörü* during the 1990s. Similar Ramadan dinners were held on January 27, 1996, and (coincidentally) the same date in 1997, both at the Hilton Hotel Exhibition Hall—yet another tony site. The 1996 event featured several Christian and Jewish speakers: Georges Marovitch (the Vatican's Istanbul representative), Kati Pelatre (the Catholic community's spiritual leader), İsa Karataş (spokesman for Turkey's Protestant Presbyterian community), and Fotis Ksidas (the Greek chief consulate). According to one of those Christian participants, the event evidenced how "mosque and church side by side" could promote peace. Another used a classical metaphor to make the point: "We're all on the same ship. If it leaks, we'll all sink together." Patriarch Bartholomew I, the Phanariot Greek Patriarch of Istanbul, also in attendance, said that "Fethullah Gülen Hodja and I love each other very much. He is an example of harmony and tolerance for all of us, a model of high values for all humanity." The evening was, in brief, a "banquet of *hoşgörü*." [117]

The Patriarch's comments set the stage for the first of several high-profile public meetings between Gülen and prominent Christian leaders. On April 4, 1996, at the request of the Patriarch, Gülen and Bartholomew I met for a brief dialogue. The site was again the Polat Hotel. Journalist Cengiz Çandar reported in *Sabah*: "I felt happy when I read in yesterday's *Zaman* about the meeting between Fethullah Gülen Hodjaefendi and the Greek Orthodox Patriarch Bartholomew I." The Patriarchate had been under fire from the Islamist press, Çandar recalled, and was looking for Muslim dialogue partners: "In one of my discussions with Patriarchate officials," Çandar went on, "I fervently recommended that they 'definitely meet with Fethullah Hodja,' who is at the head of those representing the 'Islam of the people' in Turkey." The hotel was also a significant choice, according to Çandar. It "belongs to Adnan Polat, Fethullah Hodja's 'fellow-citizen from Erzurum' who happens to be an Alawi [Alevi]. The famous 1994[sic] Ramadan dinner, which was a vehicle for

Hodjaefendi presenting his 'reconciliatory personality' to the public, also was held at this hotel."[118] So the location, and the participants, were both demonstrations of *hoşgörü*.

In an interview some years later, Gülen recalled that "When I met [the Patriarch], he had the following demand: 'I am a Turkish citizen. I would like to have the opportunity to have the [Orthodox] Seminary re-opened, so that we can train our staff and send them off to the rest of the world from Turkey. It would be beneficial to Turkey if priests were trained in Turkey and within the Turkish culture.'" This was a potentially explosive demand—the Seminary had been closed since the unrest of the 1970s. But Gülen was non-plussed. The Patriarchate had been welcomed in Istanbul since the sixteenth century. If re-opening the Seminary was a way to perpetuate this long history, he conveyed to the Patriarch, "we should not make it a problem." Turks were grown-ups and should be able to handle this diversity without rancor. In response for this supportive attitude, the Patriarch spoke highly of Gülen. He had watched Hodjaefendi on television, he said to a *Zaman* reporter, and had attended the Ramadan dinners. But "this was the first time I had the opportunity to see him up close." The Patriarch was impressed by "his humility [and] his congeniality." Gülen spoke simply and directly, he recalled, and his actions were similarly "true," the Patriarch claimed.[119] He would maintain a relationship with Hodjaefendi down to the present.

Following this successful bridge to the Orthodox world, in 1997 Gülen began a series of meetings in outreach to the Roman Catholic community. It started, interestingly, with a meeting between Gülen and Cardinal John O'Connor, Archbishop of New York. Gülen was in the U.S. in September for some medical treatment—along with some other exploratory and dialogue activities (for instance, *sohbet*s with the Turkish immigrant community). He met with O'Connor at his New York offices. That led to a meeting in November in Istanbul with Georges Marovitch—the Vatican Representative to Istanbul. Marovitch had attended the Ramadan dinners. It was through Marovitch and Francis Cardinal Arinze, President of the Pontifical Council for Interreligious Dialogue, that Gülen received a "message" from Pope John Paul II to honor the month of Ramadan in January, 1998. Then, on the first week of February, Gülen traveled to Rome to meet with the Holy Father. He did so with the blessing of the Turkish government, having met with Prime Minster

Bülent Ecevit on February 4, just prior to his departure. This was as "official" a visit, in other words, as all parties could make it. Ankara approved
Gülen's travel, and the Turkish ambassador to the Vatican, Altan Güven,
welcomed Hodjaefendi as if he were an official envoy.[120]

Gülen was accompanied by Marovitch and a few key students and
mütevelli, including at least one female journalist (who was not allowed
by Vatican officials to attend). The face-to-face meeting happened on
February 9. The Pope would live until 2005, but by 1998 was already
declining rapidly. Consequently, rather than an extended conversation,
Gülen passed along to the Holy Father after a brief meeting a letter that
outlined the matters he hoped to advance. Generally, Gülen set his conversation with the Pope in contrast to the "clash of civilizations" hypothesis that had recently been formulated by Harvard political scientist
Samuel Huntington. Gülen cut to the critical heart of that argument. He
claimed that "the idea that the world is on the threshold of new clashes
is the expectation of those whose power and continued domination depend on continuous conflict."[121] Huntington was hardly a disinterested
observer, in short. Of course, Gülen acknowledged that there was a long
history of enmity between Muslims and Christians, most notably in the
Crusades. But he also noted that new dialogue channels had been opened
after Vatican Council II, which Pope John Paul had lived out by visiting
several Muslim nations. Building on that legacy, what Gülen stressed in
his letter to the Pope was that "The Qur'an urges peace, order, and accord," and that "we [Muslims] have no intention of conquering lands or
peoples, but we are resolved to contribute to world peace and a peaceful
order and harmony."[122] The path to this, of course, was *hoşgörü*.

More specifically, Gülen proposed four specific actions to the Roman pontiff—all of them interesting, some of them unrealizable. The first
was the most immediate. Gülen suggested hosting the Pope at historic
Christian sites in Turkey—such as Antioch, Tarsus and Ephesus, and he
suggested (and had made some steps already to arrange) a mutual visit
to Jerusalem. It was the latter part of this first proposal that raised the
ire of some Turks, who accused Gülen of presenting himself as a global
leader for Muslims on par with the role of the Holy Father. Gülen deftly
deflected that charge, and the actual letter he presented to the Pope does
not admit it. The second proposal would be realized: conferences organized "with the cooperation of Christian, Jewish, and Muslim leaders,"

beginning in America. This happened within a decade. My first familiarity with Gülen and Hizmet came through an invitation to an *iftar* dinner in 2006 in Philadelphia, where the keynote speech was delivered by the Vatican Director of Interreligious Relations at the time, Fr. Thomas Michel. My first participation in an academic conference devoted to Gülen and Hizmet was in 2008 at Georgetown University—a Roman Catholic school (an even earlier conference had been organized there in 2001). So, the meeting with the Pope did bear some quite real fruit. Gülen's third and fourth proposals were ambitious. The third was to establish Jerusalem as an international district, "so that Christians, Jews, and Muslims alike would be free to go on pilgrimage with no restrictions, without even needing a visa."[123] That remains a dream, albeit a pleasant one. The last proposal Gülen made to the Pope was to establish a University in Harran—a town in Turkey traditionally associated with Prophet Abraham. This "college of divinity" would be dedicated to "a comprehensive curriculum that would satisfy the needs of all three" Abrahamic traditions, including perhaps exchange students from Jewish, Christian, and Muslim schools.[124] Although the notion seemed like a fantasy, and Gülen admitted how "problematical" it might be, such collaborative education between representatives of the three "Abrahamic monotheisms" would be a component within many Divinity Schools in coming decades, albeit not one in Harran. Cooperation between Abrahamic monotheists would also be at the heart of one of the most influential scholarly monographs to outline a religious path to peace in the Middle East—another road not yet taken—namely Rabbi Marc Gopin's *Holy War, Holy Peace: How Religion Can Bring Peace to the Middle East.*[125]

Gülen's meeting with the Pope was no doubt the apex of his *public* activities on behalf of interreligious dialogue. He nevertheless continued to meet privately with many other religious leaders (one is tempted to say ANY others), and indirectly participated in interreligious dialogues throughout his life. While still in Istanbul, for instance, he met with both Metropolitan Bishop Yusuf Çetin and Bishop Samuel Akdemir, leaders of the Syriac Orthodox Church in Turkey. And he met, in a very significant overture, with Armenian Patriarch Karekin II and Armenian Patriarch Mesrob II. Gülen's attempt to build bridges between Turks and Armenians included an initiative to build a Hizmet-related school in Armenia. As Gülen put it—"We say, 'Let us build tomorrow's intellectuals and architects of thought under the same roof. ... The Armenians were the most sincere community under the Ottomans. These current enmities are so contrived, and they do not offer us anything. Let us open schools in your countries. ... We cannot take these hostilities any further in an ever-shrinking globalized world. Let us turn these into friendships."[126] Those were, in Turkey, and in Armenia, fighting words. None of Gülen's efforts to build bridges with dialogue partners was uncontroversial, but this one was a road too far. No schools were ever built in Armenia.

Another hot topic that Gülen engaged during these years was outreach to the minority Alevi (Alawis – a branch of Shiites) community in Turkey—which had often been subjected to violence. "Alevi meeting or prayer houses [cemevi] should be supported," Gülen simply asserted. "In our history," he went on, "a synagogue, a church, and a mosque stood side by side in many places. This reflects the spirit of Islam and its inclusiveness."[127] Such an attitude made him a target from all sides. As journalist Rıza Zelyut put it in Akşam in February, 1998, some (mostly secularists) shouted "Who is this Fethullah Hodja? ... He is trying to save himself [by allying himself with Jews and Christians] because he is in difficulty." Another attack came from what Zelyut described as "the backward wing," whose members asked: "Would a true Muslim ever accept Christians as friends?" Their answer, of course, was no. "Secularists, radical Islamists, and nationalists [were] all opposed," the journalist concluded, to one or the other of Gülen's efforts for interfaith dialogue.[128]

Dialogue across faith traditions and cultures made different faith groups natural partners in dialogue. One group Gülen struggled to include was atheists, who hardly had any institutional representation in Turkey. Yet, he interacted on a regular basis with some among Turkey's secularists, who may have identified themselves as atheists. And some atheists, at least, recognized in Gülen an individual worthy of respect. Yusuf Pekmezci told the story of an Izmir neighbor of his who was an atheist and communist. He bragged to Pekmezci that 'If I saw Hodjaefendi, I'd kill him!' The braggart owned a shop not far from Pekmezci's own store. When Gülen was in Izmir, he made it a habit to stroll the streets, stopping in shops and giving the Islamic greeting of "salaam/peace," to the shopkeepers and their employees. "He'd give salaam to everyone, no matter who they were, where they came from," Pekmezci went on:

We got used to this. It became an ambition of ours to get his salaam. ... Even our communist neighbor would bow down! So, one day I said, "*Abi* [he was older than me], You say you are an enemy of the hodjas, yet when you see Hodjaefendi you respect him. Isn't this hypocrisy?' And he told me, 'If you do not see the truth and the reality what can I do? Don't you see, if it's humanity you're looking for, it's in this man. If it's a *hodja* you're looking for, it's in this man. My son, there's virtue in this man! Don't you see?'[129]

There were similar converts from among secularists who might have once thought of Gülen with violence in their hearts—although this was a difficult bridge to build by *hoşgörü* alone.

And yet Gülen was consistent that *hoşgörü* was not his, but the Prophet's way of peacebuilding. It was the revelations to the Prophet that established Islam, and since

> Islam literally means "peace, salvation, and submission," it obviously came to establish peace. This is established first in our inner worlds, so that we are at peace with God and [the] natural environment, and then throughout the world and the universe. Peace and order are fundamental in Islam, which seeks to spread in a peaceful personal and collective atmosphere. It refrains from resorting to force as much as possible, never approves of injustice, and forbids bloodshed: "Whoever kills someone ... in effect has killed humanity; whoever saves a life in effect has saved humanity." (5:32)

This was the platform for dialogue that Gülen developed in his sermons and teaching on the Prophet. Those sermons were then put into practice through interreligious dialogues that became a signal feature of the remainder of his life, and of the Hizmet movement around the globe.

Advocacy for women's rights, and death of Refia Gülen

Another perhaps surprising aspect of Gülen's bridge-building to emerge from his study and preaching on the Prophet was in advocacy on behalf of rights for women. He urged Turkish (and all) Muslims to go forward on women's rights, by going back to the most ancient and respected sources. As scholar Bernadette Andrea has suggested, it was ironic that in his commitment to returning to the most basic sources of Islam, Gülen ran into conflict with patriarchal traditions that stood as unquestioned norms in some Muslim communities today. As Andrea saw it, that made Gülen "a champion of women's rights by scrupulously following the path of the Prophet Muhammad."[130] One could go forward on women's rights by going back to the Prophet.

Gülen's chief example in this regard was the Prophet's relationship with his wives. To Westerners immune to or ignorant of the long history of polygamy in Jewish and Christian contexts, a fixation on Muhammad's plural marriage—he eventually had altogether thirteen wives over the course of his life—causes scandal. Gülen addressed the matter directly. "Some critics of Islam," he began, "either because they do not know the reasons for these marriages, or because they want to portray him as a self-indulgent libertine, have accused the Messenger of character failings."[131] In fact, Gülen went on, Muhammad was twenty-five when he married his first wife, Khadija, who was a widow fifteen-years his senior. Then, for twenty-three years Muhammad was monogamous. "The Prophet took no other wives while Khadija was alive," Gülen emphasized, "although public opinion and social norms would have allowed this." When Khadija unexpectedly died, leaving Muhammad alone with their children (they had six together), he nevertheless remained single for another five years, until he was fifty-three. At that time, he was betrothed to 'A'isha, the daughter of Abu Bakr, who was his closest friend and devoted follower. Indeed, as historians have thoroughly documented, until very recently it was family or tribal alliances and politics, more than romance, that often secured a union.[132] Several of the Prophet's wives represented tribes or regions that Muhammad hoped to convert or placate. For instance, he married three widows living in exile in Christian Abyssinia (Umm Habiba, Sawda bint Zam'a, and Hafsa) and one widow who was Jewish (Safiyya). Gülen went through similar explanations for each of Muhammad's wives, showing how his marriages helped strengthen alliances within Islam. Christian kings from the medieval era did the same kinds of things, even if they were (technically) monogamous. Several of the Prophet's marriages also, Gülen pointed out, prevented women from falling into destitution.[133]

It was not only that the Prophet was strategic and chivalric—although those were common enough ideals in the Middle Ages. Instead,

Gülen highlighted for his listeners Muhammad's egalitarianism. "The Messenger," he contended, "discussed matters with his wives as friends." Gülen highlighted especially his relationship with his first wife, Khadija, and then his marriage with 'A'isha. Muhammad and Khadija's marriage was marked by "intimacy, friendship, mutual respect, support, and consolation," Hodjaefendi preached. Khadija was the Prophet's "friend who shared his inclinations and ideals to a remarkable degree," he went on. "Their marriage was wonderfully blessed, and they lived together in profound harmony for 23 years. Through every outrage and persecution ... Khadija was his dearest companion and helper. He loved her dearly." Similarly, Gülen offered that 'A'isha was a "remarkably intelligent and wise woman," who also had "the nature and the temperament to carry forward the work of Prophetic mission." Indeed, she became a spiritual guide and teacher, Gülen put it, "one of the greatest authorities on *hadith*, an excellent Qur'anic commentator, and a most distinguished and knowledgeable expert (*faqih*) in Islamic law."[134]

All in all, as Gülen developed the Prophet's legacy in relationship to women and marriage:

> He married [his wives] to provide helpless or widowed women with a dignified subsistence; to console and honor enraged or estranged tribesmen by bringing former enemies into some degree of relationship and harmony; to gain certain uniquely gifted individuals, in particular some exceptionally talented women, for the cause of Islam; to establish new norms of relationship between different people within the unifying brotherhood of faith in God; and to honor with family bonds the men who were to be his immediate political successors.[135]

If this was not exactly a charter for Western-style feminism—it rang more than one patriarchal note that defined women by their relationship to a man—it also was a step toward "new norms" in the context of deeply patriarchal Turkish Islam.

And, at least according to many of the women I interviewed for this project, Gülen's egalitarianism extended considerably beyond most men of his generation in Turkey, including secularists ostensibly committed to women's equality, and including many of the men who followed Gülen into Hizmet. By many accounts, Gülen helped some of the men in the Hizmet movement to evolve toward egalitarianism. As one woman I interviewed, journalist Sevgi Akarçeşme put it, "by any standard, the movement has been above" the Turkish norm. Gülen had the capacity of "turning a regular Anatolian xenophobic, racist, sexist person," Akarçeşme said, "into somebody who believed in the possibility of faiths talking to each other, accepting the other as other, and advancing women's rights." Akarçeşme came into the Hizmet orbit through a FEM tutoring center in the mid-1990s, and she observed, accurately enough, that "we cannot import people from Mars or Venus and turn them into Hizmet volunteers ... Given the [raw material], the movement has been working a miracle." Kerim Balcı, who for a time worked with Akarçeşme at *Zaman*, confirmed that the miracle had worked in his case: female empowerment had "been a growing edge for me," he put it. "But when I follow Hodjaefendi ... I make gender equality a principle."[136] Akarçeşme also recalled a meeting she had with Gülen that left a strong impression on her. She had just moderated a forum at the World Women's Association in Istanbul, sponsored by the Journalists and Writers Foundation. Following the panel, several of the women asked to meet with Hodjaefendi. Gülen then hosted seven or eight of them. "He welcomed us with a smiling face," she recalled, and the group discussed together how the panel had gone. "He encouraged such initiatives," she said. It was an open forum, so "I complained about the status of women," she went on. "None of the women want to take credit for what's being accomplished," she recalled saying, "so it's always men who are visible!" Gülen listened to her complaint, and answered sympathetically, if a bit condescendingly, saying in effect that "'it's not something that's going to change overnight.' He then talked," she went on, "about how the Prophet 'A'isha had orchestrated and led and army, and then he said 'I wish we had a female chief of staff.'" The woman concluded by saying: "Hodjaefendi is beyond Hizmet and certainly beyond traditional Turkish society" regarding the rights of women.[137]

Gülen's advocacy for women's leadership may also have been inspired indirectly by a personal loss he suffered in 1993, when his mother, Refia, died on June 28. She had been ill with diabetes for several years, like her son. Since the death of Ramiz in 1974, she had alternated between living in Erzurum during summers, and then moving to the milder Izmir during winter. Gülen visited her in one place or the other at least annually—and ordinarily many more times per year—especially during his preaching rotation between Istanbul and Izmir in 1989 and 1990. Refia would also occasionally travel to visit her son, in Istanbul or at another venue. During the 1980s, when he was on the run, Refia's modest apartment in Izmir was regularly searched, on the supposition that her son might be hiding out there. Such events of course grieved her. She worried about her son's well-being, and became known for asking her friends, "Is there any news from *Hodja*?" More generally, Gülen remembered that "she was very farsighted. Sometimes she would ask about some of my friends and show interest in my service. If she felt that I was not happy with her question, she would change the subject and say to those around her, 'What are you waiting for? Make some tea for this *Hajji* and bring it!'" Refia called her son both "*Hodja*" and "*Hajji*," titles of honor as teacher and pilgrim, respectively, but they also conveyed affection. When Refia visited Fethullah in Istanbul sometime in the late '80s, Gülen recalled that "I put my head to her knees like a little child." As Refia's diabetes advanced, she shared with her son medical advice about living with dietary restrictions, and she would send updates to him regularly about her well-being, while inquiring about his. Alptekin reports that Gülen remembered how "whenever I would visit her, she would come to my side, although she was ill, touch my feet ... and say, 'Your feet are cold.'" Near the end, she called for Fethullah, and of course he came. "Come, sit next to me, I will be gone soon," she said. As they said goodbye, she asked—or rather, demanded—that her son "Send me [to heaven] like a bride." That is, send her to heaven to meet with her beloved, God—in what should be a celebration. This was a request about her funeral. When she did die, Gülen remembered, perhaps with regret, that "I was unable to be at my mother's side at her death. I had gone to Istanbul." He had worried that "I won't be able to bear my mother's death." As he reckoned with his loss, he lamented that "I cannot fill the emptiness she left." Her funeral was held at the Izmir Theology Faculty Mosque after the noon prayer, and she was buried at the Karşıyaka Örnekköy graveyard. Thousands attended, and Gülen offered prayers at the gravesite. He also penned a public "thank you" to the many in attendance that *Zaman* published on July 7, 1993. "I still feel her prayers in my life," Gülen said. She had, after all, taught him to pray. And, poignantly, in a sentiment that many a daughter or son could identify with, he said, simply: "I wish my mom was here."[138]

In her absence, Gülen became a public advocate on behalf of full inclusion for women in Islam and in Turkish society. In an interview with Ertuğrul Özkök in *Hürriyet* in January, 1995, Gülen claimed that:

> In the social atmosphere of Muslim societies where Islam is not "contaminated" with customs or un-Islamic traditions, Muslim women are full participants in daily life. For example, during the Prophet's time and in later centuries when the West gave women no place in society, when the West was debating whether or not women had souls or if they were devils or human beings, 'A'isha led an army. She also was a religious scholar whose views everyone respected. Women prayed in mosques together with men. An old woman could oppose the Caliph in the mosque in a juridical matter. Even in the Ottoman period during the eighteenth century, the wife of an English ambassador highly praised the women and mentioned their roles in Muslim families and society with admiration.[139]

That "wife" was Lady Mary Wortley Montagu, who learned while her husband was ambassador to the Ottoman court from 1716-18, that women under Islamic law could own property, could stipulate provisions in their marriage contract, and could ensure their privacy even from their husbands. "None of these rights was available to English women," according to scholar Bernadette Andrea.[140]

Andrea has documented how Gülen's views on women, like his views on anti-Semitism, underwent somewhat of an evolution. He did consistently advocate for educating girls, and he just as consistently rejected "the patriarchal logic that men's desire is women's fault." But his early writings also lauded "women's traditional position" as mothers in the home, and he tended to ascribe to women tender emotions and other romantic stereotypes. Gülen occasionally contrasted women's exalted role in the home to the liberation of women in the West that in some cases reduced them to "objects of pleasure, means of entertainment, and material for advertising." More recently, and certainly by the 1990s, Gülen moved away from such stereotypes, and moved toward far more inclusive and even radical (in an Islamic context) statements. It took a confident scholar to advocate for Muslim women and men to pray in the same place, without a separate balcony or wing for women. And yet this is precisely what Gülen argued was the practice of the Prophet:

Women and men prayed together in mosques during the time of the Prophet. It sometimes occurred that a woman would correct the Caliph who was giving [a] sermon. For example, in one [of] his sermons Caliph 'Umar warned the Muslims, saying: "Do not pay women in marriage more than 500 dirhams as dowry." A woman in the congregation objected: "O 'Umar! Should we follow the Qur'an or you?" Umar asked: "What does the Qur'an say?" The woman replied: "The Qur'an says: 'If you divorce a woman in order to wed another, and you have given her a hoarded treasure as dowry, take not the least part of it back.' (4:20) Is a hoarded treasure equal to 500 dirhams?" Umar remarked: "Umar erred, the woman said the truth." It is true that time and changing conditions have caused some changes in secondary matters. Women do not have to perform their prescribed prayers in mosques, but if they would like to, they should not be banned if there is no justifiable reason for banning them.[141]

To be sure, that left a caveat for a wide range of practices. But it also opened a door for egalitarian worship. After all, many Christian churches have had men and women pray separately, historically and down to the present, and some Jewish synagogues continue the practice today.

Succinctly, according to Andrea, Gülen has insistently claimed that "women can assume any role."[142] Indeed, in his own words, Gülen argued that

With regard to humanity and human relationships with God, there is no difference between women and men. They are equals concerning their rights and responsibilities. Woman is equal to man in the rights of freedom of religion, freedom of expression, freedom to live a decent life, and freedom of finance. Equality before the law, just treatment, marriage and founding a family life, personal life, privacy and protection are all rights of women. Her possessions, life and dignity are assured like that of men. ... Yes, woman is free and independent before the law.[143]

Not only *before* the law. Gülen had already contended in an interview in *Sabah* in 1995 that women could and should *make* the law. "There's no reason why a woman can't be an administrator. In fact, Hanafi jurisprudence says that a woman can become a judge."[144]

Such freedom was officially the case in 1990s Turkey, but in practice—notably in relationship to the headscarf—women faced restrictions that came and went as political winds blew differently over the decade. On that contentious issue, in a 1995 interview Gülen characteristically minimized, relativized, and redirected the question. He compared the headscarf to the restrictions on men's appearance and clothing. "I see the robe, turban, beard, and loose trousers as details. Muslims shouldn't drown in detail. ... Choosing not to wear a turban, robe, or loose trousers shouldn't be construed as weakening the Muslim ... identity." [145] The same logic applied to the question, "Is it necessary for women to cover their hair?" "This issue is not as important as the essentials of faith and the pillars of Islam," Gülen offered. "It's a matter of secondary importance [furu]." That left open the question, to a degree—although in my experience most women informed by Gülen's teaching have chosen to veil, drawing upon Qur'anic sources such as 24:30-31 in support of their decision.[146] Nevertheless, Gülen pointed out, it was the case that well into Muhammad's prophethood, "women's heads were still uncovered. It was not included in the pillars of Islam or the essentials of faith. Those issues which Islam gives priority should, out of our own devotion, be given priority while becoming a Muslim and communicating Islam to others."[147] In an interview in 1997 with Nevval Sevindi, Gülen gave a slightly more nuanced answer:

The covering of women is mentioned in the Qur'an, but there is no specification as to how and in what form this is to be done. Dwelling on the form would amount to narrowing Islam's broad horizon and a lack of consideration of an aesthetic dimension. In fact, it would even wrongly reduce Islam to a costume religion. Likewise, the headscarf is not one of the essentials of belief or main principles and conditions of Islam. ... It goes against the spirit of Islam to regard people to be outside the fold of religion because of these factors. Imposition and insistence in this regard is excessiveness and compulsion, even a cause for resentment.[148]

And in the early 2000s, in yet another interview with Sevindi, Gülen turned his attention to how the Prophet Muhammad could be seen, in the context of the Arabian culture of fourteen centuries ago as "having had an extraordinarily feminist approach." "The Prophet helped with housework. He would sweep the house, sew his own buttons, and tried to do his own chores." More substantively than these day-to-day matters, Gülen presented Muhammad as the opposite of any kind of violence toward women. "He never used force against any woman, and never used harsh words." In general, the principle Gülen drew out of the life of the Prophet for relations between husbands and wives, at least, was simply this: "Men are obliged to make their wives happy."[149]

What made women happy, of course, depended on the woman. For Tuba Alpat, what made her happy was preaching. She had planned to go to medical school, and in fact began her studies toward becoming an M.D. Living in a Hizmet "house of light" in the 1990s, however, she began exploring the writings of Gülen. She recalled that the daily *sohbet*s at the dormitory included conversations about Gülen's interpretations of the Qur'an, and about articles from *Zaman*, *Sızıntı*, and other sources. There were also regular prayers, of course. It was while she was still a student that she was asked to preach her first sermon. She had led the "women's circle" in her Istanbul house, but the first time she preached was in a mosque in the Istanbul neighborhood of Beyazıd. "It was actually an old church," she explained. "It was my first place to preach. It was not like an imam leading prayer—it was a woman's *masjid*—they asked for women to guide them in spirituality. The topic I spoke on was 'The Importance of Education for Women.'" Alpat never practiced medicine. She immigrated to the U.S. with her husband in 1996, after the headscarf ban came back. That ban would have forced her to choose between veiling or continuing in medical school. In her new home in Northern Virginia, where her husband was in graduate school, she hosted *sohbet*s in Turkish and English. When I interviewed her in 2017, she was preparing to become a full-time, certified hospital chaplain—neatly merging her two areas of study and vocation.

Anti-racism, including outreach to Kurds

So, through his preaching about the Prophet's *hoşgörü* Gülen encouraged equitable gender relations. Through the same sermons, and through other publications during the 1990s, Gülen also encouraged mutual relations between races. "Racism is one of our age's severest problems," Gülen preached.

Everyone has heard of how black Africans were transported across the Atlantic Ocean in specially designed ships, thought of and treated exactly like livestock. They were enslaved, forced to change their names and religion and language, were never entitled even to hope for true freedom, and were denied all human rights. The West's attitude toward non-Westerners remained unchanged until recent times. As a result ... Africans, even in the case of their descendants who lived in the West amidst non-black Americans or Europeans as theoretically equal fellow citizens, remained second-class (or even lower) citizens.[150]

In contrast to this inhumane treatment of another race by supposedly civilized Europeans and Americans, centuries earlier:

When God's Messenger, upon him be peace and blessings, was raised as a Prophet, the same kind of racism, under the name of tribalism, was prevalent in Makka. The Quraysh considered themselves in particular, and Arabs in general, superior to all the other peoples of the world. God's Messenger came with the Divine Message and proclaimed that no Arab is superior over a non-Arab, and no white is superior over black, and superiority is by righteousness and God-fearing alone (Surah al-Hujurat, 49.13). He also declared that even if an Abyssinian black Muslim were to rule over Muslims, he should be obeyed.[151]

In addition to the Qur'an, Gülen cited a *hadith* for these anti-racist insights. Delivered in the cadences typical of his preaching, he told a story about how Muhammad was sensitive even to racial slurs and what would today be called "hate speech":

Once Abu Dharr [a Companion of the Prophet] got so angry with Bilal [another Companion] that he insulted him: "You son of a black woman!" Bilal came to the messenger and reported the incident in tears. The Messenger reproached Abu Dharr: "Do you still have a sign of Jahiliya?" [lit, "ignorance," but more broadly, idolatry and non-Muslim behavior] Full of repentance, Abu Dharr lay on the ground and said: "I won't raise my head (meaning he wouldn't get up) unless Bilal put his foot on it to pass over it." Bilal forgave him, and they were reconciled. Such was the brotherhood and humanity Islam created.[152]

At the least, telling such a story challenged some of the racist stereotypes that still circulated in 1990s Turkey—and in many other places around the globe.

Challenging stereotypes without concrete action, of course, was better than nothing but not likely to end racism. Two initiatives that can be traced to Gülen from this time-period suggest that his preaching inspired more than just words. The first was the planting of schools in Africa. In an illuminating study, political scientist David H. Shinn has traced *Hizmet in Africa: The Activities and Significance of the Gülen Movement.* According to Shinn, the first Hizmet school opened in Morocco in 1994, followed by a school in Senegal in 1997, then schools in Kenya, Tanzania, and Nigeria in 1998. Shinn makes clear that throughout the 1990s to the present, Hizmet-related schools continued to be planted and to grow in Africa. Interestingly, however, Shinn could not pin down an exact number—due to the decentralized and autonomous nature of the various initiatives inspired by Gülen.[153] Indeed, in a fascinating observation that I could echo from many of the locales that I have visited, Shinn reported that "Africans who are familiar with Gülen commented to me on numerous occasions that the name [Gülen] is unknown to all but small numbers of their colleagues. ... A South African professor commented that Hizmet tends not to blow its own horn."[154] This tendency reflected Gülen's own modesty. It may also explain how Gülen has been so easily caricatured: the work took precedent over the person. This was the case even (and perhaps especially) among those closest to Gülen. Nevertheless, by 2000 Shinn estimated that there were over 30 Gülen-inspired schools in Africa, and by 2010 he estimated that the number had jumped to 95, in thirty-five different countries. All ages were included, from pre-school to high school, and there was one university, Nile University in Nigeria. Each school followed the secular curriculum of its host nation, leading some African Muslims to "complain that the Hizmet schools are not sufficiently Islamic," according to Shinn. That did not stop them from growing. Indeed, they provided what many Africans considered the elite schools in their countries. In South Africa, for instance, where the Horizon Education Trust opened its first school in 1998, by 2010 there were waiting lists for 25-30 percent more students than could be admitted, according to Shinn. A similar waiting list existed for students clamoring to attend the Fountain Educational Trust schools that were dedicated to Islamic studies, and that had opened in 2000. These were the first and only such Hizmet schools in Africa specifically dedicated to the study of Islam. Not all the students at the schools were Muslims. In Kenya, a predominantly Christian nation, Light Academy enrolled roughly 75% Christian students, albeit from a wide variety of indigenous tribal groups. In Nigeria, the percentage of Christian students was higher in predominantly Christian Lagos, but Muslim students predominated in the more heavily Muslim city of Kaduna. Generally, in other words, a school's student population represented the religious diversity of that school's region. Many of the schools were non-profits—and they employed dozens of local teachers and administrators, among other staff. The schools frequently organized international tours to competitions (especially, until recently, to Turkey, of course). They also sponsored student exchanges. Some two-hundred Turkish students were in South Africa by 2010, for example, to study English or to attend South African universities. And the schools weren't only drawing from posh regions of the country. "The Horizon International High School in Johannesburg draws about 80 percent of its 225 students from Soweto," Shin reported, "one of the poorest areas of the city."[155] If education and student exchanges were among the ideas that Gülen had suggested to the Pope to overcome *interreligious* enmity, why would such initiatives also not be worth trying to overcome racism?

People of Hizmet also followed Gülen's recommendation that the Prophet's *hoşgörü* mandated an end to racism by seeking better relations with Turkey's Kurdish population. Historically, of course, the Companions of the Prophet spread Islam to diverse cultures and people. The Ottoman Empire had been multi-cultural and multi-lingual. But when Atatürk established the Republic of Turkey, he did so on a foundation of Turkishness—often ruthlessly. Atatürk's vision of a mono-ethnic Republic was never fully realized, and imposing uniformity became particularly tempting in times of crisis, such as after the 1980 coup. At that time, many Kurdish citizens of the Republic were rounded up and imprisoned, and a series of laws made Kurds second-class citizens, at best. Even *speaking* the Kurdish language was outlawed. There were reasons for the antipathy. The Kurdistan Workers Party, better known as the PKK, was founded in 1978. Their skirmishes with the Turkish Army had escalated by the 1990s into a civil war that would cost tens of thousands of lives. In an interview in *Zaman* in 1993, Gülen carefully identified what he called "the problem of the Southeast." Government policies that responded "to violence with violence" were "highly objectionable." Even the word "Kurdish" caused something like "an allergic reaction" among some Turks, Gülen lamented. That situation would have to change for peace to ever have a chance.

Tepid as such statements might seem, in making them Gülen was walking a very fine line. On the one hand, he had to avoid alienating (more than he already had) the military and hard-line secularists. For many in those groups, Kurds were, simply, aliens who needed to assimilate into the Republican program. On the other hand, if schools in the southeast were to be planted and survive—which Gülen hoped—he needed to appeal to Kurds on the common ground of Islamic faith, without alienating Kurdish nationalists who sympathized with the PKK. It was a very delicate dance. Put more positively, what Gülen hoped to do was to bridge and to disarm both Turkish and Kurdish nationalists, by appealing to a modern version of Islam with roots in the ancient Prophet's hoşgörü. And by the early 2000s, in part through Gülen's advocacy, Turkey's Parliament passed constitutional changes that lessened some of the strictures on Kurds. This "Kurdish opening" included, for example, ending the ban on using the Kurdish language. In fact, according to sociologists Mustafa Gürbüz and Harun Akyol, people inspired by Gülen had been building some durable bridges between Turks and Kurds since at least the mid-1990s.[156] Fezalar Educational Institutions (FEI) started work among Kurds in Northern Iraq in 1993 (the Kurdish community spills across the border between Turkey, Syria, Iraq, and Iran, forming what has been historically called as "Kurdistan"). According to one Executive Director of FEI, people inspired by Gülen "love the Kurdish people. Our love and loyalty have been tested many times ... and Kurdish people love us too."[157] This was optimistic, but the schools did thrive. As Akyol put it: "Even during the civil war, (1994-1998), the FEI school extended its branches in both the KDP [Kurdistan Democratic Party] and the PUK [Patriotic Union of Kurdistan] controlled areas; Nilufer private college [high school] for girls was opened in 1996 in Erbil, which was in control of the KDP and Salahaddin Ayyubi college was opened in 1997 in Süleymaniye, which predominantly was controlled by the PUK administration."[158]

And the schools intended to promote peacebuilding. In one of the most conflicted regions of the globe, as Akyol, again, put it:

Gülen inspired Turkish schools are spreading the concept of tolerance, dialogue, democracy, and pluralism in Kurdish community[sic]. They are promoting non-violent conflict resolutions by showing how to approach to social problems through collective cooperation. Expansion of FEI educational activities open-up a political and social space for an alternative approach to the prevention of ethnic conflict. More importantly, they present an alternative way of thinking about ethnic conflict resolutions based on an increasing level of social, cultural, and trade contacts between conflicting parties. ... Turkish schools inspired by Fethullah Gülen ... have prepared and set up the preconditions for understanding each others' needs and that in doing so they are able to build confidence between antagonistic parties.

This peace-building from below, starting with individuals, was of course characteristic of Gülen's theology. Trust was the most important currency in bridging social capital. Trust was the foundation of deep peace.

By 2010, then, there were twelve FEI schools in Iraq, including a University (Ishik) founded in 2009.[159] And as we saw in Chapter One, there were even more schools—as many as three-dozen—in nearly every major city with significant Kurdish populations in southeastern Turkey. In 2009, in Erbil, Iraq, representatives of both Turkey and Iraq's Kurdish community joined with Gülen-related academics and journalists in a conference sponsored by the Journalists and Writers Foundation. It was called the Abant Platform, and it was a regular meeting for dialogue about which we'll learn more shortly. The participants at this Abant Platform in Erbil issued a joint Declaration at the close of the two-day meeting:

[Our] aim is to have sound and dynamic channels of communication in order to put an end to the lack of dialogue rather than trying to convince the parties to come to terms around a solution program. As a chief principle, we defend the free expression and discussion of any sort of ideas unless they contain open calls for violence, and [we] expect respect from everyone for the right [of] all people and groups to express their various thoughts and ideas. ... Kurds, alongside all groups in Iraq, are our brothers. We see it as a compulsory move to develop friendly ties with the federal Kurdish administration. Sustaining the democratization process in Turkey is also compulsory for solving the Kurdish problem.[160]

Over two hundred participated; and the Declaration used the language of the "Kurdistan Regional Government" to describe the prevailing administrative body for the region.[161] By 2012, even the schools in Turkey were embracing multicultural and multilingual education. As Akyol documented: "Unlike [at] standard Kurdish schools, the curriculum in all FEI schools includes the study of four languages: Turkish, Arabic, Kurdish, and English in the first year, thus improving the opportunities for effective dialogue."[162]

Although we have leaped ahead chronologically, here, it has been important to do so to get the complete picture of Gülen's anti-racism activism on this matter—given some widespread misunderstandings or misrepresentations of his actual positions. Contrary to some published opinions that identified Hizmet with opposition to the Kurdish peace-building efforts, in fact Gülen supported the ceasefire of 2013 and other initiatives that built on the "Kurdish opening." Thus, in a 2013 interview in Rudaw, the leading Kurdish-language newspaper, Gülen not surprisingly reached out to Kurds through the example of the Prophet's *hoşgörü*. Pointing out that Said Nursi was Kurdish, Gülen followed Nursi's logic to explain that:

> We have the same faith, we believe in the same God. Our food comes from the same ultimate Sustainer; we live on the same soil and under the same Sun. We breathe the same air. We have the same religion, the same destiny, and the same history. ... As Turks and Kurds, we are everywhere in Turkey, we have spread all over the country together. In a rapidly globalizing world of revolutionary advancements in transportation and communication, and in a world that is evolving into a great village, European countries that fought endless wars in the past have gotten together and even seek political unity. That is how the world is, and we know that we were born as Turks and Kurds regardless of our personal wishes. Given the fact that it is not in our hands to become a Turk or a Kurd, isn't it absurd to discriminate against people based on their Turkish or Kurdish identity or the language they speak? Isn't it to the detriment of all of us?[163]

These rhetorical questions were equally pointed to both Kurds and Turks.

From the Kurdish side, a critical question was whether Hizmet schools in "Kurdistan" were agencies for Turkish "ideological propaganda." Gülen replied by saying that he had been accused of being a propagandist within Turkey for decades—as had many humanitarian peacebuilders before him. But, he went on:

> The Hizmet movement aims at moral improvement, building and maintaining peace, and providing world-class education to catch up with the developed world while respecting local customs. These goals are the same in Iraq and Kurdistan. The concept "ideological propaganda" is foreign to us; we do not know it. It is not very easy to juxtapose ideological propaganda with what we are doing in terms of conflict resolution, dialogue, consensus building, preparing the ground for scientific and technological innovations and promoting peace and security. Hizmet schools have established close relationships with local authorities; their curriculums have been approved and they have carried out their activities under the inspection of both parents and the authorities and in a transparent fashion. Moreover, every state follows what goes on at these schools in legitimate ways. They would not tolerate anything that brought harm to their peoples. Therefore, baselessly accusing these institutions, which have been established with the efforts and sacrifices of thousands of people, of conspiratorial approaches would be unfair and illegitimate.[164]

The fact that Gülen himself used the title "Kurdistan" was significant. No matter how conspiratorial, unfair, and illegitimate, if one wants to understand why some people in Turkey believed the slander that aligned Gülen with "terrorists" like the PKK, one need look no further.[165]

And yet, of course, Gülen advocated non-violence, not terrorism, with education as the ultimate alternative to violence.

> It is impossible not to support efforts that aim to stop the tears and bloodshed of the region. It is crucial to be constructive and leave the pain of the past behind.
>
> It is also crucial to refrain from being part of any type of conflict,

fight, or provocation that is based on ethnic or sectarian grounds. People should be careful not to fuel hatred and provoke separatist ideologies. ... Any chance for solidarity, philanthropy and togetherness on a cultural and economic basis must be put into practice. ...

Specifically, educational institutions and civil society play an important role in the application of a unifying culture. Education has a specific role in generating social values that prevent material conflicts. Contrary to our experience in the modern day, the peoples of the region have a long and deeply rooted history and tradition of peaceful coexistence. The Kurds, Turks, Arabs, Christians, Muslims, and Jews used to live together in [sic] peace. We need educational models and a culture of civil society that will rediscover and put into practice the values that facilitated this togetherness. Peaceful coexistence will be more feasible if youth can find a satisfying educational system in which they would not appeal to violence, war, and terror; and thus, education will be a strong alternative to violence.[166]

And this peacebuilding found its deepest root, of course, in Islam and the Prophet—who taught Muslims to live by what the world knows as "the golden rule":

I believe that sincerity and mutual respect are crucial, as well as a characteristic expressed in a *hadith* of the Prophet (pbuh): wishing for others what we wish for ourselves and avoiding deeds that we wouldn't like to have happen to ourselves. Moreover, choosing other people over ourselves—a significant feature of the locals of Medina that is also praised in the Quran—will help us overcome hatred. Turkish and Kurdish civil society organizations can greatly contribute to peace by providing the grounds for the aforementioned values and facilitating people embracing them. On such grounds people can come together and form a kind of unity that will last. This is possible and efforts must be channeled in this direction. [sic][167]

That possibility would not be easy to achieve. By 2017, after pressure from the Turkish government, the ownership of FEI schools changed hands and they were purchased by Kurdish private investors.[168] In any event, what people of Hizmet started, others would profit from. That pattern would hold for many of the institutions or agencies of "bridging social capital" that Gülen had inspired in the 1990s, as it would for many of the businesses that Turkish Muslims inspired by Gülen had begun within Turkey, including the schools. Those agencies and businesses had been built on a foundation of the trustworthiness of the Prophet (and of Gülen), and they had engaged Muslims on behalf of interreligious dialogue, women's rights, and against racism. Gülen had moved Turkey forward, by hearkening to the *hoşgörü* in its past. Over the same years, he had also moved Turks beyond Turkey, and people had taken Hizmet to new places. As the 1990s came to an end, his own health was failing; his heart was literally breaking, even while the movement he had inspired was flourishing.

Dialogue with the world

The history of religions is filled with revival and reform movements that, for diverse reasons, failed. Missionaries travel to exotic lands, and they establish a nascent community. But they catch an unusual disease, or they fall prey to militant defenders of the old ways, and they wind up dead and forgotten. Or, a mystic proclaims a new revelation, and gains followers for a few years or generations. But then scandal or mismanagement undermines the vision, the movement falls apart, and the mystic is forgotten. Or, moral reformers hearken to some unmistakable practice at the ethical core of a tradition, and they organize movements and grow agencies to restore that practice. But the rigor and zeal of the moral reformation is too heavy for the bulk of ordinary believers, and the reform lasts for a few years and then fizzles. Had Fethullah Gülen remained content with the way The City embraced him in the 1990s, and had he kept his focus narrowly on the problems of Turkey, there is little doubt that—given recent developments in Turkish politics—there would have been no Hizmet movement in 2019. But what happened in the 1990s— culminating in Gülen's move to Pennsylvania in 1999—gave Hizmet and Gülen a global footprint that allowed both the individual and the movement, to a degree, to weather storms in Turkey's troubled political culture. While all the agencies and initiatives—educational, media, and dialogue—begun in the '80s and '90s had their origins in Turkey, by the end of the decade most of them were also putting down roots in diverse places—Africa, Asia, Europe, Eurasia, Australia, America, and beyond.

Perhaps the most important of the bridging agencies begun in the 1990s by people of Hizmet, already alluded to briefly several times, was the Journalists and Writers Foundation—JWF. Founded in 1994 at Gülen's recommendation, the JWF began its work by organizing and sponsoring the Ramadan dialogue evenings held at posh Istanbul hotels. These were, by and large, public relations efforts. Yet Gülen's intent for the agency went beyond merely improving his public image. In a speech he delivered when the Foundation was established, he expressed hope that the JWF could heal divisions within Turkey (and, by extension, around the globe): "People are divided into many different polarized camps ... such as seculars-anti-seculars, democrats-anti-democrats" Gülen offered. Turgut Özal had died suddenly in 1993, and a succession crisis followed that exacerbated dissension. "I believe, in such a period of time, an institution that has been founded by reasonable and sensible people may help to ease tensions among such groups and camps."[169] So the JWF was to be a think-tank of "reasonable and sensible people," as much as a public relations agency. In fact, those two missions of the Foundation always co-existed somewhat uneasily. As one historian has documented, some events sponsored by JWF were clearly public relations efforts for Hizmet; others were serious dialogues that actually engaged difference and dissent with intellectually critical and credible inquiry.[170] According to theologian Pim Valkenberg, the JWF eventually developed six "platforms": the Abant Platform organized a series of public forums on controversial questions; the Intercultural Dialogue Platform focused on interreligious gatherings; the Eurasian Dialogue Platform sponsored events in the former Soviet Republics and Russia; the Medialog Platform invited foreign correspondents to conferences; a Women's Platform sponsored events for female journalists, scholars, and activists; and a Research Platform. The latter was closely connected to an "Academy" located in Altunizade, and to the various publishing efforts for scholars and journalists related to Hizmet.

Of these initiatives, the Abant Platform was the most influential. Abant is a lakeside village a few hours' drive east of Istanbul, where the first Platform meetings were held in summer 1998. The topic of that first meeting was "Islam and Secularism." There could have been no hotter topic to tackle in the history of modern Turkey. The participants—several dozen prominent intellectuals and journalists—agreed on a ten-point

statement that sought to reduce mistrust between Islamists and secularists. The gist of the statement was a virtual echo of Gülen's vision of
hoşgörü: "We who are gathered at Abant believe this: people's different
views and tendencies and preferences for different lifestyles are not an
obstacle to their making sound decisions about their country. No matter how large our problems they can be solved by citizen initiatives."[171]
Abant Platform conferences or dialogues were held at least annually, often back at the lakeside setting, sometimes in Istanbul itself, and occasionally at sites around the world. The topics included, among others,
"Globalization" (2002), "Alevism" (2007), "The Kurdish Problem" (in
Abant in 2008, and, as we saw in the previous section, in Erbil, Iraq, in
2009). Another Abant Platform meeting addressed "Egypt, Stability in
the Middle East, and Turkey" in Cairo in 2009. More than thirty gatherings were held in all. The final Abant Platform to be held in Turkey
happened in Istanbul in January, 2016. It took up the topic: "Challenges
to Democracy in Turkey."[172] Within two months of that meeting, *Zaman*
and *Today's Zaman*—the daily newspapers associated with Hizmet, had,
as if in tragic fulfillment of "challenges to democracy," been closed by
the government. The JWF, in 2017, moved its primary office to New
York City, where its mission remained to promote "peaceful coexistence
through dialogue and understanding."[173] Peacebuilding through *hoşgörü*
had to involve intellectuals—journalists, writers, and academics, and the
JWF and its Abant Platform was a primary means to that end.

Hizmet in Europe

Still, well before the troubles of the twenty-first century, Hizmet *abis*
and *ablas* had been going to places where they could continue Hizmet
even when things got difficult in their native land. The migration was
inspired, in part, and not surprisingly, by Gülen's preaching. In a November 19, 1989, sermon at Süleymaniye Mosque in Istanbul, shortly
after the fall of the Berlin Wall, Gülen called for volunteers to head to
those regions that had been under Soviet control but that were opening
up (or being torn apart).[174] One of those sites was Yugoslavia. In that
country, as is well known, almost immediately after the collapse of the
Soviet Union a brutal civil war broke out as Bosnian Muslims battled
Serbian Orthodox and Croatian Roman Catholics. Into that cauldron

two Hizmet volunteers, inspired by Gülen, went to Sarajevo. Their story is documented in vivid fashion in a 2014 documentary about Gülen and the Hizmet movement, *Love Is a Verb*. The two men, who sought to build a school in Sarajevo like the schools in Turkey, reached the heart of the war-torn city by crawling through sewers.[175] They were armed with only $300. But their modest yet persistent efforts eventually bore fruit, and a school to promote peacebuilding through *hoşgörü* was founded in 1996, a year after the civil war ended. As profiled in the film, one of the first students to graduate from the Sarajevo Hizmet school was Sead Ahmiç. According to Ahmiç, the school welcomed Turkish, Bosnian, Croatian, and Serbian students, of Muslim, Roman Catholic, Orthodox and no religious affiliation—and taught them not to hate. "I'd never think like [I do] now" without those schools, Ahmiç offered, "maybe I'd still hate."[176] In a story that was repeated in country after country, the Hizmet-related schools proved popular, and multiplied. By 2015 more than a dozen schools associated with Hizmet existed in several Bosnian cities, among them Sarajevo, Zenica, Bihac, Tuzla, and Mostar. They operated under the umbrella of an agency, Bosna Sema, that also operated an International University in Sarajevo.[177]

In a heart-warming montage, the Director of *Love Is a Verb*, Terry Spencer Hesser, interviewed Mehmed Bajraktarevic, Director of the Bosnian Fatih Sultan Mehmet Orchestra. That musical group, which also featured a choir, brought together dozens of boys and girls from Hizmet schools across Bosnia's ethnic and religious diversity. Bajraktarevic explained that this kind of interreligious peacebuilding through music followed naturally from his own Islamic faith. His rationale echoed Gülen's theology, and found connections between religion, nature, the arts, and peace. "Everything God created is beautiful," Bajraktarevic offered, "also music. There's natural music. Birds sing. Water has music. The wind is musical." So, his orchestra invited "Muslims, Catholic, and Orthodox to [make music] together. We have only one God." The song the young people played and sang on the film's soundtrack was an ode to Sarajevo that then morphed into John Lennon's "Give Peace a Chance."[178] Similar efforts by Turks in Albania, Romania, and other Balkan countries soon followed leading to highly successful Turgut Özal schools in Tirana and Durres—the capital and second largest city of Albania—and Beder and Epoka Universities—both fully accredited institutions of higher education, also in Tirana. The first Özal school began even before the Bosnian initiative, in 1993.[179]

Nevertheless, it was the schools in Bosnia that received a significant financial boost when the Journalists and Writers Foundation organized a distinctive fundraiser on September 19, 1995: a charity soccer match. The game was held at Istanbul's Ali Sami Yen stadium, home of the Galatasaray football team—one of Turkey's most popular. More than 20,000 filled the stadium in the Mecidiyeköy neighborhood of Istanbul. Gülen offered brief words of thanks and appreciation for the ways that sport could promote peace. The game featured Argentine star Diego Maradona—perhaps the most famous soccer player in the world at the time—along with players from Turkey's national team and other international athletes. Millions of others were estimated to have watched the game on television. In attendance, along with Gülen, were Prime Minister Tansu Çiller, cabinet members Hasan Ekinci, Hikmet Çetin, and Yıldırım Aktuna. Halida Repovac Izetbegovic, the wife of Alija Izetbegovic, leader of Bosnia-Herzegovina, was also an honored guest, as was the mayor of Istanbul at the time, Recep Tayyip Erdoğan.[180] That Gülen appreciated sports should be no surprise; he was joined in that love by billions around the globe. And given his other peacebuilding activities of the 1990s, it should also be no surprise that he could marshal athletic competition on behalf of *hoşgörü*. "One important source of power and means of communication that can influence society is without a doubt sports," Gülen offered. Sports provided viewers with pleasure, he went on, but "a number of virtues" were also displayed by sport—excellence at one's craft, fellow feeling with others, bounded competition, grace in victory and acceptance in defeat—all of which enacted *hoşgörü*. Thus, sports "can help the ideas of dialogue and tolerance [*hoşgörü*] spread; ideas that we believe to be so essential that they must be made known to everyone and publicized by this means for the sake of the well-being of both our own people and all of humanity."[181] Gülen's interest in sport was not only pragmatic. Just two weeks after the big soccer benefit, on February 2, Gülen took in as a fan the Kırkpınar Wrestling Matches held at Sarayiçi near Edirne. This oil-wrestling contest, in which large semi-naked men contend against each other in an open, grassy field, is by some accounts the world's longest-continuing running athletic competition. It was certainly a distinctive feature of Ottoman culture—as its lineage dates at least back to the 1300s. Gülen's attendance no doubt reinforced that while he was an advocate of dialogue and a famous preacher, he also was a regular Turkish man.

We have already noted in Chapter Three how Gülen had visited Germany in 1977. Naturally, some of the thousands of Turks who emigrated to Germany in the 1990s carried with them Hizmet ideals, as they did throughout Europe. In Germany, where Turks constituted by 2000 more than two-thirds of the roughly three million new immigrants to that country, people inspired by Gülen also forged initiatives in education and dialogue. Rather than founding schools, as in Yugoslavia and other Balkan countries, Hizmet volunteers in Germany began operating "learning centers." The first—BIL Learning House (*Das Bildungshaus BIL*)—was established in Stuttgart in 1995.[182] Similar centers soon followed in Berlin, Frankfurt, Munich, and other major cities. These centers were comparable to the "tutoring centers" run by FEM within Turkey, albeit with a different curriculum. Like the FEM tutoring centers, they were often staffed by college students; some of whom were paid, many of whom volunteered. According to sociologist Jill Irvine, the centers, which were for children, youth, and adults, offered German language courses, along with classes in English, math, and science. "Integration Courses" that focused on helping Turks adapt to a new culture were also available. According to Irvine, these courses were federally-mandated, and included "six hundred hours of German language instruction and thirty hours of instruction in German language and history over a six-month period." By 2006, there were by one estimate one-hundred Hizmet-related learning centers in Bavaria alone (one of sixteen states in Germany).[183]

Already in 1995, Gülen had encouraged Turks living in Europe to seek full integration into their host societies, while also (of course) retaining Muslim practice:

> Our people who live in Europe must come off from their old situation and become a part of the European society. Their children must be orientated to universities.... Also, they must transmit our cultural and religious richness to European society. In the future, they will constitute our lobbies which we highly need today. In the past, only 2 per

Fethullah Gülen: A Life of Hizmet

cent of the Turkish immigrant population was fulfilling their religious requirements. But today, 40 or maybe 60 per cent of the young population regularly prays in the mosques. Obviously, our people didn't undergo to [sic] an assimilation process, contrary, they impressed the host societies by their conviction and culture.[184]

Exactly how "impressed" Germans were with faithful Muslim practice was open for debate.

Many of the youth interviewed by Irvine reported being bullied and otherwise harassed. Across the board, Turkish students tended to do poorly in German public schools. Few of them went on to college. Consequently, as some Turks inspired by Gülen advanced into the professional classes in Germany, and as others became successful as entrepreneurs, they sought (with varying success) to establish private schools. Irvine reported that by 2006 people inspired by Gülen had established private college-preparatory schools in Berlin, Dortmund, and Stuttgart. Similar efforts were underway by 2000 in France, Belgium, Great Britain, Ireland, the Netherlands, and Sweden. Along with learning centers and schools, of course, Hizmet individuals inspired by Gülen also set up dialogue and intercultural centers. These centers sponsored cultural festivals and exchanges that sought to bring people together around food, music, art, and inquiry. For instance, in 2016 I attended a conference on "Countering Violent Extremism: *Mujahada* and Muslim Responsibilities" in Brussels. That event was jointly organized by Dialogue Platform of Brussels and the Catholic University of Leuven. Participants from over 30 different countries with significant Muslim populations gave and listened to papers, and we engaged in dialogue around the conference topic.[185] These Hizmet-related dialogue centers also sponsored European individuals on group trips to Turkey—something that of course became impossible after 2016.

According to political sociologist Emre Demir, a student of Turkish Islam in France and Germany, Gülen's approach to "integration" of Muslims in Europe was a careful balancing between continuation of tradition and adaptation to a host culture. Unlike in the Balkans and (as we shall see) in Eastern Europe, there were in Western Europe neither established Turkish Muslim communities with values comparable to those of Gülen, nor an easy avenue to set up the kinds of initiatives that had led to the growth of Hizmet in Turkey. Gülen and those inspired by him had to negotiate both Turkish Muslim fear of becoming too "Western" (read—Jewish or Christian), and European Islamophobia, which was both deep and broad. Gülen, again, sought to chart a "middle course." Consequently, for example, Gülen advocated for Turkey's membership in the European Union:

> We should be comfortable in our outreach to the world. We will not lose anything from our religion, nationality and culture because of developments like globalization, customs union or membership in the European Union. We firmly believe that the dynamics that hold our unity are strong. Again, we also firmly believe that the Quran is based on revelation and offers solution[s] to all the problems of humanity. Therefore, if there is anybody who is afraid, they should be those who persistently live away from the invigorating climate of Quran.[186]

After 2016, as we shall see, it was this "middle-way," in a democratic Europe that was gradually opening up to Muslims, that became one of the most promising venues for a sustainable future for Hizmet.

Hizmet in Central Asia

So, if some Hizmet volunteers inspired by Gülen had in the 1990s gone south from Turkey to Africa, and others had gone northwest into the Balkans and Europe, some also went northeast, into Georgia, Azerbaijan, and Central Asia. We cannot, and do not need to, do a complete survey. A few illustrative examples will suffice. Journalist Hulusi Turgut, in an influential 1998 story, reported that Gülen told him the following:

> Turkey can't be cut off from the world. When it is cut off, it is like a branch broken off from a tree—it can't live, and so will dry up. Turkey must be integrated with the world. In such integration, the foremost countries with which we can establish sincere bonds and closeness are those of Central Asia. In one way we are a branch from the same shoot, and so I directed my friends toward that region. Maybe this is just a dream. [But] loyal Turkish people supported this idea, and schools were opened in Central Asia. Some of them are now self-supporting. ... Those [businessmen] who built mosques wanted to open Qur'an courses beside them. I said: "Mosques are wonderful; we have

the greatest respect for them. However, it would be better if you open a school." ... I was never actively involved in these efforts. I never asked for a house and home in this world. I used my friends' trust in me like a credit card for educational services.[187]

That credit card had a very high spending limit. A first delegation of eleven Hizmet volunteers started work in Georgia with a visit to Batum on January 11, 1990. The delegation met with local Muslim business and religious leaders over two days. They then repeated the meetings with representatives in Tiflis (Tbilisi)—the Georgian capital. Another delegation—in this case mostly businessmen—37 of them, set out from Istanbul on May 28. They expanded their visits from Batum and Tbilisi in Georgia by flying to Kazan (Tatarstan, in Russia), and then flying back south to Gence (Ganja) and Baku in Azerbaijan. From there they made further stops in Kazakhstan, Kyrgyzstan, Tajikistan, Uzbekistan, Afghanistan, Mongolia, and Pakistan. All of the former Soviet Republics in that list (with the exception of Tatarstan) had gained their independence in 1992. And in all these Republics, including Tatarstan, Hizmet-related schools were almost immediately opened. These schools were supported by funds from businesses started by local entrepreneurs, in partnership with Turkish business leaders (more on this model in Chapter 5). In any event, most of the schools were up and running by 1993, and had gained enough influence within a few months that President Turgut Özal, in what would be his last official State visit before dying, traveled to visit some of the businesses and schools in Central Asia in April, 1993 (he died on April 17). These were not small investments. Afghanistan saw four Hizmet-related schools established by 1998. Turkmenistan saw 20 by 1997. 5,000 students had enrolled in Turkish schools in Kazakhstan by 1998. Mongolia's six schools employed fifty teachers from Turkey, and thirty-eight from Mongolia. It was, interestingly, bread businesses that provided these schools with their "bread." "Some Turkish businessmen took over the bread market" in Mongolia, Turgut reported. The schools across Central Asia served youth from primary to high school ages, and within a few years universities were also established: Qafqaz University in Azerbaijan, International Black Sea University in Georgia, International Turkmen-Turkish University in Turkmenistan, and Süleyman Demirel University in Kazakhstan, among others.[188]

Final years in Istanbul, and exile to America

As the name of the last school suggests, these initiatives depended upon support from people in high places. Such support could turn fickle. Süleyman Demirel was not always a friend of Hodjaefendi or Hizmet. And yet Gülen clearly experienced in the 1990s an access to the highest offices in Turkey. People inspired by him parlayed that access into influence around the globe. We have already described the cordial relationship Gülen had with Turgut Özal. But similar meetings marked Gülen's calendar in the 1990s. For instance, he met twice with Prime Minister Tansu Çiller, the first (and only) female Prime Minister of Turkey, on November 30, 1994, and June 9, 1995. He met with Bülent Ecevit a few times in 1990s. The historical record will have to await another historian with greater access to the official archives to tell the full story, but Gülen almost surely discussed with Çiller a step that was to be crucial to the flourishing of Hizmet—the founding of Bank Asya. Given the range of initiatives that people inspired by Gülen were engaged in, it made sense that there be a collective financial institution both to gather and to invest the considerable resources that were accruing. The schools alone numbered over 100 by 1996 just in Turkey—and many of those campuses were built, as were the dormitories and tutoring centers, by construction companies led by people friendly to Hizmet.[189] There were private Islamic banks already in Turkey. But there was none that combined Islamic principles with the best practices of modern finance. That was to be the mission of Bank Asya, which was opened in a gala celebration on October 24, 1996. Gülen attended; Çiller spoke: the two even sat side-by-side. A picture of the ribbon-cutting shows Çiller holding the scissors, with Gülen smiling from a little behind her, over her right shoulder. Holding the ribbon and directly to Çiller's left in the picture is Recep Tayyip Erdoğan—at the time mayor of Istanbul.[190]

· Erdoğan, like Gülen, claimed legitimacy from Islam. In fact, in December 1997 he would follow Gülen in being charged for the crime of being a Muslim. More specifically, Erdoğan was charged with "inciting hatred," after he recited a portion of a poem that threatened to militarize and to mobilize Muslims. At a rally in the city of Siirt, Erdoğan had quoted these lines from poet Ziya Gökalp:

The mosques are our barracks,
the domes our helmets,
the minarets our bayonets,
and the believers our soldiers.

Erdoğan had used the lines before. He claimed that "they stirred up crowds" (which were constituted, of course, by and large by Muslims).[191] But what is often called a "postmodern coup" had happened in Turkey on February 28, 1997. A meeting of the National Security Council on that date led to a memorandum that unseated elected Prime Minister Necmettin Erbakan—the leader of the Islamist Welfare Party. Erdoğan was also a member of the Welfare Party. What followed, in policies collectively called "the February 28 Process" in Turkey, were steps to limit and rollback what secularists and some military leaders saw as an increasingly influential role of Islam in public life. To the secularists, Atatürk's sharp line between religion and politics had been getting blurry. The new policies were broad. The most visible was a ban on headscarves in schools and universities. Less obvious, but more significant, were steps that insured government officials, notably generals or ex-generals, received the financial windfalls through patronage that flowed from the increasing number of formerly-state-owned enterprises that were now going public.[192] Erdoğan, whose wife wore a headscarf, was caught up in this "coup." He eventually served four months in jail, in 1999, and was banned from politics. When he would return to public life, following an amnesty, he pledged allegiance to democracy. But he also practiced the exact forms of patronage and crony capitalism that had led to his imprisonment.

Now, these political developments post-1997 are crucial to understanding the history of Hizmet down to the present, and to understanding why Gülen left Turkey in 1999. It has often been claimed, repeatedly and inaccurately, that Gülen and Erdoğan were once "allies." Of course, the two knew each other. They occasionally appeared together at the same events. Erdoğan received an award and spoke, in fact, at a 1996 Journalists and Writers Foundation event that Gülen also attended (along with a thousand others).[193] But Gülen never sought or claimed affiliation with a political party. He also consistently stressed not political, but civic, aims. The difference was important. Gülen preached that a robust civil society—with no compulsion in religion, freedom of speech, and other human rights—was completely compatible with authentic Islam; indeed, Islam was the most secure foundation for a robust civil society. There were political implications, to be sure, to anything Gülen said or did. His life had been politicized for him. But no one has ever shown that Gülen's aims involved any active support for a politician or political party. And no one has ever discovered a Hizmet strategic plan to make Gülen caliph or sultan. Gülen consistently throughout his life had advocated for three things: for education that linked science and religion; for poverty-alleviation that harnessed capitalism to social justice; and for interreligious dialogue on behalf of conflict-resolution and peace. His advocacy for these three initiatives grew stronger and clearer over the course of his life. And when he advocated for these practices, people listened and made them actual. The best way to understand Gülen's political role, then, is as an advocate. He drew out implications for civil society from his study of Islam, and then he spoke in favor of them. He empowered and trusted people who listened to him to put those implications into practice in schools, businesses, and think-tanks. Erdoğan, on the other hand, was equally consistent in very different patterns: in exploiting popular Islam for increasingly grandiose and authoritarian political ambitions, and in manipulating and controlling people to enrich himself and his cronies, as we shall document fully at the end of Chapter Five.

It is thus telling that Gülen remembered several meetings that Erdoğan asked to have with him during the late 1990s. They happened on the 5th Floor sometime between 1997 and 1999. The Welfare Party had been abolished, and Erdoğan was planning what would become the political party that would vault him back into power, the Justice and Development Party, whose acronym in Turkish is the AKP. Erdoğan was looking for support. What he did not say openly was that he also expected obedience. As Gülen recalled the meetings, from the vantage of 2016, it was clear to him that Erdoğan was no ally of Hizmet.[194] Gülen did not promise Erdoğan any support in these meetings, but rather recalled that he expressed his "own considerations at the time." In fact, Gülen's suspicions were warranted. On the way out of one of these meetings, while still unwittingly in earshot of some of Gülen's friends, Erdoğan admitted that he needed to defeat and vanquish Hizmet first. He would eventually spend plenty in that ruthless effort.[195]

But in 1996 the two men coexisted in The City that one of them led as mayor. Gülen's public appearances were guided by his health, which was increasingly frail. He was also starting to lose to death some of his oldest friends. Perhaps his most frequent outings between 1996 and 1999 were for funerals. In April, 1997, for one example, he attended the funeral and offered a prayer for Kemal Erimez. *Hajji* (Hacı in Turkish spelling) Kemal—the title with which he was honored—was one of Gülen's wealthiest supporters. Born in 1923 in Samsun, Kemal inherited and grew wealth through olive, construction, and diamond industries. As a devout Muslim, he had always practiced the charity of zakat. But when he met Gülen in Izmir in 1966, it started a friendship that would last for thirty-one years. "*Hajji* Kemal," Gülen offered in remarks at his friends' funeral, "could talk to anyone." He helped build Yamanlar and Fatih schools in Istanbul—the first in Hizmet. Kemal helped fund Samanyolu TV—the largest television network connected to Hizmet. And Erimez actually moved to Tajikistan to help develop the schools there, along with helping to fund the schools in Uzbekistan and Azerbaijan. It was in Tajikistan that he was given the honorary title of *Hajji* Ata, *Hajji* the Father. Like Gülen, he suffered from diabetes in his advancing age. Yet Kemal also repeatedly traveled back and forth between Central Asia and Turkey, bringing delegations with him to grow businesses to support schools. He died on March 13, 1997. Gülen said about his friend that "we have lost a very important person." Whenever an opportunity arose, Gülen recalled, *Hajji* Kemal would say "I will do it." "He has passed away and gone into the ground like a seed," Gülen prayed, "And a hyacinth arose from his life. So, while he has died, twenty blossoms have bloomed from that man. The generations he has trained were not left empty."[196]

For one other example, indicating some of Gülen's broader role in The City as an advocate for a healthy civil society, on February 2, 1999, Hodjaefendi broadcast on radio a sympathetic message to mark the death of musician and television personality Barış Manço. Gülen then attended Manço's funeral. Manço was the founder of what became known as "Anatolian rock." His music combined lyrics and images from traveling Turkish folk poets with the back-beat, guitars, and bass of Western rock 'n' roll. He claimed musical influence from 1960s legends Chubby Checker and Elvis Presley, but he let his hair grow long, and he grew a Fu Manchu mustache that gave him the look (and he developed some of the sound) of what came to be called, in 1980s America, "hair bands," such as Van Halen. As his obituary in *The New York Times* put it: "He was an arresting personality who dressed in outlandish clothes he designed himself, and he covered his fingers with rings. In the 1970s, when Turkey had only a single state-owned television show, he was offered an appearance on the condition that he cut his flowing hair. He refused, and the authorities finally relented, making him the first member of the alternative youth culture to appear on Turkish television."[197] Manço appeared frequently on television thereafter, including a regular show that he hosted for nearly a decade. It featured Manço as a kind of informal diplomat for Turkey. For that show, he traveled to dozens of different countries for concerts, and then broadcast the world back to the Turkish people. Manço had been honored by the Journalists and Writers Foundation. He also appeared at several events with Hodjaefendi. At one, Manço presented Gülen a gift in honor of his educational initiatives.198 In his remarks upon Manço's passing, Gülen not surprisingly lauded the singer's contribution to tolerance—to *hoşgörü*.

And while the musician had no doubt opened up Turkey in ways compatible with Gülen's efforts, he also had a very practical reason to be grateful to Hizmet. *Today's Zaman* editor Bülent Keneş recalled the incident in a 2009 story. It is worth telling in full because it documents the extent of Hizmet's growth in the decade of the 1990s:

> In 1997, when a group of people from the Gülen Movement were trying to establish the third Turkish school in Thailand's city of Chiang Mai, the late pop star Barış Manço stopped by the city. When he learned of the sex trade being conducted in a massage parlor called the Turkish Bath, he was angered by the use of the word Turkish in the name of such an establishment and decided to cover the story for TV. Acting hastily, he forgot to obtain permission to shoot footage, mandatory under Thai law. Upon a complaint from the owners of the bath, he was detained in the hotel room where he was staying. Offended, Manço called the Turkish Embassy in Bangkok and explained the situation, demanding "urgent help." The officials at the embassy told him they would not be able to extend any immediate help since Chiang Mai is considerably far from Bangkok.
>
> While Manço went through the pangs of despair in the hotel, he

heard a knock on the door. When he opened the door, he was greeted in Turkish: "May you recover from this soon, Barış abi. We heard you were in trouble." Manço felt a big relief before asking with surprise "Who are you?" The visitor answered: "Abi, we are teachers from a Turkish school here. We will help you. Don't worry. Everything will be alright."

It soon surfaced that after receiving Manço's call for help, the Turkish Embassy phoned the executives of the Turkish school in Bangkok and told them the story. "Can your colleagues in Chiang Mai go to Barış Manço's hotel to learn about his condition?" they asked.

The teachers from the Turkish school in Chiang Mai first visited Manço and then the judge who ordered his detention, telling him that Manço is a famous singer in Turkey and would not do any harm to Thailand because he was an envoy of good will who wanted to promote Thailand in Turkey. The case against Manço was then quickly dropped. He was released from detention and was able to complete shooting footage in the city without a problem. Thus, Manço's adventure, which started as a nightmare, wound up with a happy ending— all thanks to several Turkish teachers. I can remember with clarity how Manço enthusiastically told the whole country on his TV program his adventures in Chiang Mai and his thankfulness for the help extended by the Turkish teachers.[199]

A video of Manço's homage to Gülen and to the Turkish School in Chiang Mai—called Fatih Private High School, remained on Youtube as of 2017.[200]

Such friendships, and not only at funerals, marked the last years of Fethullah Gülen's work in Istanbul. But that work was coming to an end. The political oppression that had caught up even the Mayor of Istanbul was also cracking down on Gülen. And so, on March 21, 1999, Hodjaefendi departed The City for what would be, in all likelihood, the last time. He may not have known it, but he was bidding farewell to his homeland. America would provide Gülen the best safe house he had ever visited. But the departure was still an exile. Hodjaefendi had first visited the U.S. in 1992—as part of a mini world-tour. He had also returned to the States for a visit to medical specialists in September 1997, when he had also met with a wide range of dialogue partners. But his most im-

portant visit on that occasion had been with some friends who had settled in rural Pennsylvania. Those friends had secured land for what was
at first a summer camp, and that would eventually become the twenty-
five-acre Golden Generation Retreat and Worship Center. The friends in
Pennsylvania happened to include a cardiologist that Gülen trusted, and
who could provide him with care not available in Turkey. So, officially,
and in fact, Hodjaefendi left Turkey for the U.S. for health care.

But he was also leaving behind yet another tense inquiry that followed from the "February 28 process." The rumors had swirled for two
years. Gülen had answered question after question from journalists
within and outside of Turkey about a "Military High Commission" that
had been appointed to investigate his activities. He answered charges
that ranged from his being an agent of Mossad—the Israeli secret service—to his being secret cardinal of the Pope.[201] Gradually, the pressure
increased to the point that Gülen's personal freedom was in question.
He could not, for reasons of health, endure another season on the run.
So, he left for America for treatment and for safety.

Within a month of Gülen's departure from Istanbul, on April 21,
1999, Prosecutor Nuh Mete Yüksel filed the first lawsuit that named
Gülen as a "national security" threat. Listed along with Hodjaefendi
were more than a dozen of his students and admirers—scholars, journalists, and activists.[202] Reports followed reports, documenting how Gülen
had gathered the "largest congregation" of Muslims in Turkey, and had
engaged in "secret" operations to build schools, media, finance and other
businesses. He was also accused of encouraging his people to take positions within the government—notably in police and judicial appointments. Yeni Şafak, today a pro-government newspaper, documented the
ongoing process in a 2016 article that is, contrary to much of the "journalism" in the rest of the article, accurate:

> In October 2000, Muzaffer Erkan, Head of the Intelligence Depart-
> ment of the General Directorate of Security, sent a note to the Ankara
> 11th Criminal Court titled the "National General Activities of Fetul-
> lah Gülen Group." The memorandum highlighted the financial foot-
> ing of the Gülenists' general organization in Turkey. The study, which
> included extensive information on companies, foundations, schools
> and dormitories, which were close to the Gülenists, was sent to the ...

Chief Public Prosecutor's Office. In particular, information ... about company and school administrators were included in the note that emphasized the educational structure of Gülenists.[203]

This kind of documentation of the activities of people of Hizmet would, naturally, prove extremely valuable to future governments.

But it took a while for any actual charges against Gülen to be filed. The courts were not eager to proceed with claims they recognized as baseless. Events unfolded as if the Keystone Cops were in charge:

March 8, 2000: Prosecutor Yüksel requests arrest warrant to Ankara State Security Court.
August 7, 2000: The Court (Ankara No. 1) rejects the request for a warrant.
August 11, 2000: A new request is placed to Ankara No. 2 Court.
August 23, 2000: Gülen's case is transferred to the Istanbul State Security Court
August 28, 2000: The Istanbul Court dismisses the warrant.
August 29, 2000: Gülen's case is transferred back to Ankara No. 2 Court.
August 31, 2000: The Chief Prosecutor files an indictment.
October 16, 2000: A trial begins, in absentia.[204]

This kind of bureaucratic maneuvering would continue for eight years, a hellish legal labyrinth interrupted only briefly by the resignation of the Chief Prosecutor after a sex-tape featuring the married man with a woman not his wife became public. The law under which Gülen was to be tried was Turkish Penal Code, Articles 312 and 313—the same laws that had briefly snared Erdoğan in 1999. After years of wrangling, Gülen was eventually acquitted. In 2004, a High Criminal Court was appointed to handle the case, after the military courts were closed down. That Court requested a police report detailing any criminal activities by Gülen, including the use of violence or force. The report came back indicating, of course, that Gülen had never been involved in any crime, or violence, or force. Ankara No. 11 High Criminal Court then acquitted Gülen on May 5, 2006. Appeals dragged on for another two years. The case finally reached the Supreme Court of Appeals on June 24, 2008. The

Court voted 17-6 to uphold the acquittal. It was hardly a relief. Gülen had expressed a desire and willingness to return to Turkey many times. He had wanted to face the charges against him, and even more he wanted to live again in the country he loved. But he also realized that his return was complicated. He was increasingly frail. He had retired from preaching. He no longer sought a public role that had always been difficult for him in any event. So, when he was issued a "permanent resident status" visa (I-485) by the United States Citizen and Immigration Services on October 8, 2008, what had been a lengthy and laborious application process, and yet another long-period of limbo, had appeared to be resolved. He was, in effect, in self-imposed exile. But he was, at least for the time being, in a safe place.

***

Gülen's fraught departure from The City was a fitting end to two remarkable decades of activity. The hüzün and melancholy of the 5th Floor had been transformed through the Prophet's teachings about *hoşgörü* into the global outreach of a *cemaat*—a community, dedicated to *hizmet*. As Gülen's plane left Istanbul for America, he could look out the window and see that, thank God, it was flying with two wings. Rumi had first used the metaphor of "two wings" for the spiritual life, but Gülen had also developed it. Gülen quoted Rumi that "if good deeds were a body, purity of intention would be their soul." That is, to "fly with two wings" was to do the right thing for the right reason. "Without sincerity to animate deeds spiritually," Gülen contended, "all human endeavors would remain lifeless, ephemeral, and ultimately worthless. But those who fly with the two wings of sincerity and faithfulness will fly with God's protection and will unfailingly reach their destination, that is, God's approval and pleasure."[205] Gülen made it safely to the U.S., but as he left Istanbul he no doubt reflected on how he had arrived at this juncture in his life. He had tried to do the right thing for the right reasons. He had engaged interreligious dialogue with the sincere intention of aiding both others and Turkey. He had based his positive actions on his study of the life of the Prophet, who had shared with Hodjaefendi the sincere aim of pleasing God. Yet here he was, over sixty-years-old, in failing health and fleeing his homeland.

Over his six decades, however, Fethullah Gülen had also learned that he could engage the nonviolent practices at the heart of Islam, such as prayer, from anywhere. He had learned by being on the run that he could, from anywhere, continue to advocate for literacy, for engaged empathy, and for the principled pluralism of hoşgörü. And, he was learning, through the new media that was growing in importance with every passing day, that he could, from anywhere, help friends develop businesses that would both do well and do good. Thus, in December 1999, Gülen penned perhaps his most eloquent and extended reflection on "The Necessity for Interfaith Dialogue." It was presented at the Parliament of the World's Religions in Capetown, South Africa. The essay advocated, not surprisingly, for hoşgörü:

> Our tolerance [hoşgörü] should be so broad that we can close our eyes to others' faults, show respect for different ideas, and forgive everything that is forgivable. Even when our inalienable rights are violated, we should respect human values and try to establish justice. ...
>
> Tolerance, which we sometimes use in place of respect and mercy, generosity and forbearance, is the most essential element of moral systems. It is also a very important source of spiritual discipline, and a celestial virtue of perfected men and women.
>
> Under the lens of tolerance ... believers' merits attain a new depth and extend to infinity; mistakes and faults shrink into insignificance. Actually, the treatment of [the One] Who is beyond time and space always passes through the prism of tolerance, and we wait for it to embrace us and all creation. ...
>
> Goodness, beauty, truthfulness, and being virtuous are the essence of the world and humanity. Whatever happens, the world will one day find this essence. No one can prevent this.[206]

So, Hodjaefendi would now make his home in Pennsylvania. The boy from Erzurum had traveled a long way, physically. Spiritually, however, his focus remained consistent. Life was not simply about political or economic success. Life was about seeking to please the One Who is beyond space and time. And who could say why, from that perspective— from the perspective of a hoşgörü that extended to infinity—Fethullah Gülen would not find in the United States the embrace he had also experienced from so many in The City over the past two decades?

CHAPTER FIVE

HIZMET GLOBAL - AMERICA, 1999–

In a poem entitled "Exile," penned while in America, Fethullah Gülen wrote:

> An exile poem always in my ears,
> A coolness of the northwest wind at every verse...
> My thoughts say "farewell" to these places.
>
> Since the day I left my country,
> I buried all my happiness, joy;
> Now, I'm longing for those blue days...
>
> Exile is raining in my horizon continually,
> No thunder claps in this sky;
> On the freezing cold streets like icebergs....
>
> Beauties don't live in souls here,
> Those gardens of ours are in my eyes;
> Where are those green spring days?
>
> Rise, oh light, rise from the depths of my heart!
> In these stranger countries where I wander with worry;
> Reveal to me the secrets of my soul!
>
> Present me a voice from your old songs,
> In this gloomy dawn stage by stage.
> Feed my soul that is agonizing with hunger![1]

Exile in America was a struggle for Fethullah Gülen. And yet, he also lived in hope: "Rise, oh light, rise from the depths of my heart!" Such hope in a light within is common in the history of religions, and often has consoled those who suffer. Martin Luther King, Jr. and other Civil Rights activists, for instance, found strength in singing "This Little Light of Mine" while in jail. Still, as a prison sentence extended, or as exile grew long, or even as one simply grew old and the vigor of youth faded, that light could seem to dim: "where are those green spring days?"

On one level, Gülen's story gets rather simple to tell after 1999. Once he arrived in America, Hodjaefendi almost never left the twenty-five-acre Golden Generation Retreat Center, located in the foothills of the Pocono Mountains in Saylorsburg, Pennsylvania. In newspapers, this Center is almost invariably characterized as a "compound."[2] Such a characterization is inaccurate. There is a guard house and gate where one individual monitors the driveway that leads from the narrow rural highway to the main buildings, of which there are two. One is three-story structure that houses a dining hall on its first floor, with a large meeting room on the second floor, and a third floor where Gülen's room is located. These accommodations are similar in their simplicity to Hodjaefendi's apartment in Istanbul. Gülen lives, by and large, in two very modest rooms—one a sitting room and study, the other his bedroom. The second main building on the campus is a three-story multi-purpose prayer-center, meeting space, and dormitory. It is not unlike the dormitories that Hizmet participants built in Turkey and around the world. There are eight other homes on the perimeter of the grounds. They house guests, students, and others. Staff members live nearby in private homes, with their families. The rest of the land is dedicated to gardens, a playground, walking trails, a small pond, and parking lots—all development has happened gradually over the years. It is a modest, park-like retreat center, decidedly absent the militarized features that the word "compound" conjures.

So, if on one level Gülen's life story became simple to tell after he settled into this comfortable place of retreat, on another level, Gülen's story gets more difficult to document after 1999. Lacking retroactive access to a Hizmet "Google-calendar" that does not, to my knowledge, exist, it is impossible to be sure about exactly what Gülen did in the quotidian moments of his years in Saylorsburg. What we do have are the public results—and especially the hundreds of organizations that had some connection to people of Hizmet. Perhaps some intrepid future historian will be able to work back from those results and find their origins in Pennsylvania. For while he was living in semi-seclusion, Gülen was also welcoming guests on a regular basis, and communicating with others occasionally. Most of the communication was one-way only—from Gülen to those inspired by him. For instance, Gülen began having his weekly sermons posted and eventually streamed on the internet, and he also wrote for a wide variety of publications such as *Zaman, Sızıntı,* and so forth. Regarding personal communication, he favored "old school," face-to-face meetings. When guests would visit, most stayed briefly—a day or two. Some stayed longer, for weeks, and some chose to reside nearby. Any guests who had reason to conduct business with Gülen had opportunity to witness his distinctive mode of organizational practice. It was known as *istişare (istishara)* or occasionally as *şura (shura).* These Arabic terms can be translated as "seeking advice," or "mutual consultation." When not praying or in individual supplication, when not teaching students, reading, writing, editing, or watching TV (almost exclusively news), then, Fethullah Gülen in America was likely engaged in consultation. The types and frequency of the consultations varied from day-to-day. They could be dictated by Gülen's increasingly frail health. One day *abi*s or *abla*s would come to seek his opinion about opening a school in the far east; another day Turkish businessmen would ask questions for a new venture in Africa; and on a third day his health would not permit him to meet with anyone. But after prayer and teaching, consultation was a regular part of Hodjaefendi's life in America.

We have records from only a few of these consultations from the years between 1999 and 2018. But if details of each meeting evade us— and no doubt would be interesting to conspiracy theorists—we can document consistent ways that Gülen interacted with people seeking his counsel. We can call it "the *istişare* script." He did not follow it slavishly. And people would interpret what Gülen said in a consultation; a "no" to one person might be a "yes" to another. The *istişare* process was organic. It often produced debate. Sometimes what a group thought was one decision would lead to a return visit for more consultation. But in these meetings, Gülen generally would listen more than speak. By listening, Gülen indicated that this was a meeting between equals. When he would offer his insight, it would often be couched in a phrase that began with the word "*Estağfurullah.*" This complex Turkish term can only be translated into a complete English sentence: "I ask God's forgiveness," with the additional connotation—"who am I to answer your question, since all knowledge is with God." It would seem to be an odd way to begin offering advice, and certainly nods to Gülen's modesty. But note well— the core of that sentence is simply: "I ask." So, Gülen would in some meetings ask individuals to undertake initiatives, or to take established projects in new directions. Depending upon how well the person seeking Gülen's counsel knew Hodjaefendi, a mere hint was often enough. In many cases, Gülen knew that the initiatives he was asking them to undertake could cost his friends in terms of time, comfort, and/or financial resources—hence the need to ask God for forgiveness.

But while these asks were couched in a theological context that lent them gravity, they also turned the initiative over to the individuals themselves. That was apparent in the second line of Fethullah Gülen's *istişare* script. That line was, in Turkish, *Siz bilirsiniz*: "you know [best]." Depending upon the context, the inflection in his voice, and other subtle cues, this could be Gülen's gentle way of saying "no." But more often it was, in socio-psychological jargon, Gülen's way of empowering individuals to exercise their agency. Journalist Kerim Balcı put it well, if a bit anachronistically: "Hodjaefendi came as the first Obama. He said, 'We can!' He gave us self-confidence."[3] People who came to Gülen in America brought with them not only proposals, but skills. Gülen expected them to use those skills. So, although nobody kept minutes at these consultations, and thus the details of their deliberations are not available to us other than anecdotally, what is completely clear are the results: *istişare* multiplied organizations around the globe. And then those individuals who met with Gülen at his retreat center took *istişare* with them as a model to the schools, dialogue centers, and other businesses around the globe. Hizmet-related activities and businesses were all managed, more or less, in accord with the *istişare* model. And the import for the historical record of this *istişare* model is that Fethullah Gülen was hardly a micro-managing CEO, much less a puppet-master who manipulated cult devotees. Quite simply, Fethullah Gülen taught people how to apply a central Islamic principle to community organizing and business processes. He started things, or encouraged them, and then let people use their skills to run them.

And one of the arenas of organization that became increasingly important during Gülen's time in America was humanitarian relief work. He had always paid attention to human suffering in his teaching. Gülen frequently quoted Said Nursi to the effect that there were three interrelated problems plaguing the world: ignorance, destructive conflict, and poverty.[4] "Ignorance can be defeated through education," Gülen taught. Conflict, Gülen believed, could be overcome through "dialogue and tolerance [hoşgörü]," as we saw in the previous chapter. But it was the problem of poverty that occupied especially the latter years of Gülen's life, and the activities of people of Hizmet after 1999. Poverty could be defeated, Gülen contended—again following Nursi—through "work and the possession of capital." By "work" Gülen did not mean to imply that poverty was a result of laziness. Rather, Gülen stressed—along with many sociologists and economists, that employment dignified human living, especially when it was matched with a living wage as the reward for diligent labor. And capital was not to be possessed for its own end of accumulation. Capital also should serve greater goods—notably education and conflict-resolution. And it did so through organizations to be decided upon, of course, through consultation.

So, Fethullah Gülen taught and practiced capitalism with a difference. He emphatically did not embrace the "greed is good" approach associated with unfettered "free" markets. There, in what Muhammad Yunus has identified as "profit maximizing organizations," the quarterly profit of shareholders mattered more than the long-term interests of stakeholders.[5] Gülen's organizational approach was both broader, and more focused. Naturally, he hoped that people would develop sustainable ventures that continued to generate wealth (to thereby alleviate poverty, educate people, and promote dialogue). But he was not an economist or a business leader himself. His teaching about how to alleviate poverty was never simply a set of economic arrangements. He was, always, a Muslim preacher and theologian. So, he couched whatever he had to say about economics within a theological context. The maxim, as Gülen developed it, was akin to the teachings of Christian liberation theologians: "Being with the oppressed is the same as being with God."[6]

Consequently, some individuals associated with Hizmet, and inspired (in some cases directly) by consultation with Gülen, set out to live with the oppressed—in Turkey, in Asia, in Africa, in Australia, and in the Americas.[7] While living with people who happened to be poor, then, Hizmet volunteers established with their new sisters and brothers (through consultation with them) what Muhammad Yunus would identify as social businesses—organizations designed to be sustainable but also to benefit the community. Naturally, the businesses were "social" in varying degrees, depending upon the different business leaders and structures. But the initiative for Hizmet social businesses came through what participants called *himmet*. *Himmet*, which is a Turkish version of an Arabic term, *himmah,* can be translated, narrowly, as "charity." But the term also includes the broader meanings of "resolve," "orientation," "intention," "aspiration," or even "ambition."[8] And within Hizmet the word *himmet* included not only noble and altruistic donations of money—although of course those were welcome. More broadly, *himmet* for Hizmet meant to live in mutual consultation and accountability, which usually meant, as one of the movement's maxims put it—"to live simply so that others might simply live."

Many if not most of the Hizmet leaders—for example principals and teachers in schools, presidents and administrative assistants in dialogue centers, editors and managers of publications—chose simple living to follow the example of Gülen's own austere lifestyle. Individuals who served in Hizmet associations or companies did not get wealthy. Profits from Hizmet organizations were recirculated into other Hizmet projects.[9] But individuals who supported Hizmet—factory or trade or construction-company owners, for example—had sometimes accumulated considerable wealth. They then spent or invested that wealth, sometimes large percentages of it, in other Hizmet enterprises. And, of course, they also invested in growing their private-business operations—which further worked to Hizmet's benefit. Over the years that Fethullah Gülen was in the United States, then, people of Hizmet generated wealth all over the world by living simply and by practicing *himmet* for Hizmet. To be sure, this economic dynamism interacted synergistically with economic changes across a globalizing Turkish economy. But the distinctive difference that made Hizmet agencies grow with the speed of venture start-ups elsewhere in the world, was the key process of consultation—not just with Gülen (and ordinarily not with Gülen at all), but with each other. It was through consultation that opportunities were recognized for entrepreneurial engagement. And it was through consultation that mutual accountability was practiced. The practices of *himmet* and *istişare* were not new to Hizmet in 1999. They had been taught by Fethullah Gülen for decades. And so, while in exile in America, at least until events in Turkey in 2016 changed everything, his sadness at living in a land "of freezing cold streets like icebergs" could be warmed somewhat by witnessing from afar the flourishing of Hizmet around the globe.

The work of *istişare:* "Either tell about the Beloved, or hush!"

Hizmet actually came to America before Hodjaefendi. A trickle of Turkish students had come to the U.S. at Gülen's encouragement, and some had stayed. Many settled in the New Jersey suburbs of New York City, but some also landed in Houston, and they tended to cluster wherever colleges or universities were located. One of them was Hüma Taban. She was serving, when I interviewed her in 2016, as the Vice Principal of Pinnacle Academy in Fairfax, Virginia (a school focused on STEM—science, technology, engineering, and math). She and her husband, Faruk, came to Nevada for graduate studies in 1995. Huma studied biochemistry. Her PhD dissertation examined insect pheromones, and more specifically the cotton boll weevil (anticipating developing insect-specific and environmentally-friendly pesticides). But she also worked as a Hizmet volunteer in Nevada, and she brought to Reno some of the initiatives she had experienced as a youth in Turkey. She started a "Dialogue Club." She organized "Cooking Classes" (to feature different ethnic foods). And she sponsored coffee houses, interfaith dinners with speakers from different traditions, and even movie nights. By the time she moved to Virginia, in 2007, Rumi Forum (a key Hizmet think-tank and dialogue center) was already in existence in Washington, DC. Through it, she continued her dialogue activities, while also taking on responsibilities for organizing science fairs and other science-related activities in her job as Vice-Principal at Pinnacle Academy. Her arrival in the U.S. was earlier than many of the people inspired by Gülen, but the story of how she came to study, served as a volunteer, and then worked in one of the Hizmet-related organizations would be repeated frequently.[10]

Another woman inspired by Gülen who arrived in the U.S. before he did was Nebahat Çetinkaya. She came to America in February, 1994, after her husband was accepted for graduate study in Columbus, Ohio.

They planned to stay for only eight months. "It was like a honeymoon," she said. But her husband had applied for a "green card" (a permanent visa), and when he won the lottery and received his permanent visa, the honeymoon was over. "This is our new home, now," she remembered thinking. "I wasn't ready, yet. So, I cried a lot." But very quickly the couple began to reach out: "We must do Hizmet here," she decided. "There was, like, one family [inspired by Gülen] in every state," she recalled. But various families came together in the summer of 1995 for a two-week long camp—like the camps organized by Gülen that many of them had experienced in Turkey. But this was a camp specifically for girls, and Çetinkaya, who had studied Islam as an undergraduate, became the Qur'an teacher. It was called "The Chestnut Camp," and it was held in Saylorsburg, Pennsylvania. It became the seed out of which grew the Golden Generation Retreat Center. By the next summer, some families who had moved to Pennsylvania had purchased the twenty-five acres of land, and a month-long "Chestnut Camp" was held there. In 1996, Çetinkaya traveled back to Istanbul, where she and a group of her friends visited Gülen on "the 5th floor." He gave his blessing to her endeavors in America. "He took us seriously," she recalled. "What struck me was how important to Hodjaefendi the women were. 'Women can take Hizmet to America,' he said," as she remembered the conclusion of their consultation.[11]

As this anecdote suggests, then, the learning in a consultation could go two ways. Gülen did not only give direction to peoples' activities through *istişare*, he also could become aware of a potential new direction through the activities of those with whom he met. Exactly what Gülen meant by "consultation" he made clear in a 1994 essay. *İstişare* was not an option for Muslims, according to Gülen. It was a requirement, and it was as important as prayer:

> For the [Muslims] of today, consultation [he used here the term *shura*] is a vital attribute and an essential rule, just as it was for the first [Muslims]. According to the Qur'an, it is the clearest sign of a believing community and the most important characteristic of a congregation who have given their hearts to Islam. The importance of consultation is mentioned in the Qur'an to the same degree as *salat* (prescribed prayers).[12]

Given this importance,

The most intelligent person is the one who most appreciates and respects mutual consultation and deliberation (*meşveret* – *mashwarat*), and who benefits most from the ideas of others. Those who are content with their own ideas in their plans and deeds, or who even insist or force others to accept their ideas, not only miss a very important dynamic, but also face disagreement, hostility, and hatred from the people with whom they are associated.[13]

Pragmatic criteria like avoiding hatred helped keep *istişare* from the realm of idealist fantasy.

Consultation was required in any and every activity: "Ventures and enterprises embarked on without sufficient prior consultation do not go far. ... To consultation belongs the most important mission and duty of resolving affairs concerning the individual and the community, the people and the state, science and knowledge, and economics and sociology." After all, if the Prophet had engaged in consultation, who could not? "Even if the head of state or the leader is confirmed by God and nurtured by revelation and inspiration, he [or she] is under obligation to conduct affairs by consultation." Not only a requirement, consultation proved itself in practice:

> Consultation, within its remit, promises some effects and also follows some rules which lead to positive outcomes. In this regard we may mention: [1] an increase in the level of thought and intervention in society; [2] reminding society of its own importance by taking its views on all new events; [3] by ... leading it to produce alternative ideas. ... [4] [by insuring] that the people remain aware of the necessity for questioning and calling to account the administrators whenever the situation requires them to do so; and [5] by preventing irresponsible behavior of rulers by limiting their executive power.[14]

These were not merely pious platitudes. They worked.

Of course, Gülen added—consultation could not supersede revelation or God's commands. The duty to pray could not be consulted away. Gülen was also aware, no doubt from experience, that "there may not always be unanimity (*ijma'*) in consultation." In such cases, the "conviction of the majority" must be followed. And once consultation had been concluded, it would be disagreeable to continue to contend on the matter.[15] Participating in consultation brought with it, in short, a risk. One's pet idea might not make it through the process. In a 2014 sermon, Gülen specified that in consultation "one must be able to say at appropriate times, 'I did not understand this issue thoroughly,' or 'my knowledge was mistaken,' thus not insisting or showing obstinacy at the fixed ideas in one's mind." At the heart of consultation, of course, was debate and deliberation—not "quarreling and brawling," but the civil exchange of relevant information and opinion. "The real target here is making the truth emerge in a crystal clear fashion: 'The flash of truth is born from the confrontation of ideas.'"[16] Gülen's quote here was from Namık Kemal—a nineteenth century Ottoman author and political activist.

Skeptically-speaking, anyone who has sat through a faculty or Board meeting knows how such a process can play itself out: everyone waits for the "expert" to chime in. Aware of this possibility, no doubt (again) from experience, Gülen counseled a different ideal:

> neither seniority, nor title, nor status, nor being a personage of esteem can be a factor for making another person's opinion more credible. On the contrary, when the truth has become manifest, giving weight to these other factors and using them for pressure means destroying the spirit of consultation. There must absolutely be no impositions at consultation. According to Islam, the most ideal person in this respect is the one who says to the other one ... "You are very right on this subject. I agree with every word you are saying. Besides this, however, such and such thought came to my mind. What do you think about it?" This is the person who protects the honor of consultation. ... Sometimes flawed people try to take advantage of their seniority or credit and make impositions. This way, even though unaware, they openly abuse the services they carry out in the name of faith for the sake of their seniority and status. However, no one has the right to eliminate the fruitfulness of the consultation with egotistic and selfish attitudes.[17]

İstişare was an Islamic model for doing business. The chief obstacle to its success, as it was the chief obstacle to any effort to please God, was the ego of the leader.

Gülen quoted Said Nursi to trace one lineage of his teaching: "'Respect for justice is sublime, and should not be sacrificed for anything.'"

Gülen then went on to explain: "Therefore, all words and attitudes must be accorded with truth and righteousness. That great personage [Nursi] also told his students not to accept something for the sole reason that he says it to them, for he could be mistaken too. One needs to have this degree of immensity. As none of us is a prophet who receives Divine revelation, everybody can be mistaken—one must never forget that."[18] And there was one other maxim that Hodjaefendi offered to those who sought to meet with him, or to apply consultation in their own context:

> The boundaries must be very clear while talking over certain matters, so that people will not be misled and no doors will be opened for thinking negatively about certain individuals. In order to prevent such situations from arising, even the people who speak truthfully must remain silent. They must remain silent and first ask themselves, "I wonder how I can express this truth without offending anyone?" Only then should they reveal their thoughts after thinking more deeply. Concerning a believer, silence should be reflection and speaking should be wisdom. That is, it is necessary to speak if there is some wisdom in the words to be spoken, or one must keep silent. As a *Sufi* poet [Fuzuli] expressed, "Either tell about the Beloved, or hush!"[19]

Unless one's words could build up the community, in the same way that God's activity generated creation, it was better simply to hold one's tongue.

Now, one aspect of the way Gülen described *istişare* eventually led him and people of Hizmet into trouble. In the Qur'an 4:114, one reads: "No good is there in most of their secret counsels except for [the one] who exhorts to a deed of charity, or kind equitable dealings and honest affairs, or setting things right between people. Whoever does that seeking God's good pleasure, We will grant to [that one] a tremendous reward." Now, the way Gülen interpreted this passage stressed that, generally, everything done for God's pleasure can (and should) be done openly. Yet, "at times when serving the Religion is utterly difficult and involves great patience and resistance against hardships and tribulations like the initial years of Islam and the present age," some things "must be fulfilled secretly and with secret counsels."[20] It simply made sense to keep things discrete when state repression rendered questionable even the most legitimate, ethical, and moral activities. The things being considered, Gülen repeated, were "plans and intentions to do deeds of charity ... [and] projects and strategies to do and encourage kind, equitable dealings and honest affairs; and the efforts to set things right between people." Even these, however, could be suspect to a suspicious government. Nevertheless, Gülen went on:

> Various organizations can be founded in order to support these three beneficial acts mentioned for the sake of God. It is necessary to show great care and attention to preserve their confidentiality and sacredness. The necessary consultations are held within a definite framework, and the meetings of consultation can be inaccessible to ill-intended outsiders. It is a Prophetic manner to facilitate the realization of plans and intentions concerning the community and therefore protecting the rights and good of the public by keeping it secret.[21]

This was not, to be clear, anything like the dissembling or outright lying-for-a-higher-cause (the Arabic term is *taqiyya*) that some have accused Gülen of engaging in.[22] No one associated with Gülen conspired to install "stealth *Sharia*" in Turkey or anywhere else. They did work together and practice prudential care to protect proprietary information—which was a common practice in business. But due to statements like the one above, and others that were ripped out of context, charges of a lack of "transparency" against Gülen would be common, to the detriment of Hizmet's global reputation.[23]

And yet the kinds of decisions that were kept secret were not exactly difficult to discern for anyone with an interest in doing so. For instance, beginning in the 1990s and continuing through the twenty-first century, many of the assets connected to Hizmet were taken out of the hands of foundations, which had to be authorized by the government, and were placed instead in private corporations—with Boards of Directors and shareholders (in some cases). These transfers were done quietly, without fanfare, over decades. Sociologist Helen Rose Ebaugh explained:

> When the first dormitories, prep courses and Gülen schools were established, nongovernmental foundations were established in order to raise and distribute funds to the various Gülen inspired projects. Usually, donors were not aware of the precise projects or specific students funded by their contributions. The money was given to the foundation

and then distributed to projects as needed. However, within the past decade [the book was published in 2010] the mechanism of setting up foundations has been abandoned in favor of setting up organizations to administer the fundraising operations that support various of the Gülen projects. The reason underlying the shift from foundation to business model relates to the fact that foundations are more strictly regulated than organizations and the fact that past military coups in Turkey resulted in new governmental agencies disbanding foundations and usurping financial resources. During unstable political eras, organizations are safer from being taken over than foundations. ... As organizations, the companies can also make profits but these profits are routinely used to support more [enterprises].[24]

With the privilege of hindsight, it turned out that private organizations were in some cases no more secure from government takeover than were foundations.[25] But the point, for now, is only that these are the kinds of decisions that needed to be made privately to keep Hizmet projects safe. The aim or end—to generate wealth to alleviate poverty—was consistent. There could be no negotiation of immoral ends. And the means to those *moral* ends also had to be moral; even if protected and private.

İstişare in practice—"principled capitalism"

There was a larger context to the origins of this Hizmet style of business to consider. Turkey's economy grew steadily from the 1980s to 2010, led by a phenomenon known as the "Anatolian Tigers." The "Tigers" were entrepreneurs from the Anatolian heartland or places other than Izmir and Istanbul—like Kayseri or Konya, who tried intentionally to blend Islamic practice with capitalism. Several analysts have called the attempt "green capital or Islamic capital."[26] Of course there were many styles of doing this, and Gülen's model of *istişare* was only one of them. But following the liberalization measures of Turgut Özal in the 1980s, opportunities arose for individuals who were not traditionally part of the Ankara-Izmir-Istanbul secular elite to compete for contracts and to marshal resources. Naturally, among these "Tigers," in practice if not in name, were some of the business leaders associated with Hizmet. One of them was Ahmet Haseken. Haseken's relationship with Gülen went back to

1977. He first met Gülen at a *sohbet* (see Chapter Two) in Izmir. *Sohbet*s could often morph into a consultation. After the theological and spiritual reflection was completed, business could be conducted. So, near the end of this meeting, Haseken asked a question: "To whom are we going to give our vote?" It was a loaded question—and exactly the kind of political entanglement that Gülen has been accused of engaging in. But as Haseken recalled, Gülen followed the *istişare* script: "Hodjaefendi gave a small smile," he remembered, "and said '*Estağfurullah.*' And then he said: 'You would know better than me.'" As Haseken remembered the encounter, the same question came up three times in the consultation—and

> he never gave us any direction regarding voting. And this stayed with me; it affected me. I said to myself, "this person is different." Because wherever we would go they [other spiritual leaders] would give us a direction. And give us a name. They'd say here or there and give us a name. And in this way I was struck. So, from that year, 1977, we became two people that always talked to each other.[27]

Needless to say, Haseken also helped Hizmet with financial support. He had been successful in the construction materials industry, starting with a brick factory in Turgutlu.

Once Gülen had settled in America, Haseken visited Pennsylvania regularly. He remembered one consultation (probably in 2012 or 2013) that included a group of businessmen and educators from Central America. He recalled how much he admired what they were telling him about the developments of Hizmet there. Yet, he also remembered that Hodjaefendi did not say anything; he did not praise their work, nor did he say thanks to them. Then as Gülen rose rather quickly, people around him asked why he did not say anything. He then said: "If you think these things are happening because of you, may God help you, for you're [mistaken]. Where is God in your words? It is God who is making all of this happen. Don't build anything on people. The owner of everything is God."[28] It's unclear whether this led to investment in Central America, or not. But it does reveal how Gülen could operate in a consultation. It also indicates a central principle behind the business enterprises. Christians would call it a notion of "stewardship." Haseken went on: "What Hodjaefendi is saying now is what he said years ago: the owner of everything is Allah. Hodjaefendi has seen the world, he's learned the world, and he's still saying the same thing. There's no straying in his message or life." That principle of divine ownership for resources meant that Gülen could trust that, in a consultation, resources would appear. For instance, Haseken recalled a consultation in 1987 over the building of a dormitory in Turgutlu. Money was running low. The *abi*s wanted to get the money from a man named Osman. "Osman [Aykutlar] is rich," Haseken recalled, "one of the richest men in this region." But the *abi*s were anxious about this course of action; most of them weren't used to asking for large sums. So, they asked for a consultation with Gülen. They visited him at his apartment and before they could say anything, Gülen said: "Don't forget, when everyone is going in front of God, empty handed, Osman is going to go with a dormitory." And then, Haseken remembers, Gülen turned toward the *abi*s and asked, "What did you come here for?" And we said, "Hodjaefendi, we came to visit you!" The money from Osman came through, and the dormitory got completed.

For an even earlier example, Haseken recalled that one day Gülen visited him at his brick factory in Turgutlu. A group of supporters then gathered for *istişare*. "We didn't know what *himmet* was," Haseken recalled. "We were just going door to door asking for money. The businessmen gave us money for [a] school, God bless them." But in the consultation, Haseken told Gülen, "This is how we did it. Is that OK?" Gülen said, as Haseken recalled it: "'You know best!' This is how we understood," Haseken continued, "that what we were doing was wrong." But Gülen then went on to teach that "our Prophet (pbuh) made *himmet*, and we [can] have a good *himmet* here, too." Haseken explained what he learned that day about *himmet*. "The idea was: we bring everyone together, focus on a purpose, and everyone gives what they can. Identify needs and assign tasks." This kind of task-oriented fund-raising for charity—which evolved into self-sustaining organizations, was "not a band-aid," as Haseken put it. It was demanding, and it focused on both short-term and long-term goals. "If you go home [at night] and can sleep comfortably," he put the mentality, "you didn't give enough." *Himmet* invited people to put their own money where their mouths were. Such a system had the potential for abuse. The history of religions is filled with charismatic leaders who persuaded people to give up everything for some cause. But control over resources was never in Gülen's hands. He could not possibly have managed the vast range of enterprises that eventually developed.

And unless his personal frugality is to be dismissed as a public relations stunt that was decades in the planning, and with a prescient awareness of the vast resources that Hizmet participants would eventually raise, there is little reason to doubt its sincerity. As Haseken put it: "You trusted in God; and God will give manifold in return.' You have to trust in this. People pledge numbers [of Lira] they couldn't possibly have. And they attain it! But, within Hizmet, there's also a structure of accountability. We do have accountants!"[29] As one observer put it, citing a popular Islamic proverb, *himmet* through *istişare* meant: "Trust God, but tie your camel."[30] The method was both idealistic and pragmatic. Good accountants who knew how to conduct an audit had to be part of the mix.

And there were historical precedents for social enterprise, social business, or business through consultation—and not only in the life of the Prophet. Professor Phyllis E. Bernard, a legal expert who has studied mediation, negotiation, and other ways that commerce can help resolve conflicts and organize communities, has compared the Hizmet movement and its business practices to Quaker capitalism. As is well-known, Friends—as Quakers call themselves, practice a style of living together that depends upon consensus-building through conversation. No decision is reached without considering the entire community and its needs. Far from stymying the accumulation of wealth, however, Quaker practices have led many Friends to grow quite wealthy. At the same time, especially early in the history of the movement, these Friends also channeled much of their wealth into corporations and ventures consistent with their religious commitments, such as pacifism. Bernard sees an analogy with Gülen's "*Sufi* paradigm for commerce," which she has also called his "principled capitalism." She has studied the Gülen model since 2009. She conducted interviews with business leaders, and she participated in cross-cultural exchanges between Turkish and U.S. entrepreneurs. She described, without using the Islamic word, the consultative process: "Business people committed to a cause," Bernard explains, "organize themselves into 'circles' for peer support, providing mutual encouragement, advice, and assistance." Unlike with the Quakers, who kept copious records, Bernard acknowledged that there are few detailed notes about the specific activities of these circles. This made "Hizmet circles seem more akin to bands of trusted companions sharing a quest" than to organized guilds or associations.[31]

The rise of these Gülen-inspired entrepreneurs committed to a shared quest ran roughly parallel, Bernard points out, to "the growth of today's global supply chains." Was Hizmet just a rider on a neo-liberal wave? Bernard's answer is "perhaps," but she leans towards "no." She explains: "The Hizmet focus on education and ethics created a critical mass of highly educated persons able to interact fluidly with the West while honoring traditional norms. This created a path that bridged traditional and modern, secular and sacred, building capacity on all sides of the business transaction." More explicitly, Bernard contrasts Hizmet's "principled capitalism" with traditional Western business where everything is monetized, everything negotiable, and therefore everything comes down to what gets put down in a contract on a piece of paper. Gülen helped shape a business culture that put "people before profits." This kind of "soft power" was built through practices such as hospitality, camaraderie over drinking tea, and personal relationships developed over long-periods of time. At its core, then, *istişare* as evident in Gülen-inspired organizations was about trust. "Trust is the essential ingredient," Bernard wrote. "Without trust, no business will be conducted." And trust between people had to be earned, Bernard made plain, through "a consultative, shared notion of power." It all sounds too good to be true, and many found it so until they experienced it for themselves. And what made it work, Bernard explained, was that "principled capitalism" stemmed "from a commitment to Islamic concepts of leadership."[32] It is impossible, in short, to understand accurately Gülen, and Hizmet, without continuously remembering this Islamic foundation. And what is most astonishing was not the idealism of Gülen's method. What is most astonishing is that it worked. Over the course of Gülen's life, despite repeated disruptions by the Turkish government, people did well by doing good through Hizmet.

The pragmatic side of Gülen's consultative model

İstişare had a pragmatic side. It fostered talent, and as Joshua Hendrick has cogently shown, people benefited from their relationships with Gülen and Hizmet. What they gained was not only financial security, however, but also a spiritual and moral compass, a community of purpose with many friends, and a life devoted to meaning beyond the mere accumulation of resources. Sibel Yüksel came to Houston in 2003 as a twenty-one-year-old new bride. She followed her husband who had an H-1 [worker's] visa. She began meeting with *ablas*, who welcomed her and taught her how to cook (she hadn't learned in Turkey), how to drive (it took her two months), and they helped her learn English (she spoke none when she arrived, but she was fluent when I met with her in 2017). Her first task within the community was to cook rice for a dialogue event. She then "promoted" herself to biscuit-baker. And before long (within a few years), she was asked to serve as the emcee for interfaith dialogue events. "I could make people laugh," she recalled, "and I was friendly." This kind of development of an individual happened organically through *istişare*—and is a microcosm of how Hizmet worked. It was not dictated by Gülen from Pennsylvania: how could it be? But Yüksel did learn from Hodjaefendi. She had begun practicing her faith while still in Turkey, at the age of 18. But she had been frustrated by what she heard from most Islamic preachers: "they were hell-fire this, Satan that, *haram* [forbidden], *haram, haram!*" Gülen was different. "I learned from Gülen to reach out to people by accepting them as they are. In Turkey, some people judge others harshly. He accepts people as they are. We can live so that others may live." In Yüksel's case, this meant getting her GED. She then earned first an Associate's, and shortly thereafter a Bachelor's degree, in elementary education. She also gave birth to two sons. As she raised the young boys, she worked as a babysitter to help support her husband's education, and then after gaining her credentials she began working as a teacher in the Houston Independent School District. When I interviewed her in 2017, she was beginning work on her MA in Educational Leadership, focused on English Second Language instruction. She also continued her work on behalf of interreligious dialogue, which she had discovered, in consultation with the abis and ablas, as an interest and strength. "My attitude," she put it, is "'What can I do for you?' Wherever I go, that's the idea. ... Being a neighbor means, 'What can I do for you?'" Meanwhile, her husband was working on his MBA, while working in finance. "He was supporting me, and I helped bring in money, too. It was all about love!"[33]

So mutual consultation worked not only in the macrocosm of forging transnational organizations, but also in the microcosm between husband and wife, between older sisters and younger women, and in finding a vocation. Gülen's influence was indirect. To my knowledge, Yüksel never met him. Sometimes, Gülen's influence through consultation in an individual's life-path could also be more direct. Ahmet Muharrem Atlığ was a theology student in Istanbul in 1994. He was on his way to being one of those imams who preached "hell-fire this, and Satan that." He was familiar with Gülen's thought, but he had not fully internalized it. After graduating, he met with Gülen. "Hodjaefendi asked me," Atlığ recalled, "what's your future plan?" It was a question that many young people dread. The young man and Gülen continued conversing, and then Atlığ remembered Gülen saying, "'Brother, no offense. But you have many dangerous ideas.'" Gülen then asked the young man: "'Have you only lived in this community—with people like you, the same people, the same Muslim community?'" Atlığ had to reply, "yes." He then recalled Gülen saying, "I recommend you go abroad, and experience and learn from the others." So, Atlığ did. It took a few years. Like Yüksel, he also landed in Houston, in 2000. He attended St. Mary's seminary at the University of St. Thomas, where he received an MA, while volunteering as an imam. He met there a Professor, Donald Nesti. After only a month into his studies, Atlığ received the news that his father, back in Istanbul, had died. As he sat crying in a corner of the Seminary, Fr. Nesti approached the young man. "What happened, Ahmet?" he recalls Nesti asking. Ahmet had no money to be present for his father's funeral. "Why don't you go?" Nesti said to him. "I am your father now." And Nesti paid the airfare for Atlığ's return to Istanbul. "That was when I understood," Atlığ concluded, "what Hodjaefendi said about experience and learn from the others.'" After completing his MA, Atlığ went to London, where he volunteered as an imam in the southern part of the city. He then went on to work on his PhD, also at a Catholic University, comparing the theology of Rumi with that of St. Thomas Aquinas.[34]

And sometimes, consultations could continue over an entire lifetime. Yusuf Pekmezci, whose observations we have followed in nearly every chapter, consulted with Gülen at least once every couple of months— if not in person, then on the phone. He was one of the first Turks to go to Kazakhstan in 1991. That decision came out of istişare. As he recalled it, "Hodjaefendi brought together some of our friends, and he said: 'We did not receive Islam from the hand of the Prophet. We received it from the alims [scholars] of Central Asia. ... People there are now in need.

We should go and help. ... and open up educational institutions." Still, Gülen did not dictate, Pekmezci said: "He made us think. He gave us choices. God granted me to go to Kazakhstan. I stayed in Kazakhstan for fifteen years."[35] Pekmezci was not an educator, he was a businessman. So, he started a biscuit factory. And in consultation with other Turks and with the people of Kazakhstan, Pekmezci and a local team hired teachers and administrators, arranged for buildings, planned curriculum (as directed by the State), and put out the call for applications. By the time he left Kazakhstan (in 2005), there were twenty-eight schools serving students from the many diverse races residing in the country. The biscuit factory he had started up to help fund the educational endeavors had four-hundred and fifty employees. And I must add, in a personal aside, that Pekmezci was one of the most joyful individuals I have met. Although we had to reschedule our interview in Izmir several times to evade the police, who were already (in 2015) cracking down on people close to Gülen, he seemed genuinely to be grateful for the life he had led; a "self-actualized" individual. I enjoyed his company so much that I delayed departing from him for as long as possible, and I wound up missing a flight.

The process of *istişare* included professionals as well as small business people. Şerif Ali Tekalan was an MD. He was drawn to Gülen and Hizmet in the 1970s. When I interviewed him in 2015, he was Rector of Fatih University—and a widely published researcher in otolaryngology. His medical practice began in Kayseri in the early 1980s, where he also began helping to establish schools, tutoring centers, and houses of light. "Hodjaefendi came to Kayseri a couple of times" during those years, Tekalan recalled. Gülen was on the run from the military junta, so he "didn't come for a conference, but for meetings with small groups." What happened in these consultations in Kayseri fit the pattern throughout the history of Hizmet:

> We set up Boards of Trustees, where we explained how *himmet* worked. People came together in a group, and each pledged a certain amount per year, paid in installments. ... The Boards collected the money, and businessmen governed the organizations. We did *himmet* for Hizmet. If we needed a table, chairs, and so forth, people pledged for that. We learned to trust each other. ... Governing the money is crucial. Local

people govern the money. ... And this is one of the fundamental principles of Hizmet. Until the present, we didn't get money from other Muslim countries.[36]

Tekalan recalled one consultation with Gülen that involved individuals from Kuwait and Bahrain. They were impressed by what Hizmet was doing, and they offered to help fund some of the projects. After they left, Tekalan remembered that Hodjaefendi said: "This is very important. If we take money from the outside ... there may be strings attached, or people would say our loyalty was to someone on the outside. The funding must be local, local, local." Tekalan claimed to have visited every country where a Hizmet school operated. And with the perspective of hindsight, in 2015, he expressed gratitude for a "younger generation who had learned languages, and cultures, and for whom dialogue wasn't theoretical, it was practical." In 2016, Tekalan was appointed President of North American University—a private college located in Houston. Since he met Hizmet, he estimated that he had probably consulted with Gülen "every two or three months."[37]

The structure of *istişare*: what was Gülen's role?

As these various stories of individual activity in *istişare* can suggest, there was a structure, of sorts, associated with the various Gülen-inspired initiatives. According to some, the structure could be quite tight. David Tittensor reported that several students at Hizmet schools claimed that there was a definite organizational design. As one of them put it:

> Within itself, the *cemaat* [community] is very authoritarian. You know you can't do anything without the permission of your [*abi*] or the leader of the branch you are attending. You know [small business big brothers] for instance, if you are an [*abi*] you control the [small organizations] under your branch and the small organizations without your permission can't do anything. This is a very authoritarian organization and hierarchical.[38]

As Tittensor explained, however, "this hierarchic managerial approach directly contradicts the image that the Movement seeks to display. Routinely Movement members explained that each project was autonomous and has very little to do with other projects in neighboring

cities, and that there is no top-down structure."[39] It is true that movement members often emphasized the discrete operation of various
Hizmet agencies, and not the connections between, but they did so with
good reason. For instance, Esra Koşar, who worked as a journalist for
Zaman Amerika (published in Turkish in America), and was active in
Hizmet-sponsored interreligious dialogues in the U.S. for fifteen years,
contended that:

> Hizmet is so random and disorganized—there is no organizational
> chart. There isn't the same model in every place. It's not planned
> well ahead. ... People are getting together, and consultations give
> birth to other initiatives. It's impossible for Hodjaefendi to master
> all of these things going on. People share the same values, but then
> you calibrate and adjust to the place you are and the people you are
> with.[40]

Contextualizing the differences between these two accounts of
Hizmet's authority structure is important. According to Tittensor,
there was a *strategic* reason for obscuring the structure of authority
within Hizmet agencies: "Those with greatest authority in controlling
or governing the project maintain a degree of distance from the day-to-
day activities. This gives the Movement the capacity to distance itself
from any potential scandal."[41] Joshua Hendrick made a similar claim,
suggesting that people close to Gülen intentionally or unintentional-
ly employed "strategic ambiguity" in relating to diverse publics.[42] In
fact, the ambiguity was less strategic than contextual. Projects grew organically, through *istişare* on local, national, and transnational levels.
Lines of authority were less direct in one area, more direct in others.
A student in Istanbul might see authority all the way up; a journalist
for *Zaman* might see disorganization all the way down. The degree of
organizational structure and control varied a great deal from one region to another, from one decade to another, and from one *abi* or *abla*
to another.

But what of Gülen's role at "the top?" Gülen's own words support
Esra Koşar's point of view, as do simple logistics. Gülen could not possibly have managed or controlled the vast number of enterprises that
sprang up over the decades. In 1997 he put it this way:

When our government gave permission for private schools to be established, a wave of people, rather than spinning away their days and wealth on summer and winter houses, chose to spend their energy in the service [*hizmet*] of their people. They did this not only for their country, but for all humanity and they did it with the enthusiasm that comes with an act of devotion. It would be impossible for me to know of all of the schools these volunteers have opened within Turkey and abroad. Not only do I not know most of the companies who have established these schools ... I do not even know which schools are where. As far as I can tell from the media, it is common knowledge that these schools have opened in nearly every country where the opening of a school is permitted, excluding such places as Iran, Syria, and Saudi Arabia. From Azerbaijan to the Philippines, from [St.] Petersburg ... from Moscow ... through the help of the Jewish businessman Üzeyir Garih, to the one opened in Yakutsk, they have proven to have the capacity to spring up.[43]

Some of these schools would not last; as governments cracked down on Islamic initiatives, including those associated with Gülen.

By 2005, Gülen expressed a bit of exasperation at the charge that he somehow was the mastermind who was orchestrating a vast empire of industries. Such charges were an insult to the intelligence, commitment, and agency of the people who were in fact responsible for them. And, besides, Gülen was accountable to more than just a bottom-line or a strategic plan:

> in the end I will answer to God. Only God knows the role that I have played in the hundreds of schools that have been established. I did my part to encourage it for a short time, but the matter has grown with ten times the force of what I put into it. I have no contribution there. In fact, taking credit for even one tenth of the planning that was involved would be disrespect to that service [*hizmet*]. It would be disrespect to the labors of many people. Let someone else be unfair in this way, and overlook the good work that has been done. Let someone else say that there are a handful of people who carry all of the influence of this movement, rather than the movement itself ... God is accomplishing this through the hands of people whose names and faces we will never know.[44]

And in another 2005 interview, with the journalist Mehmet Gündem, Gülen spoke to the question of why he did not visit many of the organizations or schools associated with his initiative:

In actual fact, to this movement ... my contribution is very little. Despite this truth, I am afraid that if I were to go to these places, there would be a misconception that I am somehow the author of all of those things done by these good people. I am concerned that people would assume that it was my thoughts and ideas that are the driving force behind these great works, rather than the devotion and enthusiasm of the people. Besides, people in general have a tendency to attribute the successes of others to the person who appears to be at the helm. I was also worried about what some might say. I was afraid to do anything that may provoke a reaction from certain portions of the population in those places. They might say, "Behind this is so and so," [or] "They have a hidden agenda."[45]

Now, on one level this indicates Gülen was mindful of public opinion: he did not want to give people reason to suppose the projects had "a hidden agenda." On another level, Gülen here could be strategically downplaying his contribution—and he did tend to self-deprecate. But recall—he was in the United States. The organizations had grown rapidly all over the world. Such growth at multiple sites suggests ground-up, rather than top-down, management. Even more, Gülen consistently emphasized a model, istişare, that encouraged participation, rather than hierarchical authority. All in all, the sheer scope of the global projects, and the evidence of his own words, makes plain that Gülen did not direct day-to-day operations. His distance from the grass-roots of Hizmet was not only a strategic hedge. It was a practical concession to reality, and even more it was a principled commitment to the spiritual dynamic at the heart of the movement.

Gülen spoke directly to how in some consultations people would defer to him, and how he struggled to overcome this tendency:

Some of our friends, maybe as a result of their respect, do not want always to express themselves. But [more often] they are very talkative, they express their opinions. I am always advising these friends: "Let us not say with a submissive spirit, 'so and so always says the truth.' I am making a self-criticism, by questioning if what I am doing might be wrong. My interpretations are my personal interpretations; you might not agree with them."[46]

Self-criticism was a central Islamic virtue, as Gülen taught it. The concept, in Arabic, was *muhasaba*—and it was the second topic addressed (after "repentance") in Gülen's book on *Emerald Hills of the Heart: Key Concepts in the Practice of Sufism*. He wrote there that "self-criticism attracts Divine mercy and favor, which enables one to go deeper in belief and servanthood."[47] Or as Gülen put it, more succinctly, "Those who attempt to reform the world must first reform themselves."[48]

In fact, as the years turned to decades, some of the younger people in Hizmet began to turn this self-criticism toward the tendency of some within the movement to be excessively deferential to Gülen, despite his objections to the practices: "When we talk about his ideas," this young woman reflected, "there's ... respect, but around the Hizmet community it is exaggerated. ... I don't like when people meet him, they act like he's a rock star; people are all deferential. He's just another person."[49] For this young woman, it was Gülen's ideas that were important. She was drawn especially to his emphasis on "interfaith dialogue," which she interpreted as "spreading positivity. That gave me motivation in life, and it taught me that wherever I go I could help out people."[50] This idea of "positivity," in Turkish *müspet hareket* ("positive action"), was also a central theme in Gülen's teaching. The notion again goes back to Said Nursi, who explicitly contrasted *müspet hareket* with direct political activism or violent revolution. As sociologist Caroline Tee commented, "Nursi advocated a kind of civic activism—referred to as *müspet hareket* (positive action)—that was both non-political and non-violent, yet which actively sought to integrate Islam back into the daily fabric of national life."[51] This young woman, living in the U.S., had, as she put it, found "motivation" from her encounter with Gülen's ideas, and anything but authoritarian deference to him.

"Believers, like trees, can survive only as long as they bear fruit"

So, while there were those who would defer to Gülen in a consultation, others would take away from the experience heightened motivation. That was the experience of Abdülhamit Bilici. Bilici was born in 1970, and he joined a Hizmet study group in his high school years. He stayed in touch with people in the movement on weekends while he worked on his B.A. in political science and international relations at Boğaziçi University. After graduation, he was offered a position as a foreign news reporter for *Aksiyon*—a weekly news magazine that had been started by friends of Gülen. By the time I interviewed him in 2015, he was completing a stint as General Director of Cihan News Agency (the Associated Press of Gülen-inspired media), and he had recently begun serving as Editor-in-Chief of *Zaman* newspaper. According to Bilici, Gülen motivated people through consultation because he gave them hope that their participation mattered. "His expectation was always to expect more, better, the best ... and then more."[52] When *Zaman* began, the highest expectation of many was circulation of 100,000, Bilici recalled, but Gülen said "We should aspire to a million." According to some reports, that goal was reached by 2011. There is little question that the newspaper had grown rapidly, including, according to its Editor-in Chief, "the best facilities in Istanbul" and "highest professional standards." Those aspirations too, Bilici suggested, came from Gülen's consultative example.[53]

As did, Bilici claimed, an "evolution" on gender relationships. "We have had some problems," Bilici recalled.

> There has been an evolution in Hizmet. When the newspaper was founded there were no female staff. [When] the first female staff members were hired, in the late 1980s, they were in a separate building. Then [in the 1990s] they came to be part of the main building—working here [our interview was conducted at *Zaman* headquarters]. ... Then it became normalized that men and women would work together, and as we learned to interact with others in the world, I personally learned how to develop into a more democratic and equal understanding—of course ... we are still improving. ... [But] in every section now there are women journalists, reporters, editors, designers, etc.[54]

As we noted earlier, Gülen encouraged women's full participation in professions like journalism, the sciences, and theology.

Tahsin Şimşek, an Izmir real estate and construction magnate, remembered a consultation with Gülen during his years as a preacher in the Aegean—probably the late 1970s. In the afternoon, he attended a *sohbet* with Gülen, where he remembered thinking that "Hodjaefendi's grief is

unending. I want to donate everything I have. I should donate everything
I have." But after the *sohbet*, Şimşek drove Gülen to a home where the
two were to meet with some friends—a consultation. "In the car," Şimşek
recalled, "[Hodjaefendi] said, 'Tahsin Bey, don't feel sad. Today we have
limited resources. In the future, our friends won't fit into a stadium.'" And
then during the consult, Şimşek remembered, another participant asked
Gülen: "Hodjaefendi, you tell us how to educate students, but then we do
what we think. We don't know if you are happy with it, or not? Instead
of this way [where we do what we think], can't you tell us name by name
what to do?'" And then Gülen said, Şimşek recalled: "I am pleased with
you as you are. And may God be pleased with you as well." "He then
turned to me," the businessman remembered, and said:

> "For example, if Tahsin Bey donated everything he had, this would
> be wrong. If he donated everything he had, he couldn't continue his
> business or his *hizmet*. A worldly person who cares only for the world,
> has one wing, and can continue toward a goal. But a Muslim cannot
> have only one wing. He or she must have two wings, and be able to do
> worldly things better than the worldly person. He or she must work
> for the world as long as you're in the world. He or she must work for
> the afterlife as long as you'll be in the afterlife. Find the balance. I'm
> pleased with you, and may God be pleased with you. Therefore, con-
> tinue your business and your *hizmet*."[55]

Such a direct imperative could happen in the consultative process
with Gülen. More often, though, as Şimşek put it, people were urged to
"think for themselves."

In most cases, himmet for Hizmet operated independently of
Gülen. This was especially true as the organizations multiplied. There
were only a few organizations that Gülen served as honorary president,
like the Journalists and Writers Foundation, Rumi Forum, and a few others. Some other organizations had individuals who sought *istişare* with
Gülen on occasion, including individuals from non-profit foundations,
professional associations (of which the largest was TUSKON—the Turkish Confederation of Businessmen and Industrialists, founded in 2005,
which once claimed 40,000 members), and social and educational businesses (like FEM—the tutoring centers). Then there were private companies owned by individuals inspired by Gülen, who voluntarily contrib-

uted to various projects in proportion to their commitment. Helen Rose Ebaugh documented how one of these projects—a school in Bursa, came into existence:

> One [businessman] pledged to buy the iron needed in the building and another provided the cement. They sought out their friends in other industries to provide whatever materials they could to the school construction project. In this way, they built the school for one third or one half of what it would have otherwise cost. The school . . . they estimated, was worth about $14 million.... The men were currently involved [in 2009] in building a new school on the outskirts of Bursa. One of them had donated the land for the school; another was financing one of the three buildings involved and another businessman who was not present [at her interview] was also paying for the construction of a second building.[56]

Similar stories of *himmet* could be told about dozens, hundreds, and eventually thousands of projects.

İstişare worked. Ergün Çapan—who when I interviewed him in 2015 was an Adjunct Professor in Theology at Fatih University, and editor of *Yeni Ümit* ("New Hope"), a Hizmet-related theology magazine, said that Gülen's emphasis on mutual consultation, along with his "thinking process," had "produced models that inspired."[57] İsmail Büyükçelebi, among Gülen's earliest students (1966), said as the conclusion of our interview, as his most important point: "He'd gather the ideas of his students when he was trying to organize. He'd ask about our thoughts on a situation or place. He wouldn't dictate. He'd always ask—this made people feel valuable and integrated."[58] Nevzat Savaş studied with Gülen from 1994-1999, and he was when I interviewed him editor of *Hira* (a Hizmet-related magazine published in Arabic). Savaş recalled that Gülen encouraged outreach to the Arab world—especially Morocco, Egypt, Yemen, and Sudan. "Go there!" Savaş remembered Gülen saying. And when they met with new people in the Arab world, Savaş recalled, "We'd sit down and talk and they'd say, 'we agree with you!' But then they'd say, 'This is just idealism—it can't be put into practice.'" So Hizmet benefactors paid to "bring them to Turkey," as Savaş recollected, "and they'd see that things can be realized—a positive idea could actually work. Hizmet showed to the Arabs that idealists can be practical."[59] *Hira*, founded in 2005, was published in Istanbul for ten years—before it was shut down in Turkey, and its offices moved to Cairo.[60]

So, while this book is not primarily the history of the Hizmet movement, there has been a point to documenting in this biography a few of the many individuals inspired by Fethullah Gülen's organizational model, even when he was not directly involved in the operation of the organizations they worked with. Paying attention to what these individuals said, which is what we have tried to do, leads to the conclusion that what Fethullah Gülen contributed to these individuals, and to the agencies they started or worked with, was their DNA, if you will. And that DNA was at its core nothing more, and nothing less, than the Islamic practice of *istişare*. True Muslims were to be busy with the positive action of mutual consultation. Or to mix our metaphors a bit, "Believers, like trees," Gülen once put it, "can survive only as long as they bear fruit."[61]

"Being with the oppressed is the same as being with God": Hizmet globalizes

In an essay published in 2000, Fethullah Gülen penned an impassioned "Appeal to Mercy." Mercy, of course, was a central attribute of God. Yet mercy was also an ethic, a path to peace, and a mark of a civilized society. Gülen admitted that many people, trapped in a "materialistic point of view," could not understand mercy. Materialists considered only the present. But Muslims committed to Hizmet had an eternal horizon. With that point of view, with "hopes and ideals that are concerned with eternity," it was clear that there were "antidemocratic obstacles ... as well as the propaganda of power" in the way of building a more merciful world. Any reform of society thus had to be in two directions—getting rid of the "injustice ... at the root of society's unease," and then getting rid of "personal and social repression [so as to] cease interfering with [peoples'] consciences." With unfettered consciences, and without antidemocratic obstacles, people could envision "a bright future," even "salvation as a whole society."[62] Mercy might just save us all. More prosaically, a vision of collective salvation was central to the kind of work that Gülen encouraged people of Hizmet to engage in over the last two decades of his life. Bayram Balci of the Carnegie Endowment for International Peace identified this work as the promotion of "soft power."[63] "An Appeal to Mercy" meant that for Fethullah Gülen, the salvation of society depended upon a different kind of power than sheer force.

But what kind of power was mercy? Mercy was, again, God's power—and it linked individuals and society. Thus, "I feel obliged to restate again," Gülen reiterated,

> that individual projects of enlightenment that are not planned to aid the community are doomed to fruitlessness. Moreover, it is not possible to revive values that have been destroyed in the hearts of the individual in society, nor in the conscience of the will power. Just as plans and projects for individual salvation that are independent of the salvation of others are nothing more than an illusion, so, too, the thought of achieving success as a whole by paralyzing the individual awakening is a fantasy.[64]

It was, in short, the capacity of an individual to embody or to practice God's mercy that connected individual action with community well-being: what kept "a person alive is the goal of lifting others up." Beyond personal interest—which tended to corrupt, and led to people "cringing, licking boots," people of service found their motivation in living lives of mercy.[65]

The theological perspective was crucial, as was an eternal horizon. People of Hizmet were "people of this world *and* the next, people whose contact with others ... can be considered as contact with God." Gülen here grounded human rights activism in Muslim theology. To ground peacebuilding in God's mercy, and in life beyond this life, actually made the work easy, no matter how materially hard it might have been. "The life that such people lead, with all its variants, is clear and boundless enough for them to enjoy a glimpse of the quiet of a harbor in the next world." A horizon of peace could break into the present of even the most ruthless conflict. In such situations, people of Hizmet actually had "reached the company of God." Such exalted company of course provided personal peace, not as a static state, but in a way that drove individuals to extend mercy to others. Such individuals sought "grand projects and summits. They think of mercy, speak of mercy, and seek ways to express themselves through mercy." Such lives recognized the inherent value of living, because they recognized "the fact that they are in the presence of the Supreme Power." Consequently,

Over and above the maxim, "Desire not for others what you do not desire for yourself," such people ceaselessly try harder for others so that others will benefit from what these people of heart have already found useful. With the boundlessness of the horizon of such people, they are able to revive the feeling of mercy in the hearts of tyrants. At the same time, they believe that being with the oppressed is the same as being with God, and thus support them.[66]

Here was the heart of Hizmet activism and organizing. An encounter with a person could be an encounter with God: being with the oppressed was the same as being with God. This theological maxim expressed itself through the last years of Gülen's life in manifold projects around the globe that, in effect, extended mercy to others. Such mercy, again, was not a mere accompaniment to colonializing efforts to "save" souls, and although it was "soft" compared to the hard power of force, it was also connected, Gülen believed, to the "Supreme Power" in the Universe. Mercy, in other words, was as practical as it was idealistic. Historically speaking, what Fethullah Gülen was calling for in his "Appeal for Mercy" was an Islamic variant of the Christian movement known as liberation theology, where God was for the oppressed.

Planting seeds of peace in Central Asia and elsewhere

The globalization of Hizmet took root in this theological context. As we saw in the last chapter, it began in Central Asia. Already by 2000, dozens of companies were set up in Turkey, with offices also in their host countries to support enterprises in the former Soviet Republics. Among them were the Kazak Türk Liseleri Genel Müdürlüğü (General Directorate of Kazakh-Turkish Schools), the Taşkent Eğitim Şirketi (Tashkent Educational Company—in Uzbekistan), and the Gülistan Eğitim Yayın ve Ticaret Ltd. (Gulistan Education, Publishing, and Trade, Ltd), from among many, many others. As the names of these agencies suggest, most of the Hizmet-related organizations focused on education—but some also existed to sponsor dialogue, trade, publishing, tourism, and healthcare. Some of the companies were for-profit; most were non-profit foundations (vakıf).[67] After 2016, all the Turkish offices of these companies were closed. In the host countries, many of the institutions continued, albeit under very different structures. The Kyrgyz schools, for instance, which numbered at one time twenty-eight, had become completely in-dependent, according to Nurlan Kudaberdiev, who was responsible for their operation through Sebat Foundation. He did acknowledge that it was Gülen who first had "the idea" for them, but there was "no direct influence or financing from his side anymore," he said.[68]

Victoria Clement, who taught at one of the schools in Turkmeni-stan in the early 2000s, claimed that although Gülen had no direct in-fluence on the curriculum, his ethic came through in faculty behavior. She wrote:

> Terbiye (character building) is critical to raising good Muslims and is the principal concept by which the schools are organized.... Sey-it Embel, the chair of the Başkent Educational Centre in [Ashgabat] wrote that 'enlightenment and character building are the main aims' of the combined Turkmen and Turkish efforts. One basic method for imparting terbiye in the Hizmet schools is through temsil (model liv-ing).[69]

"Model living" meant, negatively—not drinking alcohol, not smok-ing, and not engaging in illicit sex. Positively, it meant having a strong work ethic, being competent in one's discipline and being prepared, and being available to students outside of the classroom for special projects and extra-curricular activities. Clement traced these ethical behaviors directly to Gülen, who wrote, as she cited him:

> Those who lead the way must set a good example for their followers. Just as they are imitated in their virtues and good morals, so do their bad and improper actions and attitudes leave indelible marks upon those who follow them.[70]

Science Olympiads were particularly popular among Central Asian students—although students in many Hizmet-related schools around the world found competing in these contests, which often involved for-eign travel (usually to Turkey), appealing.

Many of the individuals active in Hizmet after 1999 had little or no lived experience of hearing Gülen preach, and yet they were the ones who carried Hizmet around the globe. Someone like Derya Yazıcı was perhaps typical. Yazıcı was born in Germany but grew up in the Turkish city of Bursa. She had been inspired to deepened faith during the early

1990s by a high school teacher. Although the teacher had never mentioned Gülen's name, she connected the dots in retrospect and realized the source of his influence as a role model—a not unusual story. During those years, she first paid attention to Gülen when she attended a FEM tutoring center to improve her performance on the college admissions exam. After that experience, she began reading Gülen's works and listening to recordings of his sermons. Throughout her college years, she lived in a Hizmet dormitory. Then, after graduating from Marmara University in 1997 with a degree in Turkish Literature, she married a man who also had ties to Hizmet. She then moved to Cyprus to serve as a teacher there. Her work, which lasted through 2001, was more than a job. It engaged her with what she understood to be peacebuilding—a kind of mercy. As she put it:

> In Cyprus, there was a native Turkish community that had lived there for a long time; deeply influenced by British and Greek culture. When we had a population exchange [in 1923], and Turkey sent Turks to Cyprus—to balance the population, these were low-income Turks from villages. So Turkish Cyprus now had two different strata—newcomers, low-income, pious, Anatolian and the native, more British-Greek. These two different segments almost had a "cold war" amongst them—they couldn't get along, and they lived parallel lives. But in our schools, we also had a small tutoring center—the kids started merging and getting along nicely. The teachers were both natives and newcomers. Hizmet helped create a new identity for Cyprus' Turks—uniting them.[71]

Not everyone would have been thrilled by that development. The sheer presence of Turks on what Greeks took to be their land was a consistent source of friction. In 1974, in fact, Greek assaults on Turkish citizens prompted a Turkish invasion; and no international agency recognizes Turkey's claim to Cypriot land. But Yazıcı—just out of college, and a new bride, and a first-time teacher, was no doubt less concerned with geo-political intrigue than interpersonal peacebuilding.

She saw another positive outcome, about which she could generalize, when she moved to Mongolia to teach at the Hizmet-related school there (from 2009-2013). As she put it:

In our school we had Mongolian, Turkish, Filipino, Kazak, Georgian instructors ... and we got along very nicely. Hizmet was helping to create a pluralistic identity where we were human beings first. When Hizmet enters a place, it creates an umbrella identity around being human.[72]

Gülen, of course, often made the same point. In Islam, "humanity is the vicegerent of God on Earth," an exalted position, and "we are all limbs of the same body," as he put it.[73] Nevertheless, Yazıcı was now less naive about the challenges of peacebuilding. "As a peacebuilder," she said, "we may not achieve peace in our lifetime. But there are seeds planted that will grow peace in the next generation. ... Our children are going to be the peacebuilders. ... Peace starts with one relationship at a time."[74]

Kimse Yok Mu—"Is Anybody There?"

For another example of Fethullah Gülen's influence across the generations, and around the globe, consider the story of Nurten Kutlu. Kutlu became active in Hizmet in 1993. She graduated from college in 1998, and then served for three years as a Headmaster and Dormitory Principal in the girls' school in Tirana, Albania. After returning to Turkey she worked at various tutoring centers, got married, and then in 2005 she and her husband went to Vietnam to start a school. It was a struggle. "The government didn't like it at first," she explained. But she and her husband continued to explore opportunities, and eventually received permission to open a language school—to prepare people for the burgeoning tourism business in Vietnam. From that success, followed others. By the time she left, in 2008—a school serving five-hundred students from Kindergarten through High School was in place. The government still wasn't completely sure; "they controlled us, but they loved us," as she put it. Most of her students, she explained, wanted little to do with Marx and Engels. The Communist ideology remained a mandatory part of the curriculum, but the "students were democratic," she claimed. The peacebuilding of one relationship at a time, and the peacebuilding of entrepreneurial activism, took priority over the difficulties of living under Communist ideology.[75]

But her globe-trotting for Hizmet had only begun. After another hiatus to work at home in Turkey for a few years, Kutlu went in 2012 to

Kenya. There she worked with the Lotus Foundation. The Lotus Foundation was one of several that had been set up in Kenya with the support of Turkish business leaders, most of whom lived and worked near Antalya—a Mediterranean resort city. The earliest of these Foundations was the Ömeriye [Omar] Foundation, established in 1997. It coordinated educational efforts that led to several schools in Nairobi, Mombasa, and Malindi. Another Hizmet organization in Kenya was the Respect Foundation Interfaith and Intercultural Center, opened in Nairobi in 2007. Among other activities, it organized seminars and computer courses for imams in the Kibera neighborhood of Nairobi, and it sponsored intentional peacebuilding efforts between Muslim and Christian religious leaders, and between students of diverse faiths at Jomo Kenyatta University. Kutlu's work took her immediately into Kibera—the shantytown of several square miles that was occupied by somewhere approaching 300,000 Kenyans, many of them young, most of them new arrivals to the city, and all of them poor. According to a 2012 article in *The Economist*, the residents of Kibera generally lived in extreme poverty, which is defined as earning less than $2/day.[76] Clean water was scarce, and sanitation basic. Still, "we went deeper and deeper" into the shantytown, Kutlu remembered. "You needed a guide. It was horrible." But despite her dismay at the living conditions, which are by all estimates among the roughest in the world, Kutlu engaged a project that was a classical endeavor in social enterprise: she opened a sewing school. This was "for the women," Kutlu explained. "We didn't want to just hand out money, but to train them for a job. If you buy a woman a sewing machine, and teach her to use it, she can support her family. So that's what we did."[77] Kutlu's work was connected to the work of a larger global relief agency begun by people of Hizmet, called Kimse Yok Mu. The name means, "is anybody there?" Few of the individuals who benefited from these Hizmet efforts in Kenya—the schools, dialogue centers, or direct relief efforts, had any idea of who Fethullah Gülen was, or how his theology had inspired such activism.[78] Kutlu worked in Nairobi for four years. She learned to love the country. "It was home," she simply said.

Not surprisingly, Kimse Yok Mu, the agency that Kutlu worked with in Kenya, was also at work in Sudan, and in many other nations in Africa. According to David Shinn, during the conflict in Sudan, Kimse Yok Mu contributed millions in direct assistance—notably food, but also water wells, and medical facilities, including a three-hundred bed hospital. The hospital was named for Ikbal Gürpınar—a famous Turkish television star (in fact, the host of a show entitled Kimse Yok Mu), and it was run by Turkish volunteers until the Sudanese Ministry of Health could take over.[79] In fiscal year 2013, according to Shinn, Kimse Yok Mu contributed

> about $17.5 million to 43 countries in Africa. Less than one-third was humanitarian assistance. Most of the aid went to development projects, health, education, water wells, and support for orphans. The principal recipients were Somalia ($3.8 million), Kenya ($2.8 million), Uganda ($2 million), Ethiopia ($1.9 million), Sudan ($1.8 million), and Niger ($1.7 million).

As Shinn acknowledged, this number ($17.5 million) was "modest compared to major humanitarian, international non-governmental organizations." Yet, because it went "to so many countries and relies heavily on the volunteer efforts of the local Turkish communities, it probably has a greater impact than its dollar value suggests."[80]

Kimse Yok Mu (KYM) was the broadest of the global relief agencies connected to Hizmet. At one point, it had about four-hundred employees. The agency had offices all over the world, but KYM concentrated its efforts in places of conflict and impoverishment. KYM had its beginnings in 1999 after a devastating earthquake hit the Marmara region of Turkey. The earthquake caused extensive damage to the city of Izmit—about 65 miles east of Istanbul. Over 17,000 died, and hundreds of thousands were displaced. Extensive public service programming on Samanyolu TV—the Hizmet-related network, began almost immediately, under the name of Kimse Yok Mu. The name, "Is Anybody There?" was of course what someone would shout while searching in rubble for survivors of an earthquake, or what someone buried in rubble might cry out while hoping someone would come to search. In any event, the television programming raised funds for relief efforts. It became a regular (and very popular) show that lasted for years. It focused attention on disasters and the need for assistance wherever they happened to occur. So, while the program started in Turkey, it soon broadcast stories about Turkish people from many countries taking services wherever they were needed after a disaster or conflict, such as Myanmar, Argentina, Indonesia, Pakistan, and Uganda. In 2002, Kimse Yok Mu Solidarity and Aid Association had been established as a licensed nongovernmental agency in Turkey. In 2016, that license was revoked.[81]

Naturally, while it existed KYM concentrated on poverty alleviation, and on being present for the oppressed. It often overlapped with other Hizmet-related organizations. For instance, Kimse Yok Mu administered a Sister Family project that linked middle-class or wealthy families with poorer families. The wealthier families supported especially educational opportunities for their less wealthy neighbors—including scholarships to Hizmet-related schools. Another Kimse Yok Mu project was Ramadan Tents. These tents were set up in poorer neighborhoods of major cities in Turkey, the Philippines, Indonesia, Pakistan, Lebanon, Ethiopia, and the U.S., among others. These tents provided free iftar meals to all comers. The tents were also often connected to the local dialogue agencies or foundations. They promoted dialogue with food, and they built trust without words.[82] KYM also sponsored in-kind aid to many regions around the world. These donations included food, but also clothing, stoves, fuel, and, in some areas where it operated, free medical check-ups and procedures, thereby connecting people to local Hizmet-related health-care initiatives. Money for these projects was gathered through creative kinds of *himmet*: online donations; checks or cash deposited at local offices (there were 80 in Turkey by 2007); direct deposits to bank accounts set up for aid projects; text-message donations; and cash deposited in kiosks or boxes on busy city streets. Throughout the 2000s, the number of annual donors was consistently in the hundreds of thousands. Eventually the agency operated out of a headquarters in Istanbul, with connections to the various Hizmet-related agencies around the globe. It was among the most centralized and coordinated of the various Gülen-inspired organizations. Gülen's direct involvement was, again, minimal, aside from providing the agency its DNA of compassion—although he would often be the first to donate from his royalties after a disaster, which then set an example that many followed. Most of those who received aide in countries other than Turkey knew that the aide came from Turkey, but they probably knew nothing about Fethullah Gülen.[83]

Not a Gülen "brand," but the practice of Islam

This was, in fact, how Gülen wanted it. He was not interested in a Gülen "brand." He wanted people to practice Islam. İsmail Büyükçelebi, one of Gülen's earliest and closest students, explained:

> He didn't see education only as math and physics, but education as comprehensive—trade, arts, service, and methods of service. He said he wouldn't stop with us, but would meet with others, including tradesmen. He taught them as he taught us. What he taught was based on positive action: organizations needed to help others; organizing the rich to help the poor. ... He asked for financial sacrifice. The companions of the Prophet were used as examples. ... He constantly refers back to the religion, and he says this [project] isn't about my opinion; this is Islam.[84]

The goal was not to grow for the sake of growth; the goal was to practice one's faith with integrity. Büyükçelebi continued:

> I know Hodjaefendi did not teach a class on these subjects [business or community organizing] directly, but I know of his recommendations to [many] groups. He wants to make sure that they aren't limited to a particular place [e.g., Turkey]. If you are going to build a business in America, then make sure you have an American partner.... What is key is that [Hodjaefendi] didn't recommend businessmen to go into speculation. He encouraged people to build something that produced, and to invest in your own businesses, not on credit. ... He's also promoted opening-up business foundations, and made sure to push these foundations around the globe—America, Africa, Japan.[85]

For Gülen, work was not simply work. As he put it directly in one of his sermons on the Prophet: "Islam encourages people to work, and considers our lawful attempts to earn our living and support our family acts of worship."[86] Work done with integrity and good intention was worship in Islam.

Consequently, those whose work produced excess profits were encouraged to be generous in *himmet*. Something of the capacity generated by this ethic is best studied in a microcosm—since there is no comprehensive Hizmet spreadsheet. Helen Rose Ebaugh and Doğan Koç conducted a series of interviews with Hizmet-related business leaders in Ankara in 2006.

> We asked the group of a dozen businessmen in Ankara whether each of them contributes financially to Gülen-inspired projects, and if so, approximately how much they give each year. Each of the 12 men said that they contribute as they can to the movement projects. Amounts of contributions varied from 10% to 70% of their annual income, ranging from $20,000-$300,000 per year. One man, in particular, said he gives 40% of his income every year which is about $100,000; however, he said he would like to give 95% but is not able to do so and still maintain himself and his family. Another man said, "We wish we could be like the companions of the Prophet and give everything we have. But it is not easy."[87]

Easy or not, Gülen recognized that as resources concentrated in projects connected to his teachings, some would be suspicious. In a 2005 answer to the question "Is Hizmet an alternative to the State," Gülen answered, with a bit of biting satire:

> I tell them [those who suspect Hizmet's motives] this: "Send some teachers to the four corners of the world, open up schools in every part of the world, open up cultural centers ... and when they play their own role in the future, [then you go] find the support. You do it." I would even take it a step further, despite the friends who do these services, despite those self-sacrificing people, those who are [behind] these institutions, the financiers, the businessmen; if I have the power, if my fame could reach, I would say to the whole nation: "If some are saying, 'Give those institutions to us, let us manage them,' then you give them, surrender them, let them manage everything, let us see whether [they are] managed or not." ... [Our approach is] giving without receiving anything in return.[88]

When the Turkish government started seizing Hizmet assets, this nightmare scenario came true. And, as Gülen anticipated, many of the initiatives simply ended. Their assets went into private pockets; their service stopped.

Still, in the last years of the twentieth and early years of the twenty-first centuries, there was plenty of reason for hope. The process by which *himmet* happened to raise money for work with the oppressed was described in some detail by a political scientist who "sat in" on several of the *himmet* meetings in Istanbul in the early 2000s. He wrote:

> These meetings are meticulously structured with cultural programs, soft drinks, light food and speeches from different people, especially from successful students of the movement, who recount their path to success. Those who are present are asked to donate for projects of the movement. In each of these *himmet* meetings, there is a concrete project to which participants are asked to donate.
>
> Most of the *himmet* meetings are organized by the local leader ... and he usually invites the owners of small and medium-sized businesses to participate. ... There is indirect pressure on the participants to give and, possibly, give more than they can afford in such fundraising meetings. Those participants who are most generous tend to have their children in the Gülen-run education system, or their businesses linked with the followers of other pro-Gülen business groups.
>
> The meetings usually start with a recitation from the Qur'an, and then a number of short but emotional "testimonial" speeches. ... After the speeches, the leader of the *himmet* meeting either directly asks the participants to donate, or in some cases, the fundraising follows after the showing of a video about the successful projects of the Gülen community. The participants are asked to become a partner to future projects for the sake of pleasing God, serving Islam, their community, and the wider Turkish nation. In these *himmet* fund raisers, usually one identifies the project and the cost, and then someone starts with matching gifts by declaring and asking, for example, that: "I will donate 20,000 liras for the project. Who wants to take part in its realization?"[89]

By 2007, according to sociologist Helen Rose Ebaugh, who based her estimate on documents collected at the State Department to support Gülen's "green card" application, the total value of Hizmet-related enterprises was approximately $25 billion.[90] Ebaugh's number included privately held businesses of Hizmet-supporters; not necessarily assets used directly in Hizmet activities. In 2017, the Turkish government announced that they seized $11 billion worth of assets from privately owned businesses by people allegedly affiliated with Hizmet.[91] But in any event when Prime Minister (and then President) Erdoğan started seizing

Hizmet-affiliated institutions and privately owned businesses, it became clear that funds were not unlimited, and financial struggles became daily realities for Hizmet agencies.

To Australia and the Arab world

No doubt, though, people of Hizmet between 1999 and 2016 managed to fund some serious *hizmet* around the globe. Australia was a particularly impressive case of how Hizmet globalized—with roots well before Gülen left for America. As historian of Islam Greg Barton has profiled, Hizmet came to Australia primarily through the efforts of one man, Orhan Çiçek. Çiçek was from Ankara. He encountered Gülen's thought while studying to be an imam. He was not part of the Hizmet "inner circle," since he was about fifteen years younger than most of the early participants. Nevertheless, Çiçek started participating in *sohbet*s, and when the opportunity to emigrate to Australia was presented to him, he accepted, after consulting with his *abi*. Arriving in Melbourne in 1980, he knew of no other followers of Gülen. Gradually, as more Turks arrived, a critical mass of a few people became interested in Hizmet, and Çiçek started reading circles like those he had joined in Ankara. After a few years, it came to the attention of this small group of people inspired by Gülen that many Turkish youth—that tricky second-generation of immigrants—was running into trouble with Australian police. In response, as Barton documented, in 1985 Çiçek "started a drop-in centre and youth programme which he called the New Generation Youth Association." Now, while this effort may seem far removed from the efforts of liberation theologians to develop social businesses for Kenyan women, in fact it was very much in the same spirit. Barton explains:

> Inspired by Gülen's teachings about the importance of soundly educating and developing young people and the potential for youth-driven generational change through the development of a "golden generation" (*altın nesil*), Çiçek was convinced that he should focus his efforts on trying to help second generation Turkish Australian youth. He sought to mentor the young people who he encountered and engage them in practical programmes involving sport and outings and some basic tutoring. He also began to lead *Risale-i Nur* reading groups amongst these teenagers as well as amongst their parents.[92]

Before long, by 1987, Çiçek had opened the Light Tutoring Center in inner-city Melbourne. Within a few years, after trips back to Turkey to consult with Gülen, planning for a school in Melbourne and in Sydney (where some other Turks had recently settled) began. These efforts received a further boost when Gülen visited Australia in 1992 as part of his quasi "world tour." Even before then, in 1990, a foundation called Selimiye had been set up in Melbourne—one of the first not-for-profit Muslim educational foundations in Australia, according to Barton. That group held its first *himmet* event in late 1991, and brought in AUD $70,000. That was enough to buy a building to serve as dormitory and tutoring center. Similar events were launched in Sydney, and in 1996 Şule College (High School) opened there, with Işık College in Melbourne following just a year later. By 2014, there were four Hizmet-related schools on three campuses in New South Wales, and eight schools on six campuses in Victoria. Overall, Hizmet workers in Australia had started sixteen schools across the continent that continued.[93]

Just as Gülen played an indirect but significant role in these developments in Australia, so too did he contribute to the spread of Hizmet into the Arab world. Nevzat Savaş, the Editor of *Hira* magazine, which was an Arab language version of *Sızıntı* and *The Fountain*, explained in a 2015 interview that "Hizmet [in 2015] has strength in Northern Africa—Morocco, Egypt, Yemen. Hodjaefendi said two countries were crucial—Yemen and Sudan. He saw this on TV. 'This is interesting,' he said. 'This is where we need to go.'" So, Savaş did. But, in fact, it was Morocco that provided a first opening for Gülen's teaching in the Arab world. Savaş goes on:

> The King of Morocco sent an invitation to Hodjaefendi in 2005. Abdelhak Serhane (a novelist and political activist) had read [Gülen's book] *The Infinite Light*—and he introduced it to someone close to the king. And he said: "This is the interpretation of Islam that we want." He explained it to the King. The King studied it in his palace during Ramadan. The King brings his ambassadors, brothers, Islamic scholars—and they study Hodjaefendi during Ramadan. And then the King says, "Let's call the writer of this book here." So, he extended an invitation to Hodjaefendi. And Serhane said, "If Hodjaefendi comes to Morocco, this will be a turning point for the country on the

path to peace." Of course, because Hodjaefendi was sick, he wrote a letter of thanks and sent some gifts, books. I took the books. We organized classes, on the lessons. And then we suggested that we organize a program—a conference so that people can learn about *Hira*. So, we did—and there are TV cameras, radio—I can't believe it. Scholars were looking at me; my Arabic's not that great. Here we are in the Arab world: Who are you? Why are you here? And then we went to Cairo and held a similar event.[94]

And in 2008, a similar event was held in Yemen, and a year later in Tunisia.

Savaş admitted that these conferences were challenging. "Hizmet doesn't work with professionals," he explained. "It works with amateurs who are sincere—but turns people into professionals." And there were problems to translate *hizmet* for the Arab world. "Whenever people asked, 'who's Fethullah Gülen,'" Savaş explained, "we don't say '*hizmet*.' There is no such word in Arabic. We call it a 'paradigm,' or 'model.' ... Hodjaefendi didn't want a name. He said, 'What did God name you in Islam? He called you a Muslim.' When I said this," Savaş went on, "the Arabs were really happy."[95]

Still, Gülen's teachings were clearly a contrast to Wahhabi Islam. In fact, Savaş offered, "a Moroccan writer called this 'the Hizmet shock.' It's a different paradigm.'" That paradigm had profound implications that engaged politics, but it also went beyond them. One Tunisian scholar told Savaş that "we thought we'd be able to change things with politics. But politics is like a road with spikes and mines. Now we understand the real problem is the human being and that's where we need to invest. Now we understand how Hodjaefendi can help us find a way to change society with culture and education." Peacebuilding had to engage politics. But it could not start, or end, there. As Savaş drew the implications:

> Hodjaefendi said "first spread the culture of hope. Second, spread the culture of solutions. If people are always complaining and looking negatively, make it possible for intellectuals to find solutions and alternatives to reactionaryism." ... [And that's how] the Arab world saw an alternative model [in Gülen], because it had reached a dead end ... and Hodjaefendi said, "no, there's a very wide road." He opens up horizons. His contribution is opening up the vision.[96]

Interestingly, Savaş had an opportunity to visit Gülen in 2005, but chose not to go. He wanted to wait until he had some good news about his work on *Hira* to take to Gülen.

> I want to go to a sad man with something that will make him happy. So, I went with *Hira* in 2010, as news from the Arab Spring was being broadcast. I told him, "hopefully you won't be alone anymore. In the West there are people like you who take this idea to protect it. But now there are some in the Arab world who are also protecting this idea."[97]

As the Arab Spring turned toward totalitarian winters, this hope became more fragile.

To Indonesia, Sweden, South Africa...

But in other corners of the world, people of Hizmet continued to take Gülen's ideas and translate them into practical action. In Indonesia, for instance, Gülen's teaching—brought to the world's most populous Muslim nation by just a few students in the mid-1990s, helped forge a "third-way" for Indonesia between "Islamism" or "political Islam," on the one hand, and "liberal or privatized Islam," on the other, according to political scientist Mohamed Nawab Osman.[98] Not surprisingly, given Gülen's influence, this third way was marked by openness to modernity and pluralism, in common with liberal Islam, but also rigorous adherence to Muslim practice—in common with Islamists. At the heart of the movement of those inspired by Gülen was a "commitment to organizing in a way that fostered trust," a theme we have heard repeatedly. The movement provided "'spaces of socialization' and a web of interactions for different people ... to build social capital (i.e., trust and coordination in social relations)."[99]

In Indonesia, Hizmet was planted in 1993. Three students inspired by the teachings of Gülen emigrated there to further their studies. One of them would prove particularly significant. It was this student who began building bridges with local contacts. He befriended a scholar by the name of Haji Alwi. Alwi then introduced this student to the governor of the Indonesian state bank, Burhanuddin Abdullah, and to a prominent Indonesian politician, Dr Aip Syarifuddin. Those partnerships led in 1996 to the first Gülen-inspired school in Indonesia, the

Pribadi High School in Depok (a suburb of Jakarta). All this activity was managed by the Yenbu Indonesian Foundation, which was eventually supplemented by another organization, PASIAD Indonesia (The Pacific-Asian Nations Social and Economic Development Association). The student then moved to Yogyakarta to continue studies. There an acquaintance began with Professor Siti Chamamah Soeratno—an activist holding various key positions in the women's wing of the second largest Indonesian Muslim organization, Muhammadiyah. With her help, a second school was opened in the Yogyakarta suburb of Semarang- the SMP-SMA Semesta Boarding School. Again, a foundation was set up to manage the work—the Al-Firdaus Semarang Foundation. By 2010, people connected to Hizmet, working in partnership with local contacts, had built three new schools in Bandung, Aceh and in Tangerang, on the western outskirts of Jakarta.[100] PASIAD also sponsored projects elsewhere in Asia, notably in Vietnam, Cambodia, Thailand, Laos, and Taiwan, for example.[101]

What made the developments in Indonesia significant was that this third-way had the capacity to influence the world's most populous Muslim nation. The schools quickly earned a reputation for academic excellence—especially in math and science. Parents of many (and no) religious affiliations sought to enroll their children. The schools were secular, but teachers were recruited for virtue as well as expertise. They were expected to teach by moral example as well as by technique. One alumnus of a Hizmet-related school in Indonesia echoed the mercy ethic of Gülen, in so many words: "Muslims should cease having a mindset of 'us' against 'them,'" he said. "There must be a shift in ... paradigm to start thinking of everyone as fellow human beings, rather than by their religious affiliations."[102] Over the 2000s, following the pattern from Gülen's initiatives in Istanbul, people of Hizmet in Indonesia began sponsoring interreligious iftar dinners. This was a new practice in Indonesia; previously iftars had not been open to Christians or Hindus.[103] And as schools multiplied, and graduates entered public life, political scientist Osman envisioned Hizmet alumni acquainted with Fethullah Gülen's "intellectual Sufism" serving to counter violent extremism, on the one hand, and spiritual indifference, on the other. As of late, 2016, the schools in Indonesia remained open—despite pressure from the Turkish government to close them. In reply to a question from a BBC reporter, a student named

Chilla, who attended Kharisma Bangsa High School (one of the schools in Jakarta), said: "I think it's really sad and wrong they think we're terrorists, because we're not!" Another student, named Salwa, put it quite bluntly: "If Turkey really has problems, don't involve us. We're only here to study and to pursue our dreams."[104]

There were thousands of young people around the world whose dreams came closer to realization through the work of people inspired by Fethullah Gülen, but brevity (and reader attention-span) demands some compression. Sweden saw people of Hizmet become active there in the first decade of the twenty-first century, seeking to dispel Islamophobia through "positive action." For instance, women led the way in founding Dialogslussen—a dialogue platform in the two largest Swedish cities of Stockholm and Gothenburg. Men also got into the act. Imams and priests in 2007 organized a charity football match for peace.[105] In the UK, similarly, a Foundation to support educational initiatives, Axis Educational Trust, was founded in 1994, and a Dialogue Society followed in 1999. Since 2012, England has been a significant host for Hizmet ex-pats. Some of them founded a "Centre for Hizmet Studies" in London in 2014. This think-tank has sponsored some significant research projects, especially one countering hate-speech coming from the Turkish government against Hizmet.[106] In South Africa, as noted earlier (in the previous chapter), Hizmet participants opened specifically Islamic, as well as secular, schools. At these Islamic schools, South African Muslim students could study Qur'anic interpretation and theology, along with traditional secular subjects—and, of course, they could study Fethullah Gülen's writings among other extra reading materials. Most of the schools in South Africa, however, run by Horizon Educational Trust, followed a strictly secular curriculum. Gülen's influence, again, was left to the example of good teachers. According to Yasien Mohamed, business people inspired by Gülen to support the schools in South Africa donated as much as 50% of their profits to the cause.[107] Similar patterns existed in Nigeria. As of 2018, the government of Nigeria had resisted efforts by the Turkish government to co-opt Hizmet's resources. Ufuk Dialogue Initiative—with headquarters in Abuja, has sponsored international conferences and regular award dinners to honor individuals active in fostering interreligious understanding.[108]

Healthcare efforts

Healthcare was another way that people of Hizmet in Nigeria put into practice Gülen's maxim that "being with the oppressed was the same as being with God." They opened Nizamiye Hospital in the capital city of Abuja in 2013. The hospital—among the most modern and well-equipped in Nigeria—offered full emergency, surgical, medical, and laboratory services. The medical staff, largely doctors and nurses from Turkey, also made visits to the nearby Wassa Refugee Camp, to area orphanages, and to conflict areas in the northeast of Nigeria where medical care was rare. Among the specialized initiatives of the hospital was a free cataract surgery program. When I visited in 2018, I was given a tour by the Chief Medical Officer, Dr. Osagie E. Ehanire, and sent off with a gift bag of water and hand sanitizer from Abisola Odusanya, one of the RN's with whom I met.

Healthcare had been a focus for some people within Hizmet as far back as 1979. At that time, during his last years in Izmir, Gülen was involved in a consultation that led to Şifa Hospital—the first in the Hizmet healthcare orbit. According to Yusuf Erdoğan (no relation to the President), who was Rector of Şifa University Medical College when I interviewed him in 2015, "in 1979 a doctor named Mahmud Akdoğan came to Hodjaefendi and said, 'Let's open a doctor's foundation.' Hodjaefendi said, 'Mahmud, we are people of action. Bring a piece of paper and let's get to work.'" What was eventually the Şifa Foundation was underway. Rector Erdoğan continued: "The main purpose of the Foundation was to help medical students. And then we started a clinic and a small hospital—200 square meters—with a budget of zero lira! ... Today, Şifa Hospital is 200,000 square meters ... with a budget of 150,000,000 Lira." Similar initiatives also were begun in Istanbul, in Bursa, in Erzurum, in Antalya and in other Turkish cities. In later decades hospitals were also built in Kazakhstan, Indonesia, and in various African nations, as we have already seen. "To this day," Erdoğan claimed, "we have not fully understood the way Hodjaefendi looks at health. When we were thinking about a small hospital, Hodjaefendi was thinking an international hospital. ... Hodjaefendi gives suggestions. He'd say, 'if you do this, it wouldn't be bad.' And when businessmen, doctors, have followed his suggestions, the results speak for themselves."[109]

When investigating the Sema Hospital in Istanbul, the local equivalent of Şifa in Izmir, sociologist Helen Rose Ebaugh sounded almost
surprised to discover that benevolence rather than profit marked the
ways the hospital conducted its business. Five businessmen contributed
the funds to build the facility, she learned. They remained on the Board
of Directors to stay connected to the ongoing operations. But, she also
discovered, they did not reap any profit from the project. They funneled
any return on their investment back into improving equipment. That
largesse contributed to the start-up of other hospitals, provided scholarships for medical school students, and subsidized care for the poor (Turkey has universal health care, but does not cover many beneficial procedures that must then be gained through private hospitals). The Public
Health Administrator of the Hospital, a Harvard grad Ebaugh identified
only as "Kristin," told Ebaugh that it was common for wealthier people within Hizmet to "sponsor" the care for less fortunate Istanbullus.
This administrator had to tell the sociologist about it twice: "We have
an amazing network of people who sponsor patients who come to us
for care. They sponsor our patients," she reiterated. "The system is very
informal, but it works." Such a system matched how Hizmet operated
elsewhere. People motivated by an ethic of mercy generated wealth to
alleviate suffering and to build community. Finally, Ebaugh reported,
somewhat breathlessly, that doctors took jobs at the hospital for less pay
than they would make elsewhere. Nurses were hired who saw patients
not as a nuisance, but as the reason for their vocations. Most of the staff
of the hospital, Ebaugh learned, had gone to a Hizmet-related school. All
of them were familiar with the culture where "being with the oppressed
was the same as being with God."[110] Sadly, once Erdoğan, the President
of Turkey, turned against Hizmet, all the hospitals in the Hizmet orbit in
Turkey—as many as thirty-five total, were closed.

Education, businesses, and dialogue in the U.S.

Finally, in this very compressed and selective examination of how
Fethullah Gülen's teachings inspired acts of compassion around the
world, what about in his new home—America? By many estimates, including by some who for diverse reasons are not particularly pleased by
the development, people connected to Hizmet have built over a hun-

dred charter and private schools in the US.[111] These schools, in a pattern that should be familiar by now, generally were operated by Foundations. Turkish teachers were employed in them, but so were locals (again, a pattern in most Gülen-inspired schools). And Turkish contractors or vendors were sometimes hired to do work related to the educational endeavors. Similar practices dot the history of immigrant groups in America back to the English, Dutch, Swedish, Irish—and so forth. In the end, all schools were accountable to local (and federal) judicatories, followed state-mandated curricula, and (generally) performed above local standards while also serving populations often excluded from decent public education.[112] Still, a panic about school-funding (with a tinge of Islamophobia), led to stories in ordinarily reputable sites like CBS News that asked questions such as: "Are Some U.S. Charter Schools Helping Fund Controversial Turkish Cleric's Movement?" As Alp Aslandoğan, President of the Alliance for Shared Values, put it: "If there's a proven charge that somebody illegally channeled money from public funds into some private purposes, Gülen will be first to condemn it."[113]

As for dialogue organizations and businesses, the pattern elsewhere also grew in the U.S. after 1999. *Iftar* dinners, dialogue award ceremonies, academic conferences, and (until recently) subsidized trips to Turkey helped to build bridges across communities and cultures, and cemented new friends for Hizmet (full disclosure—my wife, Lisa, and I celebrated our 30th wedding anniversary in Istanbul in 2012 as part of a tour set up by Philadelphia Dialogue Forum). It was clear to me, at least, that there were no expectations of participants on these tours. Gülen's adage—to do good things without expecting any return—was the prevailing motif. Naturally, we were offered some of Gülen's books to read, and conversation about Gülen was welcome at any of the many stops on our tour (we began in Istanbul and then went to Izmir, Bergama, Cappadocia, Konya, and then back to The City). I obviously continued to be in contact with my new friends, but most of those who were in our tour group had no further contact with Hizmet upon returning to the U.S. There were no efforts to "call in" debts of any kind.

One of the agencies in the U.S. that sponsored events and tours, and the longest-running of the Hizmet dialogue organizations in America, was Rumi Forum. Rumi Forum was founded in 1999, and has headquarters in Washington, DC, and chapters in Virginia, Maryland, Delaware, Kentucky, and North Carolina. Three Turkish men have led Rumi Forum—Zeki Sarıtoprak, Ali Yurtsever, and Emre Çelik (Emre is actually an Australian citizen of Turkish descent)—but Jena Luedtke brought a U.S. woman's perspective as a Director within the agency.[114] Finally, in regard to social businesses—Turkish entrepreneurs have set up, in addition to a variety of for-profit companies (restaurants, furniture-supply stores, marble and tile works, construction), the non-profit "Embrace Relief." Embrace Relief is basically a U.S. version of Kimse Yok Mu. In 2017 the agency provided direct aid and raised funds for Hurricane relief in Houston (where there is a large Turkish community), and Puerto Rico (where there is not). Embrace Relief efforts elsewhere continue, for instance, in Haiti.[115]

What did Fethullah Gülen have to do with all this activity in the U.S. by people inspired by him? In most cases, the answer to that question is likely "next to nothing." Even more—what did Gülen think of his new home? The poem with which we opened this chapter suggests one answer: he missed Turkey. But Gülen also saw much to admire in his new country. "Modern liberal democracy was born in the American (1776) and French (1789-99) Revolutions," he wrote. "In democratic societies," he explained the obvious, "people govern themselves as opposed to being ruled by someone above. The individual has priority over the community in this type of political system." Democracy accorded well with Gülen's emphasis on reform through individual positive action. Consequently, Gülen articulated a set of principles that came very close to those of his new land, albeit hardly as a party-line position. That set of principles had six points. And it came, Gülen claimed, directly from Islam:

1. Power lies in truth, a repudiation of the common idea that truth relies upon power
2. Justice and the rule of law are essential.
3. Freedom of belief and rights to life, personal property, reproduction, and health (both mental and physical) cannot be violated.
4. The privacy and immunity of individual life must be maintained.
5. No one can be convicted of a crime without evidence, or accused and punished for someone else's crime.
6. An advisory [consultative] system of administration is essential.[116]

İstişare or mutual consultation was the heart of democracy, after all, and therefore democracy was Islamic. Gülen appreciated the system of government in his new homeland.

He also wrote in a way that tried to represent Muslims well in American society. After the terrorist attacks of September 11, 2001, Gülen was among the first Muslim leaders to condemn them. Writing in Zaman on September 12—the day after the airplanes hit two of their targets, and shortly after in the Washington Post, Gülen said:

> I would like to make it very clear that any terrorist activity, no matter by whom it is carried out or for what purpose, is the greatest blow to peace, democracy, and humanity. For this reason, no one—and certainly no Muslim—can approve of any terrorist activity. Terror has no place in a quest to achieve independence or salvation. It takes the lives of innocent people. ...
>
> Please let me reassure you that Islam does not approve of terrorism in any form. Terrorism cannot be used to achieve any Islamic goal. No terrorist can be a Muslim, and no true Muslim can be a terrorist. Islam demands peace, and the Qur'an demands that every true Muslim be a symbol of peace and work to support the maintenance of basic human rights. ...
>
> Islam respects all individual rights and states clearly that none of these can be violated, even if doing so would be in the interest of the community. The Qur'an declares that one who takes a life unjustly has, in effect, taken all the lives of humanity, and that one who saves a life has, in effect, saved all the lives of humanity. Moreover, Prophet Muhammad stated that a Muslim is a person who does no harm with either the hands or with the tongue.
>
> I strongly condemn this latest terrorist attack on the United States. ... I feel the pain of the American people from the bottom of my heart, and I assure them that I pray to God Almighty for the victims and I pray that He give their loved-ones and all other Americans the necessary patience to endure their pain. [in Zaman newspaper][117]

***

We condemn in the strongest of terms the latest terrorist attack on the United States of America, and feel the pain of the American people at the bottom of our hearts.

Islam abhors such acts of terror. A religion that professes, "He who unjustly kills one man kills the whole of humanity," cannot condone senseless killing of thousands.

Our thoughts and prayers go out to the victims and their loved ones. [in *Washington Post*]

These would not, unfortunately, be Gülen's last statements of empathy with the citizens of his new homeland after a terrorist attack or mass trauma.

Yet, as his poem on exile made plain, Gülen did not uncritically accept the country he had chosen to live in. Thus, in an interview with journalist Nevval Sevindi, Gülen acknowledged to her that "the United States occupies the dominant position in the balance of power among the nations." But this dominance was contingent. "The continuation of this dominance depends on the maintenance of justice and equity," he said. Gülen then went on to develop a metaphor, and to issue a warning:

The wheels of this system seem to be revolving pretty well in America. However, just as every day has a night, and every spring and summer have a winter, if this system leads to a blunting of values, if America, the world champion of values such as democracy, human rights, and liberties, fails to maintain these values and does not continue to base the dominion given to it by fate on principles of equity and justice, it will be inevitable that its day will also turn into night, and its summer will be followed by winter. ... No system based on power can stand for very long. Power that is not based on equity and justice deviates into oppression, and thus prepares its own ending.[118]

This warning was not, of course, a message only to Americans. It was a general rule, drawn from Islamic theology, for political regimes generally.

Which meant that given ongoing authoritarian rule in Turkey—a likely if not certain prospect in 2019, the immediate future of Hizmet was elsewhere. If Hizmet was to survive, it would be in places like Australia, Europe, Canada, and the U.S., where open societies had institutionalized something like *istişare*, and where robust traditions of dissent, debate and mutual consultation had existed to create opportunities for "outsiders." That Gülen had come to the United States in 1999 was, at some level, a coincidence. There were friends in the U.S. who had a place for him. But he also could have gone to Brussels, or to London, or to Sydney or to Berlin. Gülen's final decades, in any event, became a foreshadowing of the fate of many of the thousands of women and men who were inspired by him. Living in exile, they could join Hodjaefendi's lament for those "blue days" of an Istanbul summer. But they also went to work to put into action *istişare* as a basic Islamic, and democratic, practice, wherever they happened to be. If being with the oppressed was the same as being with God, then Fethullah Gülen and the people of Hizmet would soon have a direct channel to the divine, as they experienced ruthless oppression from the Turkish government in the second decade of the twenty-first century.

Oppression (again), the end of a life, and hope for the future

In a 1990s sermon, delivered no doubt in response to political oppression, Fethullah Gülen once preached:

> We made a promise to God. We got onto the stony road. We will not turn back. If we turn back, we're traitors. Let this be our song. That's when the distances will be nothing. That's when the roads will be paved. That's when the bridges that cannot be crossed, will be crossed. That's when those mountains and hills will bow their heads and say, 'go on, continue!' They will be made low." And even if we have a disloyal fate and disloyal friends; and even if we feel the hatred of superpowers ... we have made a promise. We're not turning back.[119]

Such conviction did not come from political vision alone. It came from religious faith.

That faith, deepened by constant study, formed the way Fethullah Gülen saw and interacted with the world. To reduce his life to politics would be to miss its central dynamic. At times, his faith led him to utter severe, even apocalyptic, judgments. Often, in fact, Gülen's use of apocalyptic judgement was directed at efforts to reduce life to mere material matters: "In my opinion," he said in a talk in 2004, shortly after an earthquake rocked Indonesia and spurred a massive tsunami:

> If there is a greater disaster on earth than floods, earthquakes, and fires, it is people being engrossed in heedlessness and ... not discerning

the importance of their relationship with their Creator. Sooner or later the sun will definitely fold up. The stars will darken and fall. The seas will boil. Spirits will be united with their bodies. The records of deeds will open up. The sky will fall. Hell will blaze. Heaven will come close. Everyone will see what they have put forth. All of this will happen. It is inevitable. Are you prepared for this?[120]

Religious demagogues sometimes used similar reasoning to stir violence against one enemy or another, or to manipulate vulnerable listeners into facile commitments.

But Gülen's aim was loftier. His critique was spiritual. In it, politics was a decidedly ancillary pursuit:

Modern man [the original Turkish word is *insan*, which means "human"], who spends his energies in pursuit of transient material advantages, is wasting himself and all the nobler, truly human feelings in the depths of his being. It is no longer possible to find among his resources either the serenity that comes from belief, or the tolerance and depth of spirit enabled by knowledge of God, or the traces of love and spiritual joys. This is so because he weighs everything on the scales of material advantage, immediate comfort and the gratification of bodily appetites, and thinks about only how he can increase his profit or what he will buy and sell, and where and how he will amuse himself. If he is unable to satisfy his appetites through lawful means, he rarely hesitates to resort to unlawful means, however degraded and degrading.[121]

Such men may even have claimed to be pious. Such men may even have appeared frequently at Friday prayers. They were nevertheless, as Gülen depicted them, "modern Neros." The imagery he used to describe these "modern Neros" was as vivid as it was disturbing:

There are those who, while charged with healing the ills of the nation, have been too long habituated to preying on others, and sniff about for blood to drink, [and] dry the nation's veins. There are those compelled to silence in the face of every disaster. ... I watch and wonder, in profound distress, amid enraged, embittered tears.[122]

Blood-sucking vampires would masquerade as national healers. This was an apocalyptic vision; a vision of the end. But it was also a commentary on political developments in contemporary Turkey. When asked, then, about his opinion on developments in Turkey since 2010, and the government's slide into authoritarianism, Fethullah Gülen's first words were simply: "I have of course been very saddened."[123]

Contemporary history, which for some historians is anything within the past century, is tricky business. Events that are still unfolding make cause and effect, continuity and discontinuity, unclear. Most historical writing depends upon drawing trajectories of significance that only become clear with hindsight. Winners, losers, survivors, victims, heroes, and villains only become discernible as time passes. Something like a recognition of this reality is evident in Gülen's thought, although he constantly pushed to a longer horizon:

> We are about to live a new spring. The earth is pregnant with trickles of water, seeds move with germinating life, as also do snakes with poison. We shall see who is on the side of the spring and who of winter. Who will go after bargains and who will dive deep to search for [pearls]. Who will boast about their easy-to-lose possessions and who will go beyond themselves and the world, attaining to eternity. We all shall see. We shall see who will melt away like wax in the face of the transforming power of the world, and who can change the turning of this pitiless wheel. ... Time will show which of us shall be victorious in his struggle.[124]

Time, in this passage, and in the thought of Fethullah Gülen, was not merely the passing of individual lives, or even of political regimes. Gülen's language here intentionally evoked an original garden. In that garden, Prophet Adam struggled with a poisonous snake. All human struggle was connected to that struggle. The string of causes and effects playing itself out in this matter of Time was long.

So, to focus on events in Turkey in recent years, and Fethullah Gülen's role as cause, effect, villain, hero, winner or loser—would be to reduce the meaning and significance of his life to something like wax; ephemeral relations with a paltry kind of power. Still, of course Gülen had things to say about the Ergenekon and Sledgehammer Trials from 2008-2011. Those trials in effect defanged the Turkish military, and they allowed apparently devout Muslims to support an apparently democratic Prime Minister Erdoğan. And, of course Gülen had comments to make on the Mavi Marmara or Gaza Flotilla incident in 2010—in ways that enraged the Prime Minister and triggered anti-Semitic outbursts against Gülen. And, of course, Gülen felt compelled to speak about the Gezi Park protests in June 2013, especially after the Prime Minister ordered to violently suppress the spontaneous, even anarchic, outbursts of protest against the Prime Minister's plans to build a shopping mall on some of the last green space in center city Istanbul. And, naturally, Gülen had comments to make about the corruption inquiry that exposed malfeasance and greed among Erdoğan's sons and close associates, in December 2013. And, finally, Gülen of course spoke out about the claim—widely repeated as if fact, despite no evidence to support it—that he also orchestrated a failed coup on July 15, 2016. But more often than these public pronouncements about political oppression—at which we must briefly look, Fethullah Gülen prayed, and preached, and taught, and engaged in consultations. Throughout, he sought to encourage people inspired by him to live by hope. He urged them to link science and faith in educating future generations. He implored them to work to end poverty by promoting justice and supporting social businesses. And he recommended that they gravitate to friends on islands of peace around the world, where through dialogue they might experience at least glimpses of a unity that pointed toward an eternal paradise.

Between 2008 and 2016, the Turkish military—the second largest force in NATO—and long the upholder of the secular establishment that Atatürk constructed, was by and large neutered as a force in Turkish political life. In many ways, given the history of repeated coups, this was a salutary and necessary development. Through a series of trials, the military was brought to heel at the rule of law. The trials were called Ergenekon and Sledgehammer, which were the names of plots through which military officers and affiliated civilians had conducted clandestine criminal operations against religious and ethnic minorities, and allegedly conspired to overthrow the AKP government. A few hundred individuals were charged and brought to trial through Ergenekon and Sledgehammer prosecutions. Most were found guilty and imprisoned. Many of them were aging military officers. The trials riveted Turks, who saw clearly that the wheel of time was turning. To many Turks, the trials confirmed that there had existed within the democratically-elected government a conspiratorial "deep state" tied to the military that tried to pull the strings of political puppets. As the trials proceeded, observers both inside and outside Turkey began raising questions about the quality of evidence against the coup plotters, and the way the evidence had been secured (e.g., through wiretaps). When the guilty verdicts were reached, some speculated that Gülen—through judges and police beholden to him—had been the "mastermind" behind the entire operation. Clearly, Gülen had been harmed by the military in the past. Clearly, Gülen was not a fan of rigid secularism. Clearly, then, he must have taken these means to bring the military and fellow-travelers into submission.[125]

Except, there was no evidence of Gülen's involvement. His public statements directly denied the rumors of his involvement. And to have been involved in such political intrigue—supposedly conducted from rural America—would run counter to the main trajectory of his life and thought. As he put it after the fact, and after he had been rumored to be the "mastermind" behind many more supposed plots: "If [people] are looking for a mastermind of the Hizmet movement, I would say it is the solidarity and protection that God bestows on consultation. ... The Hizmet movement does not depend on any fading and mortal power or actor; it has made advances because God has been graceful."[126] This was not just pious rhetoric with a touch of satire; as the previous sections of this chapter showed, it was also accurate history; consultation *was* crucial to the movement's success. Even more, indisputably, Ergenekon and Sledgehammer were *government* projects with political aims. They were conducted through the judiciary, with the approval of the Executive and Legislative branches. Those in charge of those branches, one would think, rather than an imam residing in Pennsylvania, would be the ones most likely to be responsible for the actions of those under their jurisdiction. Any other hypothesis would need rather overwhelming evidence to secure it. According to Gülen, then, accusations that Hizmet was behind Ergenekon and Sledgehammer were ploys. Government officials scapegoated Hizmet to shield themselves from the public opprobrium that the trials might have roused (the military was still popular), *and* the officials scapegoated Gülen to maintain support for their governing among those in the military who were *not* accused as coup plotters and continued to serve. "Those [government officials] who boasted behind closed doors," Gülen wrote, "about 'making the military submit to civilians,' or 'putting an end to military tutelage,'" when they got out from behind closed doors, "told the military authorities 'We would iron out this problem, but the Hizmet Movement is preventing it.'"[127] That would hardly, alas, have been the first time that politicians had said different things to different audiences.

Gülen's own public statement about the trials was that if there were crimes committed by military officials, they should be held accountable. But he also left open the door for clemency, and compassion:

> My friends have witnessed numerous times my eyes filled with tears, seeing how those retired military officers were detained. "If only the people who wear this honorable uniform had not been faced with this situation," I had said. But I am in no position to meddle with the laws in force or make any suggestion in this context. A coup is a serious accusation and judicial authorities are supposed to, in accordance with the rules that govern them, hold those responsible accountable. But perhaps a legal remedy could have been found while taking into consideration the ages or medical condition of those people advanced in age and used to being treated with respect all their lives. This is how I feel. It has always been so. It really runs counter to the facts to say that it is the Hizmet Movement that put them in that position.[128]

Succinctly, "they [the government] attempted to blame the movement for what they actually did."[129] Erdoğan admitted as much: "I am the prosecutor of these trials," he said. He even gave the actual prosecutors armed vehicles to protect them going to and from the courthouse.[130]

Nevertheless, a narrative had emerged within Turkey that worked both to mollify public opinion and to tame the military: blame Hizmet. "The emerging trend of our time is to attribute every inexplicable event to the Hizmet Movement and use it as a scapegoat," offered Gülen. According to many, including some who should have known better, "Gülenists" had generated a "deep state." They had "infiltrated" the police, judiciary, or military, where they conspired to take over Turkish politics. What this convenient reduction omitted was that the people inspired by Gülen had also "infiltrated" furniture manufacturing, textiles, electronics, banking—and, of course, education, publishing, television, healthcare, and relief work. The language of "infiltration," repeated by journalists over and over, like the language of a "compound" to describe Gülen's retreat center, reflected intellectual laziness. It was inherently biased. "Infiltration" suggested some clandestine or nefarious intent—actual evidence of which has never been produced, and will never be produced, unless I have completely misread the historical record.

In fact, people of Hizmet generally went where the jobs were and where their skills were valued—as do most people in the world. And, yes, they participated in politically-connected roles—as police, judges, soldiers, even members of Parliament. But they did so as individuals who had been encouraged by Gülen to use their own reasoning and expert skills. That they were also connected and accountable to others in an ethically-driven community through *istişare* ought to have been a good thing, in balance, because that community explicitly and intentionally was dedicated to the rule of law, to justice and human rights, and to serving the community. Even more, given that people of Hizmet had, like members of other Muslim or minority groups in Turkey, been *persecuted* by the police, judiciary, and military for decades, it should hardly be surprising that some people inspired by Gülen sought to participate in and to reform those agencies that had oppressed them. That is, after all, how democracy is supposed to work. People participate, or democracy perishes. At one point, the conspiracy-theorizing veered onto truly sacred ground among the Turkish public. Rumors circulated that people close to Gülen were plotting to take over Fenerbahçe—one of Turkey's most popular football (soccer) teams. There was nothing to the rumors—and Gülen somewhat cheekily offered that while he liked Fenerbahçe, he also had enjoyed it when team Galatasaray saw success in the European Championships, and he also hoped that Beşiktaş, Trabzonspor and "the country's other teams are very successful." [131] Perhaps he was a politician.

More seriously, though, in 2010 an incident occurred that deepened the government's hostility to Gülen and Hizmet. On May 27, 2010, a humanitarian flotilla of six ships carrying food and medical supplies sailed from Turkey to the Gaza Strip of Palestine. At the time, Israel was blockading Gaza in retaliation for missile attacks. As the lead ship, the Mavi Marmara approached Gaza on May 31, Israeli commandoes boarded it, and engaged in a battle that led to ten Turkish deaths. The outcry in Turkey was considerable; diplomatic relations were suspended, and direct military confrontation loomed. [132] "The time has come for Israel to pay for its stance that sees it as above international laws and disregards human conscience," Foreign Minister Ahmet Davutoğlu said. "The first and foremost result is that Israel is going to be devoid of Turkey's friendship."[133] Gülen did not agree with this umbrage. In a story first published in the *Wall Street Journal*, Gülen simply called the Mavi Marmara confrontation, video of which he had seen on TV, "ugly."[134] He questioned the legality of the flotilla. Those who had organized such a direct confrontation with Israel showed "a sign of defying authority." And he speculated that the confrontation "will not lead to fruitful matters." Even more directly, and with a strong dose of common sense, he argued that "if you want to take aid supplies to a country, you should seek accordance with the authorities in that country." Such a recommendation was consistent with Gülen's long support for governmental sovereignty and his oft-stated desire for peace. Whatever the humanitarian need—and it was considerable in Gaza—such provocations could lead to war. And, finally, consistent with his public stance as an advocate for dialogue, Hodjaefendi worried that the incident would harm relations between Muslims and Jews, and, indirectly, harm relations between Turkey and the U.S.[135]

What resulted in the ensuing media firestorm was predictable, given the Islamist tilt of the Turkish regime, and given the deep hostility to Israel within the Turkish populace. Journalists, citizens, and politicians simplified Gülen's nuanced position to say that the imam had "sided with Israel." Prime Minister Erdoğan, especially, was not pleased. He said, about Gülen's statement that the flotilla organizers should have checked with the authorities first: "What was he saying? 'They didn't get permission from authority.' Who is [the] authority? Is it the ones they love in the South [i.e., the Jews] or us? If we are the authority, then we have already given permission. But [the authority] is Israel for them."[136] Many Turks repeated this anti-Semitic slur on social media and in print, where Gülen was excoriated as a "Zionist," or even as a pawn of the Israeli intelligence agency, Mossad.[137] Not surprisingly, even some within the Hizmet movement were uneasy with and/or disagreed with Gülen's comments. Gülen, however, did not back down or retract his stance.[138] The general principle he invoked was that "it is impossible to deal with illegality by relying on illegal means."[139]

However principled Gülen might have been, opposition to Hizmet was gaining populist strength. In an insightful and prescient 2010 column, journalist Mehmet Ali Birand, an outsider to Hizmet, foresaw how "a new myth was being created for Turkey—the myth of Hizmet power." As Birand saw it, Gülen's influence was exaggerated beyond its real dimensions. This was a danger to Gülen, it was a danger to people close to Gülen, and it was a danger to Turkey. Conspiracies about Hizmet influence in politics leaned toward the accusatory: "Every development in Turkey is attributed to the movement ... Ergenekon, Sledgehammer, etc. ... They seem to be found under every rock." This contradicted the facts, Birand contended, and constituted no more than rumor and legend—although powerful people were "pumping these accusations." Birand admitted that Gülen's influence had grown from 1970-2010, and that the movement "did successful work." But he also saw that in effect the movement had become "the prisoner of its own myth of power," even if Gülen and people in the movement had not been the ones to generate that myth. And Birand foresaw danger that people in the movement did not. His column was a warning, by one from the outside who at least did "not dislike the Hizmet movement." "They don't seem to know," Birand said about Gülen and people of Hizmet, "just how dangerous this myth has become."[140]

The Prime Minister knew, since he had largely created the myth, and he exploited it in the wake of yet another conflict, namely the Gezi Park protests of June, 2013. As is well-known, beginning on May 27, 2013, young people (mostly) gathered in Gezi Park in Istanbul to protest a planned shopping mall for the park. The development would have removed one of the few green spaces left in Istanbul's center city. When riot police tried to squash the protest with tear gas and water cannons, it instead escalated over the next few days from a small group of a few hundred to gatherings with thousands, not only in Istanbul but in cities all over Turkey. Over the same time, the protestors' grievances widened to include recent curbs on press freedoms, restrictions on internet access, restrictions on alcohol sales, and (especially) police brutality and the increasingly authoritarian turn in Erdoğan's government. Protestors occupied the park, lived in tents, and—in a helpful summary of the groups involved—setup zones for "Communists, Anarchists, Socialists, Nationalists, LGBT, Green, Kurdish, Muslim, and Football" to camp out (prominent players on several teams expressed their support for the protests). Conflict with police oscillated back and forth for well over a month, mostly in Istanbul, but also in other Turkish cities. Prime Minister Erdoğan ridiculed the protestors as "bandits" or "looters" (çapulcu) and refused to negotiate with them. Eleven protestors died, most from cerebral hemorrhage after being hit by tear gas canisters. One of them, a 14-year old boy, named Berkin Elvan, became somewhat of a *cause celebré* as he lay in a coma for nearly a year. Thousands were injured. The hashtag #occupyGezi linked the protest to similar mass movements happening in U.S. and European cities.[141]

Gülen's comments were not extensive, but supported the protestors' rights to assemble, to speak their minds, and to advocate for causes. Gülen tried to avoid partisanship, while also defending the human rights he had supported his entire life. The government's brutal reaction to the protests, Gülen contended, had escalated "rancor and hatred." Instead of sending riot police, the Prime Minister should have consulted (surprise!) with the protestors, or at least "not disregard them" and call them names.[142] The Prime Minister, naturally, did not take kindly to these suggestions. He began ranting against Gülen and Hizmet, claiming they had masterminded the protests, and eventually resorting to calling Gülen and those inspired by him "perverts," "hashashins," "traitors," "spies," "worse than Shiites," "leeches," and more.[143] Still, in an interview after the protests had settled somewhat, Gülen contended that

> This is not a row between the AK Party and the Hizmet Movement. There has been a serious regression in fundamental rights and freedoms over the last few years. The offensive and subversive language used by politicians is making every social segment into "the other" and polarizing society. .... [Thus], I raised my objection to the description of protestors as *çapulcu* (bandits). ... Yet, we are not and will not be a political party. Therefore, we are not the rival of any political party. We stand at an equal distance to everyone. Nevertheless, we make public our hopes and concerns about the future of our country. I think this is one of our most natural and democratic rights. I don't understand why some people do not like us enjoying this democratic right of ours. Telling people at the helm of the country "I have such and such ideas" should not be a crime. In advanced democracies, individuals and civil society organizations freely disseminate their views and criticisms about the country's political issues, and no one expresses any concern about this.[144]

Expressing this hope did not, however, heal relations between Hizmet and the Erdoğan regime.

In December, 2013, things suddenly turned much worse. A corruption inquiry—alleging rigged bids for state-driven contracts, kickbacks, bribery, and money laundering, led to the arrest on December 17 of dozens of individuals, including the sons of three ministers in Erdoğan's government. Among those indicted was Süleyman Aslan, the director of state-owned Halkbank, and Iranian-Turkish businessman Reza Zarrab.[145] All of the other individuals who were arrested had close links to Erdoğan's AKP government. The arrests seemed to take the Prime Minister by surprise, but the next day he started the sacking of people that would go on for years to come. He did not, however, fire the officials implicated in corruption—although some did resign. Instead, he labeled the investigation a "dirty operation," and fired the police, judges, and bureaucrats who had instigated and carried out the investigation and indictments. A few voices of protest arose. As reported in *The Guardian*, "the deputy chairman of the Nationalist Movement party (MHP), Oktay Vural, called the move a 'blow against the rule of law.' He added: 'Nobody will be able to cover up this shame. Let public officials do their job.'" Similarly, the leader of the pro-Kurdish Peace and Democracy party (BDP), Selahattin Demirtaş, called the sackings "'an intervention into the corruption investigation.'"[146] Not surprisingly, for accusing the Prime Minister of obstructing justice, in due course Demirtaş himself would be jailed by Erdoğan as a "terrorist." A second wave of indictments on December 25, 2013, implicated Erdoğan's own sons, Bilal and Burak. But the indictments were never acted on. The police and prosecutors involved were sacked. The investigation ground to a halt, only to be revived in U.S. courts in 2016. There, Reza Zarrab arranged a plea deal in exchange for a lesser sentence on a guilty plea, and Hakan Atilla, an official at Halkbank, was also found guilty. Hundreds of hours of leaked phone transcripts implicated Erdoğan in the case, which documented how Turkey used gold-trading to circumvent U.N. sanctions against Iran. The trading enriched Zarrab and his associates, and, as it turns out, enriched Erdoğan and his family members.[147] In the wake of the trial, the *Washington Examiner* suggested that Erdoğan "may be the most corrupt leader Turkey has ever had," which is saying something. What was fact, in any event, was that a NATO ally had intentionally undermined U.S.

interests and circumvented U.N. resolutions.[148] Turkey was becoming a rogue state.

Naturally, given how effectively the tactic had worked in the Ergenekon and Sledgehammer trials, Erdoğan blamed Hizmet and Gülen for having "masterminded" the corruption inquiries. It was right out of the Putin playbook, as described by journalist Melik Kaylan: a strategic deployment of "designated bogeys, waves of conspiracies, timed distractions, confused citizens, politicized state institutions, pyramidized economies run by oligarchs."[149] Gülen replied with exasperation:

> Some people and groups persistently continue to hurl unfounded accusations at the Hizmet Movement, although we have issued numerous denials, explanations and corrections. As I have noted previously, some prosecutors and judicial police serving under them performed the duties required of them by law, but they apparently did not know that it was a crime to hunt down criminals! ... [And then] the officials who conducted the December 17 probe and thousands of officials who had nothing to do with the probe were sent to exile and reassigned. They were victimized and the rights of their families were violated. And then, as if nothing had happened, some people started to accuse the Hizmet Movement. ... I have said this before. I have no connection to those who organized these operations. I have repeatedly stated that I do not know any of them, but they [the government and its press] continue to claim that those prosecutors and police officers are linked to me. ... [And then] Turkey launched a crackdown on those who investigated the corruption instead of on those who engaged in corrupt practices.[150]

It was like something out of Kafka, or Orwell, or 1930s Russia.

Gülen, again, tried to set the political machinations in a broader horizon of justice. It was not just this life that was at stake:

> If there are acts of bribery, theft, clientelism, bid rigging, etc., which run contrary to the interests of the nation, and if these acts are covered up, God will hold us accountable for them. But it appears that some people nurtured certain expectations.... If among those who conducted the graft investigations were some people who might be connected to the Hizmet Movement, was I supposed to tell these people, "Turn a blind eye to the corruption charges?" It appears to me that some

people were expecting me to do this. ... How can I say something that would ruin my afterlife? How else can I act? ... I have been preaching for about 60 years. I have always said the same thing. Let this be my legacy. Let my brothers and sisters who have sympathy for me—though I do not deserve it—distance themselves miles away from such corrupt practices and let them not turn a blind eye to such practices. Let them do whatever they are supposed to under the law.[151]

Gülen was right that he had, in fact, preached for about 60 years—leaving a rather clear record of public statements in support of the rule of law. What he did not say about his legacy was that it was demonstrated not only by his words, but in the lives of those non-violent teachers, entrepreneurs, and community organizers around the globe who had been inspired by him.

And it was not as if persecution was something new to him. He had experienced oppression before, and he had never reacted by getting enmeshed in political intrigue. Why would he react that way now, contradicting his entire life's work, as if he had somehow become intoxicated with power (from his retreat in Pennsylvania) and decided to meddle in Turkish politics? "We have gone through these kind of things many times," he recalled:

I was sentenced to six-and-a-half months in prison on the charge of "penetrating the state apparatus" at the time of the March 12, 1971 military memorandum. ... [Then] in the wake of the Sept. 12, 1980 military coup, the authorities tracked me for six years as if I were a criminal. Raids were carried out. Our friends were harassed. In a sense, it became a sort of lifestyle for us to live under constant surveillance in a coup atmosphere. What we are seeing today is 10 times worse than what we saw during the military coups. But despite everything, I don't complain. This time, we face similar treatment but at the hands of civilians who we think follow the same faith as us. I should acknowledge that this inflicts extra pain on us. All we can do is say, "This, too, shall pass," and remain patient.[152]

In the face of persecution, the message was not to hit back, but to keep the faith. "Return their bad actions with goodness," he had always preached. "Do not cease doing good even to those who have harmed you.... Repaying evil with evil implies a deficiency in character; the opposite is nobility."[153]

Gülen may have sought nobility, but Erdoğan was out for blood. Even prior to the graft investigations, he had threatened to shut down all prep schools, the *dershane*s such as FEM, through which Hizmet did outreach. In February 2014 he acted on his threats. As Gülen read this move, which not only targeted Hizmet-related, but all prep schools in Turkey, it was an attempt at "blackmail." Erdoğan hoped that Gülen would fall into line and be complicit with, or at least silent about, his broader power grabs and corruption. The *dershane* shutdown was a warning-shot across the Hizmet bow; a threat to its most public institutions. Gülen did not play that game. "It has now become crystal clear," he said in an interview in early 2014,

> that the plan to close the prep schools is not justified in terms of improvements to the education system. The obvious intention is to block the Hizmet Movement's educational activities. "Do not send your children to their schools and prep schools," we can hear being said at election rallies of the ruling party. In other words, the government's intention is to start with the prep school and proceed with the schools. Then they will try to ensure that the Hizmet Movement's schools abroad are shut down.[154]

That is, in fact, the scenario that developed. And it cost thousands of livelihoods, billions in assets, and damage to countless children's futures.

And then came July 15, 2016. It was called a "failed coup." There certainly was mobilization of some (incompetent) kind among some small percentage of the military. And there was also corresponding loss of life, after the Prime Minister urged citizens into the streets. And guess who drew the blame for both the "failed coup" and the lives lost? In fact, Gülen had faced a similar charge in 1997—when he was actually in Turkey, with connections to politicians, and with everyday contact with people on the ground. In that year, the so-called "Coup by Memorandum" removed the government of Necmettin Erbakan; the first "Islamist" Prime Minister in Turkey, and a mentor of Erdoğan. Gülen was on record prior to the coup recommending the government resign and hold new elections. Those who wanted to link him to the July 2016 event pointed to this prior political entanglement as evidence that he must have been "behind" the latest political intrigue. Gülen explained that he had in fact tried to warn people in government about a coming coup in 1997. "I explained to the then-Labor Minister Necati Çelik the coup atmosphere that was forming in the country at the time. Alaattin Kaya (the former owner of *Zaman* daily) and Melih Nural (a member of the Board of Trustees of Turgut Özal University), were with us during that meeting. 'They are planning to get rid of the government,' I said." No action was taken by the Erbakan government. Around the same time, Gülen also went with his concerns to former Prime Minister Tansu Çiller. She also did not take action. So, "having realized that I could not explain the danger to anyone, I was urged to say something to avert an incident that would lead to a possible coup. ... I worked hard to avert any anti-democratic development." Nevertheless, the military took charge of the government, and "the Hizmet movement was one of the main targets of the *junta*. ... Any claim to the contrary would be unfair and misguided."[155] But the narrative was out that Gülen had "sponsored" the successful 1997 coup, and (therefore) had sponsored this failed coup in 2016, as well.

It all somewhat beggared belief. Gülen had been hurt by coups before. He had opposed violence his entire life. He lived in Pennsylvania. Is it really imaginable that he would have orchestrated a violent coup, now? As theologian Philip Clayton put it:

> It would require a massive conspiracy theory to connect Gülen with the gun-carrying rebels. For example, one would have to say that all of Gülen's teachings ... were merely a hypocritical pretense. All his claims that violence is never justified in the name of religion were merely a way to mislead opponents while Gülen orchestrated violent political actions aimed at putting him and his followers in charge of the Turkish government. He only preached peace because he really wanted war. It doesn't make sense.[156]

What does make sense is that the Erdoğan regime, which almost daily since 2012 has demonstrated its ruthless, corrupt, and violent tendencies, saw in scapegoating Gülen a trope that worked, and exploited it. The details historians with more distance from the fray will have to sort out. Clayton, though, asks a poignant general question that is perhaps appropriate here: "Why do the most violent people in the world accuse the most peaceful of violence?"[157]

As for Gülen himself, from his retreat center in Pennsylvania, he penned an op-ed column in *The New York Times*, published on July 26, 2016, where he wrote:

> During the attempted military coup in Turkey this month, I condemned it [in Turkish] in the strongest terms. "Government should be won through a process of free and fair elections, not force," I said. "I pray to God for Turkey, for Turkish citizens, and for all those currently in Turkey that this situation is resolved peacefully and quickly."
>
> Despite my unequivocal protest, similar to statements issued by all three of the major opposition parties, Turkey's increasingly authoritarian president, Recep Tayyip Erdoğan, immediately accused me of orchestrating the putsch. He demanded that the United States extradite me from my home in Pennsylvania, where I have lived in voluntary exile since 1999.
>
> Not only does Mr. Erdoğan's suggestion run afoul of everything I believe in, it is also irresponsible and wrong.
>
> My philosophy—inclusive and pluralist Islam, dedicated to service to human beings from every faith—is antithetical to armed rebellion. For more than 40 years, the participants in the movement that I am associated with—called Hizmet, the Turkish word for "service"—have advocated for, and demonstrated their commitment to, a form of government that derives its legitimacy from the will of the people and that respects the rights of all citizens regardless of their religious views, political affiliations or ethnic origins. Entrepreneurs and volunteers inspired by Hizmet's values have invested in modern education and community service in more than 150 countries.
>
> At a time when Western democracies are searching for moderate Muslim voices, I and my friends in the Hizmet movement have taken a clear stance against extremist violence, from the Sept. 11 attacks by Al Qaeda to brutal executions by the Islamic State to the kidnappings by Boko Haram. ...
>
> Throughout my life, I have publicly and privately denounced military interventions in domestic politics. In fact, I have been advocating for democracy for decades. Having suffered through four military

coups in Turkey in four decades—and having been subjected by those
military regimes to harassment and wrongful imprisonment—I would
never want my fellow citizens to endure such an ordeal again. If somebody who appears to be a Hizmet supporter has been involved in an
attempted coup, he betrays my ideals.[158]

Despite such statements, there were those in the U.S. press and
around the world who "bought" and amplified the Erdoğan government's narrative.[159] As for Erdoğan himself, within hours he declared the
coup "a gift from God."[160] At the least, it is worth pointing out that by this
statement Erdoğan revealed that his God was a god of violence. A year
later, at a massive rally to mark the anniversary of his "gift from God,"
Erdoğan made plain just how deep his devotion to this devouring deity
went: "We will rip off the heads of those traitors," he screamed from his
lectern in Istanbul.[161]

Meanwhile, Gülen, writing in *The Washington Post*, lamented a
"Turkey I no longer know." "The Turkey that I once knew as a hope-in-
spiring country on its way to consolidating its democracy and a moderate
form of secularism has become the dominion of a president who is doing
everything he can to amass power and subjugate dissent." The facts here
supported Gülen. The day after the coup, "the government produced lists
of thousands of individuals whom they tied to Hizmet." The ties could
be merely circumstantial. People were fired "for having a bank account
[at Bank Asya], [for] teaching at a school or reporting for a newspaper,
for making donations to Kimse Yok Mu." The most simple affiliations
by people were considered crimes, and the government began system-
atically "destroying their lives. The lists included people who had been
dead for months and people who had been serving at NATO's European
headquarters at the time."[162] All told, from July 2016 to March 2018 (the
numbers have since increased, since the oppression has continued), the
Erdogan regime fired by state decree: 151,000 state officials, including
teachers, managers, police officers, including over 4,000 judges and public prosecutors and 5,800 academics. The government also detained over
217,971 Turkish citizens, and arrested 82,000, including 319 journalists.
All told, 3,003 schools, dormitories, tutoring centers, and universities
were closed, along with 189 media outlets—including newspapers, magazines, television and radio stations.[163] These numbers are numbing. But

they point to a purge of Stalinist proportions, albeit with a post-modern, post-truth patina (for instance, Erdoğan once claimed that he had only jailed "two" journalists).[164] Meanwhile, many of the Hizmet dormitories, and tutoring centers, now were "re-opened" either as AKP headquarters, or were operated under the auspices of an agency called Türgev (the full name was *Türkiye Gençlik ve Eğitime Hizmet Vakfı*, "Turkey Youth and Educational Services Foundation.)" Both Erdoğan's son, Bilal, and daughter Esra Albayrak, were on the Türgev national Board of Directors.[165] And the President himself had moved into his new (completed in 2014) palace. It featured 1,100 rooms. It was built at a cost of $630 million, an estimate that is probably on the low side.[166] Erdoğan had been well-prepared, it would seem, to take advantage of his "gift from God."

He also, as if in ironic fulfillment of Gülen's prediction about the behavior of "modern Neros," continued to seek ways to satisfy his blood-lust outside the rule of law. In March, 2017, *The New York Times* broke the story that Mike Flynn—a retired military officer who had served as a foreign policy advisor in Donald Trump's Presidential campaign, and then as his first National Security Advisor, had received over $500,000 from the Government of Turkey during the campaign to undertake a campaign to smear Gülen and Hizmet.[167] Such payments to a campaign official were, of course, of questionable legality, and unquestionably im-moral. A few days later, the *Wall Street Journal* broke a story describing how Flynn had discussed with Turkish officials a plot to kidnap Gülen and return him to Turkey, in exchange for payments of $15 million—stories became more widely publicized in November, as the Zarrab corruption case was also proceeding.[168] By then, of course, Flynn had been removed as National Security Advisor. He had not disclosed his Turkish entanglements, as required by law, prior to taking on his role in the NSA. Flynn had also become a target of Robert Mueller's investigation of Russian meddling in the election of Trump. It was like something out of a novel by John LeCarre—without the dramatic uncertainty about the actual villain. The consequences in the lives of millions of people within the Hizmet movement, however, were anything but fiction. As Gülen put it in his lament: "I probably will not live to see Turkey become an exemplary democracy, but I pray that the downward authoritarian drift can be stopped before it is too late."[169]

⁂

In one of his many speeches to friends as troubles began to escalate in Turkey, Fethullah Gülen interpreted a famous Qur'anic passage that reads: "Whatever good happens to you, it is from God; and whatever evil befalls you, it is from yourself" (4:79). According to Gülen, what this passage pointed toward is that "we may not always clearly see the underlying reasons behind events." In such cases—of which the current oppression of people of Hizmet surely was one, it was wisest to turn inwards, toward self-criticism, and to turn (always) towards forgiveness from God. "Blaming oneself for troubles and misfortunes depends on a consciousness of serious self-criticism—this in turn depends on a sound faith in God and the Day of Judgment." Gülen's perspective throughout his life, again, had consistently kept a horizon of eternity before believers' eyes. But, he went on, even better than any post-trouble turn toward self-criticism, was patient striving on the path of goodness: "I wish that—instead of struggling to restore their hearts and spiritual lives—people could build up barriers against their destruction from the very beginning, for it is very difficult to restore something after it has been destroyed."[170]

There were those within Hizmet who scrutinized their own behavior and relationships in the wake of events in Turkey after 2010, just as there were others who persevered in patient work as teachers, dialogue activists, and social entrepreneurs. But these practices were nothing new for them. And no matter how they responded to their oppression in Turkey, Gülen and many people of Hizmet knew that their hope for a restored Turkish democracy had dim probability of being realized by almost any reckoning of short-term history. Gülen reserved a plot in a cemetery in Pennsylvania, expecting never to return to Turkey again.[171] And yet, he kept hope, nonetheless. This, too, was nothing new for Gülen and for many within Hizmet. Finding hope in the midst of trouble had been a regular, almost routine, part of his biography. And, by now, there were islands of peace, as he called them, on every continent. Those peace islands were the schools, dialogue centers, and social enterprises wherever they operated. And those peace islands were countries where new friends could be made, and where Muslims could practice their faith without oppression.

For, if an old man might be tempted during a cold winter in exile to despair of ever again seeing those "green spring days," in fact, as

Gülen wrote, eyes again on a very long horizon, and tied to no specific nation:

> Our old world will experience an amazing "springtime" before its demise. This springtime will see the gap between rich and poor narrow; the world's riches will be distributed more justly, according to work, capital, and needs; there will be no discrimination based on race, color, language, or worldview; and basic human rights and freedoms will be protected. Individuals will come to the fore and, learning how to realize their potential, will ascend on the way to becoming "the most elevated human" on the wings of love, knowledge, and belief.
>
> In this new springtime, when scientific and technological progress has been taken into consideration, people will understand that the current level of science and technology resembles the stage of life when an infant is learning how to crawl. Humanity will organize trips into space as if they were merely traveling to another country. Travelers on the way to God, those devotees of love who have no time for hostility, will carry the inspirations within their spirits to other worlds.
>
> Yes, this springtime will rise on the foundations of love, compassion, mercy, dialogue, acceptance of others, mutual respect, justice, and rights. It will be a time in which humanity will discover its real essence. Goodness and kindness, righteousness and virtue will form the basic essence of the world. No matter what happens, the world will come to this path sooner or later. Nobody can prevent this.
>
> We pray and beg that the Infinitely Compassionate One will not let our hopes and expectations come to nothing.[172]

In a winter of brutal strongmen, such hopes for a glorious spring seemed utopian—no better than a prayer. Yet if there was one thing that Fethullah Gülen really knew how to do, it *was* to pray. So, when he also encouraged people that "difficulties increase in accordance with the greatness of the consequent reward," that, too, was a prayer.[173] But it was also a maxim that had been tested in Fethullah Gülen's life, and proven true, almost from its beginning.

To some, the oppression in Turkey signaled the death of Gülen's dream for a "golden generation." And there was, surely, a death looming. The boy from Korucuk was now a frail old man. And yet Fethullah Gülen's life was never about a short-term horizon to be measured by the brief span of four-score years and ten. He believed in heaven. He believed in resurrection. He believed in justice. These beliefs were not tied only to the next news cycle, the next election cycle, or even to an individual life-cycle. His horizon was eternal. And if the moral arc of the universe was long—and it seemed particularly long in the second decade of the twenty-first century, Gülen and people close to him also shared the belief of many people of faith that the moral arc of the universe did bend toward justice. They also were convinced that it was humanity's duty to *help bend* the moral arc of the universe in that direction. As Gülen put it often, in many publications: "Power resides in truth." Any power otherwise founded was destined to fail. And so, the end of Fethullah Gülen's earthly life—whenever it would happen—would hardly be the end of Hizmet. Eternal truth could not be contained by an authoritarian's ambitions. Fethullah Gülen had lived for a peace that surpassed understanding, because it was a peace that surpassed the superficial limits of time and space. After all, even a *Sufi* in exile whirled in a light far more substantial than mere earthly matter, caught up in an energy that was present at the very beginning of creation, and that would be there at the end of time.

NOTES

PREFACE

1. Jon Pahl, "Muslims teach lesson in sacrifice," *The Philadelphia Inquirer*, October 23, 2006, as reposted in CAIR--Philadelphia, at http://pa.cair.com/actionalert/thank-philadelphia-inquirer/
2. Jon Pahl, *Empire of Sacrifice: The Religious Origins of American Violence* (NY: New York Univer-sity Press, 2012).

INTRODUCTION

1. I realize that to some it will not be at all apparent that religious practices entail nonviolence, but I am more than happy to take on that argument: prayer promotes life (so say functional MRIs), and ritual promotes trust—which is why religious traditions have endured for millennia. They won't go away because they develop what I call "deep peace" in a person's life. Deep peace is more crucial than the absence of war—although it helps promote that absence—and deep peace is even more crucial than the kinds of peace that follow from economic and social justice, although it helps promote those kinds of peace, too.
2. See White 2015.
3. Özdalga 2005, p. 433.
4. See Eisenstadt.
5. Filkins 2016. It is as if "a year of nos" in response to his interview requests led Filkins into a resentment-laden smear campaign. His essay, while appearing well-researched, in fact is riddled with innuendo, unsubstantiated reports, and cherry-picked evidence. He shows no sensitivity to and subtle hostility to the religious dimensions of Gülen's life and work, reducing him to a "cult" leader living on a "compound" with bald political aims, which is, simply, a caricature.
6. See, for instance, Brinton 1965.
7. Yavuz 2013, p. 20.
8. See, for one of many examples, the interview of Gülen by Zeki Sarıtoprak and Ali Ünal in *The Muslim World*, 95 (July 2005): 465-6.
9. Yavuz 2003.
10. See Hatch 1987.
11. Bernard 2015, p. 168.
12. Weber 1958.
13. See Reich.
14. See Yunus Social Business, at http://www.yunussb.com/
15. See Cortright 2010.
16. The Peace and Justice Studies Association is a network of scholars dedicated to advancing understanding of the roots of and impediments to peace. See https://

www.peacejusticestudies.org/
17. See Philippians 4:7
18. Sacks 2002.
19. Eck 1993.
20. Hendrick 2013.
21. For a fuller contextual analysis of the economic contours of Hizmet, see my "Economic Crises and the Promise of Spiritually-Grounded Social Enterprise: Building Peace through Sustainable Profits, Consistent with the Prophets," delivered at Beder University, Tirana, Albania, May 17, 2013," available on request.

CHAPTER 1

1. M. Fethullah Gülen, "Any Political Aims?" in Ali Ünal and Alphonse Williams 2000, p. 331, as cited in Hunt and Aslandoğan 2006, p. 54.
2. Gülen, "The Golden Period of Time," Izmir, 1994, pp. 37-42, as cited in "Fethullah Gülen's Life: A Different Home," Fethullah Gülen, at http://fgulen.com/en/fethullah-gulens-life/about-fethullah-gulen/biography/24650-a-different-home.
3. Interview with Salih Gülen, Erzurum, Turkey. August 3, 2015.
4. Gülen, "The Golden Period of Time," Izmir, 1994, 37-42, op. cit.
5. Interview with Sabri Çolak, Erzurum, Turkey. August 5, 2015.
6. Gülen here quotes a famous Turkish poet, Mehmet Akif Ersoy. See Nuriye Akman, Sabah,1/23-30, 1995, as quoted in "Why Does He Cry?" Fethullah Gülen, at https://www.fgulen.com/en/fethullah-gulens-life/about-fethullah-gulen/biography/24660-why-does-he-cry. Mehmet Akif Ersoy (20 December 1873 – 27 December 1936) was an Ottoman born Turkish poet, writer, academic, member of parliament, and the author of the Turkish National Anthem, "Mehmet Akif Ersoy," Wikipedia, at https://en.wikipedia.org/wiki/Mehmet_Akif_Ersoy.
7. "A Different Home," op. cit.
8. While religion was being manipulated for political purposes during the Russo-Turkic War, there is no evidence that the Gülen family participated directly in any of the fighting—and plenty of evidence that they chose spirituality and education as an alternative path.
9. Alptekin 2012, pp. 2-3.
10. Gülen, 2006d, p. 12.
11. Ibid., p. 13.
12. Interview with Nurhayat Gülen, Turgutlu, Turkey, July 25, 2015.
13. This is a composite description from two sources: M. Fethullah Gülen, "Interview," as cited in Sevindi 2008, pp. 13-15, online at "The Life of Fethullah Gülen: Highlights from his Education," Gülen Movement, at http://www.gulenmovement.us/the-life-of-fethullah-gulen-highlights-from-his-education.html, and "Fethullah Gülen's Life: A Different Home," Fethullah Gülen, at http://fgulen.com/en/fethullah-gulens-life/about-fethullah-gulen/biography/24650-a-different-home.
14. See "Holding One's Tongue," Fethullah Gülen's Works: Pearls of Wisdom, at https://fgulen.com/en/fethullah-gulens-works/thought/pearls-of-wisdom/24545-holding-ones-tongue
15. Sarıtoprak, "Fethullah Gülen: A Sufi in His Own Way," in Yavuz and Esposito

2003, p. 163.
16. Ibid., pp. 28, 20, 29.
17. "The Life of Fethullah Gülen: Highlights from His Education," Gülen Movement, at http://www.gulenmovement.us/the-life-of-fethullah-gulen-highlights-from-his-education.html
18. Gülen 2006e, pp. 197-202.
19. Becker 1997.
20. See, for example, Lifton 1976.
21. As quoted in Sevindi, op. cit., pp. 2-3.
22. See "Sufism in Turkey," Harvard Divinity School Religious Literacy Project, at https://rlp.hds.harvard.edu/faq/sufism-turkey
23. See for example, Findley, "Hizmet among the Most Influential Religious Renewals of Late Ottoman and Modern Turkish History," at https://content.ucpress.edu/chapters/12909.ch01.pdf
24. Interview with Salih Gülen, Erzurum, Turkey. August 3, 2015.
25. https://fgulen.com/tr/fethullah-gulen-kimdir/gulen-hakkinda/fethullah-gulen-hayat-kronolojisi/3502-fgulen-com-1941-1959-Hayat-Kronolojisi
26. Şahin, "Turkey and Neo-Ottomanism: Domestic Sources, Dynamics and Foreign Policy," 2010.
27. Reem, "The Importance of the Mother in Islam," in *Inside Islam: Dialogue and Debates. Challenging Misconceptions, Illuminating Diversity.*
28. Interview with Alp Aslandoğan, Clifton, NJ. May 3, 2015.
29. Interview with Nurhayat Gülen, Turgutlu, Turkey. July 25, 2015.
30. See Alptekin, who includes several such accounts.
31. "A Different Home," http://en.fgulen.com/fethullah-gulen-biography/749-a-different-home
32. Özdemir 2014.
33. "A Different Home," op. cit.
34. "A Different Home," op. cit.
35. Interview with Nurhayat Gülen.
36. Gülen, "A Tribute to Mothers," *The Fountain*, 50 (April-June, 2005), online at http://en.fgulen.com/recent-articles/1940-a-tribute-to-mothers
37. Gülen 2014d, p. xix.
38. Interview with Nurhayat Gülen.
39. "Fethullah Gülen Hodjaefendi's Primary School Years as Narrated by Himself and His Teacher, Belma," *Zaman*, 24 November 2006. See also "Belma Özbatur Anlatıyor," November 23, 2006.
40. Ibid.
41. Alptekin, p. 8.
42. "Years of Education," Fethullah Gülen, at http://fgulen.com/en/home/1304-fgulen-com-english/fethullah-gulen-life/biography/24652-years-of-education
43. Alptekin, p. 11.
44. Interview with Nurhayat Gülen.
45. "Years of Education," op. cit.
46. "A Builder of Spirituality: Muhammad Lütfi Efendi, the Imam of Alvar," in M. Fethullah Gülen 2014c p. 189.
47. Ibid., p. 190.
48. Ibid., p. 192.

49. Ibid.
50. Ibid.
51. https://fgulen.com/tr/fethullah-gulenin-butun-eserleri/kirik-testi-serisi/mefkure-yolculugu/35502-fethullah-gulen-bir-gonul-mimari-alvarli-efe-hazretleri
52. "A Builder of Spirituality: Muhammad Lütfi Efendi, the Imam of Alvar," in M. Fethullah Gülen 2014c, p. 189.
53. Ibid., pp. 194-5.
54. Interview with Alp Aslandoğan, March 9, 2017.
55. Erdoğan 1997, as cited by Sevindi 2008, p. 17.
56. Gülen 2014c, pp. 195-6.
57. Ibid.
58. "Fethullah Gülen's Life Chronology: 1941-1993," Fethullah Gülen, at https://fgulen.com/en/fethullah-gulens-life/about-fethullah-gulen/life-chronology/24903-1941-1993
59. Interview with Hatem Bilgili, August 3, 2015. Erzurum, Turkey.
60. Gülen not only has cited these figures; he has also continually studied them with his students. For another summary of the works that Gülen has studied, see "Fethullah Gülen as an Islamic Scholar," Gülen Movement, at http://www.gulenmovement.com/fethullah-gulen/fethullah-gulen-as-an-islamic-scholar
61. There is a wonderful English-language site on Ghazali, at https://www.ghazali.org/
62. For one example of the approach of "civil Islam," see Hefner 2000. For a helpful and quick non-scholarly overview of the differences between "Islamism" and "Civil Islam," see "Civil Islam versus Political Islam in Two Minutes," at https://www.youtube.com/watch?v=PKLD0NJQKJA
63. On the Brotherhood, see the poorly timed but still good on the early history work by Wickham 2015.
64. Can 1996, pp. 71-89, as cited by Enes Ergene 2008, pp. 121-23.
65. Nahal Toosi, "Verbatim: Fethullah Gülen, 'I Don't Have Any Regrets,'" Politico, September 9, 2016.
66. Çetin 2010, p. 23.
67. Conveniently, as of 2017, the entire Risale-i Nur collection was available in English translation to download, here: http://www.nur.gen.tr/en.html
68. Yavuz, "Islam in the Public Sphere," in Yavuz and John L. Esposito (2003), pp. 4-5. The embedded quote from Nursi comes from Risale-i Nur Külliyatı. Vol. 2 (Istanbul: Nesil, 1996), p. 1956.
69. Alptekin, p. 17.
70. Yavuz, p. 8.
71. Çetin, p. 23, citing Erdoğan, pp. 29-49.
72. Sevindi, p. 18.
73. Rae 2015, p. 80.
74. Alptekin, p. 20.
75. Ibid., pp. 22-5.
76. "Edirne," Fethullah Gülen, at http://fgulen.com/en/fethullah-gulens-life/about-fethullah-gulen/biography/24654-edirne
77. "Military Service," Fethullah Gülen, at https://fgulen.com/en/fethullah-gulens-life/about-fethullah-gulen/biography/24655-military-service

78. Dumanlı 2014.
79. "Military Service," op. cit.
80. Findley 2010, p. 309.
81. See, with some caution, Çavdar 2014, pp. 1-12. Çavdar has little sympathy for or understanding of Gülen's theology, and her analysis reduces him to a political actor, beginning with his brief participation in anti-Communism debates in early 1960s.
82. "Military Service," op. cit.
83. Carroll 2007, p. 5.
84. "Military Service," idem.
85. Alptekin, p. 29.
86. "First Conference in Erzurum," Fethullah Gülen, at http://fgulen.com/tr/ses-ve-video/fethullah-gulen-hitabet/fethullah-gulen-hocaefendinin-vaizligi/8245-fgulen-com-Erzurumda-Ilk-Konferans.
87. Soltes 2013, p. 8.
88. Gülen 2006f, pp. 6-7.
89. Alptekin, p. 29.
90. Ibid., pp. 31-7.
91. Duran and Menderes 2013, pp. 479–500.
92. Interestingly, Kısakürek has been invoked and remembered several times by Recep Tayyip Erdoğan. See Sean R. Singer, "Erdogan's Muse: The School of Necip Fazil Kisakurek," World Affairs 176 (November-December 2013): 81-8.
93. Alptekin, pp. 37-8.
94. The Constitution was ratified in 1945. See Unesco Constitution, at http://portal.unesco.org/en. See also Narinder Kakar, "Preface," in Dahir 2015, p. xiii.
95. Aslandoğan and Çetin, "The Educational Philosophy of Gülen in Thought and Practice," in Hunt and Aslandoğan 2006, pp. 31-54.
96. See on this point Cremin, "Transformational Peace Education in the 21st Century," in Dahir 2015, pp. 63-68.
97. Gülen 2006f, pp. 202, 208.
98. Yılmaz, "Peacebuilding through Education: A Perspective on the Hizmet Movement," in Dahir 2015, p. 83.
99. Harvard Kennedy School, "Social Capital Glossary," The Saguaro Seminar: Civic Engagement in America, at https://www.hks.harvard.edu/saguaro/glossary.htm.
100. Aslandoğan and Çetin, "The Educational Philosophy of Gülen in Thought and Practice," p. 32.
101. Gülen 2006a, p. 73.
102. Gülen 2006f, pp. 198-9.
103. See Sayılan and Yıldız 2009, pp. 735-749.
104. Aslandoğan and Çetin, "The Educational Philosophy of Gülen in Thought and Practice," p. 32.
105. Gülen 2006f, p. 196.
106. Interview with Nurten Kutlu, Hasbrouck Heights. NJ, February 7, 2017.
107. Interview with Emine Eroğlu, Hasbrouck Heights, NJ. February 7, 2017. Tr. Osman Öztoprak. This is in fact a quote from Yunus Emre, a folk poet. See his poem "You Cannot Be a Dervish," excerpted at The Threshold Society, at https://sufism.org/sufism/writings-on-sufism/the-drop-that-became-the-sea-

by-yunus-emre-excerpt-2
108. Kirk 2012.
109. Ibid., pp. 18-22.
110. Ibid.
111. See Pinker 2011.
112. Kirk 2012, p. 22.
113. Ibid.
114. Ibid., p. 9.
115. See "Erzurum'dan Ayrılış ve Edirne," Fethullah Gülen, at https://www.fgulen.com/new/tr/fethullah-gulen-kimdir/hayatindan-kesitler/erzurumdan-ayri-lis-ve-edirne

CHAPTER 2

1. Irmak TV, Geçmişten İzler (Traces from the Past), "Interview with Abdullah Ünal Birlik, Episode 1," March 11, 2014.
2. Nursi 2008, p. 251.
3. Mango 2002, p. 463.
4. Gülen 2006e, p. 3.
5. Mango, idem.
6. Rausch 2008, p. 615.
7. Ibid., p. 626.
8. Ibid., p. 619.
9. Ibid., p. 620.
10. Ibid., p. 621.
11. Ibid., p. 622
12. Ibid., p. 625.
13. Ibid., p. 632.
14. Ibid., p. 632-3.
15. Alptekin, pp. 39-41.
16. The collection was compiled in the 1960s, but recently released in a beautiful edition: M. Fethullah Gülen, compiler, *Selected Prayers of Prophet Muhammad and Great Muslim Saints*. Tr. Ali Keeler (NY: Tughra Books, 2012).
17. Gülen 2014d, p. 136.
18. Any visitor to almost any mosque (Mecca is a notable exception) will recognize quickly the existence of separate spaces for men and women to pray, and, at least in Turkey, the areas for men tend to dwarf in size those for women, which are often in balconies, behind screens, etc. Women can come and join the prayers whenever they like. Yet, it is not mandatory upon them to attend congregational prayers. The separation of spaces in the mosque is about modesty, for prostration is a physical act that exposes the body. Here are divergent opinions on how much separation is required according to the Qur'an and sunnah (and how much a matter of custom). Women do not have the same obligation to attend congregational prayer in mosques as men, but they do share equal obligations to pray (at home or work) five times/day, following almost identical practices as those for men.
19. As I was in the completion of my writing, a new book by Gülen has come out in Turkish, and it is an edited volume of his sermons on salah: *Miraç Enginlikli*

İbadet: Namaz, 2018, Süreyya Yayınları).

20. Interview with İsmail Büyükçelebi, Wind Gap, PA. May 12, 2015.
21. Ibid.
22. Gülen 2006e, pp. 35-6.
23. Gülen 2014d, p. 43.
24. See Peres 2012 and Islam 2010. See also https://www.sozcu.com.tr/2019/gundem/anne-buyukelci-kardes-vekil-kizi-da-danisman-3034414/
25. Interview with Züleyha Çolak, Hasbrouck Heights, NJ. March 28, 2017.
26. Gülen, "Chaos and the Mystical World of Faith," *The Fountain*, May-June 2010.
27. Interview with Alaattin Kırkan, Izmir, July 28, 2015.
28. Interview with Yusuf Pekmezci, Izmir, July 29, 2015.
29. Ibid.
30. Ibid.
31. Naqshbandi Sufi Way, "Awrad," at http://naqshbandi.org/awrad/.
32. Gülen 2014c, pp. 190-1.
33. Yücel 2010, pp. 4-5.
34. Interview in Turkey, July 28, 2015.
35. Alptekin, p. 44-5.
36. Historian of religions Jonathan Z. Smith famously argued that "sacred places" are "focusing lenses." See Smith 1987. See also my *Shopping Malls and Other Sacred Spaces: Putting God in Place*, 2003.
37. Interview with Yusuf Pekmezci, Izmir, Turkey. July 29, 2015.
38. Gülen 2014d, p. 73.
39. Gülen, "Hajj and Praying," Weekly Sermons, The Broken Jug, 8/10/2012, at http://www.herkul.org/weekly-sermons/hajj-and-praying/. Although dated later, the sentiments reflect a consistent understanding of Hajj by Gülen evident in his own journey in 1968.
40. Ibid.
41. Ibid.
42. Gülen 2011, p. 247.
43. Ibid.
44. Ibid
45. Ibid; Tr. by Ahmet Kurucan and Osman Öztoprak, May 9, 2017.
46. Tittensor 2014, p. 96.
47. Tittensor also makes this claim.
48. Interview with Derya Yazıcı," Hasbrouck Heights, NJ. 2017. Tr. Osman Öztoprak.
49. Ibid.
50. "Malcolm X's Letter from Mecca."
51. Clingingsmith, et al, 2008.
52. Interview with Yusuf Erdoğan, Izmir, Turkey. July 28, 2015.
53. Alptekin, p. 46.
54. Irmak TV, Geçmişten İzler (Traces from the Past). "Interview with Yusuf Pekmezci, Episode 1," October 29, 2014.
55. Ibid.
56. Ibid.
57. Alptekin, p. 46.
58. Irmak TV, "Interview with Yusuf Pekmezci," idem.

59. Çetin (2010) dates the circle of intimates a little later—to 1971; but it is more likely that it was in 1971 following the coup (and the first organized persecution of Hizmet) that a movement with longer history became visible in a way it was not prior to that date.

60. Akkad 2017.

61. Irmak TV, "Interview with Yusuf Pekmezci," idem.

62. Williams 2017.

63. For instance, see "Raucous, Solemn Rites Mark Muslim Celebration of Eid al-Fitr," *Phillipine Daily Inquirer*, August 31, 2011.

64. Gülen, "Being Shaped by Ramadan," *The Fountain*, 25 (Jan-Mar 1999).

65. Gülen, "The Month Overflowing with Mercy," in *Ramadan* (NJ: Tughra Books, n.d.), pp. 10-11.

66. Gülen, "Ramadan and Softening Hearts," The Broken Jug, 10 July 2013, at https://www.fgulen.com/en/fethullah-gulens-works/thought/the-broken-jug/36142-ramadan-and-softening-hearts

67. Ibid.

68. Balcı 2011.

69. Kinzer 2015.

70. This narrative follows closely that of Çetin 2010, pp. 27-30.

71. See, from among many examples, Yunus 2007.

72. Barton et al 2013, p. 5.

73. See, for instance, the changing way zakat is woven into the general tax structure in Saudi Arabia, at "Ministry of Finance Introduces New Zakat Implementing Regulations," at *PwC, Middle East News*, April 6, 2017.

74. See Toraman et al,"Cash Awqaf in the Ottomans as Philanthropic Foundations and Their Accounting Practices."

75. Özdalga 2000, pp. 83-104.

76. The social aspects of Luther's economic ideas have been largely forgotten, leading to the kind of willy-nilly "free market" capitalism of neo-liberal regimes. For one effort to retrieve the socially-responsible kind of economics Luther imagined (and in some cases instituted), see Lindberg and Paul Wee, 2016.

77. Özdalga, 2000, pp. 83-104.

78. Yavuz, "The Gülen Movement: The Turkish Puritans," in Yavuz and Esposito 2003, pp. 19-20.

79. Ibid., p. 47.

80. Alptekin, pp. 51-2.

81. Irmak TV, Geçmişten İzler (Traces from the Past), "Interview with Sıbgatullah Gülen, Episode 1," May 29, 2014.

82. Harrington 2011, p. 97.

83. "Edirne, Kırklareli, and finally Izmir," in Fethullah Gülen's Life, at https://www.fgulen.com/en/fethullah-gulens-life/about-fethullah-gulen/biography/24656-edirne-kirklareli-and-finally-izmir

CHAPTER 3

1. See my earlier essay, "Fragments of Empire: Lessons for Americans in Orhan Pamuk's 'The Museum of Innocence,' in *Public Theology*, May 10, 2010.

2. Gardels 2011.

3. Harrington 2011, p. 97.
4. Alptekin 2012, pp. 20-2.
5. Interview with Hatem Bilgili, August 3, 2015, Erzurum, Turkey.
6. Irmak TV, Geçmişten İzler (Traces from the Past), Interview with Sıbgatullah Gülen, Episode 2," June 4, 2014.
7. Interview with Ahmet Kurucan, Hasbrouck Heights, NJ. September 8, 2017.
8. Irmak TV, Geçmişten İzler, Interview with Abdullah Birlik, Episode 1," March 11, 2014.
9. Haddad, "Ghurba as Paradigm for Muslim Life: A Risale-i Nur Worldview," in *The Muslim World* 89 (No. 3-4): 299, as cited by Yasin Aktay in Yavuz and Esposito 2003, p. 144.
10. Gülen 2011, p. 70.
11. Ibid., p. 71.
12. Ibid.
13. Ibid., p. 72.
14. Ibid., p. 150.
15. Ibid., p. 151.
16. Interview with Ahmet Tekin, July 28, 2015. Turkey.
17. The interview is recorded in Valkenberg 2015, p. 80.
18. Ibid., p. 87.
19. See, for example, Gülen, *Muhammad, the Messenger of God: An Analysis of the Prophet's Life*. Tr. Ali Ünal (NJ: Tughra Books, 2010), which was first published in Turkish in 1993, where falsehood and idolatry, among other moral boundaries, contrast sharply with the Prophet's positive action on behalf of Islam.
20. Interview with Yusuf Pekmezci, July 29, 2015. Izmir, Turkey.
21. Valkenberg 2015, p. 87.
22. Interview with Alaattin Kırkan, July 28, 2015, Izmir.
23. Interview with Esra Koşar, Hasbrouck Heights, NJ. March 27, 2017.
24. See on this theme Ergene 2008.
25. This is where analogies with revivalists in American religious history are apt; those who were also able to harness the emotion of conversion and build enduring institutions persevered. Many did not. See for instance the classic work, William G. McLoughlin, Jr., *Modern Revivalism: Charles Grandison Finney to Billy Graham*.
26. A helpful list of sermon titles and topics can be found at "1975 Yılı Vaazları," Fethullah Gülen [Turkish version], at https://fgulen.com/tr/ses-ve-video/ fethullah-gulen-hitabet/fethullah-gulen-hocaefendinin-vaizligi/3586-fgu- len-com-1975-Yili-Vaazlari. Similar lists are available for all of the years of Gülen's preaching until 1989.
27. Valkenberg 2015, p. 88.
28. Ibid., pp. 100-103.
29. See from among many others R. Scott Appleby 1999, and (for a more popular study) Kimball 2009.
30. Interview with Mehmet Doğan, Istanbul, August 4, 2015.
31. Burnett and Yıldırım 2011.
32. Alptekin 2012, p. 45.
33. Interview with Nicole Pope, *Le Monde*, 28 April 1998, as cited by Ergil 2012, p. 130.

34. Ibid., p. 55.
35. Irmak TV, Geçmişten İzler, "Interview with Sıbgatullah Gülen, Episode 2," June 4, 2014.
36. Ibid.
37. "Why Does He Cry?" Fethullah Gülen, at https://www.fgulen.com/en/fethullah-gulens-life/about-fethullah-gulen/biography/24660-why-does-he-cry, citing an interview with Nuriye Akman," Sabah Daily, 1/23-30, 1995.
38. Gülen 2014c, pp. 41-3. See also the original Turkish text in this link: http://www.herkul.org/kirik-testi/mahzun-kalblerin-aglamasi/
39. Interview with Alaattin Kırkan, July 28, 2015, Izmir.
40. Çetin 2010, p. 36.
41. Interview with Alaattin Kırkan.
42. Sevindi 2008, pp. 48-9.
43. That demographic trend which was fueled in part by mandatory conscription (the draft), has stayed largely consistent to the present. The average age of a recruit to the U.S. Marines in 2017 was just over 19, although the average age of an individual in any branch of service crept up somewhat compared to the 1970s (explainable in part by the absence of conscription, and by the growth of a permanent, professional military class).
44. See, for example, Lt. Col. David Grossman 1996, and Neitzel et al 2012).
45. Gülen, "Işık Evler [Light Houses] (1)," Fethullah Gülen, at https://fgulen.com/tr/fethullah-gulenin-butun-eserleri/cag-ve-nesil-serisi/fethullah-gulen-gunler-bahari-soluklarken/10409-Fethullah-Gulen-Isik-Evler-1. The article was first published in 1991, but the metaphor went back much further.
46. Interview with Yusuf Pekmezci, July 29, 2015, Izmir.
47. Ibid.
48. Ibid.
49. Irmak TV, Geçmişten İzler, "Interview with Tahsin Şimşek, Episode 1," December 31, 2014.
50. Yavuz, "The Gülen Movement: The Turkish Puritans," in Yavuz and Esposito 2003, p. 32.
51. Ibid.
52. Gülen 2014d, pp. 210, 212.
53. Gülen 2011, pp. 44-5.
54. Gülen, Prizma, Vol. 2 (Istanbul: Zaman, 1997), p. 12, as cited by Yavuz 2003, p. 33.
55. Ibid.
56. Irmak TV, Geçmişten İzler, "Interview with İrfan Yılmaz, Episode 1," April 1, 2015.
57. Interview with Mustafa Özcan, Wind Gap, PA, May 11, 2015. Tr. Osman Şimşek.
58. Interview with Esra Koşar, op. cit.
59. Hendrick 2013, pp. 86-7.
60. James 1910.
61. Gülen 2006c, pp. 83-4.
62. Gülen 2006f, pp. 81-3.
63. Irmak TV, Geçmişten İzler, "Interview with Yusuf Pekmezci, Episode 2," Sep. 17, 2014.
64. Interview with Mustafa Özcan, Wind Gap, PA. May 11, 2015.

65. Valkenberg 2015, p. 87.
66. See for these numbers Hermansen 2007, p. 72.
67. Interview with İsmail Büyükçelebi, Wind Gap, PA. May 12, 2015.
68. Gülen 2006c, op. cit., pp. 62-3. This teaching dates from 1998, but it reflects a consistent theme in Gülen's life, drawn from his Sufi roots.
69. "Student Selection and Placement System," at https://en.wikipedia.org/wiki/Student_Selection_and_Placement_System
70. "The Dershane Prep School Debate in Numbers," Daily Sabah, November 19, 2013, at https://www.dailysabah.com/business/2013/11/19/the-dershane-prep-school-debate-in-numbers
71. Tee 2016, p. 42.
72. Balci, Bayram, "The Gülen Movement and Turkish Soft Power," in Carnegie Endowment for International Peace, February 4, 2014.
73. Ebaugh 2010, p. 60.
74. Findley 2010, p. 341.
75. Interview with Osman Şimşek, Wind Gap, PA. May 12, 2015.
76. Interview with Esra Koşar.
77. Gülen 2006d, pp. 38-9.
78. See, for instance, Sarah El-Kazaz 2015.
79. Gülen 2006d, p. 92.
80. Yavuz and Esposito, "Introduction," in Yavuz and Esposito 2003, p. xviii.
81. Hendrick 2013, p. 108.
82. Ibid., pp. 113-14.
83. Tee 2016, pp. 39-41.
84. Interview with Emine Eroğlu, February 7, 2017. Hasbrouck Heights, NJ.
85. Irmak TV, Geçmişten İzler, "Interview with İrfan Yılmaz, Episode 1," April 1, 2015.
86. Ibid.
87. Gülen, Understanding and Belief: The Essentials of Islamic Faith (Konya/Izmir: Kaynak Publishing, 1997), p. 363, as cited by Bakar 2005, p. 363.
88. Ibid., p. 365.
89. Gülen, Understanding and Belief, p. 333, in Bakar, p. 368.
90. Interview with İrfan Yılmaz," Istanbul. August 2, 2015.
91. Ibid.
92. Gülen, Truth through Colors (Izmir: Nil, 1992), as cited by Marcia Hermansen, "Who Is Fethullah Gülen: An Overview of His Life," in Marty 2015, p. 38.
93. Interview with Yılmaz.
94. "131 Media Organs Closed by Statutory Decree," at http://bianet.org/english/media/177256-131-media-organs-closed-by-statutory-decree. Sızıntı was hardly alone. Among the casualties in the wake of the failed coup were 16 TV channels, 23 radio channels, 45 newspapers, 15 magazines, and 29 publishing houses—many (but not all) associated with Hizmet. The rationale was the "State of Emergency" declared by President Erdoğan after the failed coup.
95. "Sızıntı Celebrates 30th Year as Magazine of Love and Tolerance," at http://fgulen.com/en/home/1323-fgulen-com-english/press/news/26507-sizinti-celebrates-30th-year-as-magazine-of-love-and-tolerance
96. Fethullah Gülen's Official Website [Turkish], "1977 Yılı Vaaz ve Konferansları," at http://fgulen.com/tr/ses-ve-video/fethullah-gulen-hitabet/fethullah-gu-

len-hocaefendinin-vaizligi/3588-fgulen-com-1977-Yili-Vaaz-ve-Konferanslari
97. Ibid.
98. Interview with Mustafa Özcan.
99. Münz and Ulrich, "Changing Patterns of Immigration to Germany, 1945-1997," at Migration Dialogue, "Research and Seminars."
100. Yavuz, "The Gülen Movement," as cited by Valkenberg 2015, p. 95.
101. Zürcher 2017, p. 263.
102. Ergil 2010, Kindle 199-206.
103. Irmak TV, "Interview with İrfan Yılmaz."
104. See Kuru and Kuru 2008, pp 99-111.
105. Gülen 2006f, p. 189.
106. Interview with Safa Kaplan, *Hürriyet Daily*, 4/21/2004, as cited by Sarıtoprak, "Gülen and his Global Contribution to Peace-Building," in International Conference Proceedings: Muslim World in Transition--Contributions of the Gülen Movement 2007, p. 635.
107. Kaynak Holding, "History," at http://kaynak.com.tr/en/default.aspx
108. Irmak TV, "Interview with İrfan Yılmaz."
109. Broder 1979.
110. Kinzer 2015.
111. Sevindi 2008, p. 25.
112. Gülen, *Towards the Lost Paradise* (London: Truestar, 1996), pp. 40-2, as cited by Zeki Sarıtoprak, "Gülen and His Global Contribution to Peace-Building," op cit, p. 642.

CHAPTER 4

1. MacCulloch 2011.
2. Pamuk 2006. Kindle Edition, loc. 1201-04.
3. Ibid., 1252-55.
4. Ibid., 1266-68.
5. On how people even very close to Gülen struggle to define themselves—whether community, movement, or some other term, see Walton, "The Institutions and Discourses of Hizmet, and Their Discontents," in Marty 2015, pp. 50-65.
6. What I mean by "principled pluralism" is akin to what Simon Robinson identifies as the "plural identity" of people in Hizmet—an identity grounded in Islam, but open to the diversity of the world. See Simon Robinson, "Building Bridges: Gülen Pontifex," in Marty 2015, p. 91.
7. "The Society of Peace," [*Sızıntı*, August, 1979], in Kurt 2014, pp. 27-29.
8. Çetin 2010, p. 37.
9. Irmak TV, Geçmişten İzler (Traces from the Past), "Interview with Sıbgatullah Gülen," May 29, 2014.
10. Interview with Kesmez, July 28, 2015.
11. "Being Pursued," in Fethullah Gülen's Life, at https://www.fgulen.com/en/fethullah-gulens-life/about-fethullah-gulen/biography/24659-being-pursued. The original interview was with Nuriye Akman, Sabah daily, 1/23-30, 1995.
12. Irmak TV, Geçmişten İzler (Traces from the Past), "Interview with Sıbgatullah Gülen, Episode 1," May 29, 2014.
13. Irmak TV, Geçmişten İzler (Traces from the Past), "Interview with Sıbgatullah

Gülen," Episode 2," June 4, 2014.

14. Visiting students was a normal part of a teacher's vocation, and every Turkish male had to complete around two years of military service. In Turkish culture, if someone is sick or in the military, it is a cultural practice to visit them to offer regards. Consequently, Gülen was not doing anything unusual or suspicious by being at this military base.

15. Interview with Şerif Ali Tekalan, July 27, 2015, Izmir.

16. Interview with Abdullah Birlik, July 26, 2015, Izmir.

17. Interview with Haluk Ercan, July 27, 2015, Hisar Mosque Bazaar, Izmir. According to Alp Aslandoğan and Ahmet Kurucan, the Prime Minister, Turgut Özal, was involved in securing Gülen's release, for which he actually put at least two ministers in charge. The incident is well-known in Hizmet's collective memory.

18. Interview with Nurten Kutlu, March 11, 2017, Hasbrouck Heights, NJ.

19. Özkök 1996, as cited in Fethullah Gülen's Life, "Relation with Literature and Music."

20. Can 1995, as cited in Fethullah Gülen's Life, "Relation with Literature and Music."

21. Ibid.

22. Sevindi 1997, as cited in Fethullah Gülen's Life, "Relation with Literature and Music."

23. Özkök, at Ibid.

24. Çapan, "Fethullah Gülen's Teaching Methodology in His Private Circle," in *Mastering Knowledge in Modern Times: Fethullah Gülen as an Islamic Scholar*.

25. Ibid.

26. Tabarani, Mu'jam al-Kabir, 25/7; Ajluni, Kashf al-Khafa, 1/179.

27. See, for how Gülen meets the classical attributes of a mujtahid, İsmail Acar, "A Classical Scholar with a Modern Outlook: Fethullah Gülen and His Legal Thought," in Mastering Knowledge in Modern Times: Fethullah Gülen as an Islamic Scholar.

28. See also Yılmaz, "Ijtihad and Tajdid by Conduct: The Gülen Movement," in Yavuz and Esposito 2003, pp. 208-237.

29. Çapan, op. cit.

30. Ibid.

31. Ibid.

32. Ibid.

33. See Elder 1950. For a more recent commentary on the Commentary, see Rudolf 2014.

34. Knysh 2007.

35. Çapan, op. cit.

36. Ibid.

37. Ibid.

38. Kurt 2014, pp. 13-15. The original was in *Sızıntı*, May 1993.

39. The 5th Floor was actually a phrase in Hizmet from earlier than Gülen's time in Istanbul, back to the first Hizmet dormitory in Bozyaka, in Izmir.

40. al-Ansari 2013.

41. Hermansen 2005. See also Hermansen "The Cultivation of Memory in the Gülen Movement," 2007, p. 71.

42. Ebaugh 2010, p. 61.

43. Irmak TV, Geçmişten İzler (Traces from the Past), Interview with Tahsin Şimşek, December 31, 2014.
44. Interview with Kerim Balcı, August 5, 2015, Istanbul.
45. Ibid.
46. Irmak TV, Geçmişten İzler (Traces from the Past), Interview with Tahsin Şimşek," December 31, 2014.
47. Çetin 2010, p. 40.
48. Valkenberg 2015, p. 197.
49. Hendrick 2013, p. 137.
50. Valkenberg, "Interview with Ali Yurtsever, Izmir, August 9, 2009," as cited in Valkenberg 2015, p. 198.
51. Hendrick 2013, pp. 137-8.
52. Ibid.
53. For the voices of the students themselves, see especially Tittensor 2014.
54. Valkenberg, "Interview with Yusuf Pekmezci, Izmir, August 6, 2009," in Valkenberg 2015, p. 163.
55. Gülen 2013a, p. 115. See also Valkenberg 2015, pp. 163-5.
56. Findley 2010, p. 354.
57. Çetin 2010, p. 37.
58. Ibid.
59. Hendrick 2013, p. 135.
60. Ibid., p. 141.
61. Ibid., p. 183-4.
62. Oğurlu and Öncü, "The Laic-Islamist Schism in the Turkish Dominant Class and the Media," in Balkan et al 2015, p. 281.
63. Yavuz 2013, p. 141.
64. Gülen 2006f, p. 82.
65. Hendrick 2013, p. 187
66. https://fgulen.com/tr/ses-ve-video/fethullah-gulen-hitabet/fethullah-gulen-hocaefendinin-vaizligi/3578-fgulen-com-1986-Yili-Vaazlari
67. Alptekin 2012, p. 59.
68. Gülen 2010, p. xx.
69. On this incident, see "The Late Mehmet Özyurt," at https://fgulen.com/tr/turk-basininda-fethullah-gulen/fethullah-gulen-hakkinda-dizi-yazilar-dosyalar/fethullah-gulen-web-sitesi-ozel-dosyalar/14224-fgulen-com-merhum-mehmet-ozyurt
70. Ibid. For the circumstances of the offer to stay in Saudi Arabia, see Alptekin, pp. 57-8.
71. "1990 Sermons," at https://fgulen.com/tr/ses-ve-video/fethullah-gulen-hitabet/fethullah-gulen-hocaefendinin-vaizligi/3593-fgulen-com-1990-Yili-Vaazlari
72. Çetin 2010, p. 45.
73. Interview with Hatem Bilgili, Erzurum, August 3, 2015.
74. Gülen 2010b, p. 251.
75. Schimmel 1975.
76. Zeki Sarıtoprak reports the death threats to Gülen from an "Interview with Safa Kaplan in Istanbul's Hürriyet, 21 April, 2004," in "Fethullah Gülen's Theology of Peacebuilding," in Yılmaz and Esposito 2010, op. cit., p. 175.
77. Gülen 2010b, p. 378.

78. Ibid., p. 336. Gülen cites Muslim, "Jumu'a," 43; Nasa'i, "Idayn," 22; and Abu Dawud, "Sunna," 5 for this statement, p. 417.
79. Ibid., p. 320. Gülen here cites Muhammad 'Ajjaj al-Khatib, Al-Sunna Qabl al-Tadwin, 160.
80. Tristan Claridge, "Explanation of Types of Social Capital," *Social Capital Research*, February 13, 2013, at https://www.socialcapitalresearch.com/explanation-types-social-capital/
81. Gülen 2010b, pp. 43-46.
82. Ibid., pp. 66, 70. Gülen cites Ibn Hanbal, 1:404, for the story about the birds.
83. See Mahatma Gandhi's Writings..., "Peace, Non-Violence & Conflict Resolution: Gandhi's Views on Nonviolence—Between Cowardice and Violence," at http://www.mkgandhi.org/nonviolence/phil8.htm
84. Gülen 2010b, pp. 70-3.
85. Ibid., pp. 75-82.
86. Ibid., pp. 82, 88, 76.
87. Ibid., p. 86.
88. Ibid., pp. 84-5. Gülen cites Bukhari, "Bad'u al-Wahy" 6, for the story about the diplomatic effort with the Byzantines.
89. Ibid., pp. 91-119.
90. Ibid., p. 105.
91. Gülen 2013a, p. 135.
92. Gülen 2010b, pp. 105-6.
93. Ibid., pp. 104. Gülen cites the specific reference in Bukhari to "Iman," 4.
94. Ibid., pp. 185-6.
95. Ibid., p. 298. Gülen cites Haythami, Majma`, 9:20 as the hadith under consideration.
96. Ibid., p. 120.
97. Ibid., p. 9. Gülen here cites Muttaqi al-Hindi, Kanz al-'Ummal, 11:384.
98. Gülen 2006f, p. 43.
99. Interview with Alp Aslandoğan.
100. Aviv 2010, pp. 101-114.
101. Çiçek 2016.
102. Alarko Holding, https://www.alarko.com.tr/en/homepage
103. Gündem 2014.
104. Aviv 2010.
105. Ibid., pp. 107-8.
106. At one time, Hizmet was planning to provide the schools for Rawabi, a planned city for Palestinians in the West Bank. See Schwartz 2016.
107. Aviv, op. cit.
108. Gülen 2006f, p. 44.
109. Ibid.
110. For instance, see Gülen's interpretation of Qur'an, 2:90, "So they (disobedient Jews) have earned wrath upon wrath," in Gülen 2014d, p. 29. Gülen's mature (or post-1990) interpretation recognized the danger in generalizing about such a text, and recognized how it spoke to a specific behavior in a specific context by a specific group of people.
111. Tarabay 2103.
112. Gülen, "Jews and Christians in the Qur'an," 05/24-25, 1996, at https://fgulen.

com/en/fethullah-gulens-life/1315-fethullah-gulens-speeches-and-interviews-on-interfaith-dialogue/25142-jews-and-christians-in-the-quran

113. Gülen, "Dialogue with the People of the Book, Jews and Christians," August 25, 1995, at https://fgulen.com/en/fethullah-gulens-life/1315-fethullah-gulens-speeches-and-interviews-on-interfaith-dialogue/25141-dialogue-with-the-people-of-the-book-jews-and-christians

114. These reflections are gathered together in *Advocate of Dialogue: Fethullah Gülen*. Compiled by Ali Ünal and Alphonse Williams, 2000, pp. 208-212.

115. Ibid., pp. 201-205.

116. Sevindi, "Fethullah Gülen Ile New York Sohbeti," in Ünal and Williams 2000, p. 207.

117. Ibid., p. 219.

118. "The Patriarch and Fethullah Hodja," *Sabah*, April 6, 1996.

119. Mercan 2017, p. 190. Mercan cites an interview with Gülen in *Milliyet*, January 11, 2005 as the source for the quote from Gülen, and *Zaman*, May 13, 1996 for the words of the Patriarch.

120. Ünal and Williams 2000, p. 281.

121. "Fethullah Gülen on His Meeting with the Pope," interview in Zaman, February 13, 1998.

122. Ibid.

123. The full text of Gülen's letter is found in Gülen 2006f, pp. 258-60.

124. These four points come from Ahmet Tezcan, in *Akşam*, 11 February 1998, as summarized in Ünal and Williams 2000, p. 291.

125. Gopin 2005.

126. Mercan 2017, pp. 134-5. Mercan here cites an address by Gülen to "journalists, writers, and academics" delivered on August 16, 1996.

127. Ünal and Williams 2000, p. 69, citing Nevval Sevindi, "Fethullah Gülen Ile New York Sohbeti" [1997].

128. Mercan 2017, p. 292. The citation to the original column cites *Akşam*, 13 February 1998.

129. Irmak TV, Geçmişten İzler (Traces from the Past), "Interview with Yusuf Pekmezci," September 10, 2014.

130. Andrea, "Woman and Their Rights: Fethullah Gülen's Gloss on Lady Montagu's "Embassy to the Ottoman Empire," in Hunt and Aslandoğan 2006, pp. 145-164.

131. Gülen 2010b, p. 171.

132. See for example, Coontz 2006.

133. Gülen 2010b, pp. 159-180.

134. Ibid.

135. Ibid., p. 180.

136. Interview with Kerim Balcı, August 5, 2015, Istanbul.

137. Interview with Sevgi Akarçeşme, August 18, 2015, Istanbul.

138. See Özdemir 2014, and Alptekin 2012, pp. 61-2.

139. Gülen, "Women and Women's Rights," interview with Ertuğrul Özkök, *Hürriyet Daily*, January 23-30, 1995.

140. Andrea, "Woman and Their Rights: Fethullah Gülen's Gloss on Lady Montagu's "Embassy to the Ottoman Empire," in Hunt and Aslandoğan 2006, p. 145.

141. Gülen, "Women and Men Prayed Together at the Mosque," in Fethullah Gülen's Thoughts, at https://fgulen.com/en/fethullah-gulens-life/1305-gulens-

thoughts/25059-women-and-men-prayed-together-at-the-mosque.

142. Andrea, "Woman and Their Rights: Fethullah Gülen's Gloss on Lady Montagu's "Embassy to the Ottoman Empire," in Hunt and Aslandoğan 2006, pp. 146-154.

143. "An Interview with Fethullah Gülen," in *The Muslim World* 95 (July 2005), p. 464. Tr. Zeki Sarıtoprak and Ali Ünal.

144. Mercan 2017, p. 109. Mercan cites Interview in *Sabah Daily*, January 23, 1995.

145. Gülen, "The Beard and the Headscarf Issue," interview with Nuriye Akman, *Sabah Daily*, 1/23-30/95.

146. Thanks to colleague David G. Grafton for this citation.

147. Gülen, "The Beard and the Headscarf Issue," interview with Nuriye Akman, *Sabah Daily*, 1/23-30/95.

148. Mercan, p. 111. Mercan cites "Interview with Nevval Sevindi," 1997, but does not cite location.

149. Sevindi 2008, pp. 66-7.

150. Gülen 2010b, pp. 272-3.

151. Gülen, "Solution to the Problem of Racism," at https://fgulen.com/en/fethul-lah-gulens-works/faith/prophet-muhammad-as-commander/24896-solution-to-the-problem-of-racism Both this translation (unattributed) and the one by Ünal in *Muhammad: The Messenger of God* cite two hadiths, Hanbal, 5.441, and Muslim, 'Imarah, 37, for the sources about the life of the Prophet.

152. Gülen 2010b, p. 294. The hadith cited is Bukhari, "Iman," 22.

153. Shinn 2015, p. 46.

154. Ibid., p. 129.

155. Ibid., pp. 56-7.

156. Gürbüz, "Recognition of Kurdish Identity and the Hizmet Movement," at http://www.gulenmovement.com/recognition-of-kurdish-identi-ty-and-the-hizmet-movement.html

157. Akyol, Harun, "The Role of Turkish Schools in Building Trusting Cross-ethnic Relationships in Northern Iraq," in Esposito and Yılmaz 2010, p. 326.

158. Akyol, Harun, "An Alternative Approach to Preventing Ethnic Conflict: The Role of the Gülen's [sic] Schools in strengthening the delicate relations between Turkey and the Iraqi Kurds with particular reference to the 'Kirkuk Crisis,' in *Conference Proceedings: Islam in the Age of Global Challenges: Alternative Perspectives of the Gülen Movement*, 2008, p. 51.

159. Akyol, Harun, 2010, p. 318. Ishik University continues. See http://www.ishik.edu.iq/

160. Akyol, Harun, 2008, p. 51. Akyol cites http://www.gyc.org.tr/bpi.asp?-caid=445&cid=2366 for the full declaration, which is a dead link.

161. See Gunter 2017, pp. 259-79.

162. Ibid.

163. Kerim 2013.

164. Ibid.

165. See, for example, the story "GYV [Journalist and Writers Foundation] slams slanderous accusations seeking to link Hizmet to terrorist PKK," *Hizmet News*, April 12, 2016.

166. Kerim, op cit.

167. Ibid.

168. al-Qaher 2016.

169. "Honorary President Fethullah Gülen's Founding Speech."

170. See Yavuz 2013, pp. 143-151.

171. "1st Abant Platform Meeting Addresses Islam and Secularism," July 19, 1998.

172. Akarçeşme 2016.

173. "Journalists and Writers Foundation," at https://www.idealist.org/en/nonprofit/c623c9029a5c45068ad0bc84bc10bbf0-the-journalist-and-writers-foundation-uskudar The website still lists the Altunizade, Istanbul address for the agency.

174. The entire sermon is available on youtube [in Turkish], at https://www.youtube.com/watch?v=VgAXZuNCwU0

175. Hesser 2014.

176. Ibid., 8:41-10:00

177. Toe 2016.

178. Hesser 2014, 10:15-30.

179. Beder was not strictly a Hizmet-related institution, since it was supported by a range of Muslim groups within Albania—but Hizmet volunteers played a gradually-increasing role. See "Turgut Özal Colleges," at http://turgutozal.edu.al/, "Beder University Homepage," at http://www.beder.edu.al/, and "Epoka University," at http://www.epoka.edu.al/. So far, the Albanian government has resisted efforts by Erdoğan to close the schools. See for instance Paul Alexander, "Turkey on Diplomatic Push to Close Schools Linked to Influential Cleric," in VOA, September 21, 2017, at https://www.voanews.com/a/turkey-erdogan-gulen-schools/4010073.html and Besar Likmeta, "Albania Ignores Erdoğan's Tirade Against Gülen," in HizmetMovementNewsPortal, May 20, 2015, at https://www.voanews.com/a/turkey-erdogan-gulen-schools/4010073.html

180. Journalists and Writers Foundation, "Soccer Match Raises Money for Children's Education in Bosnia-Herzegovina," September 19, 1995, at http://jwf.org/soccer-match-raises-money-for-children-s-education-in-bosnia-herzegovina/

181. Gülen 2006f, p. 77.

182. Demir, "The Gülen Movement in Germany and France," at http://www.gulen-movement.com/gulen-movement-germany-france.html

183. Irvine, "The Gülen Movement and Turkish Integration in Germany," in Hunt and Aslandoğan 2007, pp. 62-84.

184. Akman, "Hoca'nin hedefi Amerika ve Almanya" [Hodja targets America and Germany], in Sabah, 1/28/1995, as cited by Emre Demir, "The Emergence of a Neo-Communitarian Discourse in the Turkish Diaspora in Europe: The Implantation Strategies and Competition Logics of the Gülen Movement in France and Germany," in Weller and Yılmaz 2012, p. 194.

185. See "Countering Violent Extremism: Mujahada and Muslims' Responsibility," at http://www.counteringviolentextremism.eu/

186. Kösebalaban, "The making of enemy and friend: Fethullah Gülen's national-security identity," in Yavuz and Esposito 2003, pp. 170–84, as cited by Demir, p. 193.

187. Turgut, "Fethullah Gülen and the Schools," in Yeni Yüzyıl, 15 January - 4 February, 1998, as cited in Ünal and Williams 2000, pp. 335-6.

188. Ibid.

189. See Çetin 2010, p. 44.

190. See from among many possibilities, "Tansu Çiller'den Fethullah Gülen Açıkla-

ması [A Statement by Tansu Çiller about Fethullah Gülen]," 25 July 2016, at http://www.cumhuriyet.com.tr/haber/turkiye/573852/Tansu_Ciller_den_ Fethullah_Gülen_aciklamasi.html

191. Friedman 2016.

192. See Çetin 2010, pp. 48-51, who nicely sketches the history during these years.

193. See "Tayyip Erdoğan, Fethullah Gülen, Muhsin Yazıcıoğlu ve Barış Manço'nun yıllar önceki görüntüleri: Gazeteciler ve Yazarlar Vakfı'nın 1996 yılındaki ödül töreninde Erdoğan'ın konuştuğu, Fethullah Gülen'in dinlediği video sosyal medyanın gündeminde [Pictures from years ago of Tayyip Erdoğan, Fethullah Gülen, Muhsin Yazıcıoğlu and Barış Manço: The video is of Erdoğan's speech at the award ceremony that Fethullah Gülen attended, sponsored by the Journalists and Writers Foundation in 1996," at https://www.youtube.com/ watch?v=ZhUT0Uc0wpI

194. For a commentary on this so-called "alliance" see Yeşilova 2016. For Yeşilova "such an alliance has long been overstated. The truth is, Erdoğan and Gülen only came together when Erdoğan's stated goals reflected deeply held beliefs by Gülen.... Gülen is not Erdoğan's biggest threat, nor was he his chief ally."

195. See "Interview with Fethullah Gülen," in *Herkul*, July 16, 2016. See also Mercan, *No Return from Democracy*, p. 5. In a related interview, Huner Anwer asked Gülen about the "alliance" between Gülen and Erdoğan. His answer is telling, albeit reflecting realities post-2012: "There has never been an alliance, a sincere alliance, in the sense of a political alliance between us. During the formation efforts of their party, Mr. Erdoğan visited me and I spoke with him at that time once. And I also met him when he was Istanbul's mayor when we organized a charity soccer game for the benefit of Bosnian war victims. So I met him only two or three times throughout this period. But despite the absence of an actual alliance, people outside always saw this as an alliance. The true nature of this relationship is as such that they have promised to uphold the rule of law, justice. They promised to respect the diversity of opinions. They promised to respect religious freedom. They promised to respect different opinions and worldviews. And our friends along with the majority of Turkish people supported them based on these promises, such as Mr. Süleyman Demirel who was Prime Minister and then President of Turkey, Mr. Turgut Özal who was also Prime Minister and the President of Turkey, and Mr. Bülent Ecevit who was the Prime Minister. They all received support for similar promises for democracy, and the rule of law, and freedom. So Turkish people, based on the promises of these political leaders, supported them at different times. ... We have never joined a party. We have not become political. We have simply preserved our line of thought, our core values, which are universal human values: peace in the world, unity and harmony among human beings, and to fight against poverty. These are our core values and we have not strayed from them. If we wanted, we could have taken a place in the party. We could have demanded parliamentary seats. We could have demanded seats in the Cabinet or a bureaucratic position of the government. But we have not done any of this. They have designed the Parliament, they have designed the Cabinet, they have designed bureaucratic institutions as they wished. And all of the world is a witness to this. ... So if you're going to talk about the separation or the split, this is because they strayed from their promises. We have not changed our position, our core values, but they made a U-turn.

That's why the split occurred." "There has never been a sincere alliance between Gülen Movement and Erdoğan," [n.d.], at "Gülen Movement," at http://www.gulenmovement.com/never-sincere-alliance-gulen-movement-erdogan.html

196. There is actually a blog set up to remember Erimez. See "Hacı Kemal Erimez/ Hacı Ata," at http://hacikemalerimez.blogspot.com/

197. Kinzer 1999, "Barış Manço, Turkish Pop Star and Television Personality, 56."

198. See "Barış Manço gives Fethullah Gülen a gift: The late Barış Manço admires Fethullah Gülen's schools in the Far East... [Merhum sanatçı Barış Manço da Fethullah Gülen'in Uzakdoğu'da açtığı okullar dolayısıyla hayranlığını], at https://www.izlesene.com/video/baris-manconun-fethullah-gulene-hedi-ye-takdim-etmesi/9434899

199. Keneş 2009.

200. "Rahmetli Barış Manço Fethullah GÜLEN hakkında ne dedi [What did late Barış Manço said about Fethullah Gülen], at https://www.youtube.com/watch?v=NmFd2QOK9Rg

201. It is an impressive and exhausting schedule of interviews: March 9, 1997—interview on "the southeast matter;" April 9, 1997—interview with Ali Aslan of *Zaman*; December 12, 1997—gave a briefing about the "High Military Commission" that had been organized to investigate his activities; January 6, 1998—interview with Mehmet Ali Birand, on the show "32nd Day;" January 21, 1998—interview with Özcan Ercan of *Milliyet*; February 27, 1998—interview with NTV television, hosted by Cengiz Çandar and Taha Akyol, etc. See "Fethullah Gülen's Life: About Fethullah Gülen—Life Chronology," at https://fgulen.com/en/fethullah-gulens-life/about-fethullah-gulen/life-chronology. Many of the interviews are gathered, or at least excerpted, in Mercan 2017.

202. Among them were: Mehmet Çelikel and Ahmet Ak, as well as M. İhsan Kalkavan, Latif Erdoğan, Ali Rıza Tanrısever, Orhan Özokur, Naci Tosun, Nevzat Ayvacı, Şaban Gülbahar, Mehmet Deniz Katırcı, İsmail Büyükçelebi, İlhan İşbilen and Mehmet Erdoğan Tüzün. See "July 15 Coup Attempt: FETO's Structure," at http://www.yenisafak.com/en/15-july-coup-attempt-in-turkey/fetos-structure-kurulus-en-detail

203. Ibid.

204. This list is a composite from James C. Harrington 2011, pp. 148-154 and "Fethullah Gülen Life Chronology," at https://fgulen.com/en/fethullah-gulens-life/about-fethullah-gulen/life-chronology

205. See Rumi Forum, "The Wing of the Bird—Gülen on Sincerity," at http://rumiforum.org/the-wing-of-the-bird-guelen-on-sincerity/

206. Gülen, "The Necessity of Interfaith Dialogue," in *The Fountain* 3:31 (July-Sep, 2000), pp. 7-8, as cited in M. Fethullah Gülen 2006a, pp. 51-2.

CHAPTER 5

1.   The poem can be found in its entirety in an "Appendix" to Sevindi 2008, pp. 149-50. Although written in 1997, while Gülen was in the U.S. for medical reasons, it anticipates his emotional longing for Turkey from 1999 to the present, too.

2.   Hauslohner 2016.

3.   Interview with Kerim Balcı, August 5, 2015, Istanbul.

4. See, for example, Gülen 2006f, pp. 198-99.
5. See on this thread Tittensor 2014, pp. 156-171.
6. Gülen, 2006f, p. 23.
7. In many cases, this intent had an ironic outcome; the schools and other initia-tives became attractive to elites in many of these regions, as the quality of the Hizmet offerings became apparent. The schools quickly became self-sustain-ing. The maxim was to "fry with your own oil" as soon as possible, that is, to establish initiatives that would generate indigenous support and (eventually) leadership.
8. See Orhan, Özgüç, "Islamic *Himmah* and Christian Charity: An Attempt at In-ter-faith Dialogue," in *Islam in the Age of Global Challenges: Alternative Perspec-tives of the Gülen Movement*. November 14-15, 2008. Georgetown University, Washington, DC., p. 565.
9. Helen Rose Ebaugh (2010) suggested based on her sociological research that people often contributed from 10 to 50 percent of profits, or more, to Hizmet. Not all the organizations or businesses related to Hizmet had the distinctive aim of solving a social problem. Some were more directly profit-making recog-nitions of opportunity, for instance, retail furniture. But many if not most of the Hizmet-related businesses had social aims, or were connected to social aims. See T.L. Hill and Jon Pahl, "Social Entrepreneurship as a Catalyst for Practical Social Justice in Economic Life," in *A Just World: Multi-Disciplinary Perspectives on Social Justice*, Ed. Heon Kim (Newcastle-Upon-Tyne: Cambridge Scholars Press, 2013): 39-52.
10. Interview with Hüma Taban, June 27, 2017, Washington, DC.
11. Interview with Nebahat Çetinkaya, June 27, 2017, Washington, DC.
12. Gülen 2007, p. 43.
13. Ibid., p. 44.
14. Ibid., p. 45.
15. Ibid., pp. 45-9.
16. Gülen, "Ideal Consultation-1," *Herkul*: Weekly Sermons, September 28, 2014, at http://www.herkul.org/weekly-sermons/ideal-consultation-1/
17. Ibid.
18. Idem, "Ideal Consultation-2," *Herkul*, Weekly Sermons, October 4, 2014, at http://www.herkul.org/weekly-sermons/ideal-consultation-2/
19. Ibid.
20. Gülen 2014d, p. 90.
21. Ibid, p. 91.
22. See, for example, Rodgers 2009. The article is typical of a certain right-wing suspicion (if not paranoia) that, unfortunately, has been picked up by many U.S. media agencies as the predominant narrative about Gülen. It also is marked by the bad prose, sketchy research, and poor critical thinking that also marks some of these accounts.
23. See Tittensor 2014.
24. Ebaugh 2010, p. 99.
25. Interestingly, even the worst military oppression did not seize assets in the way the Erdoğan regime has done with Hizmet organizations, which is why many people of Hizmet were surprised by and unprepared to respond to such an assault on their private wealth. Many were rendered destitute as a result. See

for the statistics, and some of their stories: "Turkey Purge: Monitoring Human Rights Abuses in Post-Coup Turkey," at https://turkeypurge.com/

26. Demir et al 2004, pp. 166-188.
27. Irmak TV, Geçmişten İzler (Traces from the Past), "Interview with Ahmet Haseken," February 24, 2014.
28. Ibid.
29. Ibid.
30. Bernard, "The Hizmet Movement in Business, Trade, and Commerce," in Marty 2015, p. 168.
31. Ibid., p. 156.
32. Ibid.
33. Interview with Sibel Yüksel, March 11, 2017, Houston, Texas.
34. Interview with Ahmet Muharrem Atlığ, August 5, 2015, Izmir.
35. Interview with Yusuf Pekmezci, August 2, 2015, Izmir.
36. Interview with Şerif Ali Tekalan, August 1, 2015, Izmir.
37. Ibid.
38. Selim, Student, Turkey, as cited by Tittensor 2014, p. 161.
39. Tittensor 2014, p. 162.
40. Interview with Esra Koşar, March 28, 2017, Hasbrouck Heights, NJ.
41. Tittensor 2014, p. 163.
42. Hendrick 2013, p. 8.
43. Gülen, "Orta Asya'da Eğitim Hizmetleri" [Educational Services in Central Asia]. Yeni Türkiye Dergisi, nr. 15. [1997], pp. 685– 692, as cited in Ergil 2012 Kindle Edition, Loc. 8074-8075.
44. "Bu Hareket Devlete Alternatif mi?" [Is This Movement an Alternative to the State?], at https://fgulen.com/en/gulen-movement/fethullah-gulen-and-the-gulen-movement-in-100-questions/48223-if-it-is-possible-to-make-a-sche-ma-of-the-areas-of-activities-of-the-gulen-movement-what-kinds-of-activi-ties-and-groups-of-activities-can-be-mentioned, as cited in Ergil 2012, Loc. 872. Here is another alternative link http://www.herkul.org/kirik-testi/bu-hare-ket-devlete-alternatif-mi-2/, where a date of November 14, 2005 is indicated.
45. Gündem 2005, pp. 163-4, as cited in Ergil 2012, Kindle Locations 908-915.
46. Akman, Nuriye, 2004. Gurbette Fethullah Gülen (Fethullah Gülen in a Foreign Land). (Istanbul: Zaman Kitap), p. 77, as cited in Ergil, Kindle Locations 1398-1402.
47. Gülen, 2013a, p. 9.
48. Gülen, 2006f, p. 91.
49. Interview with [Aisha], November 15, 2017, New York City.
50. Ibid.
51. Tee 2016, p. 3. See also Sarıtoprak, "An Islamic Approach to Peace and Nonvio-lence," in The Muslim World. Special Issue. Islam in Contemporary Turkey: The Contributions of Fethullah Gülen 95 (July 2005), pp. 418-9.
52. Interview with Abdülhamit Bilici, August 5, 2015, Istanbul.
53. Ibid.
54. Ibid.
55. Irmak TV, Geçmişten İzler (Traces from the Past), "Interview with Tahsin Şimşek," Episode 1, December 31, 2014.
56. Ebaugh 2010, p. 99.

57. Interview with Ergün Çapan, July 14, 2015, Wind Gap, Pennsylvania.

58. Interview with İsmail Büyükçelebi, May 12, 2015, Wind Gap, Pennsylvania.

59. Interview with Nevzat Savaş, August 27, 2015, Istanbul.

60. See also Heck, "Turkish in the Language of the Qur'an: *Hira'* Magazine," in Barton et al 2013, pp. 143-153.

61. Gülen 2006f, p. 172.

62. Ibid., pp. 19-21. The original citation is to *Işığın Göründüğü Ufuk*, [The Horizon Where the Light Has Appeared], Nil, Istanbul, 2000, pp. 189-195.

63. Balci, Bayram, 2014.

64. Gülen 2006f, p. 21.

65. Ibid., pp. 21-22.

66. Ibid., pp. 22-3.

67. Ünal and Williams 2000, p. 338.

68. Norton and Kasapoglu 2016.

69. Clement, "Central Asia's Hizmet Schools," in Barton et al 2013, p. 158.

70. Ibid. The citation from Gülen is to Gülen 2006a.

71. Interview with Derya Yazıcı, March 28, 2017, Hasbrouck Heights, NJ.

72. Ibid.

73. Gülen 2006f, pp. 122,7.

74. Interview with Derya Yazıcı, March 28, 2017, Hasbrouck Heights, NJ.

75. Interview with Nurten Kutlu, March 28, 2017, Hasbrouck Heights, NJ.

76. "Boomtown Slum," *The Economist*, December 22, 2012, at https://www.economist.com/news/christmas/21568592-day-economic-life-africas-biggest-shanty-town-boomtown-slum.

77. Interview with Nurten Kutlu, March 28, 2017, Hasbrouck Heights, NJ.

78. See for details, Shinn 2015, pp. 58-62, 76-8, 92.

79. See "Ikbal Gurpinar Hospital is Connecting Sudanese People to Life," in Hizmet News, February 23, 2012, at http://hizmetnews.com/420/ikbal-gurpinar-hospital-is-connecting-sudanese-people-to-life/#.WmcpT6inFPY

80. Ibid., p. 88.

81. See Thomas Michel, SJ, "Fighting Poverty with Kimse Yok Mu," in *Islam in the Age of Global Challenges: Alternative Perspectives of the Gülen Movement. Conference Proceedings*, November 14-15, 2008. Georgetown University (Washington, DC: Rumi Forum, 2008), pp. 523-533.

82. Ibid. See also Doğan Koç, "Generating an Understanding of Financial Resources in the Gülen Movement: 'Kimse Yok Mu' Solidarity and Aid Association, in *Islam in the Age of Global Challenges: Alternative Perspectives of the Gülen Movement. Conference Proceedings*, November 14-15, 2008. Georgetown University (Washington, DC: Rumi Forum, 2008), pp. 435-454.

83. See Ebaugh 2010, pp. 101-3.

84. Interview with İsmail Büyükçelebi, May 12, 2015, Wind Gap, Pennsylvania.

85. Ibid.

86. Gülen 2010b, p. 193.

87. Ebaugh and Koç, "Funding Gülen-Inspired Good Works: Demonstrating and Generating Commitment to the Movement," in *Muslim World in Transition: Contributions of the Gülen Movement. International Conference Proceedings*. London, 25-27 October 2007. (London: Leeds Metropolitan University Press, 2007), p. 545.

88. Ergil 2013, p. 301.
89. Yavuz 2013, p. 81.
90. Ebaugh 2010, p. 5
91. Srivastava 2017.
92. Barton, "How Hizmet Works: Islam, Dialogue and the Gülen Movement in Australia," in *Hizmet Studies Review* 1(Autumn 2014): 9-26.
93. Ibid.
94. Interview with Nevzat Savaş, Istanbul, Turkey, August 5, 2015.
95. Ibid.
96. Ibid.
97. Ibid.
98. Osman, "The Gülen Movement as a Civil-Islamic Force in Indonesia," in Barton et al 2013, pp. 173-4.
99. Yavuz 2013, p. 84.
100. Osman, "The Gülen Movement as a Civil-Islamic Force in Indonesia," in Barton et al 2013, pp. 173-4.
101. See Osman Cubuk and Burhan Cikili, "The Impact of Hizmet Movement on Intercultural Dialogue in Taiwan," in International Conference on the Hizmet Movement and the Thought and Teachings of Fethullah Gülen: Contributions to Multiculturalism and Global Peace. National Taiwan University, College of Social Sciences, December 8-9, 2012, pp. 194-208.
102. Ibid.
103. Ibid., p. 175.
104. Norton and Kasapoglu 2016.
105. Hällzon, "The Gülen Movement: Gender and Practice," in *Islam in the Age of Global Challenges: Alternative Perspectives of the Gülen Movement. Conference Proceedings*, November 14-15, 2008. Georgetown University, pp. 288-309.
106. See Paul Weller, "Robustness and Civility: Themes from Fethullah Gülen as Resource and Challenge for Government, Muslims and Civil Society in the United Kingdom," in *Muslim World in Transition: Contributions of the Gülen Movement. International Conference Proceedings.* London, 25-27 October 2007. (London: Leeds Metropolitan University Press, 2007): 268-284; Fatih Tedik, "Motivating Minority Integration in Western Context: The Gülen Movement in the United Kingdom," in *International Conference on Peaceful Coexistence: Fethullah Gülen's Initiatives for Peace in the Contemporary World*, Erasmus University, Rotterdam, 22-23 November 2007, at https://fgulen.com/en/gulen-movement/conference-papers/peaceful-coexistence/25871-motivating-minority-integration-in-western-context-the-gulen-movement-in-the-united-kingdom; and on the Centre for Hizmet Studies, see their website, at https://www.hizmetstudies.org/
107. Yasien Mohamed, "The Educational Theory of Fethullah Gülen and its Practice in South Africa," in *Muslim World in Transition*, pp. 552-571.
108. See Joshua Ocheja, "Understanding the Hizmet Movement in Nigeria," The Cable, 7 November 2016, reprinted at https://fgulen.com/en/press/columns/50914-understanding-the-hizmet-movement-in-nigeria. See also Ocheja, "Turkey: Erdoğan's Macabre Dance in Africa," *The Cable*, 7 December 2016, at https://www.thecable.ng/turkey-Erdoğans-macabre-dance-africa
109. Interview with Yusuf Erdoğan, Izmir, July 28, 2015.

110. Ebaugh 2010, pp. 92-3.
111. The Turkish government has also targeted these schools. See Empire of De-' ceit: An Investigation of the Gülen Charter School Network. (Amsterdam and Partners, LLP for the Republic of Turkey, 2017). The accusations try to smear Hizmet by accusing Turks of using Turkish contractors and hiring Turkish teachers—business practices rather well known in most immigrant communities. The quality of the "research" in the work can be made evident in this biographical tidbit: "Gülen's nationalist sermons focus on the reestablishment of the Ottoman Empire, whereby Turkey will rise again in prominence to become the moral, religious, and economic leader of a new world order," p. 27. For another opponent of the schools, see C.A.S.I.L.I.P.S. [the Acronym stands for Citizens Against Special Interest Lobbying in Public Schools," which sounds innocuous and even progressive, but is in fact a thoroughly Islamophobic propaganda effort, with no apparent broader purpose than to defame Hizmet schools], "A Guide to the Gulen Movement's Activities in the U.S.: Gülen Charter Schools in the U.S.," [April 17, 2017], at http://turkishinvitations.weebly.com/list-of-us-schools.html
112. See Bradley Joseph Saacks, "U.S. schools are indirectly linked to preacher, often well-regarded," Bloomberg, September 1, 2016, at https://www.bloomberg.com/news/articles/2016-09-02/u-s-schools-caught-in-turkey-s-post-coup-attempt-crackdown
113. Margaret Brennan, Jennifer Janisch, "Are some U.S. charter schools helping fund controversial Turkish cleric's movement?," CBS News, March 29, 2017, at https://www.cbsnews.com/news/is-turkish-religious-scholar-fethullah-gulen-funding-movement-abroad-through-us-charter-schools/
114. See Valkenberg 2015, pp. 215-218.
115. See Embrace Relief, at http://embracerelief.org/
116. Gülen 2006f, p. 221.
117. Ibid., pp. 161-2. Online as "Fethullah Gülen's Message on the 9/11 Terror Attacks," at http://www.gulenmovement.com/fethullah-gulens-message-on-the-911-terrorist-attacks.html
118. The online version cites Zaman, September 12, 2001. The Washington Post published an advertisement paid for by Gülen with a similar message a few days afterwards.
119. Sevindi 2008, pp. 60-1.
120. Irmak TV, Geçmişten İzler (Traces from the Past), "Interview with Hekimoğlu İsmail," April 16, 2014.
121. The talk is reported in Alptekin 2012, p. 70.
122. Gülen, Towards the Lost Paradise (Izmir: Kaynak, 1998), p. 29.
123. Ibid., p. 62.
124. Dumanlı 2015, p. 3.
125. Gülen, Towards the Lost Paradise (Izmir: Kaynak, 1998), p. 60.
126. See on the trials Dan Bilefsky and Sebnem Arsu, "Turkey Feels the Sway of Reclusive Cleric," The New York Times, April 24, 2012, at http://www.nytimes.com/2012/04/25/world/middleeast/turkey-feels-sway-of-fethullah-gulen-a-reclusive-cleric.html
127. Dumanlı 2015, pp. 56-7.
128. Ibid., p. 42.

129. Ibid., pp. 42-3.

130. Ibid., p. 11

131. "Erdoğan 'Ben bu davanın savcısıyım' demişti!" [Erdogan said 'I am the prosecutor of this case!'], in ABC Gazetesi, April 21, 2016, at http://www.abcgazetesi.com/erdogan-ben-bu-davanin-savcisiyim-demisti-13866h.htm. For the original statement, see "'Evet Ergenekon'un savcısıyım'['Yes, I am the prosecutor of Ergenekon'], Gazetavatan.com, July 16, 2008, at http://www.gazetevatan.com/-evet-ergenekon-un-savcisiyim—189246-siyaset/

132. Ibid., p. 10

133. Sezgin, İsmail Mesut, "The Mavi Marmara and Fethullah Gülen's Critics: Politics and Principles." The article was originally published in *Today's Zaman*, n.d.

134. "Mavi Marmara: Why did Israel Stop the Gaza Flotilla," BBC News, 27 June 2016, at http://www.bbc.com/news/10203726

135. Lauria, Joe, "Reclusive Turkish Imam Criticizes Gaza Flotilla," *Wall Street Journal*, June 4, 2010, at https://www.wsj.com/articles/SB10001424052748704025304575284721280274694

136. Sezgin, op. cit.

137. Bianet News Desk, "Erdoğan Changes His Mind on Mavi Marmara Crisis, *Bianet English*, June 30, 2016, at https://bianet.org/english/politics/176388-erdogan-changes-opinion-on-mavi-marmara-crisis

138. See for an example of the genre, "Gülen's Zionist Connections Exposed," *Crescent International: The Magazine of the Islamic Movement*, December 23, 2013, at https://crescent.icit-digital.org/articles/gulen-s-zionist-connections-exposed

139. Sezgin, op. cit.

140. Dumanlı 2015, p. 29.

141. Birand 2010.

142. The Wikipedia article on this is comparably good. See "Gezi Park Protests," at https://en.wikipedia.org/wiki/Gezi_Park_protests

143. Birnbaum 2013.

144. See for documentation of the sources for these terms as used by the Prime Minister, a comprehensive overview prepared by the Turkey Task Force, *Hate Speech and Beyond: Targeting the Gülen Movement in Turkey*. Rethink Paper 16, June 2014. (Washington, DC: Rethink Institute). The Rethink Institute was a Hizmet-related think-tank.

145. Ibid., pp. 35-6.

146. Letsch 17 December, 2013.

147. Letsch 18 December, 2013.

148. See Kaylan 2017.

149. Rubin 2017.

150. See Kaylan, above, who describes how "a phenomenon is at work in Turkey, as it is in the US, where partisan thinking intensifies daily and grows ever more impervious to facts, because facts themselves lose their quiddity, their lapidarian certainty in an atmosphere of widespread paranoia where nothing can be agreed on as impartially true. Here we have the triumph of a Putinization process, for he pioneered it in Russia, where regime-loyal media float one conspiracy theory after another until the population feels totally addled and people get locked into their own reality bubbles. Finally, they grow weary and fatalistic. They're grateful for a strongman at the helm."

151. Dumanlı 2015, pp. 17-18.
152. Ibid., pp. 21-22. In other interviews, Gülen admitted that he might have known 1% or so of those police and prosecutors; see his interview with BBC.
153. Ibid., p. 6.
154. Gülen 2006f, p. 218.
155. Dumanlı 2015, p. 26.
156. Ibid., pp. 8-10.
157. *What Went Wrong with Turkey? The Fountain Special Issue* (NJ: Blue Dome Press, 2017), p. 20.
158. Ibid., p. 18.
159. Gülen, "I Condemn All Threats to Turkey's Democracy," in *The New York Times*, July 25, 2016, at https://www.nytimes.com/2016/07/26/opinion/fethullah-gulen-i-condemn-all-threats-to-turkeys-democracy.html
160. Among the saner and more reasoned have been Dani Rodrik, "Is Fethullah Gülen Behind Turkey's Coup? [with update]," Dani Rodrik's weblog, July 24, 2016, at http://rodrik.typepad.com/dani_rodriks_weblog/2016/07/is-fethullah-gülen-behind-turkeys-coup.html; and Mustafa Akyol, "Who Was Behind the Coup Attempt in Turkey?," *The New York Times*, July 22, 2016, at https://www.nytimes.com/2016/07/22/opinion/who-was-behind-the-coup-attempt-in-turkey.html?action=click&contentCollection=Opinion&module=RelatedCoverage&region=Marginalia&pgtype=article. The Erdoğan government's party-line can be found at İbrahim Kalın, "The Coup Leader Must Be Held Accountable," *The New York Times*, July 24, 2016, at https://www.nytimes.com/2016/07/25/opinion/the-turkey-coup-leader-must-be-held-accountable.html?action=click&contentCollection=Opinion&module=RelatedCoverage&region=Marginalia&pgtype=article For an alternative narrative from within the Hizmet movement, see Yüksel A. Aslandogan, "What Really Happened in Turkey on July 15, 2016? An Alternative to the Turkish Government Narrative," in *What Went Wrong in Turkey*, op. cit., pp. 12-17.
161. Thoroor 2017.
162. Ibid.
163. *What Went Wrong with Turkey*, pp. 10-11.
164. See https://turkeypurge.com/, which keeps a running total as conditions change.
165. See again Belli et al 2016.
166. See http://www.turgev.org/
167. Kenyon 2014.
168. Baker and Rosenberg 2017.
169. Grimaldi et al 2017.
170. *What Went Wrong with Turkey*, p. 11.
171. Gülen 2014c, pp. 63-69.
172. Interview with Fethullah Gülen, February 30, 2018, Saylorsburg, PA
173. Gülen 2006f, pp. 231-2.
174. Gülen 2014c, p. 224.

Bibliography

"1st Abant Platform Meeting Addresses Islam and Secularism," July 19, 1998, at http://jwf.org/1st-abant-platform-meeting-addresses-islam-and-secularism/

Acar, Ismail, "A Classical Scholar with a Modern Outlook: Fethullah Gülen and His Legal Thought," in *Mastering Knowledge in Modern Times: Fethullah Gülen as an Islamic Scholar,* at https://www.fgulen.com/en/gulen-movement/on-the-movement/mastering-knowledge-in-modern-times-fethullah-gulen-as-an-islamic-scholar/47998-a-classical-scholar-with-a-modern-outlook-fethullah-gulen-and-his-legal-thought

Akarçeşme, Sevgi, "Democracy's Challenge with Turkey Debated in Abant Platform," January 30, 2016, at http://hizmetnews.com/17388/democracys-challenge-with-turkey-debated-in-abant-platform/#.WiMUM0qnFPY

Akkad, Reem, "The Importance of the Mother in Islam," in *Inside Islam: Dialogue and Debates. Challenging Misconceptions, Illuminating Diversity.* A Collaboration of the University of Wisconsin National Resource Center and Wisconsin Public Radio's "Here on Earth: Radio Without Borders," at https://insideislam.wisc.edu/2012/05/the-importance-of-the-mother-in-islam/

———. "What does a month of Ramadan fasting do, spiritually and physically?," *The Washington Post,* June 2, 2017, at https://www.washingtonpost.com/news/food/wp/2017/06/02/what-does-a-month-of-ramadan-fasting-do-spiritually-and-physically/?utm_term=.e1b973312d74

Akman, N, "Hoca'nin hedefi Amerika ve Almanya' [Hodja targets America and Germany], in *Sabah,* 1/28/1995, as cited by Emre Demir, "The Emergence of a Neo-Communitarian Discourse in The Turkish Diaspora in Europe: The Implantation Strategies and Competition Logics of the Gülen Movement in France and Germany," in *European Muslims, Civility, and Public Life: Perspectives on and from the Gülen Movement.* Ed. Paul Weller and Ihsan Yilmaz (London/NY: Continuum, 2012).

Akman, Nuriye, *Sabah,*1/23-30, 1995, as quoted in "Why Does He Cry?" *Fethullah Gülen,* at https://www.fgulen.com/en/fethullah-gulens-life/about-fethullah-gulen/biography/24660-why-does-he-cry

Akyol, Harun, "The Role of Turkish Schools in Building Trusting Cross-ethnic Relationships in Northern Iraq," in Esposito and Yilmaz 2010, pp. 311-342.

———. "An Alternative Approach to Preventing Ethnic Conflict: The Role of the Gülen's [sic] Schools in strengthening the delicate relations between Turkey and the Iraqi Kurds with particular reference to the 'Kirkuk Crisis,' in *Conference Proceedings: Islam in the Age of Global Challenges: Alternative Perspectives of the Gülen Movement.* Georgetown University President's Office. Alwaleed Bin Talal Center for Muslim Christian Understanding. Rumi Forum (November 14-15, 2008).

Akyol, Mustafa, "Who Was Behind the Coup Attempt in Turkey?" *The New York Times,* July 22, 2016, at https://www.nytimes.com/2016/07/22/opinion/who-was-behind-the-coup-attempt-in-Turkey.html?action=click&contentCollec-tion=Opinion&module=RelatedCoverage&region=Marginalia&pgtype=arti-cle.

al-Ansari, Farid, *The Return of the Cavaliers: Biography of Fethullah Gülen* (NY: Blue Dome Press, 2013).

al-Qaher, Sara, "Iraqi Kurdistan government seized, sold Gülen schools," October 5, 2016, at https://www.al-monitor.com/pulse/en/originals/2016/09/fethul-lah-gulen-kurdistan-turkey-iraq.html

Alarko Holding, https://www.alarko.com.tr/en/homepage

Alexander, Paul, "Turkey on Diplomatic Push to Close Schools Linked to Influen-tial Cleric," in *VOA*, September 21, 2017, at https://www.voanews.com/a/tur-key-erdogan-gulen-schools/4010073.html

Alptekin, Murat, *Teacher in a Foreign Land: M. Fethullah Gülen* (NJ: Tughra Books, 2012).

Andrea, Bernadette, "Woman and Their Rights: Fethullah Gülen's Gloss on Lady Montagu's "Embassy to the Ottoman Empire," in Robert A. Hunt and Yüksel A. Aslandoğan, *Muslim Citizens of the Globalized World: Contributions of the Gülen Movement* (Somerset, NJ: The Light, 2006): 145-164.

Appleby, R. Scott, *The Ambivalence of the Sacred: Religion, Violence, and Reconcilia-tion* (NY: Rowman and Littlefield, 1999).

Aslandoğan, Yüksel A. and Muhammed Çetin, "The Educational Philosophy of Gülen in Thought and Practice," in *Muslim Citizens of the Globalized World: Contributions of the Gülen Movement*, ed. Robert A. Hunt and Yüksel A. Aslan-doğan (NJ: The Light, 2006): 31-54.

Aslandoğan, Yüksel A., "What Really Happened in Turkey on July 15, 2016?: An Alternative to the Turkish Government Narrative," in *What Went Wrong in Turkey*: 12-17.

Aviv, Efrat E., "Fethullah Gülen's 'Jewish Dialogue'," in *Turkish Policy Quarterly* 9(3): 101-114 at http://turkishpolicy.com/Files/ArticlePDF/fethullah-gulens-jew-ish-dialogue-fall-2010-en.pdf.

Bakar, Osman, "Gülen on Religion and Science: A Theological Perspective," in *The Muslim World: Special Issue--Islam in Contemporary Turkey: The Contributions of Fethullah Gülen* 95(July 2005).

Baker, Peter and Matthew Rosenberg, "Michael Flynn was Paid to Represent Turkey's Interests During the Campaign," at *The New York Times*, March 10, 2017, at https://www.nytimes.com/2017/03/10/us/politics/michael-flynn-turkey.html

Balci, Bayram, "The Gülen Movement and Turkish Soft Power," in *Carnegie Endow-ment for International Peace*, February 4, 2014, at http://carnegieendowment.org/2014/02/04/g-len-movement-and-turkish-soft-power-pub-54430

Balcı, Kerim, "[Ramadan Notes] Different Levels of Fasting," in *Today's Zaman*, Fri-day, 19 August 2011, at http://hizmetmovement.blogspot.com/2011/08/rama-dan-notes-different-levels-of.html

"Barış Manço gives Fethullah Gülen a gift: The late Barış Manço admires Fethullah Gülen's schools in the Far East... [Merhum sanatçı Barış Manço da Fethullah Gülen'in Uzakdoğu'da açtığı okullar dolayısıyla hayranlığını], at https://www.izlesene.com/video/baris-manconun-fethullah-gulene-hediye-takdim-etme-si/9434899

Barton, Greg, "How Hizmet Works: Islam, Dialogue and the Gülen Movement in

Australia," in *Hizmet Studies Review* 1(Autumn 2014): 9-26.

——. Paul Weller, and İhsan Yılmaz, "Fethullah Gülen, the Movement and this Book: An Introductory Overview," in *The Muslim World and Politics in Transition: Creative Contributions of the Gülen Movement* (London/NY: Bloomsbury, 2013).

Becker, Ernest, *The Denial of Death* (NY: Free Press, 1997 [1973]).

Belli, Onur Burçak, Eren Caylan and Maximilian Popp, "A Deadly Rivalry: Erdogan's Hunt Against the Gulen Movement," *Der Spiegel Online*, August 3, 2016, at http://www.spiegel.de/international/world/erdogan-hunts-down-guelen-movement-after-coup-attempt-a-1105800.html

Bernard, Phyllis E., "The Hizmet Movement in Business, Trade, and Commerce," *in Hizmet Means Service: Perspectives on an Alternative Path within Islam*. Ed. Martin E. Marty (Berkeley: The University of California Press, 2015).

Bilefsky, Dan and Sebnem Arsu, "Turkey Feels the Sway of Reclusive Cleric," *The New York Times*, April 24, 2012, at http://www.nytimes.com/2012/04/25/world/middleeast/turkey-feels-sway-of-fethullah-gulen-a-reclusive-cleric.html

Birand, Mehmet Ali, "Cemaat, efsaneleşen gücü'nün esiri oluyor," ["Gülen Community Becomes Prisoner of its Legendary Power"], *Hürriyet*, October 6, 2010, at http://www.hurriyet.com.tr/cemaat-efsanelesen-gucu-nun-esiri-oluy-or-15970467

Birnbaum, Michael, "In Turkey Protests, Splits in Erdoğan's Base," *The Washington Post*, June 14, 2013, at https://www.washingtonpost.com/world/Erdoğan-offers-concessions-to-turkeys-protesters/2013/06/14/9a87fff6-d4bf-11e2-a73e-826d299ff459_story.html?utm_term=.b2e720ec49da

Brennan, Margaret and Jennifer Janisch, "Are some U.S. charter schools helping fund controversial Turkish cleric's movement?," *CBS News*, March 29, 2017, at https://www.cbsnews.com/news/is-turkish-religious-scholar-fethullah-gulen-funding-movement-abroad-through-us-charter-schools/

Brinton, Crane, *The Anatomy of a Revolution* (NY: Vintage Books, 1965 [1938]).

Broder, Jonathan, "Has Turkey Become the Dying Man of Europe?," *The Chicago Tribune*, August 4, 1979, at http://archives.chicagotribune.com/1979/08/04/page/40/article/has-turkey-become-the-dying-man-of-europe

Burnett, Virginia and Yetkin Yıldırım, *Flying with Two Wings: Interfaith Dialogue in an Age of Terrorism* (Cambridge, MA: Cambridge Scholars Press, 2011).

Can, Eyüp, *Fethullah Gülen ile Ufuk Turu* [Fethullah Gülen's Horizon Tour] (Istanbul: AD, 1996).

——. *Zaman Daily*, August, 1995, as cited in *Fethullah Gülen*, "Relation with Literature and Music," at https://fgulen.com/en/home/1304-fgulen-com-english/fethullah-gulen-life/biography/24661-relation-with-literature-and-music

Çapan, Ergün, "Fethullah Gülen's Teaching Methodology in His Private Circle," in *Mastering Knowledge in Modern Times: Fethullah Gülen as an Islamic Scholar*, at https://www.fgulen.com/en/gulen-movement/on-the-movement/mastering-knowledge-in-modern-times-fethullah-gulen-as-an-islamic-scholar/48072-fethullah-gulens-teaching-methodology-in-his-private-circle

Carroll, B. Jill, *A Dialogue of Civilizations: Gülen's Islamic Ideals and Humanistic Discourse*. Foreword by Akbar S. Ahmed (NJ: The Light, 2007).

C.A.S.I.L.I.P.S. [Citizens Against Special Interest Lobbying in Public Schools]," "A Guide to the Gulen Movement's Activities in the U.S.: Gülen Charter Schools in the U.S.," [April 17, 2017], at http://turkishinvitations.weebly.com/list-of-us-schools.html

Çavdar, Ayşa,"Capital and Capitalists in Turkey: Gülen Sect--Reached for the State, Got Capital Instead," in *Heinrich Böll Stiftung / Türkiye* 8(2014): 1-12, at https://www.researchgate.net/publication/310005766_Gulen_sect_Reached_for_the_state got_capital_instead

Çetin, Muhammed, *The Gülen Movement: Civic Service Without Borders* (NY: Blue Dome Press, 2010).

Çiçek, Hikmet, "İshak Alaton ve FETÖ," September 15, 2016, https://www.aydinlik.com.tr/ishak-alaton-ve-feto.

Claridge, Tristan, "Explanation of Types of Social Capital," *Social Capital Research*, February 13, 2013, at https://www.socialcapitalresearch.com/explanation-types-social-capital/

Clement, Victoria, "Central Asia's Hizmet Schools," in *The Muslim World and Politics in Transition: Creative Contributions of the Gülen Movement*. Ed. Greg Barton, Paul Weller, İhsan Yılmaz (London/NY: Bloomsbury, 2013).

Clingingsmith, David, Asim Ijaz Khwaja and Michael Kremer, "Estimating the Impact of the   Hajj: Religion and Tolerance in Islam's Global Gathering," *Faculty Research Working Papers Series, Harvard Kennedy School/John F. Kennedy School of Government*, April 2008, RWP08-022, http://ksgnotes1.harvard.edu/Research/wpaper.nsf/rwp/RWP08-022.

Coontz, Stephanie, *Marriage, A History: How Love Conquered Marriage* (NY: Penguin, 2006).

Cortright, David, *Peace: A History of Movements and Ideas* (Cambridge: Cambridge University Press, 2010).

Cremin, Hilary, "Transformational Peace Education in the 21st Century," in *Peacebuilding through Education: Challenges, Opportunities, Cases*, ed. Carol Dahir (NJ: Blue Dome Press, 2015): 63-68.

Cubuk, Osman, and Burhan Cikili, "The Impact of *Hizmet* Movement on Intercultural Dialogue in Taiwan," in *International Conference on the Hizmet Movement and the Thought and Teachings of Fethullah Gülen: Contributions to Multiculturalism and Global Peace. National Taiwan University, College of Social Sciences, December 8-9, 2012*: 194-208.

Demir, Emre, "The Gülen Movement in Germany and France," at http://www.gulen-movement.com/gulen-movement-germany-france.html

Demir, Ömer, Mustafa Acar and Metin Toprak, "Anatolian Tigers or Islamic Capital: Prospects and Challenges," *Middle Eastern Studies* 40(2004): 166-188.

"The Dershane Prep School Debate in Numbers," *Daily Sabah*, November 19, 2013, at https://www.dailysabah.com/business/2013/11/19/the-dershane-prep-school-debate-in-numbers.

Dumanlı, Ekrem, "Part 5: Gülen Says Ballot Box Not Everything in Democracy," *Today's Zaman*, March 20, 2014, at http://Hizmetnews.com/11495/part-5-gulen-says-ballot-box-everything-democracy/#.Wp8mfujwZPY

——. *Time to Talk: An Exclusive Interview with Fethullah Gülen* (NY: Blue Dome, 2015).

Duran, Burhanettin, and Çınar Menderes, "Competing Occidentalisms of Modern Islamist Thought: Necip Fazıl Kisakürek and Nurettin Topçu," in *The Muslim World*, 103 (October 2013): 479–500.

Ebaugh, Helen Rose, *The Gülen Movement: A Sociological Analysis of a Civic Movement Rooted in Moderate Islam* (Amsterdam: Springer, 2010).

——. and Doğan Koç, "Funding Gülen-Inspired Good Works: Demonstrating and Generating Commitment to the Movement," in *Muslim World in Transition: Contributions of the Gülen Movement. International Conference Proceedings. London, 25-27 October 2007.* (London: Leeds Metropolitan University Press, 2007).

Eck, Diana L., *Encountering God: A Spiritual Journey from Bozeman to Benares* (Boston: Beacon Press, 1993).

Eisenstadt, S. N. Edited with an Introduction by. *Max Weber on Charisma and Institution-Building: Selected Papers* (Chicago and London: The University of Chicago Press, 1968).

Elder, Earl Edgar, tr., *A Commentary on the Creed of Islam* (NY: Columbia University Press, 1950).

El-Kazaz, Sarah, "The AKP and the Gülen: The End of a Historic Alliance," in *Middle East Brief [Brandeis University Crown Center for Middle East Studies]*, July 2015, No. 94, at https://www.brandeis.edu/crown/publications/meb/MEB94.pdf

Empire of Deceit: An Investigation of the Gülen Charter School Network (Amsterdam and Partners, LLP for the Republic of Turkey, 2017).

"Erdoğan 'Ben bu davanın savcısıyım' demişti!" [Erdogan said 'I am the prosecutor of this case!'], in *ABC Gazetesi*, April 21, 2016, at http://www.abcgazetesi.com/erdogan-ben-bu-davanin-savcisiyim-demisti-13866h.htm

Erdoğan, Latif, *Fethullah Gülen "Küçük Dünyam"* ["My Little World"]. 40th ed. (Istanbul: AD, 1997).

Ergene, Mehmet Enes,*Tradition Witnessing the Modern Age: An Analysis of the Gülen Movement* (NJ: Tughra Books, 2008).

Ergil, Doğu, *Fethullah Gülen and the Gülen Movement in 100 Questions* (Istanbul: Blue Dome Press, 2012 – Kindle edition 2013).

Esposito, John L. and İhsan Yılmaz, *Islam and Peacebuilding: Gülen Movement Initiatives* (Istanbul: Blue Dome, 2010).

Esposito, John L., *Unholy War: Terror in the Name of Islam* (London/NY: Oxford University Press, 2003).

"'Evet Ergenekon'un savcısıyım' ['Yes, I am the prosecutor of Ergenekon'], *Gazetavatan.com*, July 16, 2008, at http://www.gazetevatan.com/-evet-ergenekon-un-savcisiyim--189246-siyaset/

"FETO's Structure," *Yeni Şafak*, at http://www.yenisafak.com/en/15-july-coup-attempt-in-turkey/fetos-structure-kurulus-en-detail

fgulen.com. "Sızıntı Celebrates 30th Year as Magazine of Love and Tolerance," at http://fgulen.com/en/home/1323-fgulen-com-english/press/news/26507-sizinti-celebrates-30th-year-as-magazine-of-love-and-tolerance

Filkins, Dexter, "Turkey's 30-Year Coup," *The New Yorker*, October 27, 2016, at http://www.newyorker.com/magazine/2016/10/17/turkeys-thirty-year-coup

Findley, Carter Vaughn, "Hizmet among the Most Influential Religious Renewals of Late Ottoman and Modern Turkish History," at https://content.ucpress.edu/chapters/12909.ch01.pdf

——. *Turkey, Islam, Nationalism, and Modernity: A History, 1789-2007* (New Haven: Yale University Press, 2010).

Friedman, Uri, "The Thinnest-Skinned President in the World," *The Atlantic*, April, 2016, at https://www.theatlantic.com/international/archive/2016/04/turkey-germany-erdogan-bohmermann/479814/

Gardels, Nathan, "A Talk with Orhan Pamuk: Caressing the World with Words," *Huffington Post Blog*, May 25, 2011, at http://www.huffingtonpost.com/nathan-gardels/a-talk-with-orhan-pamuk-c_b_353799.html

Gopin, Marc, *Holy War, Holy Peace: How Religion Can Bring Peace to the Middle East* (NY/London: Oxford University Press, 2005).

Grimaldi, James V., Dion Nissenbaum and Margaret Coker, "Ex-CIA Director: Mike Flynn and Turkish Officials Discussed Removal of Erdoğan Foe From U.S.," *The Wall Street Journal*, March 24, 2017, at https://www.wsj.com/articles/ex-cia-director-mike-flynn-and-turkish-officials-discussed-removal-of-Erdoğan-foe-from-u-s-1490380426

Grossman, Lt. Col. David, *On Killing: The Psychological Cost of Learning to Kill in War and Society* (Boston: Back Bay Books, 1996).

Gülen, M. Fethullah, "1975 Yılı Vaazları," [1975 Year Sermons], *Fethullah Gülen* [Turkish version], at "1975 Yılı Vaazları," Fethullah Gülen [Turkish version], at https://fgulen.com/tr/ses-ve-video/fethullah-gulen-hitabet/fethullah-gulen-hocaefendinin-vaizligi/3586-fgulen-com-1975-Yili-Vaazlari

——. "1977 Yılı Vaaz ve Konferansları,"[1977 Year Sermons and Conferences], *Fethullah Gülen*, [Turkish Version], at http://fgulen.com/tr/ses-ve-video/fethullah-gulen-hitabet/fethullah-gulen-hocaefendinin-vaizligi/3588-fgulen-com-1977-Yili-Vaaz-ve-Konferanslari

——. "1990 Yılı Vaazları" [1990 Year Sermons], at https://fgulen.com/tr/ses-ve-video/fethullah-gulen-hitabet/fethullah-gulen-hocaefendinin-vaizligi/3593-fgulen-com-1990-Yili-Vaazlari

——. "The Beard and the Headscarf Issue," at https://fgulen.com/en/home/1305-fgulen-com-english/fethullah-gulen-life/gulens-thoughts/25051-the-beard-and-the-headscarve-issue

——. "Being Pursued," in *Fethullah Gülen*, at https://www.fgulen.com/en/fethullah-gulens-life/about-fethullah-gulen/biography/24659-being-pursued

——. "Being Shaped by Ramadan," *The Fountain Magazine*, 25 (Jan-Mar 1999), at http://www.fountainmagazine.com/Issue/detail/Being-Shaped-by-Ramadan

——. "Bu Hareket Devlete Alternatif mi?" [Is This Movement an Alternative to the State?], at http:// tr.fgulen.com/ content/ view/ 12134/ 9/, as cited in Ergil, Loc. 872. The cited link is broken, but the essay can be found at: http://www.herkul.org/kirik-testi/bu-hareket-devlete-alternatif-mi-2/, November 14, 2005.

——. "Chaos and the Mystical World of Faith," *The Fountain Magazine*, May-June 2010a, at http://www.fountainmagazine.com/Issue/detail/Chaos-and-the-Mystical-World-of-Faith

——. "Dialogue with the People of the Book, Jews and Christians," August 25, 1995, at https://fgulen.com/en/fethullah-gulens-life/1315-fethullah-gulens-speeches-and-interviews-on-interfaith-dialogue/25141-dialogue-with-the-people-of-the-book-jews-and-christians

——. "Edirne," in *Fethullah Gülen*, at http://fgulen.com/en/fethullah-gulens-life/about-fethullah-gulen/biography/24654-edirne

——. "Edirne, Kirklareli, and finally Izmir," in *Fethullah Gülen*, at https://www.fgulen.com/en/fethullah-gulens-life/about-fethullah-gulen/biography/24656-

edirne-kirklareli-and-finally-izmir

———. *Emerald Hills of the Heart: Key Concepts in the Practice of Sufism, Volume 1.* Tr. Ali Ünal (NJ: Tughra Books, 2013a).

———. *Emerald Hills of the Heart: Key Concepts in the Practice of Sufism, Volume. 2.* Tr. Ali Ünal (NJ: Tughra Books, 2011).

———. *Essays-Perspectives-Opinions.* Compiled by The Light (NJ: The Light, 2006a).

———. "An Exile Poem," in "Appendix" to Nevval Sevindi, *Contemporary Islamic Conversations: M. Fethullah Gülen on Turkey, Islam, and the West.* Ed. with an Introduction by Ibrahim M. Abu-Rabi'. Tr. by Abdullah T. Antepli (Albany: SUNY Press, 2008): 149-50.

———. "Fethullah Gülen on His Meeting with the Pope," interview in *Zaman,* February 13, 1998, at https://fgulen.com/en/fethullah-gulens-life/dialogue-activities/meeting-with-the-pope-john-paul-ii/25152-fethullah-gulen-on-his-meeting-with-the-pope

———. "Fethullah Gülen's Message on the 9/11 Terror Attacks," at http://www.gulen-movement.com/fethullah-gulens-message-on-the-911-terrorist-attacks.html

———. "The Golden Period of Time, Izmir," *Fethullah Gülen,* at http://fgulen.com/en/fethullah-gulens-life/about-fethullah-gulen/biography/24650-a-different-home

———. "Hajj and Praying," *Weekly Sermons, The Broken Jug,* 8/10/2012, at http://www.herkul.org/weekly-sermons/hajj-and-praying/

———. "Hocaefendi's Primary School Years as Narrated by Himself and his Teacher, Belma," *Zaman,* 24 November 2006b. https://fgulen.com/tr/turk-basininda-fethullah-gulen/fethullah-gulen-hakkinda-dizi-yazilar-dosyalar/fethullah-gulen-web-sitesi-ozel-dosyalar/12561-fgulen-com-belma-ozbatur-anlatiyor

———. "Honorary President Fethullah Gülen's Founding Speech," [1994], at http://jwf.org/jwfs-honorary-president-fethullah-gulens-founding-speech/

———. "I Condemn All Threats to Turkey's Democracy," in *The New York Times,* July 25, 2016, at https://www.nytimes.com/2016/07/26/opinion/fethullah-gulen-i-condemn-all-threats-to-turkeys-democracy.html

———. "Ideal Consultation-1," *Herkul: Weekly Sermons,* September 28, 2014a, at http://www.herkul.org/weekly-sermons/ideal-consultation-1/

———. "Ideal Consultation-2," *Herkul,* October 4, 2014b, at http://www.herkul.org/weekly-sermons/ideal-consultation-2/

———. "Interview with Fethullah Gülen," in *Herkul,* July 16, 2016.

———. "Işık Evler [Light Houses] (1)," *Fethullah Gülen,* at https://fgulen.com/tr/fethullah-gulenin-butun-eserleri/cag-ve-nesil-serisi/fethullah-gulen-gunler-bahari-soluklarken/10409-Fethullah-Gulen-Isik-Evler-1

———. "Jews and Christians in the Qur'an," 05/24-25, 1996, at https://fgulen.com/en/fethullah-gulens-life/1315-fethullah-gulens-speeches-and-interviews-on-interfaith-dialogue/25142-jews-and-christians-in-the-quran

———. *Journey to Noble Ideals: Droplets of Wisdom from the Heart.* Vol. 13, The Broken Jug (NJ: Tughra Books, 2014c).

———. "Military Service," *Fethullah Gülen,* at http://fgulen.com/en/home/1304-fgulen-com-english/fethullah-gulen-life/biography/24655-military-service

———. "The Month Overflowing with Mercy," in *Ramadan* (NJ: Tughra Books, n.d.).

———. *Muhammad, the Messenger of God: An Analysis of the Prophet's Life.* Tr. Ali

Ünal (NJ: Tughra Books, 2010b).

——. "The Necessity of Interfaith Dialogue," in *The Fountain* 3:31 (July-Sep, 2000), pp. 7-8, as cited in M. Fethullah Gülen, *Essays-Perspectives-Opinions* (NJ: The Light, 2006c): 51-2.

——. "Orta Asya'da Eğitim Hizmetleri" [Educational Services in Central Asia]. *Yeni Türkiye Dergisi*, nr. 15. [1997], pp. 685– 692, as cited in Doğu Ergil, *Fethullah Gülen and the Gülen Movement in 100 Questions* (NJ: Blue Dome Press, Kindle Edition), Loc. 8074-8075.

——. "The Patriarch and Fethullah Hodja," *Sabah*, April 6, 1996, at   https://fgulen.com/en/fethullah-gulens-life/dialogue-activities/repercussions-from-gulen-bartholomeos-meeting/25144-the-patriarch-and-fethullah-hodja

——. *Pearls of Wisdom*. Tr. Ali Ünal. (NJ: The Light, 2006d).

——. *Questions and Answers about Islam,* Vol. 1. Tr. Muhammed Çetin (NJ: The Light, 2006e).

——. *Questions and Answers about Islam*, Vol. 2. Tr. Muhammed Çetin (NJ: The Light, 2005).

——. "Ramadan and Softening Hearts," *The Broken Jug*, 10 July 2013b, at https://www.fgulen.com/en/fethullah-gulens-works/thought/the-broken-jug/36142-ramadan-and-softening-hearts

——. *Reflections on the Qur'an: Commentaries on Selected Verses*. Tr. Ayşenur Kaplan and Harun Gültekin (NJ: Tughra Books, 2014d).

——. "The Society of Peace," [*Sızıntı*, August, 1979], in Erkan M. Kurt, ed. and translator, *So That Others May Live: A Fethullah Gülen Reader* (NY: Blue Dome Press, 2014e): 27-29.

——. "Solution to the Problem of Racism," at https://fgulen.com/en/fethullah-gulens-works/faith/prophet-muhammad-as-commander/24896-solution-to-the-problem-of-racism

——. *Toward a Global Civilization of Love and Tolerance*. Foreword by Thomas Michel (NJ: The Light, 2006f).

——. "A Tribute to Mothers," The Fountain Magazine, 50(April-June, 2005), at http://en.fgulen.com/recent-articles/1940-a-tribute-to-mothers

——. *Truth through Colors* (Izmir: Nil, 1992).

——. *Towards the Lost Paradise* (London: Truestar, 1996).

——. "Why Does He Cry?," *Fethullah Gülen*, at https://www.fgulen.com/en/fethullah-gulens-life/about-fethullah-gulen/biography/24660-why-does-he-cry, citing an "Interview with Nuriye Akman," *Sabah Daily*, 1/23-30, 1995.

——.Years of Education," *Fethullah Gülen*, at http://fgulen.com/en/home/1304-fgulen-com-english/fethullah-gulen-life/biography/24652-years-of-education

——. compiler, *Selected Prayers of Prophet Muhammad and Great Muslim Saints*. Tr. Ali Keeler (NY: Tughra Books, 2012).

——. *The Statue of Our Souls: Revival in Islamic Thought and Activism*. Tr. Muhammed Çetin (NJ: The Light, 2007).

——. *Understanding and Belief: The Essentials of Islamic Faith* (Konya/Izmir: Kaynak Publishing, 1977).

——. "Women and Men Prayed Together at the Mosque," in *Fethullah Gülen's Thoughts*, at https://fgulen.com/en/fethullah-gulens-life/1305-gulens-thoughts/25059-women-and-men-prayed-together-at-the-mosque.

——. "Women and Women's Rights," interview with Ertuğrul Özkök, *Hürriyet*

Daily, January 23-30, 1995, at http://www.fethullahgulen.com/en/home/1305-fgulen-com-english/fethullah-gulen-life/gulens-thoughts/25057-women-and-womens-rights

GülenMovement.com, "The Life of Fethullah Gülen: Highlights from His Education," at http://www.gulenmovement.us/the-life-of-fethullah-gulen-highlights-from-his-education.html

——. "Fethullah Gülen as an Islamic Scholar," at http://www.gulenmovement.com/fethullah-gulen/fethullah-gulen-as-an-islamic-scholar

——. "There has never been a sincere alliance between Gülen Movement and Erdoğan," [n.d.], at http://www.gulenmovement.com/never-sincere-alliance-gulen-movement-erdogan.html

HizmetNews.com. "İkbal Gürpinar Hospital is Connecting Sudanese People to Life," in *Hizmet News*, February 23, 2012, at http://hizmetnews.com/420/ikbal-gurpinar-hospital-is-connecting-sudanese-people-to-life/#.WmcpT6inF-PY

Gündem, Mehmet, *Lüzumlu Adam [An Essential Man]: İshak Alaton* (Istanbul: Alfa Yayıncılık, 2014).

——. *Fethullah Gülen'le 11 Gün* [11 Days with Fethullah Gülen] (Istanbul: Alfa, 2005).

Gunter, Michael M., "Contrasting Turkish Paradigms toward the Volatile Kurdish Question: Domestic and Foreign Considerations," in *The Kurdish Question Revisited*, ed. Gareth Stansfield and Mohammed Sharif (London: Oxford University Press, 2017): 259-79.

Gürbüz, Mustafa, "Recognition of Kurdish Identity and the Hizmet Movement," at http://www.gulenmovement.com/recognition-of-kurdish-identity-and-the-hizmet-movement.html

Haddad, Yvonne Yazbeck "Ghurba as Paradigm for Muslim Life: A Risale-i Nur Worldview," in *The Muslim World* 89(No. 3-4): 299, as cited by Yasin Aktay, "Diaspora and Stability: Constitutive Elements in a Body of Knowledge," in *Turkish Islam and the Secular State: The Gülen Movement*. Ed. M. Hakan Yavuz and John L. Esposito (Syracuse: Syracuse University Press, 2003).

"Hacı Kemal Erimez/Hacı Ata," at http://hacikemalerimez.blogspot.com/

Hällzon, Patrick, "The Gülen Movement: Gender and Practice," in *Islam in the Age of Global Challenges: Alternative Perspectives of the Gülen Movement. Conference Proceedings, November 14-15, 2008. Georgetown University*: 288-309.

Harrington, James C., *Wrestling with Free Speech, Religious Freedom, and Democracy in Turkey* (Lanham, MD: University Press of America, 2011).

Harvard Kennedy School, "Social Capital Glossary," The Saguaro Seminar: Civic Engagement in America, at https://www.hks.harvard.edu/saguaro/glossary.htm.

Hatch, Nathan O., *The Democratization of American Christianity* (New Haven, CT: Yale University Press, 1987).

Hauslohner, Abigail, "Inside the Rural PA Compound where an Influential Muslim Cleric Lives in Exile," in *The Washington Post*, August 3, 2016, at https://www.washingtonpost.com/news/post-nation/wp/2016/08/03/inside-the-rural-pa-compound-where-an-influential-muslim-cleric-lives-in-exile/?utm_term=.bdd6e17dcacd

Heck, Paul L., "Turkish in the Language of the Qur'an: *Hira'* Magazine," in *The Muslim World and Politics in Transition: Creative Contributions of the Gülen Move-

ment. Ed. Greg Barton, Paul Weller, and İhsan Yılmaz (London/NY: Blooms-bury, 2013): 143-153.

Hefner, Robert, *Civil Islam: Muslims and Democratization in Indonesia* (Princeton: Princeton University Press, 2000).

Hendrick, Joshua D., *Gülen: The Ambiguous Politics of Market Islam in Turkey* (NY: New York University Press, 2013).

Hermansen, Marcia, "The Cultivation of Memory in the Gülen Movement," in *International Conference Proceedings--Muslim World in Transition: Contributions of the Gülen Movement* (London: Leeds Metropolitan University Press, 2007).

———. "Understandings of Community in the Gülen Movement," 12 November 2005, in *Studies: Academic Works on the Risale-i Nur Collection*, at http://risaleinur.com/index.php?option=com_content&view=article&id=4341:understandings-of-community-within-the-gulen-movement&catid=79&Itemid=157.

———. "Who is Fethullah Gülen: An Overview of His Life," in *Hizmet Means Service: Perspectives on an Alternative Path in Islam*. Ed. Martin E. Marty (Berkeley: University of California Press, 2015).

Hesser, Terry Spencer, *Love Is a Verb* (NY: Global Vision Productions, 2014).

Hunt, Robert A. and Yüksel A. Aslandoğan, *Muslim Citizens of the Globalized World: Contributions of the Gülen Movement* (Somerset, NJ: The Light, 2006):

"Interview with Nicole Pope," *Le Monde*, 28 April 1998, as cited by Doğu Ergil, *Fethullah Gülen and the Gülen Movement in 100 Questions* (Istanbul: Blue Dome Press, 2012).

Irmak TV, *Geçmişten İzler* (Traces from the Past), "Interview with Abdullah Ünal Birlik," March 11, 2014. Episode 1, at https://www.youtube.com/watch?v=T89g-0bCDADQ

———. *Geçmişten İzler* (Traces from the Past), "Interview with Ahmet Haseken," February 24, 2014.

———. *Geçmişten İzler*, "Interview with İrfan Yılmaz," Episode 1, April 1, 2015.

———. *Geçmişten İzler* (Traces from the Past), "Interview with Sıgbatullah Gülen: Episode 1," May 29, 2014, at https://www.youtube.com/watch?v=0BAL-W0DYmB0.

———. *Geçmişten İzler* (Traces from the Past), "Interview with Sibgatullah Gülen, Episode 2," June 4, 2014.

———. *Geçmişten İzler*, "Interview with Tahsin Şimşek," Episode 1, December 31, 2014.

———. *Geçmişten Izler* (Traces from the Past), "Interview with Yusuf Pekmezci," Episode 1, October 29, 2014, at https://www.youtube.com/watch?v=8OnPa0Idm-NI

———. *Geçmişten Izler*, "Interview with Yusuf Pekmezci," Episode 2, September 17, 2014.

Irvine, Jill, "The Gülen Movement and Turkish Integration in Germany," in *Muslim Citizens of the Globalized World: Contributions of the Gülen Movement*. Ed. Robert A. Hunt and Yüksel A. Aslandoğan (NJ: The Light, 2007): 62-84.

Islam, Merve Kavakci, *Headscarf Politics in Turkey: A Postcolonial Reading* (NY: Palgrave-Macmillan, 2010).

James, William, "The Moral Equivalent of War," [1910], at http://www.constitution.org/wj/meow.htm

Journalists and Writers Foundation, "Soccer Match Raises Money for Children's Education in Bosnia-Herzegovina," September 19, 1995, at http://jwf.org/soccer-match-raises-money-for-children-s-education-in-bosnia-herzegovina/

Kakar, Narinda, "Preface," in *Peacebuilding through Education*, ed. Carol Dahir (NJ: Blue Dome Press, 2015).

Kalın, İbrahim, "The Coup Leader Must Be Held Accountable," *The New York Times*, July 24, 2016, at https://www.nytimes.com/2016/07/25/opinion/the-turkey-coup-leader-must-be-held-accountable.html?action=click&contentCollection=Opinion&module=RelatedCoverage& region=Marginalia&pgtype=article

Kaylan, Melik, "The Zarrab Court Case: What it means for Flynn, Trump, Erdoğan, Even Putin," *Forbes*, December 5, 2017, at https://www.forbes.com/sites/melikkaylan/2017/12/05/the-zarrab-court-case-what-it-means-for-flynn-trump-Erdoğan-even-putin/#7481559e7ecb

Kaynak Holding, "History," at http://kaynak.com.tr/en/default.aspx

Keneş, Bülent, "Sawadee Ka World Peace," *Today's Zaman*, 10 June 2009, at https://www.fgulen.com/new/en/press/columns/sawadee-ka-world-peace

Kenyon, Peter, "Turkey's President and His 1,100 Room 'White Palace,'" *All Things Considered*, National Public Radio, December 24, 2014, at https://www.npr.org/sections/parallels/2014/12/24/370931835/turkeys-president-and-his-1-100-room-white-palace

Kerim, Rebwar, "Kurdish Paper Rudaw's Interview with Fethullah Gülen," March 13, 2013, at http://hizmetnews.com/15341/kurdish-paper-rudaws-interview-with-fethullah-gulen/#.WiF8GEqnFPY

Kimball, Charles, *When Religion Becomes Evil: Five Warning Signs* (NY: Harper-Collins, 2009).

Kinzer, Stephen, "Barış Manço, Turkish Pop Star and Television Personality, 56, http://www.nytimes.com/1999/02/07/nyregion/baris-manco-turkish-pop-star-and-television-personality-56.html

——. "Süleyman Demirel, 9 Times Turkey's Prime Minister, Dies at 90," *The New York Times*, June 16, 2015, at https://www.nytimes.com/2015/06/17/world/europe/suleyman-demirel-former-prime-minister-of-turkey-dies-at-90.html

——. "Kenan Evren, 97, Dies; After Coup, Led Turkey With Iron Hand," in *The New York Times*, May 1, 2015, at https://www.nytimes.com/2015/05/10/world/europe/kenan-evren-dies-at-97-led-turkeys-1980-coup.html

Kirk, Martha Ann, *Growing Seeds of Peace: Stories and Images of Service of the Gülen Movement in Southeastern Turkey—A Travel Journal. With Historical and Geographical Context by Doğan Koç* (Houston: The Gülen Institute, 2012).

Knysh, Alexander, tr., *Al-Qusharyri's Epistle on Sufism: Al-Risala Al-qushayriyya Fi 'ilm Al-tasawwuf* [Great Books of Islamic Civilization] (NY: Garnet Publishing, 2007).

Koç, Doğan, "Generating an Understanding of Financial Resources in the Gulen Movement: 'Kimse Yok Mu' Solidarity and Aid Association, in *Islam in the Age of Global Challenges: Alternative Perspectives of the Gülen Movement. Conference Proceedings, November 14-15, 2008*. Georgetown University (Washington, DC: Rumi Forum, 2008): 435-454.

Kurt, Erkan M., ed. and tr., *So That Others May Live: A Fethullah Gülen Reader* (NY: Blue Dome, 2014).

Kuru, Zeynep Akbulut, and Ahmet Kuru, "Apolitical Interpretation of Islam: Said Nursi's Faith- Based Activism in Comparison with Political Islamism and Sufism," in *Islam and Christian-Muslim Relations* 19(2008): 99-111, at https://www.tandfonline.com/doi/abs/10.1080/13510340701770311

Lauria, Joe, "Reclusive Turkish Imam Criticizes Gaza Flotilla," *Wall Street Journal*, June 4, 2010, at https://www.wsj.com/articles/SB10001424052748704025304575284721280274694

Letsch, Constanze, "Turkish Minister's Sons Arrested in Bribery and Corruption Scandal," *The Guardian*, 17 December, 2013, at https://www.theguardian.com/world/2013/dec/17/turkish-ministers-sons-arrested-corruption-investigation

———. "Turkish PM: corruption probe part of 'dirty operation' against administration," *The Guardian*, 18 December, 2013, at https://www.theguardian.com/world/2013/dec/18/turkish-pm-corruption-probe-dirty-operation

Lifton, Robert Jay, *Revolutionary Immortality: Mao Tse-Tung and the Chinese Cultural Revolution* (NY: Norton, 1976).

Likmeta, Besar, "Albania Ignores Erdoğan's Tirade Against Gülen," in *Hizmet-MovementNewsPortal*, May 20, 2015, at https://www.voanews.com/a/turkey-erdogan-gulen-schools/4010073.html

Lindberg, Carter and Paul Wee. Eds. *The Forgotten Luther: Reclaiming the Social-Economic Dimension of the Reformation*, (Minneapolis: Lutheran University Press, 2016).

"Malcolm X's Letter from Mecca," at http://islam.uga.edu/malcomx.html

Mango, Andrew, *Atatürk: The Biography of the Founder of Modern Turkey* (NY: Overlook, 1999).

Marty, Martin E., ed., *Hizmet Means Service: Perspectives on an Alternative Path in Islam.* (Berkeley: The University of California Press, 2015).

MacCulloch, Diarmaid, *Christianity: The First Three Thousand Years* (NY: Penguin, 2011).

McLoughlin, William G., Jr., *Modern Revivalism: Charles Grandison Finney to Billy Graham.* Reprint Edition. (Eugene, OR: Wipf and Stock, 2004 [1959]).

Mercan, Faruk, *No Return from Democracy: A Survey of Interviews with Fethullah Gülen* (NJ: Blue Dome Press, 2017).

Michel, Thomas, SJ, "Fighting Poverty with Kimse Yok Mu," in *Islam in the Age of Global Challenges: Alternative Perspectives of the Gülen Movement. Conference Proceedings, November 14-15, 2008.* Georgetown University (Washington, DC: Rumi Forum, 2008): 523-533.

Mohamed, Yasien, "The Educational Theory of Fethullah Gülen and its Practice in South Africa," in *The Muslim World in Transition: Contributions of the Gülen Movement. International Conference Proceedings. London, 25-27 October 2007.* (London: Leeds Metropolitan University Press, 2007): 552-571.

Münz, Rainer, and Ralf E. Ulrich, "Changing Patterns of Immigration to Germany, 1945-1997," at *Migration Dialogue, "Research and Seminars,"* at https://migration.ucdavis.edu/rs/more.php?id=69

Naqshbandi Sufi Way, "Awrad," at http://naqshbandi.org/awrad/

Neitzel, Sonke, Harald Welzer, and Jefferson Trace (tr), *Soldiers: German POW's on Fighting, Killing, and Dying* (NY: Vintage, 2012).

Norton, Jenny and Cagil Kasapoglu, "Turkey's post-coup crackdown hits 'Gulen schools' worldwide," *BBC World Service*, 23 September 2016, at http://www.

bbc.com/news/world-europe-37422822

Nursi, Said, *Risale-I Nur Külliyatı*. (Istanbul: Nesil, 1996), at http://www.nur.gen.tr/en.html

——. *The Risale-I Nur Collection. The Gleams: Reflections on Qur'anic Wisdom and Spirituality*. Tr. By Hüseyin Akarsu (NJ: Tughra Books, 2008).

Ocheja, Joshua, "Turkey: Erdoğan's Macabre Dance in Africa," *The Cable*, 7 December 2016, at https://www.thecable.ng/turkey-Erdoğans-macabre-dance-africa

——. "Understanding the Hizmet Movement in Nigeria," *The Cable*, 7 November 2016, reprinted at https://fgulen.com/en/press/columns/50914-understanding-the-hizmet-movement-in-nigeria.

"131 Media Organs Closed by Statutory Decree," at http://bianet.org/english/media/177256-131-media-organs-closed-by-statutory-decree

Oğurlu, Anita and Ahmet Öncü, "The Laic-Islamist Schism in the Turkish Dominant Class and the Media," in *The Neoliberal Landscape and the Rise of Islamist Capital in Turkey*, ed. Nesecan Balkan, Erol Balkan, and Ahmet Öncü (Berghahn, 2015).

Osman, Mohamed Nawab, "The Gülen Movement as a Civil-Islamic Force in Indonesia," in *The Muslim World and Politics in Transition: Creative Contributions of the Gülen Movement*. Ed. Greg Barton, Paul Weller, Ihsan Yilmaz (London/NY: Bloomsbury, 2013).

Özdalga, Elisabeth, "Redeemer or Outsider? The Gülen Community in the Civilizing Process," in *The Muslim World 95* (July 2005).

——. "Worldly Asceticism in Islamic Casting: Fethullah Gülen's Inspired Piety and Activism," in *Critique* 17(2000): 83-104.

Özdemir, Şemsinur, *Hoca Anne ve Ailesi* (Istanbul: Ufuk Yayınları, 2014).

Orhan, Özgüç, "Islamic Himmah and Christian Charity: An Attempt at Inter-faith Dialogue," in *Islam in the Age of Global Challenges: Alternative Perspectives of the Gülen Movement*. November 14-15, 2008. (Washington, DC: Georgetown University, 2008).

Özkök, Ertuğrul, *Hürriyet Daily*, 1/23-30, 1996, as cited in *Fethullah Gülen*, "Relation with Literature and Music," at https://fgulen.com/en/home/1304-fgulen-com-english/fethullah-gulen-life/biography/24661-relation-with-literature-and-music

Pahl, Jon, "Economic Crises and the Promise of Spiritually-Grounded Social Enterprise: Building Peace through Sustainable Profits, Consistent with the Prophets," delivered at Beder University, Tirana, Albania, May 17, 2013," available on request.

——. "Fragments of Empire: Lessons for Americans in Orhan Pamuk's 'The Museum of Innocence,' in *Public Theology*, May 10, 2010, at http://www.pubtheo.com/page.asp?pid=1548

——. "Muslims teach lesson in sacrifice," *The Philadelphia Inquirer*, October 23, 2006, as reposted in *CAIR--Philadelphia*, at http://pa.cair.com/actionalert/thank-philadelphia-inquirer/

——. *Empire of Sacrifice: The Religious Origins of American Violence* (NY: New York University Press, 2012).

——. *Shopping Malls and Other Sacred Spaces: Putting God in Place* (Grand Rapids, MI: Brazos Press, 2003).

——. and T.L. Hill, "Social Entrepreneurship as a Catalyst for Practical Social Justice in   Economic Life," in *A Just World: Multi-Disciplinary Perspectives on Social Justice*, Ed.   Heon Kim (Newcastle-Upon-Tyne: Cambridge Scholars Press, 2013): 39-52.

Pamuk, Orhan, *Istanbul: Memories and the City*. Tr. Maureen Freely (NY: Vintage, 2006).

————. *Istanbul: Memories and the City*. Tr. Maureen Freely (NY: Vintage, 2006). Kindle Edition.

Peace and Justice Studies Association, at https://www.peacejusticestudies.org/

Peres, Richard, *The Day Turkey Stood Still: Merve Kavakci's Walk into the Turkish Parliament* (UK: Ithaca Press, 2012).

Phillipine Daily Inquirer, "Raucous, Solemn Rites Mark Muslim Celebration of Eid al-Fitr,", August 31, 2011, at http://newsinfo.inquirer.net/50645/raucous-solemn-rites-mark-muslim-feast-of-eid%E2%80%99l-fitr

Pinker, Steven, *The Better Angels of Our Nature: Why Violence Has Declined* (NY: Viking, 2011).

PwC, *Middle East News*, "Ministry of Finance Introduces New *Zakat* Implementing Regulations," April 6, 2017, at https://www.pwc.com/m1/en/services/tax/me-tax-legal-news/2017/ksa-ministry-finance-introduces-new-zakat-implementing-regulations.html

Rae, Laurelie, *Islamic Art and Architecture: Memories of Seljuk and Ottoman Masterpieces* (NJ: Blue Dome Press, 2015).

Rausch, Margaret, "Progress through Piety: Sohbetler (Spiritual Gatherings) of the Women Participants in the Gülen Movement," in *Islam in the Age of Global Challenges: Alternative Perspectives of the Gülen Movement. Georgetown University President's Office, Alwaleed bin Talal Center for Muslim Christian Understanding. Rumi Forum.* November 14-15, 2008.

Reich, Robert, "The Virtuous Cycle," in *Inequality for All*, at https://www.youtube.com/watch?v=gT3cm2eTuSg

Robinson, Simon, "Building Bridges: Gülen Pontifex," in *Hizmet Means Service: Perspectives on an Alternative Path in Islam.* (Berkeley: The University of California Press, 2015).

Rodgers, Guy, "Fethullah Gulen: Infiltrating the U.S. Through Our Charter Schools? [incl. Tarek ibn Ziyad Academy]," *Campus Watch: Monitoring Middle East Studies on Campus*, April 9, 2009, at http://www.campus-watch.org/article/id/7238.

Rodrick, Dani, "Is Fethullah Gülen Behind Turkey's Coup? [with update]," *Dani Rodrik's Weblog*, July 24, 2016, at http://rodrik.typepad.com/dani_rodriks_weblog/2016/07/is-fethullah-gülen-behind-turkeys-coup.html

Rubin, Michael,"Why the Reza Zarrab guilty plea matters to Turkey and the world," *Washington   Examiner*, November 28, 2017, at http://www.washingtonexaminer.com/why-the-reza- zarrab-guilty-plea-matters-to-turkey-and-the-world/article/2641919

Rudolf, Ulrich, *Al-Māturīdī and the Development of Sunnī Theology in Samarqand* (London/Berlin: Brill, 2014).

Rumi Forum, "The Wing of the Bird--Gülen on Sincerity," at http://rumiforum.org/the-wing-of- the-bird-guelen-on-sincerity/

Sacks, Jonathan, *The Dignity of Difference: How to Avoid the Clash of Civilizations* (NY: Continuum, 2002).

Sahin, Mustafa Gokhan, "Turkey and Neo-Ottomanism: Domestic Sources, Dynamics and Foreign Policy," PhD Dissertation, Department of International Relations, Florida International University, 2010, at http://digitalcommons.fiu.edu/cgi/viewcontent.cgi?article=1220&context=etd

Sarıtoprak, Zeki and Ali Ünal, "Interview with Fethullah Gülen," in *The Muslim World. Special Issue. Islam in Contemporary Turkey: The Contributions of Fethullah Gülen*, 95 (July 2005).

———. "An Islamic Approach to Peace and Nonviolence," in *The Muslim World. Special Issue. Islam in Contemporary Turkey: The Contributions of Fethullah Gülen* 95 (July 2005).

Schwartz, Yardena, "In New Palestinian City, Few Residents and Charges of Collusion with Israel," *The Times of Israel*, 24 January 2016, a https://www.timesofisrael.com/in-new-palestinian-city-few-residents-and-charges-of-collusion-with-israel/

Soltes, Ori Z., *Embracing the World: Fethullah Gülen's Thought and Its Relationship to Jalaluddin Rumi and Others* (NJ: Tughra Books, 2013).

Srivastava, Mehul, "Assets worth 11bn seized in Turkey crackdown," in *Financial Times*, July 7, 2017.

"Sufism in Turkey," *Harvard Divinity School Religious Literacy Project*, at https://rlp.hds.harvard.edu/faq/sufism-turkey

"Tansu Çiller'den Fethullah Gülen Açıklaması" [Tansu Ciller and Fethullah Gülen Explained]," 25 July 2016, at http://www.cumhuriyet.com.tr/haber/turkiye/573852/Tansu_Ciller_den_Fethullah_Gülen_aciklamasi.html

Toosi, Nahal, "Verbatim: Fethullah Gülen, 'I Don't Have Any Regrets,'" *Politico*, September 9, 2016, at https://www.politico.eu/article/fethullah-gulen-full-interview-politico-turkey-coup-erdogan/

Saacks, Bradley Joseph, "U.S. schools are indirectly linked to preacher, often well-regarded," *Bloomberg*, September 1, 2016, at https://www.bloomberg.com/news/articles/2016-09-02/u-s-schools-caught-in-turkey-s-post-coup-attempt-crackdown

Sarıtoprak, Zeki, "Fethullah Gülen: A Sufi in His Own Way," in *Turkish Islam and the Secular State: The Gülen Movement*, ed. M. Hakan Yavuz and John L. Esposito (Syracuse: Syracuse University Press, 2003).

———. "Gülen and his Global Contribution to Peace-Building," in *International Conference Proceedings: Muslim World in Transition--Contributions of the Gülen Movement* (London: Leeds Metropolitan Press, 2007).

Sayilan, Fevziye and Ahmet Yildiz, "The Historical and Political Context of Adult Literacy in Turkey," in *International Journal of Lifelong Learning* 28(October, 2009): 735-749, at https://www.tandfonline.com/doi/abs/10.1080/0260137090 3293203?scroll=top&needAccess=true&journalCode=tled20

Schimmel, Annemarie, *Mystical Dimensions of Islam* (Chapel Hill, NC: The University of North Carolina Press, 1975).

Sevindi, Nevval, *Contemporary Islamic Conversations: Fethullah Gulen on Turkey, Islam, and the West*. Ed. with an Introduction by Ibraim M. Abu-Rabi. Tr. Abdullah T. Antepli (Albany: SUNY, 2008).

———. *Yeni Yüzyıl Daily*, August, 1997, as cited in *Fethullah Gülen*, "Relation with Literature and Music," at https://fgulen.com/en/home/1304-fgulen-com-english/fethullah-gulen-life/biography/24661-relation-with-literature-and-music.

Sezgin, İsmail Mesut, "The Mavi Marmara and Fethullah Gülen's Critics: Politics and Principles," at https://fgulen.com/en/home/1324-fgulen-com-english/press/columns/38038-ismail-mesut-sezgin-todays-zaman-mavi-marmara-and-fethullah-gulens-critics-politics-and-principles?hitcount=0

Shinn, David H., *Hizmet in Africa: The Activities and Significance of the Gülen Movement* (Los Angeles, CA: Tsehai Publishers, 2015).

Singer, Sean R., "Erdogan's Muse: The School of Necip Fazil Kisakurek," *World Affairs* 176 (November-December 2013): 81-8.

Smith, Jonathan Z., *To Take Place: Toward Theory in Ritual* (Chicago: The University of Chicago Press, 1987).

Spencer Hesser, Terry, *Love Is a Verb* (NY: Global Vision Productions, 2014).

Tarabay, Jamie, "A Rare Meeting with Reclusive Turkish Spiritual Leader Fethullah Gülen," *The Atlantic*, Aug 14, 2013, at https://www.theatlantic.com/international/archive/2013/08/a-rare-meeting-with-reclusive-turkish-spiritual-leader-fethullah-gulen/278662/

"Tayyip Erdoğan, Fethullah Gülen, Muhsin Yazıcıoğlu ve Barış Manço'nun yıllar önceki görüntüleri: Gazeteciler ve Yazarlar Vakfı'nın 1996 yılındaki ödül töreninde Erdoğan'ın konuştuğu, Fethullah Gülen'in dinlediği video sosyal medyanın gündeminde [Pictures from years ago of Tayyip Erdoğan, Fethullah Gülen, Muhsin Yazicioglu and Barış Manço," at https://www.youtube.com/watch?v=ZhUT0Uc0wpI

Tedik, Fatih, "Motivating Minority Integration in Western Context: The Gülen Movement in the United Kingdom," in *International Conference on Peaceful Coexistence: Fethullah Gülen's Initiatives for Peace in the Contemporary World, in International Conference on Peaceful Coexistence: Fethullah Gülen's Initiatives for Peace in the Contemporary World, Erasmus University, Rotterdam, 22-23 November 2007*, at https://fgulen.com/en/gulen-movement/conference-papers/peaceful-coexistence/25871-motivating-minority-integration-in-western-context-the-gulen-movement-in-the-united-kingdom

Tee, Caroline, *The Gülen Movement in Turkey: The Politics of Islam and Modernity* (London/NY: IB Tauris, 2016).

Thoroor, Ihsan, "Turkey's Erdoğan turned a failed coup into his path to greater power," *The Washington Post*, July 17, 2017, at https://www.washingtonpost.com/news/worldviews/wp/2017/07/17/turkeys-Erdoğan-turned-a-failed-coup-into-to-his-path-to-greater-power/?utm_term=.756a110f24ed

Tittensor, David, *The House of Service: The Gülen Movement and Islam's Third Way. Religion and Global Politics.* (London/NY: Oxford University Press, 2014).

Toe, Rodolfo, "Gülen Schools Fight Provokes New Tensions in Bosnia," in *Balkan Insight*, 26 July 2016, at http://www.balkaninsight.com/en/article/gulen-schools-fight-provokes-new-tensions-in-bosnia-07-26-2016

Toraman, Cengiz, Bedriye Tuncsiper and Sinan Yilmaz,"Cash Awqaf in the Ottomans as Philanthropic Foundations And Their Accounting Practices," at http://waqfacademy.org/wp-content/uploads/2013/03/Cengiz-Toraman-Bedriye-Tuncsiper-Sinan-Yilmaz-CTBTSY.-Date.-Cash-Awqaf-in-the-Ottomans-as- Philanthropic-Foundations-Their-Accounting-Practices.-Turkey.-University.pdf

"Turgut Özal Colleges," at http://turgutozal.edu.al/

"Turkey Purge: Monitoring Human Rights Abuses in Post-Coup Turkey," at https://turkeypurge.com/

Turkey Task Force, *Hate Speech and Beyond: Targeting the Gülen Movement in Turkey*. Rethink Paper 16, June 2014. (Washington, DC: Rethink Institute).

Ünal, Ali and Alphonse Williams. Compiled by. *Advocate of Dialogue: Fethullah Gülen*. (Fairfax, VA: The Fountain, 2000).

——. "Any Political Aims?" in Ali Ünal and Alphonse Williams, eds., *Fethullah Gülen: Advocate of Dialogue* (Fairfax, VA: The Fountain, 2000), p. 331, as cited in Yüksel A. Aslandoğan and Muhammed Çetin, "The Educational Philosophy of Gülen in Thought and Practice," in *Muslim Citizens of the Globalized World: Contributions of the Gülen Movement*, ed. Robert A. Hunt and Yüksel A. Aslandoğan (NJ: The Light, 2006).

Valkenberg, Pim, *Renewing Islam by Service: A Christian View of Fethullah Gülen and the Hizmet Movement* (Washington, DC: Catholic University of America Press, 2015).

Walton, Jeremy F., "The Institutions and Discourses of Hizmet, and Their Discontents," in *Hizmet Means Service: Perspectives on an Alternative Path Within Islam*, ed. Martin E. Marty (Berkeley: The University of California Press, 2015): 50-65.

Weber, Max, *The Protestant Ethic and the Spirit of Capitalism*. Tr. Talcott Parsons (NY: Scribner, 1958).

Weller, Paul, "Robustness and Civility: Themes from Fethullah Gülen as Resource and Challenge for Government, Muslims and Civil Society in the United Kingdom," in *Muslim World in Transition: Contributions of the Gülen Movement. International Conference Proceedings. London, 25-27 October 2007.* (London: Leeds Metropolitan University Press, 2007): 268-284.

——. Greg Barton, and İhsan Yılmaz, eds., *The Muslim World and Politics in Transition: Creative Contributions of the Gülen Movement* (London/NY: Bloomsbury, 2013).

What Went Wrong with Turkey? The Fountain Special Issue (NY: Blue Dome Press, 2017).

White, Jenny B., "The Turkish Complex," in *The American Interest* 10(4): February 2, 2015, at https://www.the-american-interest.com/2015/02/02/the-turkish-complex/

Wickham, Carrie Rosefsky, *The Muslim Brotherhood: The Evolution of an Islamist Movement* (Princeton: Princeton University Press, 2015).

Williams, Jennifer, "Ramadan 2017: Nine Questions about the Muslim Holy Month You Were Too Embarrassed to Ask," *Vox*, June 23, 2017, at https://www.vox.com/2017/5/25/11851766/what-is-ramadan-2017-muslim-islam-about

Yavuz, M. Hakan, *Toward an Islamic Enlightenment: The Gülen Movement* (NY/London: Oxford University Press, 2013).

Yavuz, M. Hakan, "The Gülen Movement: The Turkish Puritans," in *Turkish Islam and the Secular State: The Gülen Movement*, ed. M. Hakan Yavuz and John L. Esposito (Syracuse, NY: Syracuse University Press, 2003): 19-47.

Yeşilova, Hakan. "Debunking the Gülen-Erdoğan Relationship," *The Daily Caller*, September 22, 2016. https://dailycaller.com/2016/09/22/debunking-the-gulen-erdogan-relationship.

Yılmaz, İhsan, "Peacebuilding through Education: A Perspective on the Hizmet Movement," in *Peacebuilding Through Education: Challenges, Opportunities,*

Cases, ed. Carol Dahir (NJ: Blue Dome Press, 2015).

——. "*İjtihad* and *Tajdid* by Conduct: The Gülen Movement," in *Turkish Islam and the Secular State: The Gülen Movement*, ed. M. Hakan Yavuz and John L. Esposito (NY: Syracuse University Press, 2003): 208-237.

Yücel, Salih, "Fethullah Gülen: Spiritual Leader in a Global Islamic Context," in *Journal of Religion and Society* 12 (2010), at https://fgulen.com/en/home/1326-fgulen-com-english/press/review/26887-fethullah-gulen-spiritual-leader-in-a-global-islamic-context

Yunus, Muhammad, *Creating a World without Poverty: Social Business and the Future of Capitalism* (NY: Public Affairs, 2007).

Yunus Social Business, at http://www.yunussb.com/

Zürcher, Erik J., *Turkey: A Modern History*. Library of Modern Turkey Series. New Edition. (London/NY: I.B. Tauris, 2017).

Interviews

- Abdullah Birlik, Izmir, Turkey. July 26, 2015.
- Ahmet Kurucan, Hasbrouck Heights, NJ. September 8, 2017.
- Ahmet Muharrem Atlığ, Izmir, Turkey. July 29, 2015.
- Ahmet Tekin, Turkey. July 28, 2015.
- [Aisha], New York City. November 15, 2017.
- Alaattin Kırkan, Izmir, Turkey. July 28, 2015.
- Alp Aslandoğan, Clifton, NJ. May 3, 2015.
- Derya Yazıcı, Hasbrouck Heights, NJ. February 7, 2017.
- Esra Koşar, Hasbrouck Heights, NJ. March 27, 2017.
- Emine Eroğlu, Hasbrouck Heights, NJ. February 7, 2017.
- Ergün Çapan, Wind Gap, Pennsylvania. July 14, 2015.
- Fethullah Gülen, Wind Gap, PA. February 30, 2018.
- Haluk Ercan, Hisar Mosque Bazaar, Izmir. July 27, 2015.
- Hatem Bilgili, Erzurum, Turkey. August 3, 2015.
- Huma Taban, Washington, DC. June 27, 201.
- İsmail Büyükçelebi, Wind Gap, PA. May 12, 2015.
- Kerim Balcı, Istanbul. August 5, 2015.
- Mehmet Doğan, Istanbul. August 4, 2015.
- Mustafa Özcan, Wind Gap, PA, May 11, 2015. Tr. Osman Şimşek.
- Nebahat Çetinkaya, Washington, DC. June 27, 2017.
- Nevzat Savaş, Istanbul, August 27. 2015.
- Nurhayat Gülen, Turgutlu, Turkey. July 25, 2015.
- Nurten Kutlu, Hasbrouck Heights. NJ, February 7, 2017.
- Osman Şimşek, Wind Gap, PA. May 12, 2015.
- Salih Gülen, Erzurum, Turkey. August 3, 2015.
- Sabri Çolak, Erzurum, Turkey. August 5, 2015.
- Şerif Ali Tekalan, Izmir, Turkey. July 27, 2015.
- Sevgi Akarçeşme, Istanbul. August 18, 2015.
- Sibel Yüksel, Houston, Texas. March 11, 2017.

- Yusuf Erdoğan, Izmir, Turkey. July 28, 2015.
- Yusuf Pekmezci, Izmir, Turkey. July 29, 2015.
- Züleyha Çolak, Hasbrouck Heights, NJ. March 28, 2017.

INDEX